Practical Issues in Cointegration Analysis

Practical Issues in Cointegration Analysis

Edited by Les OXLEY
and Michael MCALEER

University of Waikato, New Zealand; University of Western Australia and Adjunct Professor, Australian National University

BLACKWELL
Publishers

Published simultaneously as Vol. 12, No. 5 of
Journal of Economic Surveys December 1998

This edition first published 1999

Blackwell Publishers Ltd
108 Cowley Road
Oxford OX4 1JF, UK

Blackwell Publishers Inc
350 Main Street
Malden, Massachusetts 02148, USA

British Library Cataloguing in Publication Data

Library of Congress Cataloging in Publication Data
Practical issues in cointegration analysis / edited by Les Oxley and Michael McAleer.
p. cm.
"Published simultaneously as vol. 12, no. 5 of Journal of economic surveys, December 1998"—T.p. verso.
Includes index.
ISBN 0–631–21198–5
1. Cointegration. I. Oxley, Les. II. McAleer, Michael.
HB137.P69 1999
330'.01'5195—dc21 99-19757
CIP

CONTENTS

EDITORIAL PREFACE

The *Journal of Economic Surveys* was conceived in 1985 and the first issue was produced in 1987. From its inception, it was hoped that collections of recent contributions in an area could be arranged to reflect particular themes. The first of these, the edited volume *Surveys in Econometrics*, was published in 1995. That particular collection of articles on econometric methodologies, pre-testing, diagnostics, cointegration, ECMs, ARCH modelling, non-linearities, semi-and non-parametric testing, and issues in rational expectations and generated regressors, has become a well-cited volume with a number of classic contributions.

Continuing the innovative and dynamic ethos of the *Journal*, a special issue on a particular theme will be published annually in the *Journal* and also as a Blackwells Book. The first such issue and book is *Practical Issues in Cointegration Analysis*. In this special issue, seven papers on recent developments in unit root testing and cointegration are surveyed by some of the most influential experts in the area. Each paper was fully refereed and revised accordingly.

The field has expanded enormously since the publication of *Surveys in Econometrics* in 1995, including a range of Bayesian-based unit root tests and the investigation of series which are integrated of order two, or I(2). The notion of what cointegration may mean and how cointegrating vectors might be interpreted, has also been subject to considerable discussion. Each contribution in the special issue has been chosen to reflect recent developments in a fast-moving and dynamic field, and has been written so as to be accessible to the technically competent non-specialist and specialist alike.

Practical Issues in Cointegration Analysis is the first of a new series of special issues from the *Journal of Economic Surveys*, to be followed by *Issues in Non-linear Modelling* which will be edited by Donald George, Les Oxley and Simon Potter.

We wish to thank all those involved at Basil Blackwell Ltd., for facilitating these developments, and once again thank Mike Grover of Tieto Ltd., who had the vision to see that the *Journal of Economic Surveys* was a venture worth backing.

Les Oxley and Michael McAleer

COINTEGRATION IN PRACTICE

Michael McAleer
University of Western Australia
and
Osaka University

Les Oxley
University of Waikato

1. Introduction

The publication of Dickey and Fuller (1979) and Johansen (1988), among others, opened the area of non-stationary time series estimation and testing to serious academic investigation. In the interim, the area has undoubtedly become one of the most intensely researched in econometrics, with the frontiers continuing to be expanded with a consideration of I(2) and partially cointegrated systems.

Surveys in Econometrics, published in 1995, included two papers which explicitly considered cointegration, unit roots and Error Correction Mechanisms (ECMs), with others citing issues relating to problems caused by nonstationary in testing (see, for example, McAleer (1995)). These two articles, Muscatelli and Hurn (1995), and Alogoskoufis and Smith (1995), have become exceedingly well-cited contributions and have also acted as excellent teaching devices. However, in the few years since their publication, the discipline has advanced considerably. Thus, a single issue devoted to cointegration and unit roots is not only feasible, but also necessary.

In *Practical Issues in Cointegration Analysis*, we have been most fortunate to have collected a series of up-to-date surveys on both unit root testing and the estimation of cointegration systems, as well as related issues on the interpretation of 'shocks'. The papers are both state-of-the-art surveys of developments as well as scholarly contributions to the literature. Starting with a survey (Primer) on unit roots (Phillips and Xiao), the contributions progress logically through 'new' approaches to interpreting cointegrating VARs (Pesaran and Smith), to seasonal unit roots (Franses and McAleer), I(2) series (Haldrup), and finally a new way of determining critical values for I(1) processes, I(2) series and cointegrating systems (Doornik). Within this progression, Levtchenkova, Pagan and Robertson focus on the issue of decomposing shocks in multivariate systems, and relate this to cointegration. Doornik, Hendry and Nielsen provide a 'case study' in how to undertake the formulation, estimation and testing of models for potential cointegration, a paper all aspiring applied econometricians should read carefully.

Throughout each of these papers, there is a concerted attempt to bring theoretical issues and contributions to life via practical applications and examples. Recently developed software is referenced, and some readers may find McAleer and Oxley (1998a,b), McAleer *et al.* (1999) and McKenzie (1998) as useful adjuncts to this *Issue*. A more detailed introduction and overview to these contributions is given below.

2. Overview

The first survey paper by Peter Phillips (Yale University) and Zhijie Xiao (University of Illinios at Urbana-Champaign) is 'A Primer on Unit Root Testing'. Given the immense literature and diversity of unit root tests, based on parametric, semi-parametric and non-parametric methods which employ both classical and Bayesian principles of statistical testing, the various procedures and methodologies can be confusing to the specialist, and prove even more daunting to the uninitiated. As a result, much empirical work continues to use the simplest testing procedures because the literature has not made it clear which tests, if any, are superior to others. This review paper examines unit root theory, with an emphasis on testing principles, the most commonly used tests in empirical research, a comparison of the finite sample properties of the various tests, and recent developments. The general framework adopted by the authors makes it possible to consider tests of stochastic trends against trend stationarity and trend breaks of a general type. The authors list the main tests, and asymptotic distributions are given in a simple form to emphasize common features in the theoretical developments. Classical unit root tests such as the Dickey-Fuller, augmented Dickey-Fuller, and the semi-parametric Z tests of Peter Phillips and his associates, are analysed comprehensively. Methods of improving the efficiency of unit root tests are considered, as are fractional integration, seasonal unit root tests, and bootstrapping unit root tests. Some simulation results are reported, and the authors also provide an extensive list of references and an annotated bibliography on unit root non-stationarity in textbooks, review articles and computer software, which should prove invaluable to both the specialist and novice.

'Structural Analysis of Cointegrating VARs', the second survey paper in volume, is by M. Hashem Pesaran (University of Cambridge and University of Southern California) and Ron P. Smith (Birkbeck College, London and University of Colorado at Boulder). The survey paper uses a number of recent developments in the analysis of cointegrating vector autoregressions (VARs) to examine their links to the older and venerable structural modelling traditions using both AR distributed lag (ARDL) models and simultaneous equations models. The authors emphasize, in particular, the importance of using judgment and economic theory to supplement statistical information. After a brief historical overview, the paper presents a structural vector ARDL model, gives a detailed analysis of the statistical framework, discusses the identification of impulse responses using the generalized impulse response function, reviews the analysis of cointegrating VARs, including the treatment of the deterministic components, and highlights the large number of choices facing the practitioner in determining a particular specification. The paper also considers the problem of specification of intercepts and trends, and the size of the VAR, in greater detail, and examines the advantages of using exogenous variables in cointegrating VARs. The various issues are well illustrated with a small macroeconomic model for the US, which examines the number and list of the endogenous and exogenous variables to be included in the analysis, the nature of the deterministic variables (such as intercepts, trends and seasonals), and whether their coefficients are to be restricted, the order of the vector ARDL, the orders of integration of the variables, the number of cointegrating vectors, the specification of identifying restrictions, and the identification and estimation of impulse responses to economic shocks.

'Shocking Stories', by S. Levtchenkova (Australian National University), Adrian Pagan (Australian National University) and J. C. Robertson (Federal Reserve Bank of Atlanta and Australian National University), provides a survey of various methods that decompose multivariate series into permanent and transitory components by using ideas that are drawn from the cointegration literature. When long run relations arise in systems of variables that are not cointegrated, the emphasis is on the effects of permanent and transitory shocks upon variables rather than cointegration itself. As much of modern macroeconomics involves studying such shocks, the authors suggest that the shock analysis literature (or shocking stories) might be expected to be closely connected with cointegration. They argue, however, that many papers in econometrics provide permanent and transitory decompositions with little apparent references to economics or a theoretical model. The authors provide just such a connection between theory and the various solutions, and adopt a two stage procedure to effect the decomposition into the two components. In the first stage, a basic set of permanent and transitory components is formed by using standard definitions of the shocks from which they are constituted. The authors show that the resulting measurements are not unique, and that additional information is required to achieve uniqueness. Such information can arise in many forms, but a particularly important form involves the values of the long run multipliers for permanent shocks that are available from many calibrated models. A comparison of the methods of effecting the decomposition is performed on six macroeconomic variables from a well know data set using quarterly observations.

Jurgen Doornik (University of Oxford), David Hendry (University of Oxford) and Bent Nielsen (University of Oxford) address the practical determination of cointegration rank in 'Inference in Cointegrated Models: UK M1 Revisited'. As the literature on the formulation, estimation and testing of models for potential cointegrated economic time series is extensive, the authors focus their attention on determining the cointegration rank of a linear dynamic system. From a practical perspective, the determination of cointegration rank is difficult for a number of reasons, including the following: deterministic terms (such as constants and trends) play a crucial role in the limiting distributions; the system may not be formulated to ensure the asymptotic similarity of key test statistics to nuisance parameters; alternative choices of test statistics may deliver apparently conflicting inferences; finite-sample critical values may differ substantially from their asymptotic equivalents; the asymptotic distributions themselves are usually approximations, obtained by simulation and possibly summarized by response surfaces; dummy variables can alter critical values, often greatly; the lag length selected may not remove all residual serial correlation, or it may be too long; multiple cointegration vectors must be identifiable for valid inference; the data may be I(2), or near I(2), rather than I(1), which will again alter the relevant limiting distributions; and in the presence of non-modelled variables, conditioning to create 'partial' systems must be done with care. The paper addresses many of these important issues of inference in the empirical application of multivariate cointegration, illustrating the analysis with a well-known four-equation model of narrow money, M1, prices, aggregate expenditure, and interest rates in the UK. The useful modelling exercise raises a number of typical problems faced by empirical researchers in economics.

Although the following paper is not a standard survey paper, it does provide an analysis of current research to approximate the asymptotic distributions of some tests of cointegration with non-standard distributions. Jurgen Doornik (University of Oxford) addresses this topic in 'Approximations to the Asymptotic Distributions of Cointegration Tests'. As the distributions of the test statistics involve Brownian motions, for which no closed-form solutions are available, tables have been published for specific quantiles, based on simulation experiments. Current econometric software packages do not report probability-values, but rather list the conventional quantiles based on the published tables, or on a response surface fitted to the tables. As both applied modellers and Monte Carlo experimenters are interested in being able to compute probability-values and quantiles easily, the current paper addresses this need. It is clear that non-standard distributions need to be approximated in a form which can be implemented on a computer in a straightforward manner. The approximations in some well-known papers can involve a very large number of coefficients, whereas the present paper uses only a fraction of the number of coefficients. Thus, it would seem to be particularly suitable for econometric software packages. It has been found in previous research that a (scaled) chi-squared distribution is a reasonably accurate approximation of the likelihood ratio test, and that the gamma distribution also provides a close approximation to the squared Dickey-Fuller distribution. The author confirms that the gamma distribution is a good approximation to the tests for cointegration rank, with the fitted distributions being used to compute probability-values and quantiles. Moreover, the proposed approximate procedures are straightforward to use and are more accurate than the existing procedures.

The focus of the previous survey papers has been on I(1) time series processes, that is, series with a single unit root. In 'An Econometric Analysis of I(2) Variables', Niels Haldrup (Aarhus University) provides a selective survey of the recent literature dealing with I(2) variables in economic time series, namely processes that need to be differenced twice in order to render the series stationary. Although processes with a single unit root appear quite adequate to describe the behaviour of most economic time series, there are numerous examples of economic time series with double unit roots, such as prices, wages, money balances and stock variables, which appear to be more smooth and change more slowly over time. Such series are potentially I(2), so that double differencing is required to render the series stationary. As both the levels and growth rates of economic time series are important for many economic theories, the complicated interaction between I(1) and I(2) series is important in the econometric analysis of models including such variables. The author demonstrates why I(2) processes are a relevant class of models to be considered in economics, and reviews different econometric tools that are available in the literature to analyse models with I(2) variables. In the context of particular economic models, intuition is provided as to why I(2) and polynomial cointegration are features which are likely to occur in economics. The properties of I(2) series are discussed, and the following topics are reviewed: testing for double unit roots; representations of I(2) cointegrated systems; hypothesis testing in single equations; and hypothesis testing in systems of equations. Different data sets, such as German hyperinflation data, US housing data and Danish money data, are used to illustrate the various economic and statistical techniques.

In the final paper, Philip Hans Franses (Erasmus University Rotterdam) and Michael McAleer (University of Western Australia and Osaka University) review various recent approaches to 'Cointegration Analysis of Seasonal Time Series'. This survey highlights the main distinguishing properties of various methods of estimation and testing, without elaborating on the technical details. Some of the important empirical applications in the literature are also reviewed. This review is directed towards practitioners who, when faced with a set of quarterly observed economic time series variables, intend to construct a cointegration model which can be used for tackling important economic questions. A large number of decisions facing the practitioner are reviewed, and it is shown how alternative decisions can lead to alternative empirical models. The focus of the analysis is primarily on the VAR model as this appears to the authors to be the most useful for cointegration analysis. In addition to the usual practical decisions concerning data transformations and univariate time series properties, the authors argue that it is necessary to decide how seasonal variation is included in the multivariate model, and how standard cointegration methods should accordingly be modified. Seasonal cointegration and periodic cointegration methods are discussed, as are some of their recent refinements. The authors present an empirical example related to non-nested testing of periodic autoregressive models. An overview of further research topics is also provided, with attention directed toward the important problems which a practitioner might be expected to face. These issues include the use of monthly or weekly data, the choice of appropriate data transformation for seasonal and periodic integration, nonlinear seasonal patterns, and common seasonal patterns.

Acknowledgements

The first author wishes to acknowledge the financial support of the Australian Research

Council and the Japan Society for the Promotion of Science, and the research support of the Osaka School of International Public Policy, Osaka University.

References

Alogoskoufis, G. and Smith, R. (1995) On error correction models: Specification, interpretation and estimation, chapter 6 in L. Oxley *et al.* (eds), *Surveys in Econometrics*, Blackwell, Oxford, 139–70.

Dickey, D. and Fuller, W. (1979) Distribution of the estimators for autoregressive time series with a unit root, *Journal of the American Statistical Association*, vol. 84, 427–31.

Johansen, S. (1988) Statistical analysis of cointegration vectors, *Journal of Economic Dynamics and Control*, 12, 231–54.

McAleer, M. (1995) Sherlock Holmes and the search for truth: A diagnostic tale, chapter 5 in L. Oxley *et al.* (eds), *Surveys in Econometrics*, Blackwell, Oxford, 91–138.

McAleer, M. and Oxley, L. (1998a) Review of Microfit 4.0 — DOS version, *Economic Journal*, 108, 924–38.

McAleer, M. and Oxley, L. (1998a) Review of Microfit 4.0 for Windows, *Economic Journal* (to appear).

McAleer, M., McKenzie, C. R. and Oxley, L. (1999) Clash of the Titans: Microfit 4.0 for Windows and PcGive Professional compared, *Journal of Economic Surveys* (to appear).

McKenzie, C. R. (1998) Review of Microfit 4.0, *Journal of Applied Econometrics*, 13, 77–89.

Muscatelli, A. and Hurn, S. (1995) Econometric modelling of cointegrated time series, chapter 7 in L. Oxley *et al.* (eds), *Surveys in Econometrics*, Blackwell, Oxford, 171–214.

A PRIMER ON UNIT ROOT TESTING

Peter C. B. Phillips
Yale University

Zhijie Xiao
University of Illinois at Urbana-Champaign

Abstract. The immense literature and diversity of unit root tests can at times be confusing even to the specialist and presents a truly daunting prospect to the uninitiated. In consequence, much empirical work still makes use of the simplest testing procedures because it is unclear from the literature and from recent reviews which tests if any are superior. This paper presents a survey of unit root theory with an emphasis on testing principles and recent developments. The general framework adopted makes it possible to consider tests of stochastic trends against trend stationarity and trend breaks of a general type. The main tests are listed, and asymptotic distributions are given in a simple form that emphasizes commonalities in the theory. Some simulation results are reported, and an extensive list of references and all annotated bibliography are provided.

Keywords. Autoregressive unit root; Brownian motion; Functional central limit theorem; Integrated process; LM principle; Model selection; Moving average unit root; Nonstationarity; Quasi-differencing; Stationarity; Stochastic trend.

1. Introduction

At a casual level, many observed time series seem to display nonstationary characteristics. For economic time series nonstationary behavior is often the most dominant characteristic. Some series grow in a secular way over long periods of time, others appear to wander around as if they have no fixed population mean. Growth characteristics are especially evident in time series that represent aggregate economic behavior like gross domestic product and industrial production. Random wandering behavior is evident in many financial time series like interest rates and asset prices. Similar phenomena arise in data from other social sciences like communications and political science, one example being opinion poll data on presidential popularity. Any attempt to explain or forecast series of this type requires that a mechanism be introduced to capture the nonstationary elements in the series, or that the series be transformed in some way to achieve stationarity. Yet this is often much easier to say than it is to do in a satisfactory way. The problem is particularly delicate in the multivariate case, where several time series may have nonstationary characteristics and the interrelationships of these variables are the main object of study.

Before 1970, a very popular way of modeling nonstationarity was to use deterministic trending functions like time polynomials to capture the secular movements in the series. Regression methods were commonly used to extract this trend and the residuals were then analyzed as a stationary time series. A model of the form

$$y_t = h_t + y_t^s,\ h_t = \gamma' x_t,\ t = 1, \ldots, n, \tag{1}$$

where y_t^s is a *stationary time series* and x_t is a k-vector of deterministic trends, is known as a *trend-stationary* time series. The trend function h_t may be more complex than a simple time polynomial. For example, time polynomials with sinusoidal factors and piecewise time polynomials may be used. The latter corresponds to a class of models with structural breaks in the deterministic trend. The outline of the theory of unit root tests that is given here will allow for these possibilities.

A major limitation of models like (1) is that the trending mechanism is non-stochastic. One way of introducing a stochastic element into the trend is to allow the process y_t^s to be generated as follows:

$$y_t^s = \alpha y_{t-1}^s + u_t,\ t = 1, \ldots n, \text{ with } \alpha = 1,\ u_t = C(L)\varepsilon_t, \tag{2}$$

and

$$C(L) = \sum_{j=0}^{\infty} c_j L^j,\ \sum_{j=0}^{\infty} j^{1/2} |c_j| < \infty,\ C(1) \neq 0, \tag{3}$$

where L is the lag operator for which $Ly_t = y_{t-1}$. The initial condition in (2) is set at $t = 0$, and y_0^s may be a constant or a random variable. In the latter case, we can even allow for distant initial conditions (see Phillips and Lee, 1996, and Canjels and Watson, 1997), so that y_0^s has a comparable stochastic order to the terminal data point y_n^s, viz. $O_p(\sqrt{n})$. If $\varepsilon_t \equiv \text{iid}(0, \sigma^2)$, then u_t in (2) is a *linear process*, and y_t^s has an autoregressive unit root. It is common to make the more general assumption that ε_t is a stationary martingale difference sequence with respect to the natural filtration $(\mathcal{F}_t)$ with $E(\varepsilon_t^2 | \mathcal{F}_{t-1}) = \sigma^2$, a.s. The second and third conditions of (3) ensure that u_t is *covariance stationary* and has positive *spectral density* at the origin, thereby ensuring that the unit root in y_t does not cancel (as it would if u_t had a *moving average unit root*). The $\frac{1}{2}$-summability condition in (3) is useful in validating the following expansion of the operator $C(L)$

$$C(L) = C(1) + \tilde{C}(L)(L - 1), \tag{4}$$

where $\tilde{C}(L) = \sum_{j=0}^{\infty} \tilde{c}_j L^j$ and $\tilde{c}_j = \sum_{j+1}^{\infty} c_s$. This expansion gives rise to an explicit martingale difference decomposition of u_t

$$u_t = C(1)\varepsilon_t + \tilde{\varepsilon}_{t-1} - \tilde{\varepsilon}_t, \quad \text{with } \tilde{\varepsilon}_t = \tilde{C}(L)\varepsilon_t, \tag{5}$$

This decomposition is sometimes called the martingale decomposition in the probability literature (see Hall and Heyde, 1980) because the first term of (5) is a martingale difference and the partial sums $\sum_{s=1}^{t} u_s$ correspondingly have the leading martingale term $C(1) \sum_{s=1}^{t} \varepsilon_s$. The expansion (4) was obtained, but not validated, in the work of Beveridge and Nelson (1981) on decomposing aggregated economic data into long run and short run components and is significant in this context. Thus, if y_t^s is generated by (2) then (5) reveals that

$$y_t^s = C(1)\sum_{s=1}^{t} \varepsilon_s + \tilde{\varepsilon}_0 - \tilde{\varepsilon}_t + y_0^s = Y_t^s + \eta_t,$$

where $Y_t^s = C(1)\sum_{s=1}^{t} \varepsilon_s$ and $\eta_t = \tilde{\varepsilon}_0 - \tilde{\varepsilon}_t + y_0^s$ are the long run and short run components of y_t^s respectively. The decomposition (5) was justified in a simple algebraic way using (3) by Phillips and Solo (1992), who showed how to use it to prove strong laws, central limit theorems, functional laws, and laws of iterated logarithms for time series. It is now commonly used in this way in the development of an asymptotic theory for nonstationary time series.

The output of (2) can be written as the accumulated process $y_t^s = \sum_{j=1}^{t} u_j + y_0^s$, and is called a *stochastic trend* by virtue of the fact that it is of stochastic order $O_p(t^{1/2})$. The process y_t^s is *difference stationary* in the sense that $\Delta y_t^s = u_t$ is a stationary process where $\Delta = 1 - L$ is the differencing operator. The terminology *integrated process* of order one (written as $I(1)$) is in common use because of the above representation. In consequence, we call a stationary time series an $I(0)$ process (integrated of order zero). The assumptions given above are sufficient to ensure that y_t^s satisfies a *functional central limit theorem* (see Phillips and Solo, 1992, for a demonstration), which is an important element in the development of the asymptotic theory of all unit root tests. As a result, $n^{-1/2} y_{[nr]}^s \Rightarrow B(r)$, a Brownian motion with variance $\omega^2 = \sigma^2 C(1)^2$, where $[nr]$ signifies the integer part of nr and $r \in [0, 1]$ represents some fraction of the sample data. The parameter $\omega^2 = 2\pi f_u(0)$ is called the *long-run variance* of u_t.

In contrast to stationary or trend stationary time series, models with a stochastic trend have time dependent variances that go to infinity with time, are persistent in the sense that shocks have permanent effects on the values of the process, and have infinite spectrum at the origin. These properties of stochastic trends have considerable relevance in economic applications. For instance, under the real business cycle hypothesis, policy actions are required to bring real GNP back to its original path due to the persistent effects of innovations. However, less policy intervention is needed in trend stationary models because shocks only have a transitory effect.

Testing for the presence of a stochastic trend in the model (1) is equivalent to testing the null hypothesis that the autoregressive parameter $\alpha = 1$ in (2), and is known as a *unit root test*. The alternative hypothesis that $|\alpha| < 1$ corresponds to the version of the model in which y_t is trend stationary. The test can be interpreted as a test of difference stationarity versus trend-stationarity in the time series y_t. There are now a wide variety of such tests, based on parametric, semi-parametric and non-parametric methods and employing both classical and Bayesian principles of statistical testing. The literature is immense. This paper seeks to cover the main principles of testing, the most commonly used tests in practical work, a comparison of the finite sample properties among these tests, and recent developments.

2. Classical unit root tests

2.1. *The Dickey-Fuller tests*

Combining (1) and (2) gives the regression model

$$y_t = \beta' x_t + \alpha y_{t-1} + u_t. \tag{6}$$

In (6) the deterministic component is constructed so that $\Delta h_t = \gamma' \Delta x_t = \gamma' A x_t = \beta' x_t$, for some matrix A and vector β. This usually involves raising the degree of the deterministic trends to ensure that the maximum trend degrees in (6) and (1) are the same. Then, at least one element of the parameter vector β is zero and, consequently, there are surplus trend variables in the regression equation (6). It will subsequently be useful to make this redundancy explicit, and this can be done by rewriting the trend component in (6) as $\Delta h_t = \beta' x_t = \breve{\beta}' \breve{x}_t$, where $\breve{x}_t = S x_t$ for some eliminator matrix S that eliminates redundant rows of x_t. The formulation (6) therefore results in some inefficiency in the regression because $\breve{x}_t$ is of smaller dimension than x_t. There is an alternative approach that avoids this problem of redundant variables and it will be discussed in Sections 3.1 and 3.2 below. The regression (6) does have the advantage that the detrended data is invariant to the parameters in the trend function in (1).

To develop an asymptotic theory it is assumed that there exists a scaling matrix D_n and a piecewise continuous function $X(r)$ such that $D_n^{-1} x_{[nr]} \to X(r)$ as $n \to \infty$ uniformly in $r \in [0, 1]$. For example, if h_t is a p-degree time polynomial, then $D_n = \text{diag}(1, n, \ldots, n^p)$ and $X(r) = (1, r, \ldots, r^p)'$. Correspondingly, it is also assumed that there exists a matrix F_n for which $F_n^{-1} \breve{x}_{[nr]} \to \breve{X}(r)$ as $n \to \infty$, uniformly in $r \in [0, 1]$. In general, $\breve{X}(r) = SX(r)$.

The Dickey-Fuller tests (Dickey and Fuller, 1979, 1981) dealt with Gaussian random walks with independent residuals. Let $\hat{\alpha}$ be the OLS estimator of α in (6) and $t_{\hat{\alpha}}$ be the corresponding t-ratio statistics, under the null hypothesis $\alpha = 1$, the large sample theory for these quantities involves functionals of Brownian motion, some of which are stochastic integrals. The limit theory forms the basis of the unit root tests. If the shocks u_t are $iid(0, \sigma^2)$ random variates, the large sample theory for the coefficient estimator $\hat{\alpha}$ and its regression t-ratio statistic $t_{\hat{\alpha}}$ are given by the following functionals of Brownian motion,

$$n(\hat{\alpha} - 1) \Rightarrow \left[\int_0^1 W_X(r) dW(r)\right]\left[\int_0^1 W_X(r)^2\right]^{-1}, \tag{7}$$

$$t_{\hat{\alpha}} \Rightarrow \left[\int_0^1 W_X(r) dW(r)\right]\left[\int_0^1 W_X(r)^2\right]^{-1/2}, \tag{8}$$

where $\Rightarrow$ signifies weak convergence, W is standard Brownian motion, and $W_x(r) = W(r) - \int_0^1 WX' (\int_0^1 XX')^{-1} X(r)$ is the Hilbert projection in $L_2[0, 1]$ of W onto the space orthogonal to X. In the special case where there is no deterministic component x_t, these limit distributions reduce to the commonly known

Dickey-Fuller distributions given by the functionals $[\int_0^1 WdW][\int_0^1 W^2]^{-1}$ and $[\int_0^1 WdW][\int_0^1 W^2]^{-1/2}$. Dickey and Fuller (1979, 1981) did not themselves use these representations, but used equivalent $\mathbb{R}_\infty$ formulations in terms of linear combinations of functions of iid $N(0, 1)$ variates, rather than stochastic process representations on function spaces. The latter first appeared, but were unproved, in White (1958), and were later developed in progressive degrees of generality by Lai and Wei (1982), Solo (1984) and Phillips (1987). Multivariate regression cases were dealt with using these methods in Phillips (1986) and Phillips and Durlauf (1986).

In the more general case where the residual process u_t is stationary, the limit distributions of $\hat{\alpha}$ and $t_{\hat{\alpha}}$ have additional bias terms due to the presence of serial correlation. These were explored in Phillips (1987a). As a result, the limiting distributions of the two statistics in (7) and (8) become dependent on the nuisance parameters. Such a problem can be solved in a parametric or non-parametric way, leading to two major classes of unit root tests that are distinguished by their treatment of the autocorrelation in the stationary residual process u_t. One approach, proposed by Phillips (1987a), adjusts $\hat{\alpha}$ and $t_{\hat{\alpha}}$ based on nonparametric estimates of the nuisance parameters to account for the serial correlation. This approach is said to be semi-parametric since its treatment of the regression coefficient α is parametric but it deals with the stationary residual nonparametrically. The second approach, the augmented Dickey-Fuller (ADF) test, adds lags to the autocorrelation to eliminate the effect of serial correlation on the test statistics. Such a device relies on specifying the stationary part of the process in terms of a parametric model (commonly an autoregression) and is therefore fully parametric. This approach was explored by Said and Dickey (1984).

2.2. *The semi-parametric Z_α and Z_t tests*

The semiparametric Z_α and Z_t tests were developed in Phillips (1987a) and extend the original unit root tests of Dickey and Fuller (1979, 1981), which were based on the statistic $n(\hat{\alpha} - 1)$ and t_α in the Gaussian AR(1) model. Phillips and Perron (1988), Ouliaris *et al.* (1989), and Park and Sung (1994) give various extensions of these semiparametric tests. Following Phillips (1987a), when the residual process u_t in (4) is a general stationary time series, the asymptotic distributions are given as follows:

$$n(\hat{\alpha} - 1) \Rightarrow \left[\int_0^1 B_X(r)dB(r) + \lambda\right]\left[\int_0^1 B_X^2(r)dr\right]^{-1}, \tag{9}$$

and

$$t_{\hat{\alpha}} \Rightarrow \sigma_u^{-1}\left[\int_0^1 B_X(r)dB(r) + \lambda\right]\left[\int_0^1 B_X^2(r)dr\right]^{-1/2}, \tag{10}$$

where $\sigma_u^2 = \mathrm{var}(u_t)$, $B(r)$ is Brownian motion with variance $\omega^2 = \sigma^2 C(1)^2$, $\lambda = \sum_{j=1}^{\infty} E(u_0 u_j)$ and $B_X(r)$ is detrended Brownian motion defined by the $L_2[0, 1]$

Hilbert space projection of $B(r)$ onto the space orthogonal to the span of $X(r)$, viz., $B_X(r) = B(r) - (\int_0^1 BX')(\int_0^1 XX')^{-1}X(r)$. In (9) and (10), ω^2 and λ are nuisance parameters and may be consistently estimated by nonparametric *kernel* techniques, analogous to those that are used in the estimation of the spectral density (e.g., see Andrews, 1991). Let $\hat{\omega}^2$ and $\hat{\lambda}$ be such estimates. Using the limit theory in (9) and (10) and these nonparametric estimates of the nuisance parameters, the following statistics are formed to test the unit root hypothesis:

$$Z_\alpha = n(\hat{\alpha} - 1) - \hat{\lambda}\left(n^{-2}\sum_{t=2}^{n} y_{X,t-1}^2\right)^{-1} \Rightarrow \left[\int_0^1 W_X dW\right]\left[\int_0^1 W_X^2\right]^{-1}, \tag{11}$$

$$Z_t = \hat{\sigma}_u \hat{\omega}^{-1} t_\alpha - \hat{\lambda}\left\{\hat{\omega}\left(n^{-2}\sum_{t=2}^{n} y_{X,t-1}^2\right)^{1/2}\right\}^{-1} \Rightarrow \left[\int_0^1 W_X dW\right]\left[\int_0^1 W_X^2\right]^{-1/2}, \tag{12}$$

where $y_{X,t}$ is the residual from a regression of y_t on x_t. The limit variates shown in (11) and (12) involve standard Brownian motion $W(r) = (1/\omega)B(r)$ and the standardized process $W_X(r) = (1/\omega)B_X(r)$, so they are free of nuisance parameters and produce similar tests for a unit root.

The limit variates (11) and (12) simplify to those of the original Dickey-Fuller tests in the case of a fitted intercept or linear trend and can be used to construct critical values for the tests. This is typically done by large scale simulations, since the limit distributions are non-standard. Fuller (1976/1996) gives some numerical tabulations for the intercept and linear trend cases. Computerized tabulations are given in Ouliaris and Phillips (1994) for the case of polynomial trends. These limit distributions are asymmetric and have long left tails. In the case of the Z_α test, for instance, we reject the null hypothesis of a unit root at the 5% level if $Z_\alpha < cv(Z_\alpha; 5\%)$, the 5% critical value of the test. Both the Z_α and Z_t tests are one-sided. They measure the support in the data from a unit root against the alternative that the data are stationary about the deterministic trend x_t. When there is no deterministic trend in the regression model, the alternative hypothesis is just stationarity. In this case, the limit variates involve only the standard Brownian motion W, and $W_X = W$ in (11) and (12).

2.3. *The parametric ADF tests*

The most common parametric unit root test is the augmented Dickey-Fuller (ADF) test. This test was originally proposed by Dickey and Fuller (1979, 1981) for the case where u_t in (6) is an AR(p) process. The unit root hypothesis in (6) corresponds to the hypothesis $a = 0$ in the following regression:

$$\Delta y_t = a y_{t-1} + \sum_{j=1}^{k-1} \varphi_j \Delta y_{t-i} + \beta' x_t + \varepsilon_t. \tag{13}$$

This hypothesis can be tested by means of the regression coefficient $\hat{a}$ or its t-ratio statistic $t_{\hat{a}}$, which have the same limiting distributions as those given in (7) and

(8). For more general time series processes, we can expect that, as $k \longrightarrow \infty$, the autoregressive approximation will give an increasingly accurate representation of the true process. In an important extension of Dickey and Fuller (1979), Said and Dickey (1984) prove the validity of the ADF t-ratio test (ADF_t) in general ARMA processes of unknown order, provided the lag length in the autoregression increases with the sample size at a rate less than $n^{1/3}$, where $n =$ sample size. This statistic has the same limit distribution as the Z_t test given in (12) and thus the same critical values can be used in practical applications.

The limit distribution of the coefficient estimate $\hat{a}$ is dependent on nuisance parameters even as the lag length goes to infinity. Specifically,

$$n\hat{a} \Rightarrow \left[\sigma \int_0^1 W_X dW\right]\left[\omega \int_0^1 W_X^2\right]^{-1},$$

which depends on unknown parameters σ and ω. However, ω and σ can be consistently estimated. In particular, $\hat{\sigma}^2 = \sum \hat{\varepsilon}_t^2/n$ is a consistent estimator of σ^2, and ω^2 can be consistently estimated by the AR estimator (Berk, 1974) $\hat{\omega}^2 = \hat{\sigma}^2/(1 - \sum \hat{\varphi}_j)^2$. Under the null hypothesis that $a = 0$, it is apparent that the modified coefficient-based test statistic, $ADF_a = (\hat{\omega}/\hat{\sigma})n\hat{a}$, has the same limit distribution as that of the Z_a test and that of the original Dickey-Fuller coefficient test. This ADF_a test was developed in Xiao and Phillips (1997).

3. Towards efficient unit root tests

3.1. *The von Neumann ratio and LM tests*

The regression equations of classical unit root tests like (6) and (13) involve redundant trend variables. It is to be anticipated that elimination of redundant components in the deterministic trend may bring an efficiency gain to the unit root tests. One such test that successfully avoids the problem of redundant trend variables is the von Neumann (VN) ratio test.

The von Neumann (VN) ratio is the ratio of the sample variances of the differences and the levels of a time series. For Gaussian data this ratio leads to well known *tests of serial correlation* that have good finite sample properties. Sargan and Bhargava (1983) suggested the use of this statistic for testing the Gaussian random walk hypothesis, and Bhargava (1986) extends it to the case of a time trend. Using nonparametric estimates of the nuisance parameter ω^2, it is a simple matter to rescale the VN ratio to provide a unit root test for model (1) and (2) above. Stock (1995) does this for the case where there is a linear trend. Using a different approach and working with polynomial trends, Schmidt and Phillips (1992) show that for a Gaussian likelihood the Lagrange multiplier (LM) principle leads to a VN test, and can be generalized by using a nonparametric estimate of ω^2. The following discussion gives a generalized VN unit root test for the model (1) and (2), allowing for trends and trend breaks.

If y_t^s were observable, the VN ratio would take the form $VN = \sum_{t=2}^{n}(\Delta y_t^s)^2/$

$\sum_{t=1}^{n}(y_t^s)^2$. The process y_t^s is, in fact, unobserved but may be estimated from (1). Note that, under the null hypothesis and after differences are taken, we get

$$\Delta y_t = \Delta h_t + \Delta y_t^s. \tag{14}$$

This equation is trend stationary, so that by the Grenander–Rosenblatt theorem (Grenander & Rosenblatt, 1957, Chapter 7) the trend function can be efficiently estimated by an OLS regression. Doing so avoids the problem mentioned earlier of having surplus trend variables in the detrending regression. Intuition suggests that this should increase the power of the test, at least in the neighborhood of the null, and simulations in Schmidt & Phillips (1992) confirm this.

Let $\Delta\hat{y}_t^s = \Delta y_t - \Delta\hat{h}_t$ be the residuals from the efficient detrending regression (14) and let $\hat{y}_t^s = \sum_{j=2}^{t}\Delta\hat{y}_j^s$ be the associated estimate of y_t^s. Let $\hat{\omega}^2$ and $\hat{\sigma}_u^2$ be consistent estimates of ω^2 and σ_u^2. (These may be obtained in the same way as in the construction of the Z_t test, i.e. by using the residuals from the regression (6).) Finally, let $\tilde{y}_t^s = \hat{y}_t^s - \beta' x_t$ be the residuals from an OLS regression of $\hat{y}_t^s$ on x_t. Rescaling the von Neumann ratio then leads to the following two test statistics

$$R_{VN} = \frac{\hat{\omega}^2}{\hat{\sigma}^2}\,\frac{n^{-1}\sum_{t=2}^{n}(\Delta\hat{y}_t^s)^2}{n^{-2}\sum_{t=1}^{n}(\hat{y}_t^s)^2} \Rightarrow \left[\int_0^1 \hat{V}_X^2\right]^{-1}, \tag{15}$$

$$\tilde{R}_{VN} = \frac{\hat{\omega}^2}{\hat{\sigma}^2}\,\frac{n^{-1}\sum_{t=2}^{n}(\Delta\tilde{y}_t^s)^2}{n^{-2}\sum_{t=1}^{n}(\tilde{y}_t^s)^2} \Rightarrow \left[\int_0^1 \tilde{V}_X^2\right]^{-1}. \tag{16}$$

The limit process $\hat{V}_X(r)$ in (15) is a detrended generalized *Brownian bridge*, whose precise form depends on the deterministic trend h_t in (1). Specifically,

$$\hat{V}_X(r) = \check{V}_X(r) - \left(\int_0^1 \check{V}_X\check{X}'\right)\left(\int_0^1 \check{X}\check{X}'\right)^{-1}\check{X}(r) \tag{17}$$

is the projection residual of the process $\check{V}_X$ on the space spanned by $\check{X}(r)$, and

$$\check{V}_X(r) = W(r) - \left(\int_0^1 dW\check{X}'\right)\left(\int_0^1 \check{X}\check{X}'\right)^{-1}\int_0^r \check{X} \tag{18}$$

is a generalized Brownian bridge process. When $\check{X}$ has a constant element (as it usually will), it is easy to see that the process $\check{V}_X$ is tied down to the origin at the ends of the $[0,1]$ interval just like a Brownian bridge, so that both $\check{V}_X(0)=0$ and $\check{V}_X(1)=0$. In the case of a simple linear trend, $\check{V}_X(r) = W(r) - rW(1)$ is a standard Brownian bridge, and $\hat{V}_X(r) = \check{V}_X(r) - \int_0^1 \check{V}_X$ is a detrended Brownian bridge. Consonant with the efficient detrending regression $\Delta\hat{y}_t^s = \Delta y_t - \Delta\hat{h}_t$, the limit process $\hat{V}_X$ in (15) is detrended using the limiting trend function $\check{X}(r)$, which, like $\check{x}_t$, involves no redundant trend variables.

Critical values of the limit variates shown in (15) and (16) must be obtained by simulation. The statistics are positive almost surely and the tests are one sided.

Schmidt & Phillips (1992) provide tabulations for $\tilde{R}_{VN}$ in the case where h_t is a linear trend. The presence of a unit root is rejected at the 5% level if $\tilde{R}_{VN} > cv(\tilde{R}_{VN}, 5\%)$.

3.2. *Quasi-difference detrended unit root tests and joint estimation of the local parameter and trend*

As discussed in Section 3.1 above, the von Neumann ratio test R_{VN} is constructed using an efficient detrending regression under the null hypothesis in contrast to the regression (6), where there are generally redundant trending regressors. One way to improve the power of unit root tests is to perform the detrending regression in a way that is efficient under the alternative hypothesis as well, an idea that was suggested in Elliot *et al.* (1996) in the context of the removal of means and linear trends. For alternatives that are distant from a unit root, this can be done directly by means of a regression on (1) because y_t^s is stationary with a spectral density that is continuous at the origin and then the Grenander–Rosenblatt theorem applies. To obtain large sample approximations, we can consider alternatives that are closer to unity. Such alternative hypotheses can often be well modelled using the local alternative

$$\alpha = \exp(n^{-1}c) \sim 1 + n^{-1}c \tag{19}$$

for some fixed $c = \bar{c}$, say, given the sample size n. In this case, in order to efficiently estimate the trend coefficient under the alternative hypothesis, we should use quasi-differencing rather than differencing in the construction of the detrending regression. It is known that such a regression leads to estimates of the trend coefficients that are asymptotically more efficient than an OLS regression in levels (Phillips and Lee, 1996), and this result justifies the modified test procedure that follows.

Define the quasi-difference operator as $\Delta_{\bar{c}}$, $\Delta_{\bar{c}} y_t = (1 - L - n^{-1}\bar{c}L) y_t = \Delta y_t - n^{-1}\bar{c} y_{t-1}$, take quasi-differences of (1) and run the detrending regression

$$\Delta_{\bar{c}} y_t = \tilde{\gamma}' \, \Delta_{\bar{c}} x_t + \Delta_{\bar{c}} \tilde{y}_t^s. \tag{20}$$

We call such detrending procedures quasi-difference (QD) detrending. Using the fitted coefficients $\tilde{\gamma}$ from this OLS regression, the levels data are detrended according to

$$\tilde{y}_t = y_t - \tilde{\gamma}' x_t. \tag{21}$$

The detrended data $\tilde{y}_t$ may be used in the construction of unit root tests. For example, we can construct the modified semi-parametric Z_α test by running the regression of the QD detrended variable $\tilde{y}_t$ on its one-period lagged value $\tilde{y}_{t-1}$ without deterministic trends in the regression, giving

$$\tilde{y}_t = \tilde{a}\tilde{y}_{t-1} + \text{residual}.$$

The modified Z_α test statistic has the following form

$$\tilde{Z}_a = n(\tilde{\alpha} - 1) - \tilde{\lambda}\left(n^{-1}\sum_{t=2}^{n}\tilde{y}_{t-1}^2\right)^{-1}$$
$$\Rightarrow \left\{\left[\int_0^1 dW\tilde{W}_{\bar{c}}\right] - \left[\int_0^1 dW_{\bar{c}}X_{\bar{c}}'\right]^{-1}\left[\int_0^1 X_0\tilde{W}_{\bar{c}}\right]\right\}\left[\int_0^1 \tilde{W}_{\bar{c}}^2\right]^{-1} \tag{22}$$
$$= \left[\int_0^1 \tilde{W}_{\bar{c}}^2\right]^{-1}\int_0^1 \tilde{W}_{\bar{c}}d\tilde{W}_{\bar{c}},$$

where $\tilde{W}_{\bar{c}}(r) = W(r) - \int_0^1 dW_{\bar{c}}X_{\bar{c}}'(\int_0^1 X_{\bar{c}}X_{\bar{c}}')^{-1}X(r)$ is the weak limit of $n^{-1/2}\tilde{y}_{[nr]}$, $W_{\bar{c}}(r) = W(r) - \bar{c}\int_0^r W(s)$, $\tilde{\lambda}$ is a consistent estimator of λ, $X_{\bar{c}}(r) = X'(r) - \bar{c}X(r)$ is the limit function of the quasi-differenced deterministic trend and $X_0 = X'(r)$ is the limiting deterministic trend function with $\bar{c} = 0$. Note that the simple form of (22) follows because

$$d\tilde{W}_{\bar{c}}(r) = dW(r) - \int_0^1 dW_{\bar{c}}X_{\bar{c}}'\left(\int_0^1 X_{\bar{c}}X_{\bar{c}}'\right)^{-1} X_0(r)dr, \tag{23}$$

since $dX(r) = X'(r)dr = X_0(r)dr$. From expression (23) it is further apparent that $(d\tilde{W}_{\bar{c}}(r))^2 = (dW(r))^2 = dr$. While similar in form to (11), the limit formula (22) depends on the process $\tilde{W}_{\bar{c}}(r)$, rather than $W_X(r)$. One difference here is the dependence of $\tilde{W}_{\bar{c}}(r)$ on $\bar{c}$. A second and more significant difference is that $\tilde{W}_{\bar{c}}(r)$ is formed by taking a non orthogonal Hilbert projection residual of $W(r)$ on the space spanned by $X(r)$ in $L_2[0,1]$. Such projections appear infrequently in Hilbert space analysis, but this is an important example where they do appear, arising from the idempotent operator that gives the optimal direction of the projection in $L_2[0,1]$ function space — see Phillips (1996a) for more discussion.

Using the same idea, we can construct the modified Z_t tests and ADF tests and the corresponding limit theory for these tests is

$$ADF_t, \tilde{Z}_t \Rightarrow \left[\int_0^1 \tilde{W}_{\bar{c}}^2\right]^{-1/2}\int_0^1 \tilde{W}_{\bar{c}}d\tilde{W}_{\bar{c}}. \tag{24}$$

By a simple application of stochastic calculus using the fact that $(d\tilde{W}_{\bar{c}}(r))^2 = (dW(r))^2 = dr$, it is apparent that the limit distribution (24) can be written in the alternate form

$$\frac{1}{2}\left[\int_0^1 \tilde{W}_{\bar{c}}^2\right]^{-1}[\tilde{W}_{\bar{c}}(1)^2 - 1].$$

In the special case where x_t is a constant or a linear trend, these formulae reduce to those given in Stock (1994).

Since the limit theory in (22) is different from that of (11), new critical values are needed for this test. The limit theory depends explicitly on the trend functions, as it does in (11), but it also depends on the posited value of the localizing parameter $\bar{c}$ that is used in the quasi-differencing. A reasonable default choice of $\bar{c}$ seems to be the value for which local asymptotic power (see Section 3.4 below) is 50% (see King, 1988, and Elliot *et al.*, 1996).

The QD detrending procedure involves the choice of the prespecified local parameter c. There is another way to proceed that does not appear in the literature to date which we will now exposit. If we incorporate the local to unity hypothesis (19) in models (1) and (2), we obtain the following nonlinear regression:

$$\Delta y_t = \beta'\Delta x_t - x\beta'\left(\frac{x_{t-1}}{n}\right) + c\left(\frac{y_{t-1}}{n}\right) + \varepsilon_t. \tag{25}$$

This nonlinear regression provides for joint estimation of the local parameter c and the trend coefficient β. If we denote the nonlinear estimate of β and c in the above regression by $\tilde{\beta}_{nl}$, and $\tilde{c}_{nl}$, denote the limit of $n^{-1/2}D_n(\tilde{\beta}_{nl} - \beta)$ by ξ and the limit of $\tilde{c}_{nl}$ by η, then the asymptotic behavior of these quantities is governed by the following equations:

$$\xi = [\int X_\eta(r)X_\eta(r)'dr]^{-1}\,[\int X_\eta(r)dB(r) + (c-\eta)\int X_\eta(r)J_c(r)dr],$$
$$\eta = c + [\int \underline{J}_{c\xi}(r)^2 dr]^{-1}\,[\int \underline{J}_{c\xi}(r)dB(r) - \xi'\int \underline{J}_{c\xi}(r)X_c(r)dr],$$

where

$$X_\eta(r) = g(r) - \eta X(r),$$
$$X_c(r) = g(r) - cX(r),$$
$$\underline{J}_{c\xi}(r) = J_c(r) - \xi' X(r),$$

and $D_n^{-1}x_{[nr]} \rightarrow X(r)$, $nD_n^{-1}\Delta x_{[nr]} \rightarrow g(r)$, $J_c(r) = \int_0^r e^{(r-s)c}dB(s)$. There is no direct analytic solution to these equations, but the equations determine (ξ, η) and thereby the limit distributions of $\tilde{\beta}_{nl}$ and $\tilde{c}_{nl}$, which can be found by numerical methods.

Although the local parameter c can not be consistently estimated because of the asymptotic collinearity between y_{t-1} and x_{t-1} in the above nonlinear regression, this regression will still provide a more efficient estimate of the deterministic trend (i.e., the parameter β) than regressions which do not take into account the parameter restrictions in (25). Actually, when the u_t are $N(0, \sigma^2)$ variates, this nonlinear regression delivers the maximum likelihood estimates of β and c for model (1), (2) and (19). The improvement in efficiency from this joint estimation procedure has been confirmed by the authors in Monte Carlo experiments, which we do not report here due to space constraints. Because we do not know the true value of the local parameter c, this maximum likelihood estimate of the deterministic trend can not achieve the efficiency level that applies when the local parameter is known. Nevertheless, the approach certainly seems worthy of use.

3.3. *A point optimal test*

In the simplest framework where the model is a Gaussian AR(1) with unit error variance, the Neyman-Pearson lemma can be used to construct the most powerful test of a unit root against a simple point alternative. Such a test is point optimal for a unit root at the specific point alternative that is selected. King (1988) provides a general discussion of such point optimal invariant tests, and Dufour and King (1991) developed the family of exact most powerful invariant tests. Elliot *et al.* (1996) apply this idea in the context of unit root tests by using the local alternative (19) for a particular value of $c = \bar{c}$.

If we assume $u_t \equiv \text{iid}N(0, \sigma^2)$ in (2), $y_0^s = 0$, and σ^2 is known, then the likelihood function for the autoregression coefficient α is proportional to

$$L(\alpha) \sim -\tfrac{1}{2}\sigma^{-2}\sum_t (y_t^s - \alpha y_{t-1}^s)^2,$$

where $y_t^s = y_t - h_t$. If h_t were known, then the likelihood function could be calculated and a most powerful test could be constructed directly by the Neyman–Pearson lemma. However, as discussed in Section 3.1, h_t is not known and y_t^s has to be estimated. Moreover, u_t may be a general $I(0)$ process and thus the limit distribution of the point optimal test statistic depends in general on nuisance parameters. In this case, corrections have to be made on the original *LR* test so that the adjusted test statistic is free of nuisance parameters. As Dufour and King (1991) and Elliot *et al.* (1996) discuss, the point optimal invariant test (POI) statistics can be constructed based on the ratio of the sum of squared residuals from the efficient detrending regressions under the null and alternative hypothesis. Specifically, taking a local alternative $\alpha = 1 + n^{-1}c$ with $c = \bar{c}$, using quasi-differencing to detrend, and using a consistent nonparametric estimate $\hat{\omega}^2$ of the nuisance parameter ω^2, the POI test statistic for a unit root in (1) and (2) has the following form:

$$\tilde{P}_{\bar{c}} = \hat{\omega}^{-2}\left\{\bar{c}^2 n^{-2}\sum_{t=2}^{n}(y_{t-1}^s)^2 - \bar{c}n^{-1}\tilde{y}_n^s\right\} \Rightarrow \bar{c}^2\int_0^1 \tilde{W}_{\bar{c}}^2 - \bar{c}\tilde{W}_{\bar{c}}(1), \tag{26}$$

where the notation is the same as that defined above in Section 3.2. The test is performed by comparing the observed value of the statistic with the critical value obtained by simulation. The presence of a unit root in the data is rejected if the calculated value of the statistic $\tilde{P}_{\bar{c}}$ is too small. Note that in the construction of $\tilde{P}_{\bar{c}}$, the estimate $\hat{\omega}^2$ is used and this is obtained in the same way as in the Z_t test, i.e., using residuals from the regression (6). This point is of some importance and affects the consistency of the test — see Section 3.4 below.

3.4. *Asymptotic properties and local power*

All of the above test statistics are asymptotically *similar* in the sense that their limit distributions are free of nuisance parameters. However, the limit distributions do depend on whether the data has been prefiltered in any way by preliminary regression. Thus, if deterministic trends are removed by regression as in (6) or (20), then the limit distributions of the unit root test statistics depend on limiting versions of the deterministic trends that are used in the detrending regressions.

The tests are also consistent against stationary alternatives provided that any nonparametric estimator of ω^2 that is used in the test converges in probability under the alternative to a positive limit as $n \to \infty$. The latter condition is important, and it typically fails when estimates of ω^2 are constructed using first differences or quasi-differences of the data rather than regression residuals. This is because, under the alternative hypothesis, the data are stationary and first differences (or quasi-differences) of stationary data have zero spectrum at the origin. (See Phillips and Ouliaris, 1990, for further discussion of this issue.) The point is especially important when 'detrending after quasi-differencing' is used, as outlined in Section 3.2 above, as in this case there is a natural tendency to estimate ω^2 from the residuals of this regression. In effect, while an efficient regression in quasi-differences may be run to detrend the data, an inefficient regression such as (6), where the autoregressive coefficient is estimated, must be run to estimate the long-run variance parameter ω^2. Thus, some care is needed in the formulation of tests that rely on nonparametric estimates of ω^2. The problem also arises in certain parametric unit root tests when nuisance parameters are estimated using first differenced data (as in the case of Solo's, 1984, LM test — see Saikonnen and Luukkonen, 1993).

Rates of divergence of the statistics under the alternative are also available. For instance, when $|\alpha|<1$, Z_α, $\tilde{Z}_\alpha$, ADF_α, $VN = O_p(n)$, and Z_t, $ADF_t = O_p(n^{1/2})$ as $n \to \infty$. Thus, coefficient-based tests that rely on the estimated autoregressive coefficient and the von Neumann ratio/LM tests diverge at a faster rate than tests that are based on the regression t-ratio. We may therefore expect such tests to have greater power than t-ratio tests, and this is generally borne out in simulations. Heuristically, the t-ratio tests suffer because there is no need to estimate a scale parameter when estimating the autoregressive coefficient α. The autoregressive estimators $\hat{\alpha}$, and $\tilde{\alpha}$, on the other hand, are already scale invariant. Note also that while $ADF_t^2 = O_p(n)$ and therefore has the same divergence characteristics as Z_α, $\tilde{Z}_\alpha$, ADF_α, and VN, the statistic ADF_t^2 produces a nondirectional test, whereas the coefficient-based tests are directional (against stationarity, or explosive behavior).

Under the local alternative hypothesis (19), the limit theory for the above statistics can be derived and used to analyze local asymptotic power. When (2) and (19) hold, y_t^s behaves asymptotically like a linear diffusion, i.e., $n^{-1/2}y_{[nr]}^s \Rightarrow J_c(r) = \int_0^r e^{(r-s)c}dW(s)$ (see Phillips, 1987b). The limit distributions of the unit root test statistics then involve functionals of $J_c(r)$. For example, the Z_α statistic has the limit

$$Z_\alpha \Rightarrow c + \left[\int_0^1 J_{cX}dW\right]\left[\int_0^1 J_{cX}^2\right]^{-1}, \tag{27}$$

where $J_{cX}(r) = J_c(r) - (\int_0^1 J_c X')(\int_0^1 XX')^{-1}X(r)$. This limit is identical to that of the Dickey-Fuller test that is based directly on the coefficient estimator $n(\hat{a} - 1)$ when u_t has no serial correlation and no corrections are required to make the statistic asymptotically similar. Thus, the corrections for residual serial correlation in the statistic Z_α do not lead to any loss in asymptotic power.

The local asymptotic theory can be used to construct asymptotic power envelopes for unit root tests. Under the hypothesis that the data is Gaussian, the best test of a unit root against the specific local alternative with $c = \bar{c}$ is given by the point optimal test by virtue of the Neyman-Pearson lemma. When efficient detrending under this alternative is used, the resulting test statistic is $\tilde{P}_{\bar{c}}$ as given in (26). The limit distribution of this statistic under the specific local alternative $c = \bar{c}$ is

$$\tilde{P}_{\bar{c}} \Rightarrow \bar{c}^2 \int_0^1 \tilde{J}_{\bar{c}}^2 - \bar{c}\tilde{J}_{\bar{c}}(1), \tag{28}$$

where $\tilde{J}_{\bar{c}}(r) = J_{\bar{c}}(r) - X(r)(\int_0^1 X_{\bar{c}} X_{\bar{c}}')^{-1}(\int_0^1 X_{\bar{c}} dW - \bar{c}\int_0^1 X_{\bar{c}} J_{\bar{c}})$. As we vary the parameter $\bar{c}$, this distribution delivers a power envelope against which other tests may be compared. Note that the limit given in (28) is attainable by the POI test (26) only when $c = \bar{c}$ exactly. In general, the chosen value of c that is used in the QD detrending procedure on which (26) is based will be different, and hence the power of the POI test will generally be less than that delivered by (28). In the special case of a linear tend, computations in Stock (1995) indicate that the POI test (26) has power that is very close to the power envelope for a wide range of local alternatives.

3.5. *Further issues on size and power*

Two further issues relating to the size and power of unit root tests deserve attention. The first of these arises from some recent work of Phillips (1998a, b) showing that nonstationary time series admit many different representations. The most obvious representation comes directly from the model formulation (2) itself. However, Phillips (1998a) shows that there are valid alternative representations in terms of deterministic functions. These representations originate in the corresponding representation of the limiting Brownian motion for which $n^{-1/2}y_{[nr]}^s \Rightarrow B(r)$. Indeed, for $B(r)$ we have the following L_2-representation

$$W(r) = \omega\sqrt{2}\sum_{k=1}^{\infty} \frac{\sin[(k-1/2)\pi r]}{(k-1/2)\pi}\,\xi_k = \omega\sum_{k=1}^{\infty}\varphi_k(r)\xi_k, \tag{29}$$

where the components ξ_k are independently and identically distributed (iid) as $N(0, 1)$ and the functions $\varphi_k(r)$ form an orthogonal set in $L_2[0, 1]$. Phillips shows that empirical regressions of y_t^s on $\varphi_{K,t} = (\varphi_1(t/T), \ldots, \varphi_K(t/T))'$ accurately reproduce in the limit the first K terms of the expansion (29). Further, when $K \to \infty$ and $K/T \to 0$ as $T \to \infty$, such regressions succeed in reproducing the entire representation (29). It follows that these deterministic functions are capable of successfully representing a nonstationary time series like y_t^s in the limit as $T \to \infty$.

Such regressions on deterministic functions then become an alternate way of modelling a nonstationary time series. A fascinating implication of this work is that unit root tests which involve deterministic functions, like (1) above, will inevitably lead to the rejection of the unit root hypothesis when $K, T \longrightarrow \infty$ and in this sense the conventional critical values used in unit root tests (like those based on the limit functionals (11) and (12)) are invalid asymptotically when the competing deterministic functions that appear in the maintained hypothesis provide an alternative mechanism of modelling the non-stationarity, as in cases like polynomial trends and trend break polynomials they will. These issues are further explored in ongoing research in Phillips (1998b). It is too early to comment on the full implications of this work, but the results are of obvious importance in the empirical assessment of trend/trend-break stationarity versus persistence in economic time series.

The second issue emerges from some recent work by Faust (1996). Faust pointed out that while unit root tests like the Z_a, Z_t, and ADF_t tests have limit distributions under the null that are invariant to the nuisance parameters σ^2, ω^2 and λ, the non-parametric nature of the maintained hypothesis can cause difficulties. In particular, the key condition that underlies the unit root null hypothesis in (2) is that $C(1) \neq 0$. In fact, using the BN expansion of the operator $C(L)$, we have, as in (5) above

$$u_t = C(1)\varepsilon_t + \tilde{\varepsilon}_{t-1} - \tilde{\varepsilon}_t, \quad \text{with } \tilde{\varepsilon}_t = \tilde{C}(L)\varepsilon_t. \tag{30}$$

It follows that if $C(1) = 0$, then $y_t^s = \tilde{\varepsilon}_0 - \tilde{\varepsilon}_t + y_0^s$, which is stationary. Of course, in the $I(1)$ class for y_t^s there will be some error processes u_t satisfying (3) for which $C(1)$ is arbitrarily close to zero. Indeed, Faust shows for any real a, the set of sequences

$$\mathscr{C}_a = \{c = (c_j)_1^\infty : c_j = 0 \text{ for all but a finite number of } j;\ C(1) = a\}$$

is dense in l_2, the space of square summable sequences. It follows that given a sequence $c = (c_j)_1^\infty$ of coefficients in the Wold representation of u_t for which $C(1) = a \neq 0$, there is a sequence $c' = (c_j')_1^\infty$ that is arbitrarily close to c in l_2 but for which $C'(1) = \sum_{j=0}^\infty c_j' = 0$. Faust concludes that the $I(1)$ sequences, for which $C(1) \neq 0$, and the $I(0)$ sequences, for which $C(1) = 0$, are both dense in l_2, and hence these classes of processes are nearly observationally equivalent. (Campbell and Perron, 1991, and Blough, 1992, also indicated that this property may affect unit root tests.) One implication of this near observational equivalence, is that the size of semi-parametric unit root tests will not converge to the nominal size given by the limit distribution, at least when the size is computed by taking the supremum of the rejection probability of the unit root test over the set $\mathscr{G}_\eta = \{c \in \mathscr{C}_a : |C(1)| > \eta > 0\}$ for any η. (In fact, Faust shows that the actual size of the test converges to unity). In view of (30), the restriction $\eta > 0$ would normally be interpreted as setting up a buffer zone between the class of $I(1)$ and $I(0)$ processes. Faust's result shows that even this buffer zone does not prevent size distortions in a general enough nonparametric setting for the error process.

The reason for the size distortion is that the nonparametric (composite) form of the null hypothesis is too broad as it stands. As is apparent from (30), the error processes that lead to the size distortion involve sequences like $c' = (c_j')_1^\infty$ that are arbitrarily close in l_2 to a null sequence c (for which $C(1) \neq 0$) but which have $C'(1) = \sum_{j=0}^{\infty} c_j' = 0$. However, for these sequences c' to produce data y_t^s that have $I(1)$-like properties, the second component $\tilde{\varepsilon}_t' = \tilde{C}'(L)\varepsilon_t$ in the BN decomposition of

$$u_t' = C'(L)\varepsilon_t = C'(1)\varepsilon_t + \tilde{\varepsilon}_{t-1}' - \tilde{\varepsilon}_t'$$

must also have $I(1)$-like properties. It is, in fact, quite easy to exclude this possibility by placing a smoothness requirement on spectrum of $\tilde{\varepsilon}_t'$. This can be accomplished by a summability condition on the allowable sequences $\{\tilde{c}_j'\}$, which is in turn assured by a summability condition on the original sequence c'. It turns out that a strengthening of the summability condition used in Phillips and Solo (1992) to validate the BN decomposition is sufficient to rule out the pathology of $I(0)$ sequences with near $I(1)$ behavior.

4. Finite sample properties of unit root tests

Extensive simulations have been conducted to explore the finite sample performance of unit root tests (inter alia, Schwert, 1989; Diebold and Rudebusch, 1991; DeJong *et al.*, 1992; Phillips and Perron, 1988; Ng and Perron, 1995; and Stock, 1995). One general conclusion to emerge is that, although differences exist across tests and these depend on the models generating the data, the discriminatory power in all of the tests between models with a root at unity and a root close to unity is generally low. For instance, power is usually less than 30% for $\alpha \in [0.90, 1.0)$ and $n = 100$. Power is reduced further by detrending the data — even larger values of the test statistics are required to achieve a rejection of the null and the power curve is lower. Both these features mirror the asymptotic theory. However, as the discussion in the previous section indicates, some of the observed power reduction is spurious, because the critical values of the tests are inappropriate when extensive deterministic detrending is done prior to testing for unit roots.

Another interesting finding from simulation studies is the extent of the finite sample size distortion (the difference between the nominal asymptotic size of the test and the actual finite sample size) of the tests in cases where the true model is close to a trend stationary process (Schwert 1989). For example, if u_t in (2) follows a moving average process $u_t = \varepsilon_t + \theta\varepsilon_{t-1}$ whose parameter is large and negative, then the sample trajectories of y_t^s more closely resemble those of a stationary process than a random walk. In such cases there is a tendency for all of the tests to over-reject the null of a unit root. This is an outcome that may not be so serious in practical work if the data are indeed better modeled by a trend stationary process, and so it is easy to overstate the importance of size distortions in such cases.

Tests that are based directly on autoregressive coefficient estimates like the Z_α tend to be more affected by size distortion than the other tests because the bias in the first order autoregressive estimator is large in this case, not only in finite samples but even in the asymptotic distribution (9), where the miscentering is measured by the bias parameter $\lambda = \theta\sigma_\varepsilon^2$. This is large when θ is large, and good estimates of the bias parameter are needed to control the size distortion. The one sided covariance parameter λ is usually estimated in a nonparametric way by kernel methods which often give confidence intervals with low coverage probabilities, especially when the time series has substantial temporal dependence. The parameter is also estimated at a slower rate than $\sqrt{n}$, and it is therefore often difficult to estimate well with samples of the size that are typical in many econometric applications (with $n \leqslant 200$). Similar comments apply to the estimation of the long run variance parameter ω^2, which appears in the other semi-parametric tests.

Recent attempts to improve the estimation of this parameter using data-determined bandwidth choices (Andrews, 1991) coupled with prewhitening (Andrews & Monahan, 1992), and data-based model selection and prewhitening (Lee & Phillips, 1994) offer some promise in this direction, as does pretesting for lag length in ADF regressions (Ng and Perron 1998). In particular, prewhitening is shown to bring better accuracy and less variance to kernel estimators. The idea behind prewhitening is to transform the data to reduce temporal dependence before applying kernel estimation. The transformed data typically have a flatter spectrum which can be estimated with less bias than the original spectrum. The kernel density estimator for the original data can then be obtained by applying the inverse transformation. Andrews and Monahan (1992) introduced a class of VAR prewhitened kernel estimators. In the scalar case, Lee and Phillips (1994) extend this idea by employing model selection techniques in the prewhitening stage and implement the Hannan-Rissanen recursion to efficiently estimate an ARMA model prefilter prior to estimating the long run variance ω^2 by kernel techniques. It is shown that, with this method, $\sqrt{n}$-rates of estimation are achievable with nonparametric estimates when consistent *model selection* techniques are used to determine the prefilter and the model for the errors lies within the prefiltering class (in this case the class of finite parameter ARMA models).

The parametric ADF t-ratio test is less affected by size distortions when the true model is close to stationarity, but generally has less power than the other tests. As shown by simulation experiments, the coefficient-based tests and VN ratio tests typically have better power properties than the ADF t-ratio test. Although on theoretic grounds it is known that the lag length of the ADF regression can grow at a rate $o(n^{1/3})$, not much information is provided in this rate criterion about lag length selection for specific sample sizes. With these tests, power is further reduced by the inclusion of additional lagged dependent regressors in (13). It has been found in many Monte Carlo studies that lag length selection has important effects on the finite sample performance of ADF tests. DeJong *et al.* (1992) show in their simulation results that increasing the lag length typically lowers the power in a systematic way, although it may also reduce size distortion. Again, the use of model selection methods like BIC (Schwarz, 1978; Rissanen, 1978) are useful in this respect and provide some improvement in the finite sample performance of the ADF tests. Ng and Perron (1995, 1998) studied the choice of lag length in constructing the ADF t-test and compared information-based model selection rules, such as BIC and AIC (Akaike, 1977), with classical sequential tests in determining lag length, such as F- and t-tests for the significance of the lag coefficients. They show that data-dependent rules which take sample information into account have beneficial effects on the finite sample performance of unit root tests.

Since detrending the data reduces power, it is to be expected that the inclusion of surplus trend variables in regressions like (6) will do so also. Hence, efficient detrending procedures like those discussed in Section 3.2 can be expected to benefit all tests, and this is partly confirmed by simulations in Stock (1995). Of all the procedures studied so far, efficient detrending by regression in quasi-differences seems to be the most successful in increasing finite sample (and asymptotic) power.

We provide some Monte Carlo results here, partially illustrating the findings in existing simulation studies, with an emphasis on studying the effect of the procedures mentioned above on the finite sample performance of common unit root tests. In particular, we examine the effect of model selection procedures, bandwidth selection methods, prewhitening and detrending procedures on the finite sample power of the following unit root tests: ADF_α, ADF_t, Z_α, Z_t tests combined with various detrending procedures; and VN and POI tests. For the ADF tests, the BIC criterion of Schwarz (1978) and Rissanen (1978) is used in selecting the appropriate lag length of the autoregression and the AR spectral estimator of Berk (1974) is used for the estimation of the long run variance parameter. Thus, in this Monte Carlo experiment, the ADF tests are all parametric. For the Z tests, the Andrews and Monahan prewhitened kernel estimation of the long run variance parameter is used. Although comparison has been made for different kernel choices, only those results using the Parzen kernel function are reported because no unambiguous ranking could be found among different kernels. Size-corrected power is reported in the simulations to provide a comparison among the different tests, although it does not reflect empirical rejection frequencies based on the use of asymptotic critical values. The finite sample critical values are calculated as quantiles in the simulations under the null hypothesis of a unit root, given the model selection rules and kernel choices.

The simulation results suggest some general findings. First, using data-based bandwidth choice coupled with prewhitening procedures in the estimation of nuisance parameters significantly improves the finite sample performance of the Z tests. Second, the use of model selection procedures like BIC in choosing lag length helps to improve the ADF tests. Third, unit root tests based on QD detrending have reasonably good finite sample properties, especially in the case where the deterministic trend includes a constant term.

Table A reports the size-corrected power of ADF and Z tests for the case without deterministic trends. Four designs for the data generating process are considered here. In each case, $y_t = y_t^s$, $y_t^s = \alpha y_{t-1}^s + u_t$, and initial values are set to be 0. The four different error structures are: an AR(1) process $u_t = \rho u_{t-1} + \varepsilon_t$, with $\rho = 0.5, -0.5$ and an MA(1) process $u_t = \varepsilon_t - \theta\varepsilon_{t-1}$, with $\theta = 0.5, -0.8$, where ε_t are iid standard normal variates. For the case with a deterministic trend, the size corrected power properties are reported in Figures 1 to 10. Figure 1 depicts the power of four (OLS detrended) unit root tests (Z_α, Z_t, ADF_α, ADF_t) when the error process is AR(1) with $\rho = 0.5$, and Figure 2 reports the results for these tests when u_t is MA(1) process with $\theta = 0.5$. Figures 3 and 4 compare different tests based on the same detrending procedures, and Figures 5 to 8 compare the effects of different detrending procedures on the same tests. All these experiments study the case where u_t is an iid standard normal process. Specifically, power comparisons among five tests (Z_α, Z_t, ADF_α, ADF_t and VN) are given in Figure 3. The power envelope is also provided in the graph for convenience of comparison. The power of the QD detrended versions of these tests are given in Figure 4. Figure 5 compares the power of the OLS detrended Z_α test with those of the QD detrended Z_α tests for different choices of the prespecified local parameter $\bar{c}$, and Figures 6, 7, and 8 compare the power of Z_t, ADF_α, and ADF_t tests respectively for different choices of detrending procedures. Figures 9 and 10 give the power of these tests for another form of deterministic trend.

DeJong *et al.* (1992) find from their Monte Carlo study that the semiparametric Z tests have very low power when there is positive serial correlation, while the ADF_t test is reasonably well-behaved in this case. Their results were obtained based on commonly used estimators of the nuisance parameters without

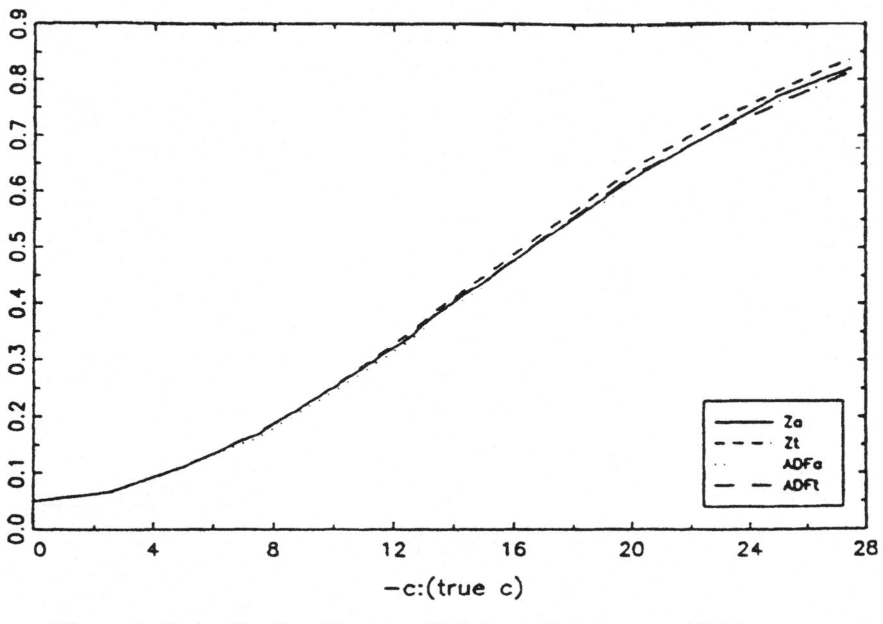

Figure 1. Power for Four Tests — OLS detrending case — AR(1) error

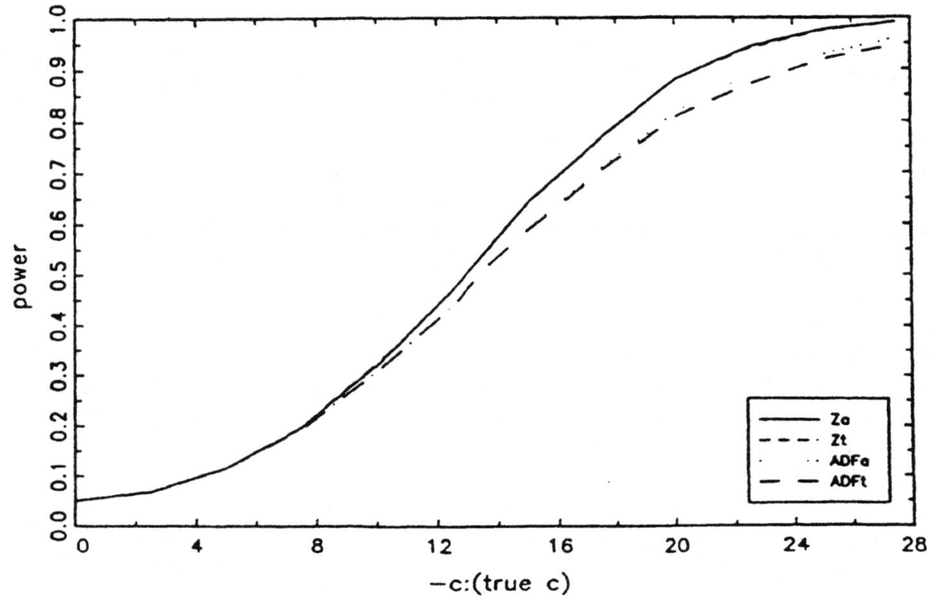

Figure 2. Power for Four Tests — OLS detrending case — MA(1) error

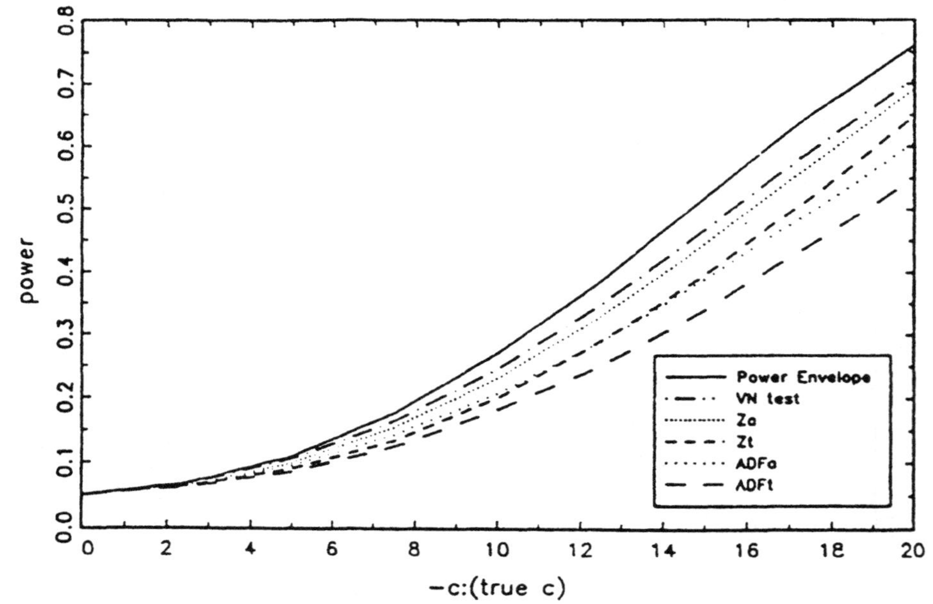

Figure 3. Power for Five Tests — OLS detrending case

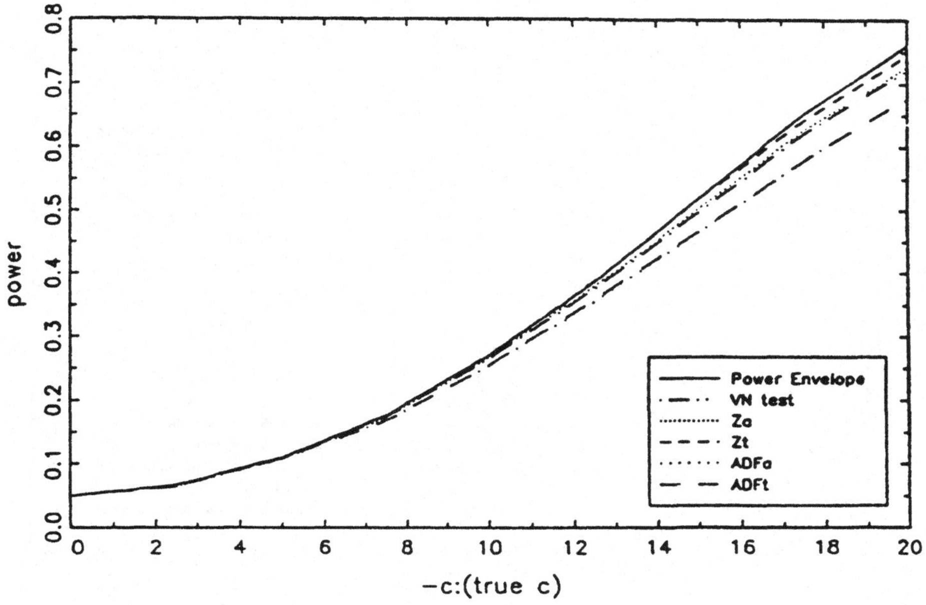

Figure 4. Power for Five Tests — GLS detrending case (c = −10)

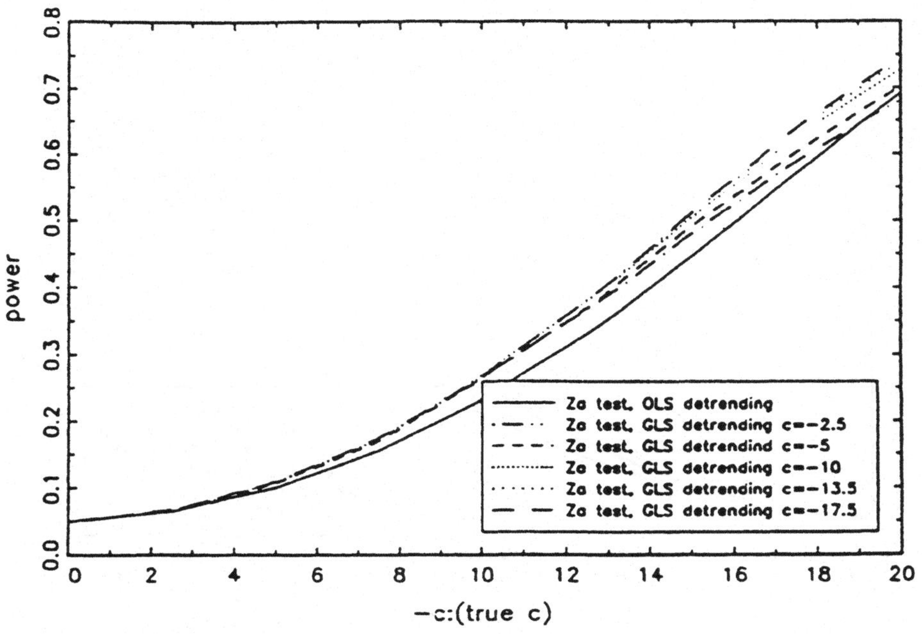

Figure 5. Power of Za tests based on different detrending procedures

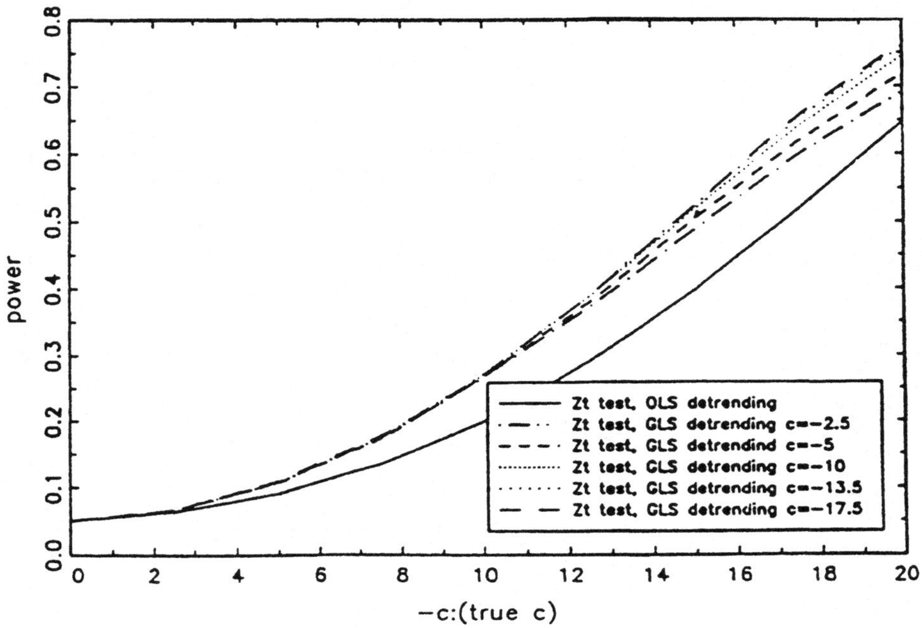

Figure 6. Power of Zt tests based on different detrending procedures

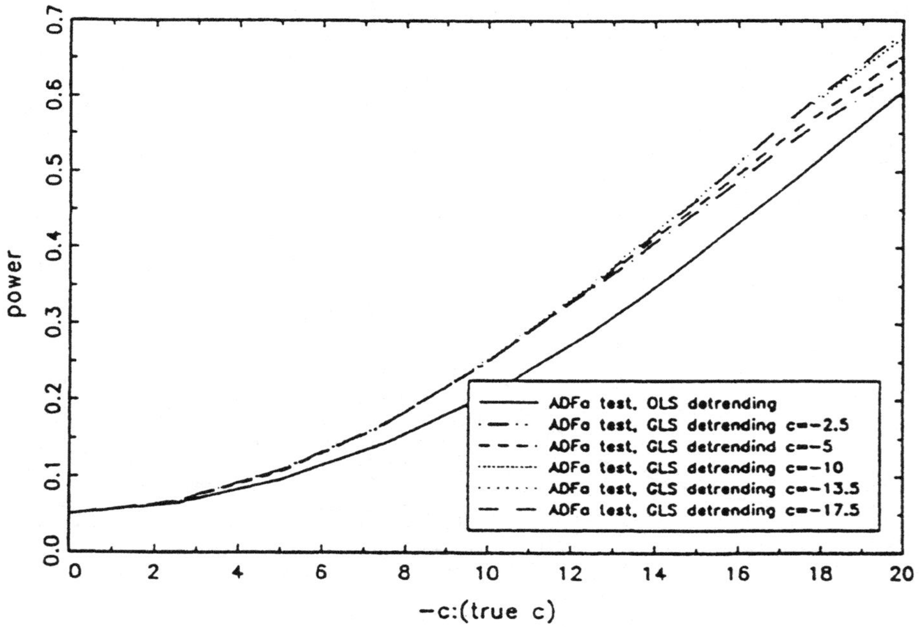

Figure 7. Power of ADFa tests based on different detrending procedures

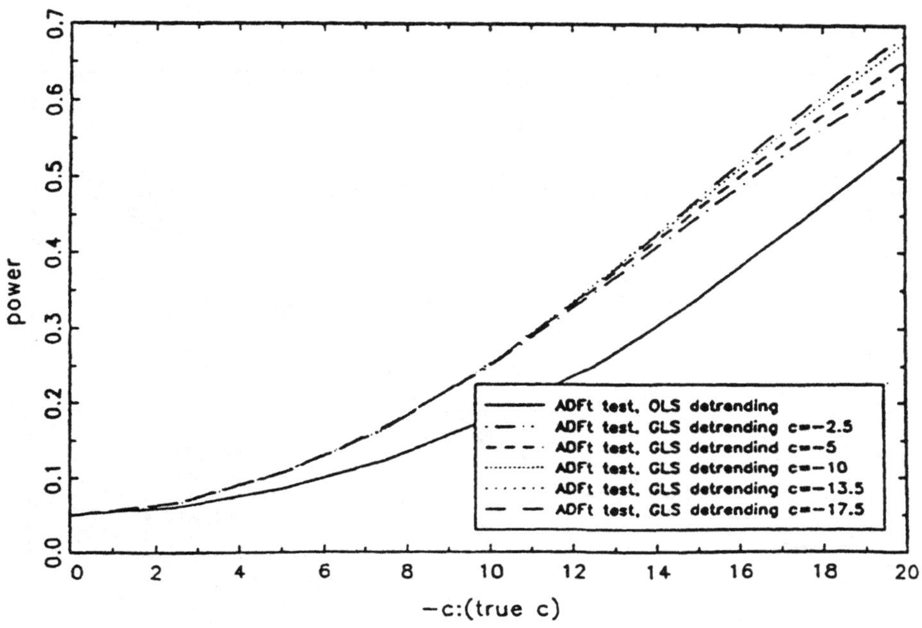

Figure 8. Power of ADFt tests based on different detrending procedures

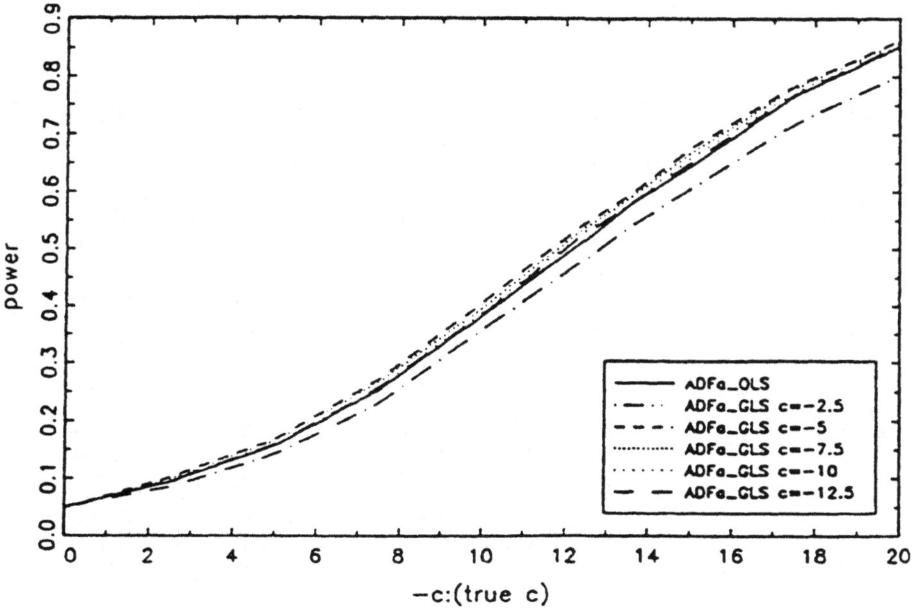

Figure 9. Effect of GLS detrending on ADFa test — iid error

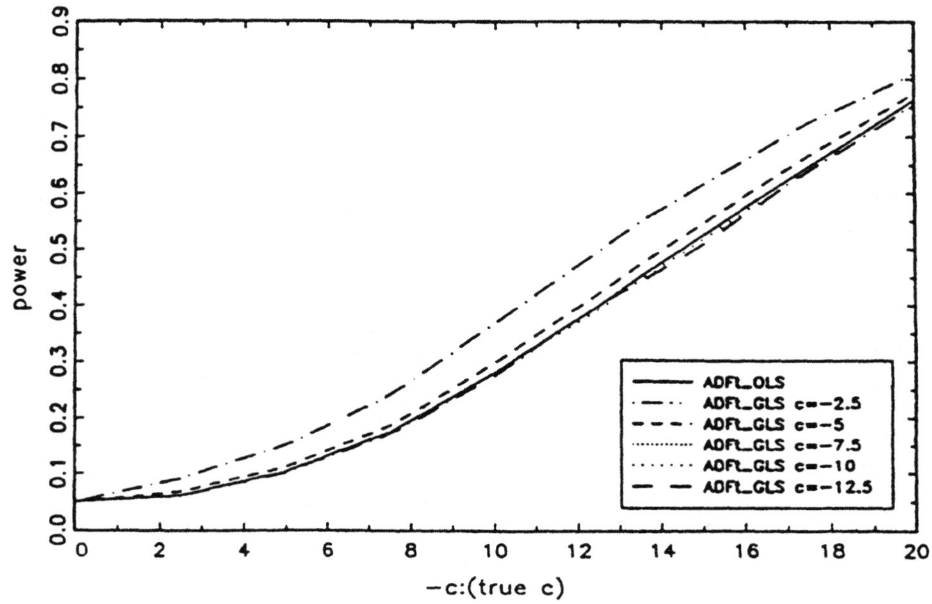

Figure 10. Effect of GLS detrending on ADFt test — iid error

Table A. Size corrected power of unit root tests 5% level, no deterministic trend

Test	α	AR(1) $\rho = 0.5$	AR(1) $\rho = -0.5$	MA(1) $\theta = 0.5$	MA(1) $\theta = -0.8$
ADF_α	0.95	0.216	0.234	0.181	0.251
	0.9	0.458	0.524	0.478	0.566
	0.85	0.622	0.717	0.650	0.758
ADF_t	0.95	0.211	0.233	0.171	0.248
	0.9	0.448	0.522	0.472	0.565
	0.85	0.618	0.716	0.649	0.761
Z_α	0.95	0.228	0.268	0.198	0.268
	0.9	0.536	0.615	0.520	0.619
	0.85	0.718	0.792	0.698	0.792
Z_t	0.95	0.222	0.268	0.196	0.266
	0.9	0.538	0.618	0.516	0.611
	0.85	0.718	0.806	0.707	0.792

prewhitening and without data-based bandwidth selection. We apply the Andrews-Monahan procedure for estimating the long run variance parameter in the Z tests and found that the data-based bandwidth selection and prewhitening procedures have very important effects on the Z tests. The finite sample performance of the Z tests improves significantly with the use of this estimator of the long run variance, especially for the case with positive serial correlation. The size distortion, although still present, is also decreased after using the prewhitening procedure. Table A shows that the Z tests, with data-based bandwidth choice coupled with prewhitening, generally have higher size corrected power than the *ADF* tests. Qualitatively similar results can also be found in Figures 1 and 2 when a deterministic trend is included. The results from Figure 1 to Figure 3 also confirm the findings in other simulation experiments that coefficient based tests generally have higher power than the t-ratio tests, at least in large samples, and they show the relatively good finite sample properties of the *VN* test.

Figures 3 to 10 show the effect of different detrending procedures on the finite sample power of unit root tests. Two forms of deterministic trend were considered in the experiment. The first case, $x_t = a + bt$, includes both an intercept term and a time trend, while the second case, $x_t = t$, does not have a constant term. Figures 3, 4, 5, 6, 7, and 8 correspond to the first case with both a constant term and a time trend, and Figures 9 and 10 correspond to the second case with no constant term. These figures show that QD detrending increases the finite sample power of unit root tests, especially when the deterministic trend includes a constant term. Among the four tests, Z_α, Z_t, ADF_α, and ADF_t, QD detrending brings the largest power gains to the t-ratio based tests. Different choices of the prespecified local parameter $\bar{c}$ were tried and the results show that, in the case $x_t = a + bt$, for quite a wide range of choices of $\bar{c}$, the QD detrended tests have reasonably good power properties against alternatives close to the unit root. Differences among the tests using different $\bar{c}$ occur when the true local parameter c becomes larger (in absolute value), corresponding to alternatives that are distant from a unit root. As the true value of $|c|$ becomes large, a QD detrended test with $\bar{c} = -2.5$ has power lower than tests using a larger $\bar{c}$ (in absolute value). This phenomenon is expected because, from the perspective of a point optimal test, the power should be higher when the prespecified $\bar{c}$ is closer to the true c value.

Another important phenomenon we see from these figures is the difference between the case with a constant term in the deterministic trend and the case with no constant term. Figures 7, 8, 9, and 10 compare the *ADF* tests combined with different detrending procedures for the two kinds of deterministic trend removal. The QD detrended tests seem to be more sensitive to the choice of $\bar{c}$ in the case without a constant term. A larger power gain from QD detrending is found in the presence of a constant term. Phillips and Lee (1996) provide an analysis of the effects of a fitted intercept. In most practical applications, an intercept will be included in the deterministic trend and so QD detrending can be expected to be successful in improving the finite sample power of unit root tests.

5. Unit root tests against trends with structural breaks

Just as dummy variables are used in regression to deal with unusual observations and shifts in the mean, breaks in deterministic trend functions can be employed to capture changes in trend. This possibility is already included in the specification of h_t in (1). For instance, the trend function

$$h_t = \sum_{j=0}^{p} f_j t^j + \sum_{j=0}^{p} f_{m,j}\, t^j_m, \text{where } t^j_m = \begin{cases} 0 & t \in \{1, \ldots, m\} \\ (t-m)^j & t \in \{m+1, \ldots, n\} \end{cases} \tag{31}$$

allows for the presence of a structural change in the polynomial trend at the data point $t = m + 1$. Suppose $\mu = \lim_{n\to\infty}(m/n) > 0$ is the limit of the fraction of the sample where this structural change occurs. Then the limiting trend function $X_\mu(r)$ corresponding to (31) has a similar break at the point μ. The unit root tests and power functions considered above, including those that make use of efficient detrending procedures, all continue to apply as given for such broken trend functions. Indeed, (31) may be extended further to allow for multiple break points in the sample and in the limit process without affecting the theory. The tests may be interpreted as tests for the presence of a unit root in models where broken trends may be present in the data. The alternative hypothesis in this case is that the data are stationary about a broken deterministic trend of degree p.

In order to construct unit root tests that allow for breaking trends like (31) it is necessary to specify the break point m. (Correspondingly, the limit theory depends on the limit processes $X(r)$ and $\check{X}(r)$ and these depend on the break point μ.) In effect, the break point is exogenously determined. Perron (1989) considered linear trends with single break points in this way. An alternative perspective is that the break point(s) is (are) endogenous to the data and unit root tests should take account of this fact. In this case, alternative unit root tests have been suggested (e.g., Banerjee *et al.*, 1990, and Zivot & Andrews, 1992) that endogenize the break point by choosing the value of m that gives the least favorable view of the unit root hypothesis. This has been done for the parametric ADF test and for linear trends with breaks. If $ADF(m)$ denotes the ADF statistic given by the t-ratio for α in the ADF regression (13) with a broken trend function like (31), then the trend break ADF statistic is

$$ADF(\hat{m}) = \min_{\underline{m} \leq m \leq \overline{m}} ADF(m), \text{ where } \underline{m} = [n\underline{\mu}],\ \overline{m} = [n\overline{\mu}] \text{ and } 0 < \underline{\mu} < \overline{\mu} < 1, \tag{32}$$

and $[\cdot]$ signifies the integer part of its argument. The limit theory for this trend break ADF statistic is given by

$$ADF(\hat{m}) \Rightarrow \inf_{\mu \in [\underline{\mu}, \overline{\mu}]} \left[\int_0^1 W_{X\mu} dW\right]\left[\int_0^1 W^2_{X\mu}\right]^{-1/2}, \tag{33}$$

where the limit process $X_\mu(r)$ that appears in this functional on the right side is now dependent on the trend break point μ over which the functional is minimized. Similar extensions to trend breaks are possible for the other unit root tests considered above. Critical values of the limiting test statistic (33) are naturally further out in the tail than those of the exogenous trend break statistic, so it is harder to reject the null hypothesis of a unit root when the break point is considered to be endogenous.

Asymptotic and finite sample critical values for the endogenized trend break *ADF* unit root test are given in Zivot & Andrews (1992). Simulations studies indicate that the introduction of trend break functions leads to further reductions in the power of unit root tests and to substantial finite sample size distortion in the tests. Sample trajectories of a random walk are often similar to those of a process that is stationary about a broken trend for some particular breakpoint (and even more so when several break points are permitted in the trend). So continuing reductions in the power of unit root tests against competing models of this type is to be expected. In view of the fact that Brownian motion can be represented as an infinite linear random combination of deterministic functions of time, as shown in (29) above, there are good theoretical reasons for anticipating this outcome. Carefully chosen trend stationary models can always be expected to provide reasonable representations of given random walk data, but such models are certain to fail in post sample projections as the post sample data drifts away from the final trend line. Phillips (1998a,1998b) explores these issues in a systematic way.

6. Fractional integration

Although most attention has been focused on $I(1)$ and $I(0)$ processes in econometric applications, the concept of an integrated process generalizes to higher order integration and fractional integration. These concepts are embodied in the following extended version of (2)

$$(1 - L)^d y_t^s = u_t, \tag{34}$$

where d may be fractional and the operator $(1 - L)^d$ is defined by the formal binomial expansion

$$(1 - L)^d = 1 + \sum_{j=1}^{\infty} \frac{(-d)_j}{j!} L^j, \quad (a)_j = (-a)(-a + 1), \ldots, (-a + j - 1) \tag{35}$$

whose convergence properties depend on the value of d. Note that (35) terminates when d is a positive integer. The process y_t^s is said to be an $I(d)$ process. With this generalization, there may be one or several unit roots (d integer $\geqslant 1$) or fractional integration ($0 < d < 1$). Such processes have been the subject of intensive recent research and are reviewed in Robinson (1994a) and Baillie (1996). When $0 < d < 1/2$, y_t^s is stationary but *strongly correlated* in the sense that its lag-j autocovariance γ_j decays at the rate $|j|^{2d-1}$, which is slower than that of stationary linear processes like u_t. When $1/2 \leqslant d \leqslant 1$, y_t^s is nonstationary, and the value $d = 1/2$ provides the nexus between stationary and nonstationary regions. When d is an integer $\geqslant 2$, it is called higher order integration. In this case, y_t^s has two or more real autoregressive unit roots and is stationary after differencing d times. A process with $d \geqslant 1/2$ has nonstationary long-memory and a variance that explodes as $t \longrightarrow \infty$. Such processes are, in fact, not mean reverting, although their impulse responses, which are obtained from the expansion

$$(1 - L)^{-d} = 1 + \sum_{j=1}^{\infty} \frac{(d)_j}{j!} L^j$$

and have the form

$$\frac{(d)_j}{j!} = \frac{1}{\Gamma(d)} \frac{\Gamma(d+j)}{\Gamma(j+1)} \sim \frac{1}{\Gamma(d)} \frac{1}{j^{1-d}} \text{ as } j \to \infty,$$

decay to zero provided $d < 1$, and so shocks in (34) are not persistent in this case.

Within the family (34) it is possible to test for 'unit root' nonstationarity by estimating d and testing the null hypothesis $d = 1$ against the alternative $d < 1$, or to test for stationarity $d < 1/2$ against $d = 1/2$. At present, the literature has focussed on parametric tests, because of the difficulties of a general treatment that covers both stationary and nonstationary cases in the semiparametric case, i.e., when u_t is treated nonparametrically in estimation and inference about d.

Robinson (1994b) took model (1) and (34) and proposed a unit root test against fractional alternatives based on the LM principle. Consider a test of the null hypothesis H_{d_0}: $d = d_0$ in the simple case where the u_t are iid $N(0, \sigma^2)$ variates. Let $L(\eta)$ be the negative of the log-likelihood of u_t, where $\eta = (d, \gamma, \sigma^2)$, then an LM (score) statistic is

$$\tilde{R} = \frac{\partial L(\eta)}{\partial \eta'} \left[E\left(\frac{\partial L(\eta)}{\partial \eta} \frac{\partial L(\eta)}{\partial \eta'} \middle| H_{d_0} \right) \right]^{-1} \frac{\partial L(\eta)}{\partial \eta} \bigg|_{d = d_0, \gamma = \tilde{\gamma}, \sigma^2 = \tilde{\sigma}^2} = \tilde{r}'\tilde{r}.$$

Let $\Delta^d = (1 - L)^d$ and take fractional differences of equation (1) under the null, leading to

$$\Delta^{d_0} y_t = \gamma' \, \Delta^{d_0} x_t + \Delta^{d_0} y_t^s. \tag{36}$$

Under H_{d_0}, $\Delta^{d_0} y_t^s = u_t$. Estimating the trend coefficient γ by (36) and calculating the fitted residuals $\tilde{u}_t$ using this trend estimator, we obtain $\tilde{\sigma}^2 = n^{-1} \sum_t \tilde{u}_t^2$. The LM test statistic $\tilde{R}$ can then be calculated. Under certain regularity conditions, Robinson showed that the statistic $\tilde{r}$ has a standard normal limit distribution, and thus the LM test $\tilde{R}$ is asymptotically distributed as χ^2. The asymptotic theory justifies a one-sided test for a unit root H_0: $d = 1$ against a fractional alternative H_1: $d < 1$ which rejects the null hypothesis when $\tilde{r} < z_\alpha$, where z_α is the corresponding critical value of standard normal distribution. Tanaka (1999) considered similar parametric LM tests for the nonstationary case $d \geqslant 1/2$.

Under Gaussian assumptions, efficient parametric estimation of d can be obtained based on the maximum likelihood principle, provided the model is fully specified. However, since calculating these Gaussian estimates requires numerical methods of estimation and the good large sample properties rely on correct specification of the short memory components of the model, simpler estimates have been suggested that do not rely on full specification of the short memory components.

If u_t in (34) were a white-noise sequence with spectrum $f_u(\lambda) = (\sigma^2/2\pi)$, then the spectral density of $y_t^s, f(\lambda, d, \sigma^2)$ satisfies

$$\log f(\lambda, d, \sigma^2) = \log(\sigma^2/2\pi) - d \log|1 - e^{i\lambda}|^2. \tag{37}$$

If we denote the periodogram of y_t^s by $I(\lambda_j) = (2\pi n)^{-1} |\sum_{t=1}^n (y_t^s - \bar{y}^s) e^{it\lambda_j}|^2$, with $\lambda_j = 2\pi j/n$, and $\bar{y}^s = n^{-1} \sum_{t=1}^n y_t^s$, then, the form of (37) suggests a log periodogram regression of the type

$$\log I(\lambda_j) = c - d \log|1 - e^{i\lambda}|^2 + v_s. \tag{38}$$

If we confine attention to a set of $m < n$ fundamental frequencies $\{\lambda_j\}_{j=1}^m$ in this regression, then we can expect this procedure to give satisfactory results even when the spectrum of u_t is quite general because in that case $\log(f_u(\lambda)) \sim \log(f_u(0)) = c$ for $\lambda \to 0+$, which holds provided $m/n \to 0$. Such log periodogram regressions have been extensively used in empirical research largely because they are so convenient. However, the asymptotic properties of such estimates of d have only recently been obtained (Robinson, 1995; Hurvich *et al.*, 1998) and then only in the stationary Gaussian case. The essential difficulty was pointed out by Kunsch (1986), viz. that the periodogram ordinates $I(\lambda_j)$ in (38) are asymptotically correlated for fixed j. At present, there is no published asymptotic theory for the nonstationary case.

Another approach is to use an explicit model, like the following, to approximate the spectrum of a process with long-range dependence (see Robinson, 1994a)

$$f(\lambda, d, \beta) = \exp\left[\sum_{k=1}^{p-1} \beta_k \cos\{(k-1)\lambda\}\right] |1 - e^{i\lambda}|^{-2d}.$$

Notice that $\log|1 - e^{i\lambda}| = \sum_{k=1}^{\infty} (\cos k\lambda/k)$, so the above representation can be reparameterized as

$$f(\lambda, d, \beta) = \exp\left[\sum_{k=1}^{p-1} \theta_k \cos\{(k-1)\lambda\} - 2d \sum_{k=1}^{\infty} \frac{\cos k\lambda}{k}\right],$$

where $\theta = (\theta_1, \ldots, \theta_{p-1}, d)'$. Thus, the logarithm of $f(\lambda, d, \theta)$ is a linear function of θ and linear regression of $\log I(\lambda_j)$ on these components can be applied to estimate the parameters.

Another quite different approach is to locally approximate the Gaussian likelihood in the frequency domain, leading to the following objective function suggested by Künsch (1986)

$$Q_m(G, d) = \frac{1}{m} \sum_{j=1}^{m} \left[\log(G\lambda_j^{-2d}) + \frac{\lambda_j^{2d}}{G} I_x(\lambda_j)\right] \tag{39}$$

where $I_x(\lambda_j) = w_x(\lambda_j) w_x(\lambda_j)^*$ and m is some integer less than n. The parameters in

(39) are d and $G = f_u(0)$ and are estimated by minimizing $Q_m(G, d)$, so that

$$(\hat{G}, \hat{d}) = \arg \min_{0 < G < \infty,\, d > 0} Q_m(G, d),$$

which involves numerical optimization. Concentrating (39) with respect to G, we find that the estimate $\hat{d}$ satisfies

$$\hat{d} = \arg \min_{d} R(d),$$

where

$$R(d) = \log \hat{G}(d) - 2d \frac{1}{m} \sum_{j=1}^{m} \log \lambda_j, \quad \hat{G}(d) = \frac{1}{m} \sum_{j=1}^{m} \lambda_j^{2d} I_x(\lambda_j).$$

Recently, Robinson (1995a) analyzed the above estimators in the stationary case where $d \in (-\frac{1}{2}, \frac{1}{2})$. Under rather weak regularity conditions on the smoothness of $f_u(\lambda)$, the innovations in the Wold representation of u_t and an expansion rate condition on m, which requires that $m \to \infty$ but $(m/n) \to 0$ as $n \to \infty$, Robinson showed that $\hat{d} \to_p d_0$ and $\hat{G}(\hat{d}) \to_p G_0$. Under a slight strengthening of these conditions, Robinson also established that $\hat{d}$ is asymptotically normally distributed with the limit distribution

$$m^{1/2}(\hat{d} - d) \xrightarrow{d} N(0, \tfrac{1}{4}). \tag{40}$$

This limit theory makes testing and the construction of confidence intervals for d_0 a straightforward matter in the stationary case.

In recent unpublished work, Phillips (1998c) has dealt with the nonstationary case where $d \in (\frac{1}{2}, 1]$ and, under regularity conditions that are broadly similar to those of Robinson (1995b), has established that

$$\hat{d} \xrightarrow{p} d, \quad \hat{G}(\hat{d}) \xrightarrow{d} G_0 + C(d), \tag{41}$$

and

$$m^{1/2}(\hat{d} - d_0) \Rightarrow MN\left(0, \frac{1}{4} \frac{G_0^2}{(G_0 + C(d_0))^2}\right), \tag{42}$$

where $C(d) > 0$ is a random and depends on the true value of d. Since the variance in (42) is smaller than $1/4$, conservative confidence intervals can be constructed for d that utilize the limit theory (40) and apply for both stationary and nonstationary d.

Another approach to estimation of d stems from the properties of the autocovariances. If we approximate the spectral density $f(\lambda)$ by $c\lambda^{-2d}$ for λ close to 0, and denote $\mathrm{cov}(y_j, y_{j+h})$ by γ_h, then, under certain conditions (Yong, 1974), the relation $f(\lambda) \sim G\lambda^{-2d}$ as $\lambda \to 0$ is equivalent to '$\gamma_h \sim gh^{2d-1}$ as $h \to \infty$', for suitable g, providing semiparametric estimates of d based on estimates of γ_h for large h. For example, if $\hat{\gamma}_h$ are consistent estimates of γ_h, d can be consistently estimated by the following semiparametric estimate

$$\hat{d} = \frac{-\frac{1}{2}\sum_{h=n-p}^{n-1} \log \hat{\gamma}_h(\log h - \overline{\log h})}{\sum_{h=n-p}^{n-1} (\log h - \overline{\log h})^2},$$

where $\overline{\log h} = p^{-1} \sum_{h=n-p}^{n-1} \log h$, p increase suitably with n. Alternatively, d can be estimated by minimizing $\sum_{h=n-p}^{n-1}(\hat{\gamma}_h - Ch^{2d-1})^2$.

Other procedures than the ones discussed above are available and the subject is still under intensive study. Two recent surveys on the topic are given by Beran (1992) and Robinson (1994), and Baillie (1996) reviews many of the empirical aspects of fractional integration. Some applications to conditional heterogeneity are discussed in Baille *et al.* (1996).

7. Seasonal unit root tests

Another important extension of (2) is the seasonal unit root model

$$(1 - L^4)y_t = u_t. \tag{43}$$

Notice that the polynomial $1 - L^4$ can be expressed as $(1 - L)(1 + L)(1 + L^2)$. Thus, the unit roots (or roots on the unit circle) in (43) are 1, -1, i, and $-i$, corresponding to the annual ($L = 1$) frequency, the semi-annual ($L = -1$) frequency, and the quarter and three quarter annual ($L = i, -i$) frequency respectively. The model (43) is often relevant in practical work with quarterly data. Quarterly differencing, as in (43), is sometimes used as a seasonal adjustment device, and it is of interest to test whether the data supports the implied hypothesis of the presence of unit roots at these seasonal frequencies. Other types of seasonal processes, say monthly data, can be analyzed in the same way.

Dickey *et al.* (1984) proposed a test for the presence of a single unit root at a seasonal lag by considering the following model

$$y_t = \alpha y_{t-s} + \varepsilon_t.$$

The null hypothesis is $\alpha = 1$, and the alternative is $\alpha < 1$. The limit distribution of the least squares estimate of α is given and small-sample distributions for several values of s are provided based on Monte Carlo experiments. A more general case was studied by Hylleberg *et al.* (1990), extending the parametric *ADF* test to the case of seasonal unit roots. In order to accommodate fourth differencing as in (43) the autoregressive model is written in the new form

$$\Delta_4 y_t = \alpha_1 y_{1t-1} + \alpha_2 y_{2t-1} + \alpha_3 y_{3t-2} + \alpha_4 y_{3t-1} + \sum_{J=1}^{p} \varphi_j \Delta_4 y_{t-j} + \varepsilon_t, \tag{44}$$

where $\Delta_4 = 1 - L^4$, $y_{1t} = (1 + L)(1 + L^2)y_t$, $y_{2t} = -(1 - L)(1 + L^2)y_t$, $y_{3t} = -(1 - L^2)y_t$. The transformed data y_{1t}, y_{2t}, y_{3t} retain the unit root at the zero frequency (long run), the semi-annual frequency (two cycles per year), and the annual frequency (one cycle per year). When $\alpha_1 = \alpha_2 = \alpha_3 = \alpha_4 = 0$, there are unit roots at the zero and seasonal frequencies. To test the hypothesis of a unit root ($L = 1$) in this seasonal model, a t-ratio test of $\alpha_1 = 0$ is used. Similarly, the test for a semi-annual root ($L = -1$) is based on a t-ratio test of $\alpha_2 = 0$, and the test for an annual root on the t-ratios for $\alpha_3 = 0$ or $\alpha_4 = 0$. If each of the α's is different from zero, then the series has no unit roots at all and is stationary. Details of the implementation of this procedure are given in Hylleberg *et al.* (1990) and the limit theory for the tests is developed in Chan and Wei (1988).

As an alternative approach to the conventional seasonal unit root analysis, periodic models have been used in the study of seasonality. Under the framework of a periodic model, parameters are allowed to vary according to the time at which the series are observed. A definition of periodic integration and some testing procedures are provided in Osborn *et al.* (1988). Franses (1996) provides a useful reference on periodicity in the context of models with stochastic trends. There has also been work on seasonal versions of the fractional integration model (Porter Hudak, 1990), and seasonal versions of error correction models and reduced rank regressions (McAleer and Franses 1998). Hylleberg (1994) is a useful general reference on the topic.

8. Bayesian unit root tests

While most practical work on unit root testing has utilized classical procedures of the type discussed above, Bayesian methods offer certain advantages that are useful in empirical research. Foremost among these is the potential that these methods offer for embedding the unit root hypothesis in the much wider context of model specification. Whether or not a model such as (4) has a unit root can be viewed as part of the overall issue of model determination. Model comparison techniques like *posterior odds* and *predictive odds* make it easy to assess the evidence in the data in support of the hypothesis $\alpha = 1$ at the same time as decisions are made concerning other features of model specification, such as the lag order in the autoregression (6), the degree of the deterministic trend component, and the presence of trend breaks. A common asymptotic theory (see Phillips and Ploberger, 1996) further facilitates this approach to model selection and leads to an extension of the Schwarz (1978) BIC criterion to models with some nonstationary data that is based on the idea of selecting the model that is *a posteriori* the most probable. The approach has connections with *prequential probability* (Dawid, 1984) and *stochastic complexity* (Rissanen, 1986). It can be shown that model choices that are made in this way are completely consistent in the sense that the probability of type I and type II errors goes to zero as $n \rightarrow \infty$ (Phillips and Ploberger, 1994).

In the context of Bayesian analysis, a model may be selected based on the posterior odds ratio

$$\left(\frac{\pi_2}{\pi_1}\right) \frac{\Pr[Y^n \mid \mathcal{M}_2]}{\Pr[Y^n \mid \mathcal{M}_1]}$$

where $\mathcal{M}_1$ and $\mathcal{M}_2$ are the two candidate models, and π_1 and π_2 are corresponding prior weights on $\mathcal{M}_1$ and $\mathcal{M}_2$. If $\mathcal{M}_1$ and $\mathcal{M}_2$ are specified as $I(0)$ and $I(1)$ models respectively, the unit root hypothesis can be tested by choosing between models $\mathcal{M}_1$ and $\mathcal{M}_2$. More rigorously, consider a linear regression

$$y_t = \theta' z_t + \varepsilon_t,$$

where y_t and ε_t are real valued stochastic processes on a probability space $(\Omega, \mathcal{F}, P)$, and $\mathcal{F}_t \subset \mathcal{F}(t = 0, 1, 2, \ldots)$ is a filtration to which y_t and ε_t are adapted, z_t is a $k \times 1$ vector defined on the same space and is $\mathcal{F}_{t-1}$ measurable). Suppose $\varepsilon_t \equiv$ iid $N(0, \sigma^2)$ and then, conditional on $\mathcal{F}_0$ and θ, the joint density of $Y_n = [y_1, \ldots, y_n]'$ with respect to Lebesgue measure v is

$$\begin{aligned} \mathrm{pdf}(Y_n \mid \mathcal{F}_0, \theta) &= dP_n^\theta / dv \\ &= (2\pi\sigma^2)^{-n/2} \exp\{-(1/2\sigma^2)[\hat{U}_n'\hat{U}_n + (\hat{\theta}_n - \theta)' A_n (\hat{\theta}_n - \theta)]\}, \end{aligned} \tag{45}$$

where $\hat{U}_n = Y_n - Z_n\hat{\theta}_n$, $\hat{\theta}_n = [Z_n'Z_n]^{-1} Z_n'Y_n$, $Z_n = [z_1, \ldots, z_n]$, $A_n = Z_n'Z_n$, and P_n^θ is the probability measure of Y_n. Combining (45) with a prior density, $\pi(\theta)$, for θ, we get the joint density of (θ, Y_n). Conditional on $\mathcal{F}_0$, the data density for Y_n can then be obtained by integrating out θ in the joint density of (θ, Y_n). For $\pi(\theta) = \pi_0$,

$$\mathrm{pdf}(Y_n \mid \mathcal{F}_0) = \pi_0 (2\pi\sigma^2)^{-(n-k)/2} |A_n|^{-1/2} \exp\{-(1/2\sigma^2)\hat{U}_n'\hat{U}_n\}.$$

Let Q_n be the (probability) measure whose density with respect to v is $\mathrm{pdf}(Y_n \mid \mathcal{F}_0)$ and choose $P_n = P_n^0$ as the reference measure, then

$$\begin{aligned} \frac{dQ_n}{dP_n} &= \int \pi(\theta) \frac{dP_n^\theta}{dP_n} \, d\theta \\ &= \pi_0 (2\pi\sigma^2)^{k/2} |A_n|^{-1/2} \exp\{(1/2\sigma^2)\hat{\theta}_n' A_n \hat{\theta}_n\}. \end{aligned}$$

For all $n > k$, Q_n as given above leads to a proper conditional probability measure and this measure can be interpreted as the Bayesian version of the data generating mechanism. In other words, Q_n gives us the Bayesian model for the data.

A natural measure of model adequacy is provided by the data density dQ_n/dP_n. If we denote Q_n^k as the 'Bayes model' measure given by Q_n for a model with k parameters and incorporate the index 'k' in what follows to signify the number of regressors, then

$$\frac{dQ_n^k}{dP_n} = |(1/2\sigma^2) A_n(k)|^{-1/2} \exp\{(1/2\sigma^2)\hat{\theta}_n'(k) A_n(k) \hat{\theta}_n(k)\}, \quad k = 1, 2, \ldots, K.$$

Let K be some maximum number of regressors, then Q_n^K corresponds to the 'least restricted' option and we may use it as the reference measure. Multiplying the Radon-Nikodym derivatives we obtain the likelihood ratio

$$\frac{dQ_n^k}{dQ_n^K} = \left(\frac{dQ_n^k}{dP_n}\right)\left(\frac{dP_n}{dQ_n^K}\right)$$

corresponding to the two 'Bayes models'

$$H(Q_n^k):\ y_{n+1} = \hat{\theta}_n(k)' z_{n+1} + v_{n+1}^k,$$

$$H(Q_n^K):\ y_{n+1} = \hat{\theta}_n(K)' z_{n+1} + v_{n+1}^K.$$

In model (13), if we set $K = p + q$, and $k = p + q - 1 = K - 1$, where q is the dimension of the deterministic trend x_t, we get the following two 'Bayes models':

$$H(Q_n^{K-1}) : \Delta y_{n+1} = \sum_{j=1}^{p-1} \tilde{\varphi}_{jn} \Delta y_{n+1-j} + \tilde{\beta}'_n x_{n+1} + \varepsilon_{n+1}, \text{ and}$$

$$H(Q_n^K) : \Delta y_{n+1} = \tilde{a} y_n + \sum_{j=1}^{p-1} \hat{\varphi}_{jn} \Delta y_{n+1-j} + \hat{\beta}'_n x_{n+1} + \varepsilon_{n+1}.$$

The first model incorporates a unit root. If we assign equal prior odds to the two models we can test the hypothesis of a unit root, i.e., $H(Q_n^{K-1})$, against trend stationarity, i.e., $H(Q_n^{K})$, using the criterion:

$$\text{Accept } H(Q_n^{K-1}) \text{ in favor of } H(Q_n^K) \text{ if } dQ_n^{K-1}/dQ_n^K > 1. \tag{46}$$

Thus, under the wider context of model specification, testing for a unit root becomes an issue of whether or not to include the lag variable (y_n above) as a regressor in the *ADF* regression. This criterion, as shown in Phillips and Ploberger (1994), gives a completely consistent 'Bayes model' test in the sense that the probabilities of both types of error tend to zero as $n \rightarrow \infty$.

A second advantage of Bayesian techniques in nonstationary models with unit roots is that the asymptotic form of the posterior density is normal under rather general conditions, a result that facilitates large sample Bayesian inference and that contrasts with the non-standard asymptotic distribution theory of classical estimators and tests. The fact that posterior densities have limiting normal forms in a wider class of models than those for which the maximum likelihood estimator is asymptotically normal has long been known (Heyde and Johnstone, 1979) but its relevance for models with unit roots has only recently been recognized (Sims, 1990; Kim, 1994; Phillips and Ploberger, 1996). For instance, a large sample Bayesian confidence set for the autoregressive parameter α in (11) can be constructed in the conventional way without having to appeal to any nonstandard limit theory. In this respect, Bayesian theory (which leads to a symmetric confidence set for α) differs from classical statistical analysis where the construction of valid confidence regions is awkward because of the discontinuity of the limit theory at $\alpha = 1$ (but may be accomplished using local asymptotics as in Stock, 1991). This divergence can lead to quite different inferences being made from the two approaches with the same data even when the influence of the prior is negligible, as it is in very large samples. In small samples, the role of the prior is important and time series models raise special concerns about the construction of uninformative priors, primarily because a great deal is known about the properties of simple time series models like autoregressions and their characteristic features in advance of data analysis. How this knowledge should be used or ignored is a matter on which there is ongoing debate (see Phillips, 1991, and two themed issues of the *Journal of Applied Econometrics*, 1991, and *Econometric Theory*, 1994).

Third, Bayesian methods offer flexibility and convenience in analyzing models with possible unit roots and endogenous trend breaks. In such cases, a prior distribution of break points is postulated (a uniform prior across potential break points may be appealing in the absence of other information), the posterior mass function is calculated, and the Bayes estimate of the break point is taken as the one with highest posterior mass (Zivot and Phillips, 1994). This approach makes the analysis of multiple break points straightforward, a problem where classical asymptotic theory is much more complex (For a classical analysis of multiple breaks, see Bai, 1997; Lumsdaine and Papell, 1995, among others).

9. Bootstrapping unit root tests

The study of bootstrapping time series regression models was started by Freedman (1984). Bose (1988) shows that under certain regularity conditions, the bootstrap approximation to the distribution of the least squares estimator in a stationary autoregressive model is of order $o(n^{-1/2})$ a.s., thereby improving the normal approximation. The validity of the bootstrap for unit root models has been studied by several authors recently. Basawa *et al.* (1991a) show that the standard bootstrap least squares estimate is asymptotically invalid in unit root models, even if the error distribution is assumed to be normal. Consider the following AR(1) process:

$$y_t = \alpha y_{t-1} + u_t,\ y_0 = 0,\ u_t \equiv \text{iid } N(0, 1).$$

Let $\hat{\alpha}$ be the OLS estimator of α, then under the null hypothesis of a unit root and when $n \longrightarrow \infty$,

$$Z_n = \left[\sum y_{t-1}^2\right]^{-1/2} (\hat{\alpha} - \alpha) \Rightarrow \tfrac{1}{2}\{W(1)^2 - 1\}\left\{\int_0^1 W(r)^2 dr\right\}^{-1/2}. \tag{47}$$

A parametric bootstrap sample y_t^* is obtained recursively from the following recursion:

$$y_t^* = \hat{\alpha} y_{t-1}^* + u_t^*,\ y_0^* = 0, \tag{48}$$

where $\{u_t^*\}$ is a random sample from $N(0, 1)$. The bootstrap estimator of $\hat{\alpha}$ can then be calculated from the bootstrap sample $\{y_t^*\}$, as $\hat{\alpha}^* = [\sum y_t^* y_{t-1}^*] \times [\sum y_{t-1}^{*2}]^{-1}$, and the bootstrap version of Z_n is $Z_n^* = [\sum y_{t-1}^{*2}]^{1/2}(\hat{\alpha}^* - \hat{\alpha})$. Basawa *et al.* (1991a) show that the limit distribution of Z_n^* is not the same as that of Z_n, thus invalidating the bootstrap. Specifically, consider the triangular array

$$y_{k,n} = b_n y_{k-1,n} + u_k, \quad y_0 = 0, \tag{49}$$

where ε_k are independent $N(0, 1)$ variates and $\{b_n\}$ is a sequence of numbers such that $n(b_n - 1) \longrightarrow \lambda$. Then, (49) is a triangular system with roots $b_n = 1 + (\lambda/n)$

that are local to unity. It follows from our earlier analysis that if $b_n^* = [\sum_k y_{k,n} y_{k-1,n}][\sum_k y_{k-1,n}^2]^{-1}$, and $\tau_n(b_n) = [\sum_k y_{k-1,n}^2]^{1/2}(b_n^* - b_n)$ is the corresponding sequence of scaled and centered estimators from (49), then

$$\tau_n(b) \Longrightarrow Z_n = \left[\int_0^1 J_\lambda(r)^2 dr\right]^{-1/2} \int_0^1 J_\lambda(r) := \eta(\lambda),$$

where $J_\lambda(r) = \int_0^r e^{(r-s)\lambda} dW(s)$ is a linear diffusion. If the bootstrap approximation were asymptotically valid, then along almost all paths $\tau_n(\hat{\alpha})$ would converge to the same distribution as that of $Z_n = [\sum y_{t-1}^2]^{1/2}(\hat{\alpha} - \alpha)$ itself, viz. (47). However, in fact, $\tau_n(\hat{\alpha}) \Longrightarrow \eta(\xi)$, as $n \longrightarrow \infty$, where

$$\xi = \tfrac{1}{2}\{W(1)^2 - 1\}\left\{\int_0^1 W(r)^2 dr\right\}^{-1}$$

since $n(\hat{\alpha} - 1) \Longrightarrow \xi$. A similar invalidity of the bootstrap occurs for the coefficient based bootstrap statistic $n(\hat{\alpha}^* - \hat{\alpha})$.

To circumvent the asymptotic invalidity of the bootstrap, there are several possibilities. Basawa *et al.* (1991b) suggested resampling the restricted residuals under the null hypothesis of a unit root. If u_t^{**} is the restricted residual $y_t - y_{t-1}$ and the bootstrap sample is generated from the following resampling scheme under the null

$$y_t^* = y_{t-1}^* + u_t^{**},$$

then the bootstrap t-ratio statistic Z_n^* has the same asymptotic distribution as Z_n. As an alternative, Ferretti and Romo (1994) consider the unrestricted residuals $u_t^* = y_t - \hat{\alpha} y_{t-1}$ and generate the pseudo data y_t^* under the null of a unit root. They show that the corresponding bootstrap test statistics are asymptotically valid. Another possibility is to use model selection to determine whether to sample from a unit root process or the fitted regression. In this case, a natural procedure is to use the model selection method outlined in (46) above, which gives a consistent model choice procedure in which the type I and type II errors both tend to zero in probability as $n \longrightarrow \infty$. In consequence, the correct model is chosen asymptotically and the resulting bootstrap test statistics are asymptotically valid.

None of the above methods work when the underlying model is a near integrated process, because there in this case there is no way in which the localizing parameter can be consistently estimated from the sample data.

For unit root models with deterministic trends, the problem of redundant deterministic trend variables discussed in Section 2 surfaces again. Although we use regression models like (6), which include redundant trend variables, to calculate the DF test statistics and to obtain the bootstrap residuals ε_t^*, the redundant variables should be excluded from the resampling scheme to make the bootstrap DF test asymptotically valid. Nankervis and Savin (1994) present some simulation results on bootstrapping unit root tests for the following model

$$y_t = \mu_0 + \mu_1 t + \alpha y_{t-1} + \varepsilon_t$$

under different error distributions. Their sampling scheme is based on restricted residuals and the bootstrap sample data is generated under the null hypothesis. The bootstrap DF test has basically the same power as the original DF test, except for some non-Gaussian distribution cases where the bootstrap tests perform slightly better. Another study of the asymptotic properties of bootstrap procedures in unit root models with a drift is Giersbergen (1995).

10. Testing stationarity

Many empirical analyses, like those of Nelson and Plosser (1982) and subsequent studies, lead to the conclusion that aggregate economic time series are unit root nonstationary. One explanation that has been suggested for these empirical outcomes is that the standard tests are all based on the null hypothesis of a unit root, which assures that the hypothesis will be accepted at conventional significance levels (of 5% and 1%) unless there is strong evidence against it. As a result, there is considerable interest in tests for which the null hypothesis is trend stationary.

Such tests are easily developed by working from the components representation of the time series y_t. In particular, if we add a stationary component v_t to (1) and (2), we get the so-called *components* model

$$y_t = h_t + y_t^s + v_t, \quad y_t^s = y_{t-1}^s + v_t, \tag{50}$$

which decomposes the time series y_t into a deterministic trend h_t, a stochastic trend y_t^s, and a stationary residual v_t. The stochastic trend in (50) is annihilated when $\sigma_r^2 = \text{var}(r_t) = 0$, which therefore corresponds to a null hypothesis of trend stationarity. Under Gaussian assumptions and iid error conditions, the hypothesis can be tested in a simple way using the LM principle. Let $\hat{e}_t$ be the residuals from the regression of y_t on the deterministic trend x_t and $\hat{\sigma}_v^2 = n^{-1} \sum \hat{e}_t^2$, then the LM statistic can be constructed as follows:

$$LM = \frac{n^{-2} \sum S_t^2}{\hat{\sigma}_v^2},$$

where S_t is the partial sum process of the residuals $\sum_{j=1}^{t} \hat{e}_j$. Under the null hypothesis of stationarity, this LM statistic converges to $\int_0^1 V_X^2$, where $V_X(r) = W(r) - [\int_0^r X'][\int_0^1 XX']^{-1}[\int_0^1 XdW]$ is a generalized Brownian bridge process, like (18) above. This procedure can easily be extended to more general cases where there is serial dependence by replacing $\hat{\sigma}_v^2$ with corresponding estimates of the long run variance of v_t based on nonparametric methods. This was done in Kwiatkowski *et al.* (1992), where a general approach was developed.

Defining $w_t = y_t^s + v_t$ and writing differences as $\Delta w_t = (1 - \theta L)\eta_t$, where η_t is stationary, it is clear that $\sigma_u^2 = 0$ in (50) corresponds to the null hypothesis of a moving average unit root $\theta = 1$ in this representation. Thus, there is a formal correspondence between testing for stationarity and testing for a moving average unit root (Saikonnen and Luukkonen, 1993). The asymptotic theory for the maximum likelihood estimator in the moving average unit root case is known, but has a complex point process representation (Davis and Dunsmuir, 1995). This makes a likelihood ratio approach awkward and the LM test attractive in practice. Leybourne and McCabe (1994) suggested a similar test for stationarity which differs from the test of Kwiatkowski *et al.* (1992) in its treatment of autocorrelation and applies when the null hypothesis is an $AR(k)$ process.

11. Applications and empirical evidence

Most empirical applications of unit root tests have been in the field of economics. Martingales play a key role in the mathematical theory of efficient financial markets (Duffie, 1988) and in the macroeconomic theory of the aggregate consumption behavior of rational economic agents (Hall, 1978). In consequence, economists have been intrigued by the prospect of testing these theories. In the first modern attempt to do so using unit root tests, Nelson and Plosser (1982) tested fourteen historical macroeconomic time series for the United States by the ADF test. The time series start around 1860 to 1909 and end in 1970. Nelson and Plosser analyzed the logarithms of all of these series (except for interest rates, which was treated in levels) and found empirical evidence to support a unit root for thirteen of them (the exception being unemployment). Since then, these series have been re-tested hundreds of times with other methods, and thousands of other time series have been examined in the literature. Meese and Singleton (1982) studied various exchange rate time series and could not reject the null hypothesis of a unit root; and Perron (1988) applied the semiparametric Z tests to the Nelson–Plosser data and some other macroeconomic time series and basically confirmed the conclusion reached by Nelson and Plosser. While it is recognized that the discriminatory power of unit root tests is often low, there is a mounting body of evidence that many economic and financial time series are well characterized by models with roots at or near unity.

Although standard tests of the unit root hypothesis against trend stationary alternatives usually cannot reject the null hypothesis, other approaches do find different results. For example, performing a test for the null hypothesis of stationarity against the alternative of a unit root, Kwiatkowski *et al.* (1992) revisited the Nelson-Plosser data and could not reject the hypothesis of trend stationarity in many of these time series (including real per capita GNP, employment, unemployment rate, GNP deflator, wages and money). Tests based on efficient detrending by quasi-differencing have also been applied to macroeconomic time series and various results have been reported. For instance, applying the QD detrended ADF test to the U.S. GNP data, Cheung and Chin (1995) could not reject the unit root hypothesis in quarterly data but did get different results with annual data.

Gil-Alana and Robinson (1997) applied the LM test for a unit root against fractional alternatives to the extended Nelson-Plosser series (Schotman and van Dijk, 1991). Although their results vary across the fourteen series and across different model structures for the stationary component u_t, they found the most nonstationary evidence for the consumer price and money stock series, trend stationary evidence for industrial production and stationary evidence for the unemployment rate data.

Using the Nelson-Plosser data and a U.S. postwar quarterly real GNP series, Perron (1989) argues that if the Great Depression in 1929 and the oil price shock in 1973 are treated as exogenous events that caused structural changes, then a trend stationary representation with structural change is favored over a unit root representation with structural change. By allowing for these structural breaks, Perron rejected the unit root hypothesis at the 5% level of significance for all of the Nelson-Plosser series except consumer prices, velocity, and bond yields. Christiano (1992), Banerjee *et al.* (1990), and Zivot and Andrews (1992) argue that Perron's tests for a unit root with structural change are biased because the choices of the break points are correlated with the data. Christiano (1992) suggested that the date of the break should be treated as unknown and, by using tests based on bootstrap critical values, reached different conclusions from Perron (1989). Zivot and Andrews (1992) allowed the breakpoint to be endogenous and suggested pre-testing procedures to estimate the structural change points, finding less compelling evidence against the unit root hypothesis.

In recent years, various Bayesian analyses have been conducted on unit root-testing. Using flat prior Bayesian techniques, DeJong and Whiteman (1989a,b,c) tested the Nelson-Plosser series, stock prices and dividend data, and postwar quarterly real GNP for the U.S.A{50 }. Their results challenged the classical unit root tests results in many cases. Schotman and van Dijk (1991) analyzed the random walk hypothesis for real exchange rates and found more evidence in favor of the trend stationary model than classical unit root tests. Contrary to the conclusion of DeJong and Whiteman, Phillips (1991) provided an alternative Bayesian approach using a Jeffreys' prior, and found more support for the unit root model for some series. Using a modified information matrix-based prior, Zivot and Phillips (1994) considered autoregressive models with fitted deterministic trends allowing for certain types of structural change. Their results are generally in accord with those of Phillips (1991). In addition, their Bayesian analysis also shows evidence of trend breaks in some of the macroeconomic series with breaks occurring around 1929, partially supporting the conclusion reached by Perron (1989). It is also shown in Zivot and Phillips (1994) and in other work that the choice of prior can be important in distinguishing between different models. Using the extended Nelson-Plosser data and a Bayesian procedure that consistently classifies the time series as $I(1)$ or $I(0)$, Stock (1994) obtain results largely supporting the unit root hypothesis. Applying the model selection criterion 'PIC' to the Nelson-Plosser data and allowing for model selection of deterministic trend components and lag length in the autoregressions, Phillips and Ploberger (1994) found eleven out of the fourteen time series to be stochastically nonstationary.

Of course, unit root issues in multivariate time series have also attracted a good deal of research, and the *ADF* and semi-parametric Z tests have been extensively used to test for the presence of cointegration using residual based approaches. The tests are used in the same way as standard unit root tests and have the same null hypothesis, but the data are the residuals from a least squares cointegrating regression, and the alternative hypothesis (of cointegration) is now the main hypothesis of interest (Engle and Granger, 1987; Phillips and Ouliaris, 1990). The model is analogous to (1), but both variables y_t and x_t have unit roots and y_t^s is stationary under the alternative hypothesis and unit root nonstationary under the null. The limit theory for these residual based tests was developed in Phillips and Ouliaris (1990). There are also approaches to cointegration testing that rely on likelihood ratio methods (Johansen, 1996) in vector autoregressions and these lead to tests with asymptotic distributions that are simple multivariate analogues of those given in (8) and (12). A large empirical literature has developed around these techniques. More recently, model selection methods have been advocated in Phillips (1996) and Chao and Phillips (1996, 1997). In this work, model selection is used to simultaneously choose the lag length and cointegrating rank in a VAR of possible reduced rank. The method is extremely easy to use and like the PIC test for a unit root that is discussed in Section, produces consistent estimates of lag length and cointegrating rank. The methods have been used with some success in simulations (Phillips, 1998d) and in ex ante forecasting exercises with macroeconomic data for the USA and several Asia-Pacific countries (Phillips, 1995).

Unit root theory plays a major role in modern time series econometrics and weak convergence methods and function space asymptotics have opened up the econometric analysis of nonstationary regression models. While a multitude of test procedures are available for evaluating evidence in support of unit root nonstationarity, fractional integration and short memory stationarity, the main principles of statistical testing are analogous to those in stationary time series and many of the same issues figure in the analysis. However, the nonstandard limit theory of unit root tests does complicate classical inference and there are important new issues that arise from the nonparametric treatment of the stationary component and the existence of valid alternative models for nonstationary data, as discussed in Section 3.5. Further, unit root models provide an interesting case of divergence between the asymptotic behavior of Bayesian and classical estimators and tests. They also provide an instance of the asymptotic failure of the bootstrap. With these interesting characteristics, it is hardly surprising that the field has attracted so much attention in the last 15 years. Additionally, most economic time series have clearly evident nonstationary empirical characteristics, and there are strong reasons in economic theory for giving attention to the martingale hypothesis and for wanting to distinguish between models with persistent and non persistent shocks. For all these reasons, the field has attracted a full spread of participants from empirical macroeconomists interested in growth and finance theorists interested in efficient markets, through to econometricians and statisticians interested in the development of new testing procedures, asymptotic theory and unified methods of inference for data of this type.

Acknowledgements

This review paper is a considerably expanded version of 'A primer on Unit Root Tests' by Phillips and draws on material published in the brief review of unit root testing given in Phillips (1997). We thank Les Oxley and Michael McAleer for comments on an early version of this paper. The paper was keyboarded by the authors in Scientific Word 2.5. Phillips thanks the NSF for research support under grant no. SBR94-22922 and Xiao thanks the Cowles Foundation for hospitality during a visit in May–June 1998.

References

Akaike, H. (1977) On entropy maximization principle, In P. R. Krishnarah (ed.), *Applications of Statistics*. Amsterdam: North-Holland, 1977, pp. 27–41.

Andrews, D. W. K. (1991) Heteroskedasticity and autocorrelation consistent covariance matrix estimation, *Econometrica*, **59**, 817–858.

Andrews, D. W. K. and J. C. Monahan (1992) An improved heteroskedasticity and autocorrelation consistent covariance matrix estimator, *Econometrica*, **60**, 953–966.

Bai, Jushan (1997) Estimating multiple breaks one at a time, *Econometric Theory*, **13**, 315–352.

Baillie, R., T. (1996) Long memory processes and fractional integration in econometrics, *Journal of Econometrics*, **73**, 5–59.

Baillie, R., T. Bollerslev and H. Mikkelsen (1996) Fractionally integrated generalized autoregressive conditional heteroskedasticity, *Journal of Econometrics*, **74**(1), September, 3–30.

Banerjee, A., R. L. Lumsdaine and J. H. Stock (1990) Recursive and sequential tests for a unit root: Theory and international evidence, manuscript, Harvard University, Cambridge, MA.

Beran, J. (1992) Statistical Models for Data with long-range dependence (with discussion), *Statistical Science*, **4**, 404–427.

Berk, K. N. (1974) Consistent Autoregressive Spectral Estimates, *Annals of Statistics*, **2**, 489–502.

Basawa, I. V., A. K. Mallik, W. P. McCormick and R. L. Taylor (1991a) Bootstrapping unstable first order autoregressive process, *Annals of Statistics*, **19**, 1098–1101.

Basawa, I. V., A. K. Mallik, W. P. McCormick and R. L. Taylor (1991b) Bootstrapping test of significance and sequential bootstrap estimation for unstable first order autoregressive processes, *Communication in Statistics*, **20**, 1015–1026.

Beveridge, S. and R. Nelson (1981) A new approach to decomposition of time series in permanent and transitory components with particular attention to measurement of the 'business cycle', *Journal of Monetary Economics*, **7**, 151–174.

Bhargava, A. (1986) On the theory of testing for unit roots in observed time series, *Review of Economic Studies*, **53**, 369–384.

Blough, S. R. (1992) The relationship between power and level for generic unit root tests in finite samples, *Journal of Applied Econometrics*, **7**, 295–308.

Bose, A. (1988) Edgeworth correction by bootstrap in autoregressions, *Annals of Statistics*, **16**, 1709–1722.

Canjels, N. And M. Watson (1997) Estimating deterministic trends in the presence of serially correlated errors, *Review of Economics and Statistics*, **79**, 184–200.

Chan, N. H. and C. Z. Wei (1987) Asymptotic inference for nearly nonstationary AR(1) processes, *Annals of Statistics*, **15**, 1050–1063.

Chan N. H. & C. Z. Wei (1988) Limiting distributions of least squares estimates of unstable autoregressive processes, *Annals of Statistics*, **16**, 367–401.

Chao, J. and P. C. B. Phillips (1994) Bayesian model selection in partially non-stationary

vector autoregressive processes with reduced rank structure, Yale University, mimeographed.
Chao, J. and P. C. B. Phillips (1996). An empirical Bayesian approach to cointegration rank selection and test of the present value model for stock prices. In J. C. Lee and A. Zellner (eds.), *Prediction, Forecasting and Modeling in Statistics and Econometrics*. Springer-Verlag, 1996.
Chao, J. and P. C. B. Phillips (1997) Model selection in partially nonstationary vector autoregressive processes with reduced rank structure, Cowles Foundation Discussion Paper No. 1155.
Cheung, Y. and M. Chinn (1996) Deterministic, stochastic and segmented trends in aggregate output, *Oxford Economic Papers*, **48**, 134–167.
Christiano, L. (1992) Searching for a break in GNP, *Journal of Business and Economic Statistics*, **10**, 237–250.
Davis, R. A. and W. T. M. Dunsmuir, (1996) Maximum likelihood estimation for MACD processes with a root on or near the unit circle, *Econometric Theory*, **12**, 1–29.
Dawid, A. P. (1984) The prequential approach, *Journal of Royal Statistical Society A*, **147**, 278–292.
DeJong, D. N. and C. H. Whiteman (1989a) Trends and random walks in macro-economic time series: A reconsideration based on the likelihood principle, Working Paper No. 1989–4, University of Iowa.
DeJong, D. N. and C. H. Whiteman (1989b) The temporal stability of dividends and stock prices: Evidence from the likelihood function, *American Economic Review*, **81**, 600–617.
DeJong, D. N. and C. H. Whiteman (1989c) Trends and cycles as unobserved components in real GNP: A Bayesian perspective, *Proceedings of the American Statistical Association*, 63–70.
DeJong, D. N., J. C. Nankervis, N. E. Savin and C. H. Whiteman (1992) The power problems of unit root tests for time series with autoregressive errors, *Journal of Econometrics*, **53**, 323–43.
Dickey, D. A. and W. A. Fuller (1979) Distribution of estimators for autoregressive time series with a unit root, *Journal of the American Statistical Association*, **74**, 427–431.
Dickey, D. A. & W. A. Fuller (1981) Likelihood ratio tests for autoregressive time series with a unit root, *Econometrica*, **49**, 1057–1072.
Dickey, D. A., H. P. Hasza, and W. A. Fuller (1984) Testing for unit roots in seasonal time series, *JASA*, **79**, 355–367.
Diebold, F. and G. D. Rudebusch (1991) On the power of Dickey-Fuller tests against fractional alternatives, *Economic Letters*, **35**, 155–160.
Dufour, J. and M. L. King (1991) Optimal invariant tests for the autocorrelation coefficient in linear regressions with stationary and nonstationary AR(1) errors, *Journal of Econometrics*, **47**, 115–143.
Duffie, D. (1988) *Security Markets: Stochastic Models*. San Diego: Academic Press.
Durlauf, S. and P. C. B. Phillips (1988) Trends versus random walks in time series analysis, *Econometrca*, **56**, 656–676.
Elliot, G., T. J. Rothenberg and J. H. Stock (1996) Efficient tests for an autoregressive unit root, *Econometrca*, **64**, 813–836.
Engle, R. F. and C. W. J. Granger (1987) Cointegration and error correction: representation, estimation and testing, *Econometrica*, **55**, 251–276.
Evans, G. B. A. and N. E. Savin (1981) The calculation of the limiting distribution of the least squares estimator of the parameter in a random walk model, *Annals of Statistics*, **9**, 1114–1118.
Faust, J. (1996) Near observational equivalence and theoretical size problems with unit root tests, *Econometric Theory*, **12**, 724–731.

Ferretti, N. and J. Romo (1994) Unit root bootstrap tests for AR(1) models, working paper, Division of Economics, Universidad Carlos III de Madrid.

Freedman, D. A. (1984) On bootstrapping two-stage least squares estimates in stationary linear models, *Annals of Statistics*, **12**, 827–842.

van Giersbergen, N. P. A. (1995) Bootstrapping unit root tests in the AR(1) model with drift, manuscript, University of Amsterdam.

Gil-Alana, L. A. and P. M. Robinson (1997) Testing of unit root and other nonstationary hypothesis in macroeconomic time series, *Journal of Econometrics*, 241–268.

Grenander, U. and M. Rosenblatt (1957) *Statistical Analysis of Stationary Time Series*. New York: John Wiley.

Hall, R. E. (1978) Stochastic implications of the life cycle-permanent income hypothesis: Theory and evidence, *Journal of Political Economy*, **86**, 971–987.

Hall, P. and C. C. Heyde (1980) *Martingale Limit Theory and its Applications*. New York: Academic Press.

Hasan, M. N. and R. W. Koenker (1997) Robust rank tests of the unit root hypothesis, *Econometrica*, **65**, 133–161.

Heyde, C. C. and I. M. Johnstone (1979). On asymptotic posterior normality for stochastic processes, *Journal of the Royal Statistical Society* **41**, 184–189.

Hurvich, C. M., R. Deo and J. Brodsky (1998) The mean squared error of Geweke and Porter Hudak's estimator of the memory parameter of a long-memory time series, *Journal of Time Series Analysis*, **19**, 19–46.

Hylleberg, S., R. F. Engle, C. W. J. Granger and S. Yoo (1990) Seasonal integration and cointegration, *Journal of Econometrics*, **44**, 215–238.

Hylleberg, S. (ed.) (1992) *Modelling Seasonality*. Oxford: Oxford University Press.

Jeganathan, P. (1991) On the asymptotic behavior of least squares estimators in AR time series with roots near the unit circle, *Econometric Theory*, **7**, 269–306.

Jeganathan, P. (1995) Some aspects of asymptotic theory with applications to time series models, *Econometric Theory*, **11**, 818–887.

Kashyap, R. and K. Eom (1988) Estimation in long-memory time series models, *Journal of Time Series Analysis*, **9**, 35–41.

Kim, J-Y. (1994) Bayesian asymptotic theory in a time series model with a possible nonstationary process, *Econometric Theory*, **10**, 764–773.

King, M. L. (1988) Towards a theory of point optimal testing, *Econometric Reviews*, **6**, 169–218.

Kunsch, H. R. (1986) Discrimination between long range dependence and monotonic trends, *Journal of Applied Probability*, **23**, 1025–1030.

Kwiatkowski, D., P. C. B. Phillips, P. Schmidt and Y. Shin (1992) Testing the null hypothesis of stationarity against the alternative of a unit root: How sure are we that economic time series have a unit root?', *Journal of Econometrics*, **54**, 159–178.

Lai, T. L. and C. Z. Wei (1982) Least squares estimation in stochastic regresssion models with applications to identification and control of dynamic systems, *Annals of Statistics*, **10**, 154–166.

Lai, T. L. and D. Seigmund (1983) Fixed accuracy estimation of an autoregressive parameter, *Annals of Statistics*, **11**, 478–485.

Lee, C. C. and P. C. B. Phillips (1994) An ARMA pre-whitened long run variance estimator, Yale University, mimeographed.

Leybourne S. J. and B. P. M. McCabe (1994) A consistent test for a unit root, *Journal of Business and Economic Statistics*, **12**, 157–166.

Lumsdaine, R. L., and D. H. Papell (1995) Multiple trend breaks and the unit root hypothesis, manuscript, Princeton University.

MacNeill, I. B. (1978) Properties of sequences of partial sums of polynomial regression residuals with applications to tests for change of regression at unknown times, *Annals of Statistics*, **6**, 422–433.

McAleer M. and P. H. Franses (1998) Cointegration Analysis of Seasonal Time Series, in *Practical Issues in Cointegration Analysis*, Blackwell, Oxford (forthcoming).

Meese, R. A. and K. J. Singleton (1982) On unit roots and the empirical modeling of exchange rate, *Journal of Finance*, **37**, 1029–1035.

Nankervis, J. C. and Savin, N. E. (1994) The level and power of the bootstrap t-test in the AR(1) model with trend, manuscript, Department of Economics, University of Surrey and University of Iowa.

Nelson, C. R. and C. Plosser (1982) Trends and random walks in macro-economic time series: some evidence and implications, *Journal of Monetary Economics*, **10**, 139–162.

Nabeya, S. and K. Tanaka (1988) Asymptotic theory of a test for the constancy of regression coefficients against the random walk alternative, *Annals of Statistics*, **16**, 218–235.

Ng, S. and P. Perron (1995) Unit root tests in ARMA models with data dependent methods for the selection of the truncation lag, *Journal of the American Statistical Association*, **90**, 268–281.

Ng. S., and P. Perron (1998) Properties of the autoregressive spectral density estimator at frequency zero in ARIMA process, forthcoming, *Econometric Theory*.

Osborn, D. R., A. P. L. Chui, J. P. Smith, and C. R. Birchenhall (1988) Seasonality and the order of integration for consumption, *Oxford Bulletin of Economics and Statistics*, **50**, 361–368.

Osborn, D. R. and J. P. Smith (1989) The performance of periodic autoregressive models in forecasting seasonal U. K. consumption, *Journal of Business and Economic Statistics*, **7**, 117–128.

Ouliaris, S., J. Y. Park and P. C. B. Phillips (1989) Testing for a unit root in the presence of a maintained trend. In B. Raj (ed.), *Advances in Econometrics and Modelling*. Amsterdam: Kluwer, pp. 7–28.

Ouliaris, S. and P. C. B. Phillips (1994) *Coint 2.0*. Maple Valley, WA: Aptech Systems.

Park, J. Y. and J. Sung (1994) Testing for unit roots in models with structural change, *Econometric Theory*, **10**, 917–936.

Perron, P. (1988) Trend and random walks in macroeconomic time series: Further evidence from a new approach, *Journal of Economic Dynamics and Control*, **12**, 297–332.

Perron, P. (1989) The great crash, the oil price shock and the unit root hypothesis, *Econometrica*, **57**, 1361–1401.

Phillips, P. C. B. (1986) Understanding spurious regression in econometrics, *Journal of Econometrics*, **33**, 311–340.

Phillips, P. C. B. (1987a) Time series regression with a unit root, *Econometrica*, **55**, 277–302.

Phillips, P. C. B. (1987b) Towards a unified asymptotic theory of autoregression. *Biometrika*, **74**, 535–547.

Phillips, P. C. B. (1991) To criticize the critics: an objective Bayesian analysis of stochastic trends, *Journal of Applied Econometrics*, **6**, 333–364.

Phillips, P. C. B. (1995), Automated forecasts of Asia-Pacific economic activity, *Asia Pacific Economic Review*, **1**, 92–102.

Phillips, P. C. B. (1996a) Example of an optimal idempotent non orthogonal projector in $L_2[0, 1]$, research note, Yale University.

Phillips, P. C. B. (1996b) Econometric model determination, *Econometrica*, **64**, 763–812.

Phillips, P. C. B. (1998a) New tools for understanding spurious regression, *Econometrica* (forthcoming).

Phillips, P. C. B. (1998b) The invalidity of critical values of tests for unit roots against trend alternatives, in progress.

Phillips, P. C. B. (1998c) Gaussian semiparametric estimation of fractional integration — the nonstationary case, Yale University, under construction.

Phillips, P. C. B. (1998d) Impulse response and forecast error variance asymptotics in nonstationary VAR's, *Journal of Econometrics*, **83**, 21–56.

Phillips, P. C. B. And C. C. Lee (1996) Efficiency gains from quasi-differencing under nonstationarity. In P. M. Robinson and M. Rosenblatt (eds.), *Athens Conference on Applied Probability and Time Series: Essays in Memory of E.J. Hannan*, Springer-Verlag: New York.

Phillips, P. C. B. and S. Ouliaris (1990) Asymptotic properties of residual based tests for cointegration, *Econometrica*, **58**, 165–194.

Phillips, P. C. B. and P. Perron (1988) Testing for unit roots in time series regression, *Biometrika*, **75**, 335–346.

Phillips, P. C. B. and W. Ploberger (1994) Posterior odds testing for a unit root with data-based model selection, *Econometric Theory*, **10**, 774–808.

Phillips, P. C. B. and W. Ploberger (1996) An asymptotic theory of Bayesian inference for time series, *Econometrica*, **64**, 381–412.

Phillips, P. C. B. and V. Solo (1992) Asymptotics for linear processes, *Annals of Statistics*, **20**, 971–1001.

Porter-Hudak, Susan (1990) An application of the seasonal fractionally differenced model to the monetary aggregates, *Journal of the American Statistical Association*, **85**, 338–344.

Rissanen, J. (1978) Modeling by shortest data description, *Automatica*, **14**, 465–471

Rissanen, J. (1986) Stochastic complexity and modeling, *Annals of Statistics*, **14**, 1080–1100

Robinson, P. (1994a) Time series with strong dependence. In C. Sims (ed.), *Advances in Econometrics*, Sixth World Congress. Cambridge: Cambridge University Press.

Robinson, P. M. (1994b) Efficient tests of nonstationary hypothesis, *Journal of the American Statistical Association*, **89**, 1420–1437.

Robinson, P. M. (1995a) Log periodogram regression of time series with long range dependence, *Annals of Statistics*, **23**, 1048–1072.

Robinson, P. (1995b) 'Gaussian semiparametric estimation of long range dependence', *Annals of Statistics*, **23**, 1630–1661.

Said, S. E. and D. A. Dickey (1984) Testing for unit roots in autoregressive-moving average models of unknown order, *Biometrika*, **71**, 599–608.

Saikkonen, P. and R. Luukkonen (1993) Testing for a moving average unit root in autoregressive integrated moving average models, *Journal of the American Statistical Association*, **88**, 596–601.

Sargan, J. D. and A. Bhargava (1983) Testing residuals from least squares regression for being generated by the Gaussian random walk, *Econometrica*, **51**, 153–174.

Schmidt, P. and P. C. B. Phillips (1992) Testing for a unit root in the presence of deterministic trends, *Oxford Bulletin of Economics and Statistics*, **54**, 257–288.

Schotman, P. and H. K. van Dijk (1991) A Bayesian analysis of the unit root in real exchange rates, *Journal of Econometrics*, **49**, 195–238.

Schwarz, G. (1978) Estimating the dimension of a model, *Annals of Statistics*, **6**, 461–464.

Schwert, G. W. (1989) Tests for unit roots: A Monte Carlo investigation, *Journal of Business and Economic Statistics*, **7**, 147–159.

Sims, C. A. (1990) Asymptotic behaviour of the likelihood function in an autoregression with a unit root, mimeographed, Yale University.

Sims, C., J. Stock and M. Watson (1990) Inference in linear time series models with some unit roots, *Econometrica*, **58**, 113–144.

Solo, V. (1984) The order of differencing in ARIMA models, *Journal of the American Statistical Association*, **79**, 916–921.

Stock, J. H. (1991) Confidence intervals for the largest autoregressive root in U.S. economic time series, *Journal of Monetary Economics*, **28**(3), 435–460.

Stock, J. H. (1994) Deciding between I(1) and I(0), *Journal of Econometrics*, 63, 105–131.

Stock, J. H. (1995) Unit roots, structural breaks and trends. In R. F. Engle and D. McFadden (eds.), *Handbook of Econometrics*, Vol. 4, 2739–2841, Amsterdam: North-Holland.

Tanaka, K. (1999) The nonstationary fractional unit root, *Econometric Theory*, (forth coming).

White, J. S. (1958) The limiting distribution of the serial correlation coefficient in the explosive case, *Annals of Math. Statist.*, **29**, 1188–1197.

Xiao, Z. and P. C. B. Phillips (1997) An ADF coefficient test for ARMA models with unknown orders, Cowles Foundation Discussion Paper No. 1161.

Young, C. H. (1974) 'Asymptotic behaviour of trigonometric series, Chinese University of Hong Kong.

Zivot, E. and D. W. K. Andrews (1992) Further evidence on the great crash, the oil price shock, and the unit root hypothesis, *Journal of Business and Economic Statistics*, **10**, 251–270.

Zivot, E. and P. C. B. Phillips (1994) A Bayesian analysis of trend determination in economic time series. *Econometric Reviews*, **13**, 291–336.

Annotated bibliography on unit root nonstationarity — textbooks, review articles and computer software

Abadir, K. (1999) *Mathematics of Unit Root Econometrics*, New York: John Wiley. (Forthcoming introduction to the mathematics of unit root distribution theory).

Banerjee, A., J. Dolado, J. W. Galbraith and D. F. Hendry (1992) *Cointegration, Error Correction, and the Econometric Analysis of Non-Stationary Time Series*. Oxford: Oxford University Press. (A textbook introduction to unit roots and cointegration that is designed to be accessible to graduate students of economics.)

Campbell, J. Y. and P. Perron (1991) Pitfalls and opportunities: What macroeconomists should know about unit roots *NBER Macroeconomics Annual*, 141–200. (A survey of research on unit roots in the 1980's that is intended for applied researchers.)

Davidson, J. (1994) *Stochastic Limit Theory: An Introduction for Econometricians*. Oxford University Press. (An introduction to asymptotic theory for econometricians, including functional limit theory and stochastic integration with an emphasis on mixing sequences and functions of mixing sequences).

Dhrymes, P. (1998) *Time Series, Unit Roots and Cointegration*. San Diego: Academic Press. (A rigorous treatment of time series methods that deals with unit root theory and cointegration).

Diebold, F. X. and M. Nerlove (1990) Unit roots in economic time series, *Advances in Econometrics*, **8**, 3–70. (A survey of unit root literature in the 1980s.)

Dolado, J., T. Jenkinson and S. Sosvilla-Rivero (1990) Cointegration and unit roots, *J. Economic Surveys*, **4**, 249–273. (A general survey of literature in the field of unit roots and cointegration in the 1980s.)

Econometric Theory, **10**(3&4) (1994) (Symposium of recent work in the field of Bayesian unit roots.)

Econometric Reviews (1994) (Two special issues on unit roots and cointegration reporting recent research.)

Franses, P. H. (1996) *Periodicity and Stochastic Trends in Economic Time Series*, Oxford University Press, Oxford. (A general reference on periodic models for seasonally observed time series with stochastic trends)

Fuller, W. A. (1976) *Introduction to Statistical Time Series*. New York: Wiley. (Accessible technical introduction to time series. The first textbook treatment of unit roots. Contains the original tabulations of the critical values of the Dickey-Fuller tests.)

Fuller, W. A. (1996) *Introduction to Statistical Time Series*. New York: Wiley. (2nd

Edition of Fuller, 1976, expanded to include some coverage of systems with several unit roots)

Hamilton, J. D. (1994) *Time Series Analysis*. Princeton: Princeton University Press. (A textbook treatment of time series with coverage of unit root theory and cointegration with examples and applications. Designed mainly for graduate students in economics.)

Hatanaka, M. (1996) *Time-Series Based Econometrics*. Oxford: Oxford University Press. (Textbook of univariate tests for unit roots and cointegration analysis, which relates the econometric methods to economic ideas and empirical applications).

Journal of Applied Econometrics, **6**(4) (1991) (A special issue on Bayesian unit root models with a focus on the formulation of priors in stationary and nonstationary time series models.)

Journal of Business and Economic Statistics, **10** (1992) (A special issue devoted to structural change models and unit roots with broken trends.)

Johansen, S. (1995) *Likelihood Based Inference in Cointegrated Vector Autoregressive Models*. Oxford: Oxford University Press. (Textbook coverage of Gaussian maximum likelihood estimation and inference in vector autoregressive models with reduced rank structure, dealing with sequential tests for cointegrating rank and restrictions on the cointegrating space.)

Ouliaris, S. and P. C. B. Phillips (1993) *COINT 2.0: GAUSS Procedures for Cointegrating Regression*. Aptech Systems, Washington. (A suite of GAUSS computer programs for nonstationary time series and model selection, which provides routines for all of the major unit root tests and has built in kernel procedures for long run variance estimation and spectral density estimation.)

Oxford Bulletin of Economics and Statistics, **48** and **54** (1986 and 1992) (Two special issues of empirical and theoretical articles on cointegration and unit roots.)

Phillips, P. C. B. (1988) Multiple Regression with Integrated Time Series, *Contemporary Mathematics*, **80**, 79–105. (A detailed review article that covers functional limit theory, weak convergence to stochastic integrals, the asymptotic theory of unit roots, regression with integrated processes, spurious regression, cointegration, and local-to-unity asymptotics.)

Phillips, P. C. B. (1992) Unit roots, *New Palgrave Dictionary of Money and Finance*. London: Macmillan. (A short introduction to unit root testing and unit root models in economics and finance, written for economists.)

Phillips, P. C. B. (1995) Cointegration and unit roots: Recent books and themes for the future, *Journal of Applied Econometrics*, **10**, 87–94. (Reviews recent themes in the literature and points to directions of future research.)

Phillips, P. C. B. (1997) Unit Root Tests, *Encyclopedia of Statistical Science, Update*, Volume 1, pp. 531–542. (Review of unit root tests and overview of the field with an empirical illustration).

Reinsel, G. (1993) *Elements of Multivariate Time Series Analysis*. New York: Springer-Verlag. (A modern treatment of multivariate time series with some attention to VAR models with reduced rank structure and cointegration.)

Stock, J. H. and M. W. Watson (1988) Variable Trends in Economic Time Series, *Journal of Economic Perspectives*, **2**(3), 147–174. (Introductory outline of stochastic trends and unit roots and cointegration for economists.)

Tanaka, K. (1996) *Time Series Analysis: Nonstationary and Noninvertible Distribution Theory*. New York: Wiley. (Textbook coverage at an advanced level of the limit distribution theory for unit root models and small cointegration systems, with a focus on the Fredholm approach to characterising the distribution of functionals of stochastic processes like Brownian motion.)

STRUCTURAL ANALYSIS OF COINTEGRATING VARs

M. Hashem Pesaran

Cambridge University and University of Southern California

Ron P. Smith

Birkbeck College, London and University of Colorado at Boulder

Abstract. This survey uses a number of recent developments in the analysis of cointegrating Vector Autoregressions (VARs) to examine their links to the older structural modelling traditions using Autoregressive Distributed Lag (ARDL), and Simultaneous Equations Models (SEMs). In particular, it emphasizes the importance of using judgement and economic theory to supplement the statistical information. After a brief historical review it sets out the statistical framework, discusses the identification of impulse responses using the Generalized Impulse Response functions, reviews the analysis of cointegrating VARs and highlights the large number of choices applied workers have to make in determining a specification. In particular, it considers the problem of specification of intercepts and trends and the size of the VAR in more detail, and examines the advantages of the use of exogenous variables in cointegration analysis. The issues are illustrated with a small U.S. Macroeconomic model.

Keywords. Autoregressive Distributed Lag Models; Simultaneous Equations Models; Cointegrating VARs; Long-Run Relations; Impulse Response Analysis and Error Variance Decomposition.

1. Overview

Much of the literature on unit roots and cointegration seems to imply that the traditional procedures of dynamic structural econometric modelling are invalid. Recent developments indicate that this is not the case and that many of the procedures used in Autoregressive Distributed Lag (ARDL) and the dynamic Simultaneous Equation Model (SEM) approaches, suitably interpreted, remain valuable. This paper will use a number of recent developments in the analysis of cointegrated systems to examine the links to the older traditions, in particular to their use of economic theory.[1] The paper will be essentially pedagogical; systematically going through the issues that confront applied modellers.[2] In the process it will emphasise the role of economic theory in the development of the econometric model and the role of judgement in combining statistical and theoretical information.[3] The issues will be illustrated using the U.S. macroeconomic data analysed in King, Plosser, Stock and Watson (1991) hereafter referred to as KPSW.[4] This paper, which has been very widely cited, uses U.S. data to examine the long-run relationships between a set of macroeconomic variables and to identify the stochastic trends in the U.S. economy. We use this example because we regard KPSW as being within the tradition which effectively combines economic and statistical information.

The remainder of the introduction describes the historical background. Section 2 sets out the structural framework starting from a structural Vector ARDL model with exogenous variables, discusses the identification of impulse responses using the Generalized Impulse Response function, reviews the analysis of cointegrating VARs and emphasizes the appropriate specification of intercepts and trends in these models. It also highlights the importance of the use of economic theory in identification of the long relations. Section 3 reviews some of the choices that applied researchers have to make. Section 4 considers one of the choices, the size of the VAR, in more detail. Section 5 returns to the use of exogenous variables and Section 6 contains some concluding comments.

Almost as soon as regression analysis was developed in the late 19th century, it was applied to economic problems. Probably the first application was Yule's use of cross-section data to investigate the effect of the British Poor Law. But as soon as regression analysis was applied to time series, it was realised that it often gave the wrong answers, since the assumptions required for regression analysis to be appropriate often did not apply to economic time series. This was partly a consequence of problems of identification, discussed by Morgan (1990), and partly a consequence of the trended nature of many data series. The classic statement of the latter problem was advanced in Yule's seminal paper, Yule (1926). Yule's warnings about the pitfalls in interpretation of (static) regressions based on economic time series did not stop economists from using time series regression, but they were taken very seriously. Keynes in his 1938 *Economic Journal* review of Tinbergen's econometric estimates used Yule's critique to attack time series estimation.[5] This attack had substance, since as Orcutt (1948) showed by Monte Carlo methods, Tinbergen's data might have been obtained from a population of series generated by a first order autoregression in first differences; in modern terminology the series were I(1).[6] Although Mann and Wald (1943) had provided an asymptotic basis for the estimation of stationary linear stochastic difference equations, the practical relevance of these assumptions had to be established. To quote Geary (1948, p. 149) 'It is scarcely an exaggeration to state that statisticians of the writer's generation were so frightened by Udny Yule's famous paper on "Nonsense Correlations" that we came to regard economic time series as so much dynamite, to be handled at all times with extreme caution and not to be handled at all if one could avoid it.'

In the late 1940s, the dynamite was defused by the establishment of the text book econometric model. In confronting the lack of independence in time series data the focus was shifted from concern with the autocorrelation structure of the data to the autocorrelation structure of the disturbance or equation error. Tests, like the Durbin–Watson statistic, were developed to detect such dependence; and procedures like the Cochrane–Orcutt transformation were developed to remove the dependence.[7] By the early 1950s, the text book econometric model was established. The main elements were the Cowles Commission SEM (which dealt with the identification problem) and the dynamic linear regression or ARDL (which modelled the dynamics explicitly in terms of the variables, rather than in terms of the unobservable disturbance). Hendry *et al.* (1984) provide a 'pre-cointegration' survey of ARDL modelling.

However, the skeleton Yule had discovered lay buried in the cupboard of econometrics until Granger and Newbold (1974) brought it out again. Using Monte Carlo techniques they; showed that spurious regressions could result from the regression of one independent random walk on another.[8] Phillips (1986) provided a theoretical basis for the Granger–Newbold result and showed that the R^2 of the regressions involving $I(1)$ variables tend to one and the t-ratios to non-zero random variables as the sample size increases, even if the underlying $I(1)$ variables are statistically independent. It should be noted that ARDL models, particularly when written in their Error Correction Model (ECM) form are much less vulnerable to this problem. Some of the literature gives the impression that regressions in which the R^2 was larger than the Durbin–Watson statistic were almost universal in economics before Granger and Newbold pointed out the problems. Although such regressions were undoubtedly published, most economists took dynamic specification more seriously and general practice was rather better than the caricature.

Fear of spurious regression, the fact that difference stationary and trend stationary variables had very different theoretical implications and the availability of tests for unit roots, e.g. Dickey and Fuller (1979), led to a proliferation of testing for the order of integration. The initial conclusion was that for most economic time series the null hypothesis of a unit root could not be rejected; the classic study is Nelson and Plosser (1982). However, given the generally low power of the tests, their sensitivity to possible breaks in the series and a variety of auxiliary statistical assumptions, the characterisation of the order of integration of most economic time series remains uncertain. For instance, Diebold and Senhadji (1996) present evidence which suggests that U.S. GNP, the series most investigated, is trend stationary, $I(0)$, rather than $I(1)$. To further complicate the issue, most of the unit root tests assume linear adjustment processes, and series found to be $I(1)$ by such tests may turn out to be stationary once possible non-linearities in the adjustment process are allowed for in the analysis, e.g. Michael *et al.* (1997).

The other element of text book econometrics, the structural SEM was attacked by Sims (1980), who argued that these models embodied incredible identifying restrictions. He advocated using a low order Vector Autoregression (VAR) to analyse economic time series. VARs appeared to have the advantage that they did not depend on an arbitrary division of the variables into endogenous and exogenous and did not require the 'incredible' identifying assumptions required by SEMs. The VAR approach was closely linked to the issue of spurious regression, since the condition for regressions between $I(1)$ variables not to be spurious is that at least one linear combination of them is $I(0)$, i.e. that they cointegrate. Cointegration, the existence of a long run relationship between the I(1) variables, imposes restrictions on the VAR.[9]

The initial applications of VARs, unit root tests and cointegration analysis tended to be relatively atheoretical, whereas the ARDL and SEM approaches used economic theory more extensively. However, economic theory can also be used to construct structural cointegrating VARs. The next section provides the statistical framework within which the long-run relationships from the economic theory can be incorporated, starting from a structural simultaneous Vector ARDL model.

2. Statistical framework

This section sets out the statistical structure, bringing out the relationship between the various representations of the processes and the identification issues. The various representations are useful for different purposes. Starting from a structural vector ARDL model we then examine how the time profile of the effect of shocks to the exogenous variables or errors can be measured. We then move to a cointegrating VAR without exogenous variables. In this case treatment of the deterministic elements raises special issues that we discuss before considering the measurement of dynamic effects in cointegrating VARs. Finally we illustrate some of the issues with an applied example.

2.1. *A structural vector ARDL model*

We begin from a traditional structural Vector ARDL (VARDL) model. Suppose the $m_y \times 1$ vector of endogenous variables y_t, is determined by:[10]

$$A_0 y_t = A_1 y_{t-1} + \cdots + A_p y_{t-p} + B_0 x_t + B_1 x_{t-1} + \cdots + B_p x_{t-p} + D d_t + \varepsilon_t, \quad (2.1)$$

for $t = 1, 2, \ldots, T$, where d_t is a $q \times 1$ vector of deterministic variables (e.g. intercept, trend and seasonal variables), x_t is an $m_x \times 1$ vector of exogenous variables, $\varepsilon_t = (\varepsilon_{1t}, \varepsilon_{2t}, \ldots, \varepsilon_{m_y t})'$ is a serially uncorrelated $m_y \times 1$ vector of errors distributed independently of x_t with a zero mean and a constant positive definite variance-covariance matrix, $\Omega = (\omega_{ij})$, where ω_{ij} is the (i, j) element of Ω. For given values of d_t and x_t, the above dynamic system is stable if all the roots of the determinantal equation

$$|A_0 - A_1\lambda - A_2\lambda^2 - \cdots - A_p\lambda^p| = 0, \quad (2.2)$$

lie strictly outside the unit circle. This stability condition ensures the existence of long-run relationships between y_t and x_t, which will be cointegrating when one or more elements of x_t are integrated, namely contain unit roots. The assumption, however, rules out the possibility that the endogenous variables, y_t, will themselves be cointegrating when the model contains no exogenous variables.

The above VARDL model is structural in the sense that it explicitly allows for instantaneous interactions between the endogenous variables through the contemporaneous coefficient matrix, A_0. It can also be written as

$$A(L) y_t = B(L) x_t + D d_t + \varepsilon_t \quad (2.3)$$

where L is the lag operator such that $Ly_t = y_{t-1}$; and

$$A(L) = A_0 - A_1 L - \cdots - A_p L^p; \qquad B(L) = B_0 + B_1 L + \cdots + B_p L^p.$$

Of particular interest are the system long-run effects of the exogenous variables:

$$A(1)^{-1}B(1) = \left(A_0 - \sum_{i=1}^{p} A_i\right)^{-1} \sum_{i=0}^{p} B_i.$$

Notice that since by assumption all the roots of (2.2) fall outside the unit circle, the inverse of $A(1)$, which we have denoted by $A(1)^{-1}$, exists.

The reduced form of the system, which expresses the endogenous variables in terms of the predetermined and exogenous variables, is given by

$$y_t = \Phi_1 y_{y-1} + \cdots + \Phi_p y_{t-p} + \Psi_0 x_t + \Psi_1 x_{t-1} + \cdots + \Psi_p x_{t-p} + \Psi d_t + u_t, \quad (2.4)$$

where $\Phi_i = A_0^{-1}A_i$, $\Psi_i = A_0^{-1}B_i$, $\Psi = A_0^{-1}D$, $u_t = A_0^{-1}\varepsilon_t$ is *i.i.d.* $(0, \Sigma)$,

$$\text{with } \Sigma = A_0^{-1}A_i\Omega A'^{-1}_0 = (\sigma_{ij}).$$

When there are no exogenous variables, $B_i = 0$, $i = 0, 1, \ldots, p$, and the VARDL model reduces to a VAR(p) that has been the focus of the cointegration literature and to which we shall return below. Given that the same variables appear in each equation and there are no cross-equation restrictions, the reduced form parameters, Φ_i, Ψ_i, Y, and Σ, can be efficiently estimated by Ordinary Least Squares (OLS) applied to each equation separately.

The classical identification problem is how to recover the structural form parameters

$$\{A_i, B_i, i = 0, 1, \ldots, p; \text{ D and } \Omega\},$$

from the reduced form parameters,

$$\{\Phi_i, \Psi_i, i = 0, 1, 2, \ldots, p, \Psi, \text{ and } \Sigma\}.$$

The resolution of this identification problem formed the basis of the Cowles Commission approach to structural modelling in econometrics. Exact identification of the structural parameters requires m_y^2 *a priori* restrictions, of which m_y restrictions would be provided by normalisation conditions. The restrictions typically involved setting certain elements of the structural coefficient matrices to zero. These were the *a priori* restrictions criticised by Sims (1980), particularly when such identifying restrictions were obtained by restricting the short run dynamics. Most of the traditional macro models were heavily over-identified and while, in principle, these over-identifying restrictions could be tested, in practice the number of exogenous and predetermined variables was so large that it was impossible to estimate the reduced form.[11] There are a variety of other ways of imposing identifying restrictions. For instance, if after a suitable ordering, it is assumed that A_0 is triangular *and* Ω diagonal (though there is no general theoretical reason to expect it to be so) the structural system becomes a recursive causal chain, each equation of which can be consistently estimated by OLS. The assumptions that A_0 is triangular and Ω is diagonal each provide $m_y(m_y-1)/2$ restrictions, which together with the m_y normalisation restrictions just identify the system. As we shall see below these assumptions are also equivalent to the use of the Cholesky decomposition of Σ originally advocated by Sims for identification of impulse responses.

2.2. *Impulse response analysis*

One of the main outputs of the traditional macro models was their dynamic multipliers, which measured the effect of a shock to an exogenous variable, e.g. a policy change, or a shock to one of the structural errors, ε_t, on the (expected) future values of the endogenous variables. We will briefly review how one can measure the dynamic effects of shocks or impulse response functions. Under the stability assumption (namely that the roots of (2.2) lie strictly outside the unit circle), $\mathbf{A}(L)$ is invertible and the time profile of-the effect of a shock can be calculated from the 'final form' of the structural model:

$$y_t = A(L)^{-1}B(L)x_t + A(L)^{-1}Dd_t + A(L)^{-1}\varepsilon_t. \tag{2.5}$$

This expresses each endogenous variable in terms of an infinite distributed lag on the exogenous variables and an infinite moving average process on the structural errors. Notice that the dynamic multipliers, the effects of a shock to x_t, can be derived from the reduced form coefficients, but to measure the dynamic effect of a shock to the structural errors we have to identify the structural coefficients. The equivalent final form representation from the reduced form is:

$$y_t = \Phi(L)^{-1}\Psi(L)x_t + \Phi(L)^{-1}\Psi d_t + \Phi(L)^{-1}u_t, \tag{2.6}$$

where[12]

$$\Phi(L) = I_{m_y} - \Phi_1 L - \cdots - \Phi_p L^p,$$

I_{m_y} is an identity matrix of order m_y, and

$$\Psi(L) = \Psi_0 + \Psi_1 L + \cdots + \Psi_p L^p,$$

Since $\Phi(L)$ is invertible we have the following moving-average representation of the structural errors:

$$\Phi(L)^{-1}u_t = \sum_{i=0}^{\infty} C_i u_{t-i} = \sum_{i=0}^{\infty} C_i A_0^{-1}\varepsilon_{t-i}, \tag{2.7}$$

where the C_i's can be calculated from the recursive relations:

$$C_i = \Phi_1 C_{i-1} + \Phi_2 C_{i-2} + \cdots + \Phi_p C_{i-p}, \quad \text{for } i = 0, 1, 2, \ldots \tag{2.8}$$

where $C_i = 0$, for $i < 0$ and $C_0 = I_{m_y}$.

Although these infinite moving average representations exist only when the model is stable, it turns out that similar results can be obtained even in the unstable case where one or more roots of (2.2) are on the unit circle. Irrespective of whether the model is stationary or contains unit roots, one can derive impulse response functions for the responses of the endogenous variables to a 'unit' displacement in the particular elements of either the exogenous variables, x_t, or the errors (u_t or ε_t). The former represents the time profile of the response of the system to changes in the observed forcing variables of the system, while the latter examines the responses of the system to changes in the unobserved forcing variables. The impulse response functions for the errors can be defined either with respect to the 'primitive/structural' errors, ε_t, or with respect to the reduced form errors, u_t. All these impulse responses can be obtained using the generalized impulse response approach advanced in Koop *et al.* (1996) for non-linear models and discussed in more detail for linear models in Pesaran and Shin (1998a). The generalised impulse response function measures the change to the n period ahead forecast of each of the variables that would be caused by a shock to the exogenous variable, structural or reduced form disturbance.

To define the generalised impulse response functions, denote the information set containing current and all lagged values of y_t and x_t by $\mathfrak{F}_t = (\mathrm{y}_t, \mathrm{y}_{t-1}, \ldots; \mathrm{x}_t, \mathrm{x}_{t-1}, \ldots)$. Consider a shock to the i-th structural error, ε_{it}, and let $\mathfrak{g}(n, \mathrm{z}: \varepsilon_i)$, be the generalized impulse responses of $\mathrm{z}_{t+n} = \mathrm{y}_{t+n}, \mathrm{x}_{t+n}$ or ε_{t+n}, respectively, to a unit change in ε_{it}, measured by one standard deviation, namely $\sqrt{\omega_{ii}}$. Then at horizon n we have

$$\mathfrak{g}(n, \mathrm{z}: \varepsilon_i) = E(\mathrm{z}_{t+n} \mid \varepsilon_{it} = \sqrt{\omega_{ii}}, \mathfrak{F}_{t-1}) - E(\mathrm{z}_{t+n} \mid \mathfrak{F}_{t-1}).$$

Clearly, since the x_t are assumed to be strictly exogenous the impulse response functions are zero, i.e. $\mathfrak{g}(n, \mathrm{x}: \varepsilon_i) = 0$ for all n and i,[13] and since the ε_{it} are serially uncorrelated then the impulse response functions are non-zero only at horizon zero when $\mathfrak{g}(n, \varepsilon: \varepsilon_i) = E(\varepsilon_t \mid \varepsilon_{it} = \sqrt{\omega_{ii}})$, for $n = 0$.

If the structural errors are correlated a shock to one error will be associated with changes in the other errors. As shown by Koop *et al.* (1996) in the Gaussian case where $\varepsilon_t \sim N(0, \Omega)$

$$E(\varepsilon_t \mid \varepsilon_{it} = \sqrt{\omega_{ii}}) = \frac{1}{\sqrt{\omega_{ii}}} \begin{pmatrix} \omega_{1i} \\ \omega_{2i} \\ \vdots \\ \omega_{m_y i} \end{pmatrix},$$

which can be written more compactly as[14]

$$E(\varepsilon_t \mid \varepsilon_{it} = \sqrt{\omega_{ii}}) = \left(\frac{1}{\sqrt{\omega_{ii}}}\right) \Omega \mathrm{e}_i,$$

where e_i is an $m_y \times 1$ selection vector of zeros except for its i-th element which is set to unity. This gives the predicted shocks in each structural error given a shock to ε_{it}, based on the typical correlation observed historically between the structural errors. In the case where the structural errors are orthogonal, the shock only changes the i th error and we have

$$E(\varepsilon_t \mid \varepsilon_{it} = \sqrt{\omega_{ii}}) = \sqrt{\omega_{ii}}\,\mathrm{e}_i.$$

Application of the generalized impulse response analysis to the VARDL specification, (2.1), now yields

$$\mathrm{A}_0 \mathrm{g}(n, \mathrm{y} : \varepsilon_i) = \mathrm{A}_1 \mathrm{g}(n-1, \mathrm{y} : \varepsilon_i) + \cdots + \mathrm{A}_p \mathrm{g}(n-p, \mathrm{y} : \varepsilon_i) + \mathrm{g}(n, \varepsilon : \varepsilon_i)$$

for $n = 0, 1, 2, \ldots$, with the initial values $\mathrm{g}(n, y : \varepsilon_i) = 0$ for $n < 0$ and as we saw above the last term is non-zero only for $n = 0$.

The identification of $\mathrm{g}(n, y : \varepsilon_i)$ requires the identification of the structural coefficients A_i, $i = 0, 1, \ldots, p$, and the covariance matrix Ω. It is also possible to identify $\mathrm{g}(n, y : \varepsilon_i)$ by a mixture of identification restrictions on A_0 and Ω. To see this pre-multiply both sides of the above relationship by A_0^{-1} to obtain

$$\mathrm{g}(n, \mathrm{y} : \varepsilon_i) = \Phi_1 \mathrm{g}(n-1, \mathrm{y} : \varepsilon_i) + \cdots + \Phi_p \mathrm{g}(n-p, \mathrm{y} : \varepsilon_i) + \mathrm{A}_0^{-1} \mathrm{g}(n, \varepsilon : \varepsilon_i) \quad (2.9)$$

where as before $\Phi_i = \mathrm{A}_0^{-1}\mathrm{A}_i$ $i = 1, 2, \ldots, p$, and the last term is non-zero only for $n = 0$. The Φ_i can be estimated from the reduced form, thus the indeterminacy is confined to the contemporaneous interaction of the structural errors $\mathrm{A}_0^{-1}\mathrm{g}(0, \varepsilon : \varepsilon_i)$, and is resolved up to a scalar coefficient if $\mathrm{A}_0^{-1}\Omega$ can be estimated consistently. However, to identify (or consistently estimate) $\mathrm{A}_0^{-1}\Omega$ involves the imposition of m_y^2 *a priori* restrictions on the elements of A_0 and/or Ω. Evidently, the identification of the structural impulse responses does not require A_0 and Ω to be separately identified, and it is possible to trade off restrictions across A_0 and Ω. But in cases where there are no *a priori* grounds for restricting Ω, since $\mathrm{A}_0^{-1}\Omega \mathrm{A}'^{-1}_0 = \Sigma$, then $\mathrm{A}_0^{-1}\Omega = \Sigma \mathrm{A}'_0$, and the identification of the impulse responses with respect to structural errors requires complete knowledge of the contemporaneous effects, A_0.

The standard approach to deriving impulse response functions is to start from the moving average representations of the final form, (2.6). The reduced form disturbances are correlated and the covariance matrix of u_t, which can be estimated, is $\Sigma = \mathrm{A}_0^{-1}\Omega \mathrm{A}'^{-1}_0$. The Sims (1980) orthogonalised impulse response function uses the Cholesky decomposition of $\Sigma = \mathrm{PP}'$, where P is a lower triangular matrix. This can be used to create a new sequence of errors, $\mathrm{u}_t^* = \mathrm{P}^{-1}\mathrm{u}_t, t = 1, 2, \ldots, T$, which are orthogonal to each other, contemporaneously uncorrelated with unit standard errors, namely $E(\mathrm{u}_t^* \mathrm{u}_t^{*\prime}) = \mathrm{I}_{m_y}$. Thus the effect of a shock to one of these orthogonalized errors, $\mathrm{u}_t^* = (u_{1t}^*, u_{2t}^*, \ldots, u_{m_y t}^*)'$, say u_{1t}^*, is unambiguous, because it is not correlated with the other orthogonalized errors. The impulse response analysis is also often supplemented by the forecast error variance decomposition; where the error variance of forecasting the ith variable n periods ahead is decomposed into components accounted for by innovations in different variables in the VAR. There are two problems with orthogonalised impulse response functions and variance decomposition. The impulse responses obtained refer to the effects on the endogenous variables, y_{it}, of a unit displacement (measured by one standard error) in the orthogonalised error, u_{jt}^*, and not in the structural or even the reduced form errors, ε_{jt} and u_{jt}. Second, notice that the choice of P is only made unique by the ordering of the variables in the VAR. Unless Σ is diagonal, or close to diagonal, different orderings will give different estimates of the impulse response functions. In fact, the particular ordering of the variables in the VAR and the Cholesky decomposition procedure used constitute an implicit identification assumption, which turns out to be equivalent to the recursive identifying assumptions discussed above.

It was quickly recognised, e.g. Cooley and LeRoy (1985), that orthogonalised impulse response functions actually employed traditional identification assumptions. The Structural VAR approach, or what Sims (1996) calls 'weakly identified time-series models', attempts to identify the impulse responses by imposing *a priori* restrictions on the covariance matrix of the structural errors and the contemporaneous and/or long-run impulse responses themselves. This approach was developed by Bernanke (1986), Blanchard and Watson (1986), Sims (1986), Shapiro and Watson (1988) and Blanchard and Quah (1989). The restrictions include requiring certain shocks to have zero long-run impacts, or by assuming contemporaneous effects of certain other shocks to be zero on certain variables. Under this approach it is also typically assumed that the structural (or economic) errors, ε_t, are uncorrelated, which may not be reasonable in many macroeconometric applications of the structural VAR methodology.[15] Furthermore, while this approach can be used in very small systems, the number of restrictions required, $m_y(m_y - 1)/2$, grows rapidly with m_y, the number of endogenous variables in the system, making it non-feasible in larger systems.

When plausible *a priori* information to identify the effects of structural shocks is not available, it would still be of some interest to examine the effect of shocks to the reduced form errors, $\mathrm{u}_t = \mathrm{A}_0^{-1}\varepsilon_t$. The generalised impulse response function provides a natural way to do this since it measures the effect on the endogenous variables of a typical shock to the system, based on the estimated covariance between the reduced form shocks in the estimation period. Notice that the generalized impulse responses of y_{t+n} with respect to u_{it} (the i-th element of u_t) are given by

$$\mathfrak{g}(n, \mathrm{y} : u_i) = \boldsymbol{\Phi}_1 \mathfrak{g}(n-1, \mathrm{y} : u_i) + \cdots + \boldsymbol{\Phi}_p \mathfrak{g}(n-p, \mathrm{y} : u_i) + \mathfrak{g}(n, \mathrm{u} : u_i), \quad (2.10)$$

where the last term is non-zero only for $n = 0$, when it is

$$\mathfrak{g}(n, \mathrm{u} : u_i) = \left(\frac{1}{\sqrt{\sigma_{ii}}}\right) \Sigma \mathrm{e}_i, \quad \text{for } n = 0,$$

and where $\Sigma = \mathrm{A}_0^{-1}\Omega\mathrm{A}'^{-1}_0$. These impulse responses can be uniquely estimated from the parameters of the reduced form and unlike the orthogonalized impulse responses are invariant to the ordering of the variables in the VAR. One can also construct a comparable forecast error decomposition.

In the case of stationary variables the generalised impulse response function, as defined by (2.9) or (2.10), will tend to zero as n tends to infinity. In the case of $I(1)$ variables it will tend to a non-zero constant as n goes to infinity. When the variables are $I(1)$ and cointegrated, there will be linear combinations of the generalised impulse response function that tend to zero and we discuss this further below. The relationships between the generalized impulse response functions and the orthogonalized impulse responses are discussed in Pesaran and Shin (1998a).

The above impulse responses consider the effect of a shock to a *particular* exogenous variable, x_{it}, or an error term, ε_{it} or u_{it}. An alternative approach developed in Lee and Pesaran (1993) would be to consider the effect of system-wide shocks at time t on the evolution of the system at time $t+n$. Under this approach the generalized impulse responses are derived with respect to the whole vector of shocks, ε_t or u_t, and viewed as random variables. The probability distribution function of these random variables are then examined as a function of n. In the case where ε_t (or u_t) are Gaussian, the generalized impulse responses with respect to the system-wide shocks are also Gaussian with a zero mean and the covariance matrix $C_n \Sigma C_n'$. The diagonal elements of $C_n \Sigma C_n'$ (appropriately scaled) are called the persistence profiles by Lee and Pesaran (1993). It is easily seen that the same persistence profiles are obtained for the structural as well as the reduced form errors. For a stationary VAR, the persistence profiles tend to zero as $n \rightarrow \infty$. For VARs with unit roots the persistence profiles tend to the spectral density function (apart from a scalar constant) of Δy_t at zero frequency.

2.3 *Cointegrating VARs*

Most of the analysis of cointegration has been done in the context of a VAR(p), where all the variables are regarded as endogenous. Initially we follow the literature and assume that the VAR model *only* contains endogenous $I(1)$ variables and linear deterministic trends. Setting $B_i = 0$ in (2.1), we have:

$$y_t = \Phi_1 y_{t-1} + \cdots + \Phi_p y_{t-p} + a_0 + a_1 t + u_t, \tag{2.11}$$

where a_0 and a_1 are $m \times 1$ vectors of unknown coefficients.[16] To cover the unit root case we now allow for the roots of

$$|I_m - \Phi_1 \lambda - \Phi_2 \lambda^2 - \cdots - \Phi_p \lambda^p| = 0, \tag{2.12}$$

to fall on and/or outside the unit circle, but rule out the possibility that one or more elements of y_t be $I(2)$.[17] We shall return to the case where the model also contains exogenous $I(1)$ variables in Section 5. The model can be reparameterized as a Vector Error Correction

$$\Delta y_t = -\Pi y_{t-1} + \sum_{i=1}^{p} \Gamma_i \Delta y_{t-i} + a_0 + a_1 t + u_t, \tag{2.13}$$

where

$$\Pi = I_m - \sum_{i=1}^{p} \Phi_i, \quad \Gamma_i = -\sum_{j=i+1}^{p} \Phi_j, \quad i = 1, \ldots, p-1. \tag{2.14}$$

If the elements of y_t were $I(0)$, Π will be a full rank $m \times m$ matrix. If the elements of y_t are $I(1)$ and not cointegrated then it must be that $\Pi = 0$ and a VAR model in first differences will be appropriate. If the elements of y_t are $I(1)$ and cointegrated with $\text{rank}(\Pi) = r$, then $\Pi = \alpha\beta'$, where α and β are $m \times r$ full column rank matrices and there will be $r < m$ linear combinations of y_t, the cointegrating relations, $\xi_t = \beta' y_t$, which are $I(0)$. The variables ξ_t are often interpreted as deviations from equilibrium.

Under cointegration, the VECM can be written as:

$$\Delta y_t = -\alpha\beta' y_{t-1} + \sum_{i=1}^{p-1} \Gamma_i \Delta y_{t-i} + a_0 + a_1 t + u_t, \tag{2.15}$$

where α is the matrix of adjustment or feedback coefficients, which measure how strongly the deviations from equilibrium, the r stationary variables $\beta' y_{t-1}$, feedback onto the system. If there are $0 < r < m$ cointegrating vectors, then some of the elements of α must be non zero, i.e. there must be some Granger causality involving the levels of the variables in the system to keep the elements of y_t from diverging.

The unrestricted estimate of Π can be obtained using (2.13). In the restricted model, (2.15), which is subject to $r < m$ cointegrating vectors we need to estimate the two $m \times r$ coefficient matrices, α and β. It is clear that α and β are not separately identified without some additional restrictions, since for any non-singular matrix Q we could define $\Pi = \alpha Q Q^{-1} \beta'$ and $\alpha^* = \alpha Q$ and $\beta^{*\prime} = Q^{-1}\beta'$ would be equivalent matrices of adjustment coefficients and cointegrating vectors. Put differently, any linear combination of the $I(0)$ variables, $\xi_t = \beta' y_t$, are also $I(0)$ variables. To avoid this indeterminacy, we require r independent restrictions on each of the r cointegrating relations, a total of r^2 restrictions, r of which are provided by normalisation conditions. Thus in the restricted model we estimate $2mr - r^2$ free parameters, and cointegration imposes $(m - r)^2$ restrictions. Johansen (1988, 1991), who provides procedures for testing for the rank of Π and estimating α and β, uses the identifying restrictions that β are eigenvectors, i.e. have unit length and are orthogonal. While mathematically natural given the statistical structure of the problem, these restrictions have no economic meaning, since in general there is no reason to expect economic cointegrating vectors to be orthogonal. When $r > 1$, economic interpretation of the Johansen estimates of the cointegrating vectors is almost impossible. The alternative is to use economic theory to provide the restrictions, which allows the cointegrating vectors to be interpreted as familiar long-run economic relations. These restrictions are usually similar to Cowles Commission type restrictions (e.g. that a particular variable does not appear in a particular equation) but apply only to the long run, getting around the Sims critique of the use of restrictions on the dynamics to identify the equations. Pesaran and Shin (1997) provide a general treatment of such identifying or overidentifying restrictions, which can be linear or non-linear.

2.3.1. *Treatment of the deterministic components*

If there are linear trends in the unrestricted VAR, in general there will be quadratic trends in the level of the variables when the model contains unit roots. To avoid quadratic trends the linear trend coefficients must be restricted.[18] Below we discuss this issue. As shown, for example, in Pesaran, Shin and R. J. Smith (1997), using (2.11) Δy_t can be represented by an infinite moving average representation.[19]

$$\Delta y_t = C(L)(a_0 + a_1 t + u_t), \tag{2.16}$$

where

$$C(L) = \sum_{j=0}^{\infty} C_j L^j = C(1) + (1 - L)C^*(L), \tag{2.17}$$

$$C^*(L) = \sum_{j=0}^{\infty} C_j^* L^j, \quad C_j^* = C_{j-1}^* + C_j, \quad \text{with } C_0^* = C_0 - C(1), \tag{2.18}$$

and C_j given by the recursive relations (2.8).[20] It is now easily seen that

$$\Delta y_t = b_0 + b_1 t + C(1)u_t + C^*(L)\Delta u_t, \tag{2.19}$$

where

$$b_0 = C(1)a_0 + C^*(1)a_1, \qquad b_1 = C(1)a_1.$$

Cumulating (2.19) forward we obtain the 'level MA representation':

$$y_t = y_0 + b_0 t + b_1 \frac{t(t+1)}{2} + C(1)s_t + C^*(L)(u_t - u_0),$$

where s_t denotes the partial sum $s_t = \sum_{s=1}^{t} u_s$, $t = 1, 2, \ldots$, and rank $[C(1)] = m - r$. Consequently, it is immediately seen that since $b_1 = C(1)a_1$, in general y_t will contain m different linear deterministic trends, $b_0 t$, $m - r$ different (independent) deterministic quadratic trends given by $(t(t+1)/2)C(1)a_1$, $m - r$ unit root (or permanent) components given by $C(1)s_t$, and m stationary components given by $C^*(L)(u_t - u_0)$.[21] With a_1 unrestricted, the quadratic trend term disappears only in the full rank stationary case where there are no unit roots, namely if $rank(\Pi) = m$, and $r = m$.

To remove the quadratic trends and ensure that the trend in the deterministic part of y_t is linear for all values of r, we need to restrict the trend coefficients so that $a_1 = \Pi\gamma$, where γ is an arbitrary $m \times 1$ vector of fixed constants. For this choice of a_1 it is easily seen that $b_1 = C(1)\Pi\gamma = 0$.[22] Under this restriction on the trend coefficients we have

$$y_t = y_0 + b_0 t + C(1)s_t + C^*(L)(u_t - u_0). \tag{2.20}$$

The associated error correction formulation is given by

$$\Delta y_t = \alpha\beta'(y_{t-1} - \gamma t) + \sum_{i=1}^{p-1} \Gamma_i \Delta y_{t-i} + a_0 + u_t, \tag{2.21}$$

where the deterministic trend is now specified to be a part of the cointegrating relations, $\beta'(y_{t-1} - \gamma t)$. This ensures that the y_t only have linear and not quadratic trends.

The cointegrating relations will not contain deterministic trends when $\beta'\gamma = 0$. These provide r further restrictions, known as 'co-trending' restrictions which are testable. A similar conclusion also follows from the 'level MA representation', (2.20). Pre-multiplying both sides of these relations by β' we have

$$\beta' y_t = \beta' y_0 + (\beta' b_0)t + \beta'(1)s_t + \beta' C^*(L)(u_t - u_0).$$

But $\beta' C(1) = 0$, and it is also easily established that

$$\beta' b_0 = \beta' C(1)a_0 + \beta' C^*(1)a_1 = \beta' C^*(1)\Pi = \beta'\gamma.$$

Hence

$$\beta' y_t = \beta' y_0 + (\beta'\gamma)t + \beta' C^*(L)(u_t - u_0), \tag{2.22}$$

and in the case of VAR models with linear trends, the cointegrating relations will also contain deterministic trends, unless the co-trending restrictions $\beta'\gamma = 0$ are imposed.

So far we have focused on cointegrating VAR models with linear deterministic trends. A similar consideration also applies to cointegrating VAR models that contain intercepts only. Once again to ensure that the level variables do not contain different numbers of independent linear deterministic trends as the cointegrating rank changes, the intercepts in these models must also be accordingly restricted. It is also possible that different elements of y_t may have different trend characteristics. For example, output and interest rates are often included in the same VAR, while it is clear that these variables have different trend characteristics. Although there are a large number of possible treatments of the deterministic elements, it will be convenient to distinguish between five different cases often encountered in practice:

Case I: no intercept or trend;

Case II: r restricted intercepts which enter the cointegrating relations and no trend;

Case III: m unrestricted intercepts and no trends;

Case IV: m unrestricted intercepts and r restricted trends;

Case V: m unrestricted intercepts and m unrestricted trends.

As argued in Pesaran, Shin and R. J. Smith (1997), cases II and IV are likely to be particularly relevant in practice and are preferable to the corresponding unrestricted cases III and V. For ease of reference we index these five cases by $d = 1, 2, \ldots, 5$.

2.3.2. *Impulse response analysis in cointegrating VARs*

Using the level MA representation, (2.20), generalized impulse response functions can be calculated for the cointegrating VECM in a way similar to the VARDL discussed above. In particular using (2.20), for the effect of a unit shock to the i-th structural form error, ε_{it}, we have[23]

$$g(n, y : \varepsilon_i) = \left(\frac{1}{\sqrt{\omega_{ii}}}\right)\tilde{C}_n A_0^{-1}\Omega e_i,$$

where $\tilde{C}_n = (\sum_{j=0}^{n} C_j)$, and as before e_i is a selection vector of zeros with unity as its i-th element. For the effect of a unit shock to the i-th reduced form error, u_{it}, we have

$$g(n, y : u_i) = \left(\frac{1}{\sqrt{\sigma_{ii}}}\right)\tilde{C}_n \Sigma e_i,$$

In particular, $g(\infty, y : \varepsilon_i) = \omega_{ii}^{-1/2}C(1)A_0^{-1}\Omega e_i$ and $g(\infty, y : u_i) = \sigma_{ii}^{-1/2}C(1)\Sigma e_i$, and unlike the stationary case shocks will have permanent effects on the $I(1)$ variables, though not on the cointegrating relations. The generalized impulse response function for the cointegrating relations $\xi_t = \beta' y_t$ with respect to a unit shock to the structural errors, for example, is given by

$$g(n, \xi : \varepsilon_i) = \left(\frac{1}{\sqrt{\omega_{ii}}}\right)\beta'\tilde{C}_n A_0^{-1}\Omega e_i.$$

Since $\beta'\tilde{C}_\infty = \beta' C(1) = 0$, it then follows that $g(\infty, \xi : \varepsilon_i) = 0$, and ultimately the effects of shocks on the cointegrating relations will disappear. Nevertheless, estimation of $g(n, \xi : \varepsilon_i)$ for a finite n still requires *a priori* identification of $A_0^{-1}\Omega$. Once again a variety of identification schemes can be used for this purpose. Alternatively, we could focus on the impulse response functions of $\xi_t = \beta' y_t$ with respect to the i-th reduced form shock, u_{it}. In this case

$$g(n, \xi : u_i) = \left(\frac{1}{\sqrt{\sigma_{ii}}}\right)\beta'\tilde{C}_n \Sigma e_i,$$

which is uniquely determined from the knowledge of the reduced-form parameters.

Finally, we could examine the effect of system-wide shocks on the cointegrating relations using the persistence profiles discussed above in Section 2.2. Pesaran and Shin (1996) suggest using the persistence profiles to measure the speed of convergence of the cointegrating relations to equilibrium. For convenience of interpretation these are scaled to have a value of unity on impact. The (unscaled) persistence profile of the cointegrating relations is given by

$$\beta'\tilde{C}_n \Sigma \tilde{C}_n' \beta, \qquad \text{for } n = 0, 1, \ldots$$

The profiles tend to zero as $n \rightarrow \infty$, and provide a useful graphical representation of the extent to which the cointegrating (equilibrium) relations adjust to system-wide shocks. Once again the main attraction of persistence profiles lies in the fact that they are uniquely determined from the reduced form parameters and do not depend on the nature of the system-wide shocks considered. Using (2.22), the cointegrating relations in terms of the structural errors may be written as

$$\beta' \mathrm{y}_t = \beta' \mathrm{y}_0 + (\beta'\gamma)t + \beta' \mathrm{C}^*(L)\mathrm{A}_0^{-1}(\varepsilon_t - \varepsilon_0),$$

and the persistence profile of $\beta' \mathrm{y}_t$ with respect to the structural errors is given by

$$\beta'(\tilde{\mathrm{C}}_n \mathrm{A}_0^{-1})\Omega(\tilde{\mathrm{C}}_n \mathrm{A}_0^{-1})'\beta.$$

But, since $\Sigma = \mathrm{A}_0^{-1}\Omega \mathrm{A}_0'^{-1}$, this persistence profile is in fact identical to the one derived using the reduced-form errors, namely $\beta' \tilde{\mathrm{C}}_n \Sigma \tilde{\mathrm{C}}_n' \beta$.

2.4. *An example*

As an example consider the cointegrating VAR(p) models analysed by KPSW using the six variables, c_t: private consumption, i_t: private investment, $m_t - p_t$: real money balances, q_t: private output, R_t: the nominal interest rate, and Δp_t: the rate of inflation. Except for R_t and Δp_t, the variables are in logarithms. Output, consumption, investment and money balances are measured on a per capita basis using civilian non-institutional population. KPSW treat all the six variables as endogenous $I(1)$, although the unit-root evidence on the inflation rate seems to be rather weak. They estimate two VARs, one with $m = 3$, including only the real variables (c_t, i_t, q_t) and one with $m = 6$ containing both real and nominal variables. They use two samples. The first, 1949:1–1988:4, is used for models which involve only real variables and the second, 1954:1–1988:4, is used for models which also include nominal variables. The shorter period is used for nominal variables to avoid observations that occurred during periods of price control, the Korean War and the Treasury-Fed accord which may have disrupted the normal price transmission mechanisms. When $m = 6$, they expect three cointegrating vectors: a consumption function, an investment function and a money demand function; thus they need 9 just identifying restrictions, 3 on each cointegrating vector. They provide this by the 3 normalisation conditions, plus the restrictions that investment and real money balances do not appear in the consumption function, consumption and real money balances do not appear in the investment function and that consumption and investment do not appear in the real money demand function. Thus for $\mathrm{y}_t = (c_t, i_t, m_t - p_t, q_t, R_t, \Delta p_t)'$ the matrix of cointegrating vectors has the form:

$$\beta' = \begin{pmatrix} -1 & 0 & 0 & \beta_{41} & \beta_{51} & \beta_{61} \\ 0 & -1 & 0 & \beta_{42} & \beta_{52} & \beta_{62} \\ 0 & 0 & -1 & \beta_{43} & \beta_{53} & \beta_{63} \end{pmatrix}.$$

Other natural restrictions, which KPSW use as overidentifying restrictions to be tested, or which could be used as alternative just-identifying restrictions, are: $\beta_{41} = \beta_{42} = \beta_{43} = 1$, (unit income elasticities); $\beta_{63} = 0$ (the effect of inflation on money demand is captured by nominal interest rates) and $\beta_{51} = -\beta_{61}$ and $\beta_{52} = -\beta_{62}$ (consumption and investment are determined by real interest rates).

One can also test restrictions on trends and intercepts, which are not treated explicitly by KPSW.

Of course, being able to identify the long-run coefficients does not allow one to identify stochastic trends or structural disturbances. With six variables and three cointegrating vectors there are three stochastic trends. They partition the vector of structural errors, ε_t, into two components, ε_t^p, which contains the three disturbances that have permanent effects and, ε_t^s, which contains the three disturbances that have only short-term or transitory effects. Such a decomposition is clearly arbitrary, and there are many other possible linear combinations of the structural errors, ε_t, that could have been used. Therefore, in addition to the usual problem of identifying the contemporaneous effects of structural errors, $A_0^{-1}\Omega$, further *a priori* information is needed with which to identify the permanent from the transitory shocks. Levtchenkova *et al.* (1998) discuss in more detail this and other problems associated with the identification of the effects of shocks in the KPSW model.

3. Applied choices: in the context of a simple application

The previous section set out the standard structure for the analysis of cointegrating VAR models. It is clear from this presentation that the applied economist has to make a number of difficult choices. For instance, he/she has to determine:

1. The number and list of the endogenous variables to be included, (m_y, y_t).
2. The number and list of the exogenous variables (if any) to be included, (m_x, x_t).
3. The nature of the deterministic variables (intercepts, trends, seasonals) and whether the intercepts and/or the trend coefficients need to be restricted, d.
4. The order of the VARDL.
5. The order of integration of the variables.
6. The number of cointegrating vectors, r.
7. The specification of r^2 just-identifying, and possibly additional over-identifying restrictions on β.
8. The identification and estimation of impulse responses to shocks of economic relevance and interest.

This is a highly simplified version of the actual decision problem in applied work, which usually involves more dimensions. Firstly, the assumption that the lag length is common to each variable in each equation is arbitrary. It can be relaxed as discussed in Pesaran, Shin and R. J. Smith (1997), but this just adds more choices. Secondly, we have just assumed intercepts and trends, but as Perron (1989) makes clear it may be important to include dummy variables which allow the coefficient of intercept or trend to shift in response to large rare shocks. Thirdly, the sample size has been taken as given, but in many applications, such as that considered by KPSW, choice of an appropriate sample (or 'observation window') plays an important role and it is not clear how it should be selected in practice. Many researchers appeal to data availability, and *ad hoc* recourse to special events when deciding on the choice of the observation window. These and many other applied choices make our presentation highly simplified, but even these limited choices raise difficult statistical problems.

The first six choices in the above list change the maximised value of the log-likelihood (MLL). Thus in principle these choices could be made on the basis of either hypothesis testing exercises or by means of model selection criteria such as the Akaike Information Criterion (AIC), or the Schwarz Bayesian Criterion (SBC). However, different significance levels, different forms of the tests and different model selection criteria may well give conflicting conclusions. This has been most extensively studied in the case of choice 5, the order of integration of the variables. In many cases little is known about the small sample properties of these procedures and what is known is often not reassuring (e.g. the low power of many tests). Little is also known about the properties of the tests or model selection criteria when the range of models considered does not include the data generation process. Each of these choices is likely to be sensitive to each of the others. For instance, it is known that choice of r, the number of cointegrating vectors, is sensitive to m, the dimension of the system; p, the order of the VAR; and the treatment of intercepts and trends indexed by d, (see Section 2.3). The combination of these choices gives us a very large space of possible models and there is no reason to expect a series of sequential choices (e.g. fix m, then choose p conditional on m, etc.) to adequately explore the possible model space. Joint tests may lead to different inferences from a sequence of individual tests. Sequential procedures are likely to suffer from pre-test bias, while general to specific searches face the difficulty that the unrestricted models are profligate with parameters. Nor is the order above, which corresponds to the development of the theoretical model, necessarily the right one. It is not clear whether one should decide on the order of integration at the beginning, as is common practice; when moving from VAR to reduced rank VECM as above; or after completing the cointegration analysis to determine whether any of the cointegrating vectors identify single variables. In certain circumstances one may not need to determine the order of integration. For instance, bounds tests are available to determine the existence of a long-run relation in a single equation ARDL model, which except for a region of indeterminacy do not require the variables to be classified as $I(0)$ or $I(1)$, see Pesaran, Shin and R. J. Smith (1996).

While data dependent decision procedures are extremely important, given the complexity of the applied modelling problem they have to be supplemented with other considerations. In particular, choices will be informed by the purpose of the exercise and by prior information from economic theory; theory being interpreted widely. In principle, this combination could be done formally by embodying the purpose of the exercise in an explicit loss function and the theory information in a prior probability distribution for the parameters, and then applying Bayesian techniques. In practice the difficulty of formalising the loss function and prior probability distributions makes an informal use of these other considerations more attractive except for relatively simple problems. The strength of the ARDL and

SEM traditions was that they developed a range of informal but effective procedures for integrating economic and statistical information. Statistically insignificant variables were retained when they were economically important and statistically significant variables were deleted when they were likely to be economically unimportant. Misleading statistical significance can arise for many reasons, e.g. significant effects at lags which are multiples of seasonal frequencies arise to remove the effect of separate seasonal adjustment of each variable. Chance correlations with omitted variables, like cold winters or policy announcements, can make variables significant. It is a matter of judgement whether these variables or lags are regarded as economically important.

Given the size of the potential model space, defined by the choices discussed above, it is important to investigate a range of specifications. At present full exploration of the model space is likely to be highly data-intensive and computationally burdensome, if not infeasible. Even much simpler problems, like determining the lag order in an ARDL, discussed in Pesaran and Shin (1998a) requires many hundred regressions. Given that full exploration is not feasible, organised sensitivity analysis plays an important role. The sensitivity analysis should investigate both the statistical significance and the economic importance of the restrictions, as KPSW do.

To illustrate these choices, we will examine the data used by KPSW and estimate a number of different VAR models in $y_t = (c_t, i_t, q_t)'$. In particular, we consider the choice of p, r and the nature of intercepts and deterministic trends included in the VAR. It should be emphasised that we are not trying to show that KPSW made the wrong judgements about these choices; merely that such choices are based on a combination of economic theory and statistical evidence and that the statistical evidence is not decisive. KPSW make this quite clear; they use economic theory very effectively to choose between specifications, they present a wide range of statistical results which allow the reader to investigate the likelihood function, and their judgements are always qualified (conclusions are described as 'can be characterised as' or 'are consistent with').

We estimated the VAR models over the period 1949:1–1988:4, the same sample as used by KPSW, giving $T = 160$.[24] Our results are identical to those reported by KPSW, though the Maximised Log-Likelihood (MLL) is lower than that reported in KPSW by the constant $-3 \times 160/2 \ln(2\pi + 1) = -681$. Whereas the likelihood function is informative in exploring alternative parameter estimates it is less informative when exploring alternative specifications, since the number of parameters changes. In these circumstances, model selection criteria, which adjust the maximised log-likelihood for the number of parameters estimated, are more useful. This raises two different issues. Firstly, what weight should be put on parsimony (the numbers of parameters estimated) relative to statistical fit of the data (the MLL)? We use two criteria, the AIC, which for model i is $\text{MLL}_i - k_i$, where k_i is the number of parameters estimated and the SBC which is $\text{MLL}_i - (0.5 \ln T)k_i$, where T is the sample size.[25] The second issue is that model selection criteria treat all parameters equally, but in economic applications one might wish to put different weights on extra parameters generated by additional lags than extra parameters generated by additional cointegrating vectors because the economic implications of the restrictions may be quite different. From a statistical viewpoint, the use of AIC and SBC in the case of models with non-stationary regressors is also complicated by the fact that the ML estimates of the short-run and long-run parameters converge to their true (or pseudo-true) values at different rates, depending on the choice of r. The extent of this problem varies with the value of r. Both of these economic and statistical considerations might underlie the common practice of using different criteria for the different choices: choose lag length, p, by AIC or SBC; choose the specification of intercepts and deterministic trends *a priori*, and choose the number of cointegrating vectors, r, by Likelihood Ratio (LR) tests in the light of predictions of the long-run economic theory. In what follows we illustrate both approaches and compare their outcomes.

Using the KPSW data we first investigated the choice of p and r over the range of $p = 7, 6, \ldots, 1$ and $r = 0, 1, 2, 3$, according to the two model selection criteria, assuming four different specifications of the intercept/trends, $d = 2, 3, 4, 5$.[26] We also examined the choice of r, conditional on p and intercept/trend specifications, by Likelihood Ratio tests, using Johansen's maximum eigenvalue and trace statistics. Economic theory suggests $r = 2$, which is what KPSW chose. They also chose $p = 6$, while the model selection criteria reported below suggest a much lower order for the VAR. However, there are a number of other considerations which KPSW may have taken into account in choosing a higher order. There is some suggestion of lag 6 effects in the extended model where $m = 6$, and having a common lag order between the real and nominal models allows consistent comparison between them. The size of many of these tests is sensitive to lag order and over-parameterisation may avoid biasing the size, though it may have negative effects on the power. As KPSW make clear, it is a matter of judgement how one trades off these effects.

The results for the AIC are not reported because they are very clear-cut and can be summarised briefly. For any value of p (lag order) and the chosen characterization of intercepts/trends, the AIC always chooses $r = 3$, implying that all three variables (c_t, i_t, q_t) are $I(0)$. The global maximum for the AIC over the range investigated is for a second order lag ($p = 2$), three cointegrating vectors ($r = 3$) and models with restricted or unrestricted intercepts, but without deterministic trends. The AIC would suggest that the concern over spurious regression among $I(1)$ variables is misplaced, since on this criteria they all appear $I(0)$. There is some ambiguity over the choice of intercepts/trends which arises because for $r = m$ the restrictions on intercepts and on trend coefficients will not be binding and Cases II and III, as well as Cases IV and V will yield identical likelihoods. This can be seen in Table 1, which gives the values of SBC for alternative values of p and r, under Cases II to V. When $r = 0$, the SBC for models with $d = 3$ and $d = 4$ are identical. Similarly when $r = m$, the models with $d = 2$ and $d = 3$ have identical SBC values as do models with $d = 4$ and $d = 5$. There is a tendency for the number of cointegrating vectors identified to fall as one moves to higher values of d, a less restricted treatment of intercept and trend.

Table 1.[1] Values of the Schwarz–Bayesian criterion for a VAR(p) in $y_t = (c_t, i_t, q_t)'$ for alternative choices of p, r and d

		Choice of intercepts and/or deterministic trends (d)			
VAR(p)		$d=2$	$d=3$	$d=4$	$d=5$
$p=7$	r				
	0	1355.0	1359.0	**1359.0**	**1353.1**
	1	1356.4	**1359.1**(3)	1356.8(4)	1353.0(4)
	2	1355.8	1357.6(1)	1352.8	1351.4
	3	**1356.8**(4)	1356.8	1350.7	1350.7
$p=6$	r				
	0	1373.9	**1378.7**(1)	**1378.7**(4)	**1372.8**(4)
	1	**1375.1**	1376.2(2)	1373.9	1369.9
	2	1372.8	1374.8(1)	1370.1	1368.6
	3	1373.9(4)	1373.9	1367.6	1367.6
$p=5$	r				
	0	**1392.9**	**1397.0**	**1397.0**	**1390.8**
	1	1392.0	1394.9(4)	1392.5(4)	1388.5(4)
	2	1391.5	1392.8	1387.9	1386.5
	3	1391.9(4)	1391.9	1385.9	1385.9
$p=4$	r				
	0	1407.2	1412.5	**1412.5**	1406.2
	1	1407.3	**1414.3**(2)	1411.9(4)	**1408.0**(4)
	2	1410.9	1413.4(2)	1408.4	1407.0
	3	**1412.5**(4)	1412.5	1406.6	1406.6
$p=3$	r				
	0	1422.3	1428.6	1428.6	1422.1
	1	1423.7	**1432.2**(4)	**1429.7**(4)	**1425.7**(4)
	2	**1428.8**	1429.3	1424.6	1422.9
	3	1428.3(4)	1428.3	1422.7	1422.7
$p=2$	r				
	0	1429.6	**1445.8**	1445.8	1439.5
	1	1440.4	1450.3(4)	**1447.9**(4)	1444.2(4)
	2	1447.3	1448.6	1444.0	1442.6
	3	**1447.8**(4)	1447.8	1442.1	1442.1
$p=1$	r				
	0	1410.8	**1430.7**	**1430.7**	**1424.2**
	1	1425.8	1429.5(4)	1427.0(4)	1422.9(4)
	2	1425.9	1427.4	1422.9	1421.3
	3	**1426.4**(4)	1426.4	1420.8	1420.8

[1] p is the order of the VAR, r is the number of the cointegrating vectors, $d=2$ refers to r restricted intercepts and no trends, $d=3$ refers to m unrestricted intercepts and no trends, $d=4$ refers to m unrestricted intercepts and r restricted trends, $d=5$ refers to m unrestricted intercepts and m unrestricted trends. For given p and d, the maximum value of SBC over $r=0,1,2,3$ is highlighted. Figures in brackets give the number of LR tests which selected a particular value of r.

In Table 1, the r which gives the highest value of the SBC for given p and d is highlighted. The table also gives the number of Likelihood Ratio tests which choose a particular value of r in parentheses. Of the large number of possible tests, the table considers four: the Johansen maximum eigenvalue test at the 95% and 90% level and the Johansen trace test at the 95% and 90% level. The eigenvalue tests tend to identify fewer cointegrating vectors than trace tests and 95% tests identify fewer cointegrating vectors than 90% tests. The global maximum for the SBC over this range is $p = 2$, $r = 1$, $d = 3$. For these values of p and d, all four of the Johansen tests agree with the SBC that $r = 1$, rather than $r = 2$ which is suggested by economic theory. At the higher lags used by KPSW, the position is less clear cut. For $p = 6$, $d = 3$; the AIC suggests $r = 3$, the SBC suggests $r = 0$, the 95% maximum eigenvalue test suggests $r = 0$, the 90% eigenvalue test and the 90% trace test suggests $r = 1$ and the 90% trace test suggests $r = 2$, which is what the theory predicts.

In this example, the economic parameter of interest is the number of cointegrating vectors, r. But it is clear that the data are not very informative about r; when one adjusts for the number of parameters estimated the likelihood function is fairly flat in this dimension. Choice of r varies over the possible range between $r = 0$ and $r = 3$ with different specifications of p and d, and with the particular statistical criteria used. Given this, the KPSW judgement on economic criteria that $r = 2$ is probably sensible; but it is an economic judgement made after investigating the statistical information.

Fixing the number of cointegrating relations at 2, say on theoretical grounds, and then using the SBC values in Table 1 to select p and d, it is seen that the value of p which maximizes SBC is equal to 2, for all choices of d. Now fixing $r = 2$, and $p = 2$, we find that the value of d which maximizes SBC is $d = 3$. This yields a VAR(2) with unrestricted intercepts and no deterministic trends. But as we have already pointed out in Section 2.3, given the trended nature of variables (c_t, i_t, q_t) a VAR(2) with restricted trend coefficients (namely $d = 4$) may be more appropriate.

There is another reason for not abandoning the VAR(2) with $d = 4$ at this early stage in the analysis. For given values of r and p, the SBC values in Table 1 provide a reasonable basis to select d only if we are happy to ignore the (economic) theory restrictions and their associated trade-offs. In the present example there are two types of theory restrictions — the over-identifying restrictions on the cointegrating vectors, and the co-trending restrictions. It is therefore more appropriate to base the choice of d on VAR(2) models estimated subject to the theory restrictions. For $d = 3$, the VAR(2) model can be written as

$$\Delta \mathbf{y}_t = \mathbf{a}_0 - \alpha\beta'\mathbf{y}_{t-1} + \Gamma_1 \Delta \mathbf{y}_{t-1} + \mathbf{u}_t, \tag{3.1}$$

and for $d = 4$ as

$$\Delta \mathbf{y}_t = \mathbf{a}_0 - \alpha\beta'(\mathbf{y}_{t-1} - \gamma t) + \Gamma_1 \Delta \mathbf{y}_{t-1} + \mathbf{u}_t, \tag{3.2}$$

where $\mathbf{y}_t = (c_t, i_t, q_t)'$. In both formulations the intercepts, $\mathbf{a}_0$, are unrestricted. Neoclassical growth theory would predict that in the long run consumption-output and investment-output ratios are stationary around constant means, or more specifically $c_t - q_t$ and $i_t - q_t$ are $I(0)$ variables with constant means. Therefore, an exactly-identified formulation of β is given by

$$\beta_E' = \begin{pmatrix} -1 & 0 & \beta_{31} \\ 0 & -1 & \beta_{32} \end{pmatrix}.$$

with the coefficients β_{31} and β_{32} being subject to the following *two* over-identifying restrictions:

$$\beta_{31} = \beta_{32} = 1. \tag{3.3}$$

Furthermore, the theory also predicts the following two co-trending restrictions (recall that $r = 2$):

$$\beta'\gamma = 0. \tag{3.4}$$

The two specifications (3.1) and (3.2) are clearly equivalent when the above co-trending restrictions are satisfied. But the trend restricted model, (3.2), offers a more general framework within which the co-trending restrictions can be tested. As it happens in the present application the co-trending restrictions are not rejected and so the problem of a choice between $d = 3$ and $d = 4$ does not arise. Setting $r = 2$, $p = 2$, and $d = 4$, we obtained the following ML estimates

$$\hat{\beta}_E' = \begin{pmatrix} -1 & 0 & \begin{matrix} 1.1131 \\ (0.16994) \end{matrix} \\ 0 & -1 & \begin{matrix} 1.3519 \\ (0.33067) \end{matrix} \end{pmatrix}.$$

The figures in brackets are the asymptotic standard errors. The MLL value for this model is equal to 1499.9, which is the same as the relevant entry in Table 1. The value of MLL under the co-trending restrictions (3.4) is 1499.3. Thus yielding a log-likelihood ratio of around 1.06, which is well below the 95% percent critical value of the Chi-squared distribution with 2 degrees of freedom. Notice also that the SBC values for the models defined by ($r = 2$, $p = 2$, $d = 3$) and ($r = 2$, $p = 2$, $d = 4$) are the same when the co-trending restrictions are imposed on the latter.

We are now in the position to test the remaining theory restrictions given by (3.3). Estimating the model under these and the co-trending restrictions yield the MLL of 1496.2, with an associated LR statistic of 7.34 [=2(1499.9–1496.2)], which is distributed as a Chi-squared variate with 4 degrees of freedom. Hence the joint theory restrictions are not rejected by the data. One could also test the restrictions (3.3) conditional on the co-trending restrictions (3.4) being true. The outcome of this test will be identical to that of testing (3.3) in the context of ($r = 2$, $p = 2$, $d = 3$). Using the above MLL values the LR statistic for this test is given by 6.2 [=2(1499.3–1496.2)], which is just above the 95% critical value of the Chi-squared distribution with 2 degrees of freedom. This simple exercise also clarifies the differences in test outcomes that could result from the different choices of d. Our analysis favours the use of the trend restricted models when one or more underlying variables are trended, and the intercept restricted models when none of the underlying variables are trended.

Having arrived at a model which seems to be in accordance with the long-run predictions of the economic theory and at the same time does not seem to be rejected by the available time series data, we could examine some of its short-run dynamic properties by considering the estimates of the error-correction coefficients, α and Γ_1 that appear in (3.2) or (3.1). The ML estimates of these parameters are given by

$$\hat{\alpha} = \begin{pmatrix} -0.0223 & 0.0300 \\ (0.0285) & (0.0161) \\ -0.2417 & 0.1627 \\ (0.0830) & (0.0468) \\ -0.1446 & 0.0097 \\ (0.0440) & (0.0248) \end{pmatrix},$$

and

$$\hat{\Gamma} = \begin{pmatrix} -0.1694 & 0.0381 & 0.1716 \\ (0.0940) & (0.0340) & (0.1716) \\ -0.0454 & 0.2927 & 0.7294 \\ (0.2739) & (0.0990) & (0.2003) \\ 0.1706 & 0.1646 & 0.0857 \\ (01451) & (0.0525) & (0.1061) \end{pmatrix}.$$

These estimates suggest particularly strong and statistically significant feedbacks from the lagged error correction terms, $c_{t-1} - q_{t-1}$ and $i_{t-1} - q_{t-1}$, on investment and, to a lesser extent, on output changes. In contrast, the effects of these terms on consumption changes are rather weak and only marginally significant statistically.

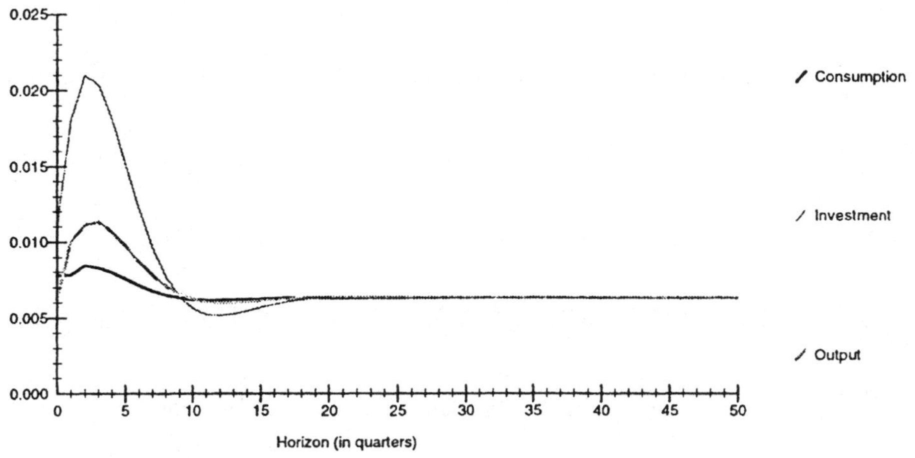

Figure 1. Generalized impulse response(s) to one S.E. shock in the equation for C

The same is also true of the coefficient estimates for the effects of lagged changes given in $\hat{\Gamma}_1$, and can be readily seen in Figures 1–3 which display the generalized impulse responses of unit shocks to the consumption, investment and output equations.

4. The dimensions of the VAR

It has long been recognised that for most empirical analysis VARs are over-parameterised: each equation of the VAR involves estimating *mp* lag coefficients plus one or more parameters for the deterministic components. Even moderate

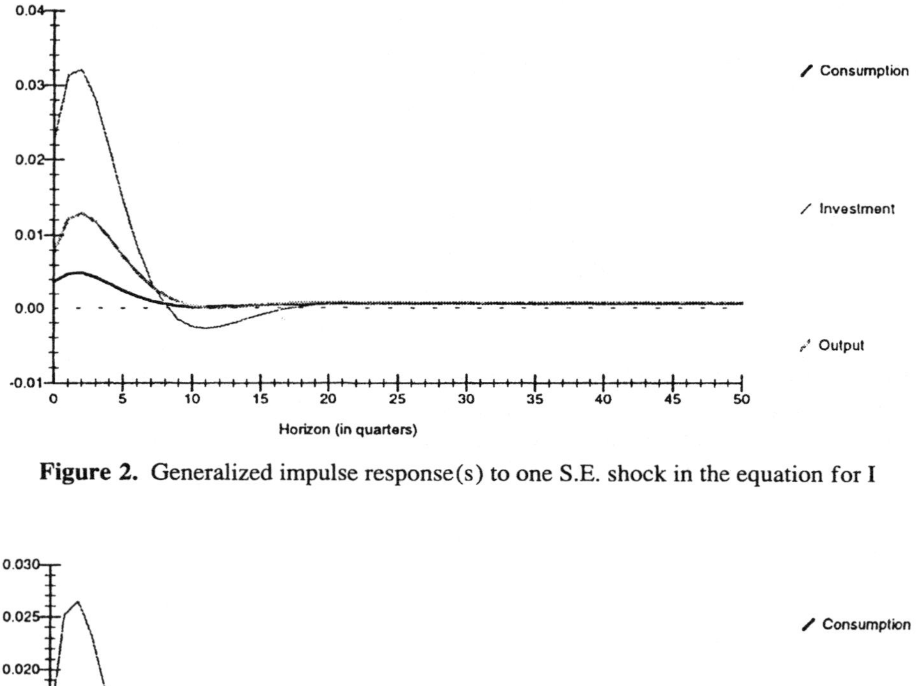

Figure 2. Generalized impulse response(s) to one S.E. shock in the equation for I

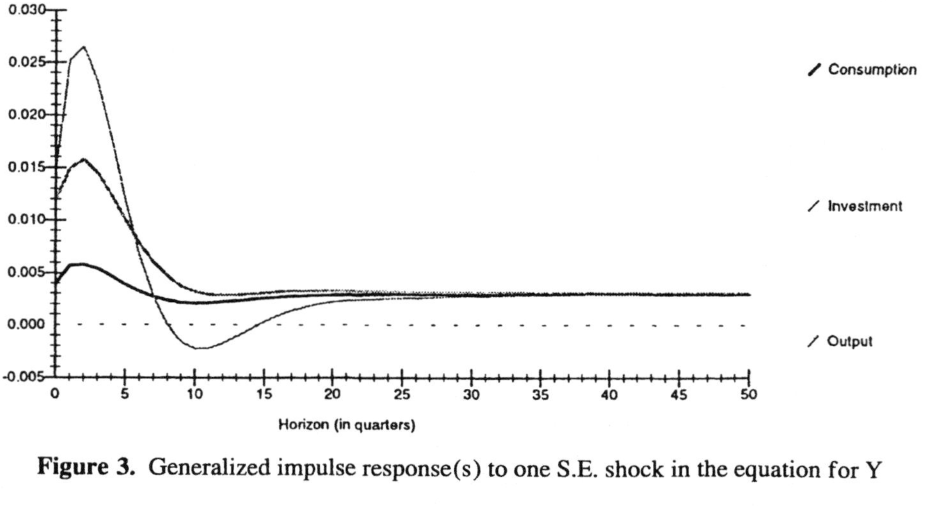

Figure 3. Generalized impulse response(s) to one S.E. shock in the equation for Y

values of m and p will quickly exhaust typical samples available for macro-econometric research. For instance, each equation in the six variable VAR(p) model estimated by KPSW involves estimating 38 parameters from 140 observations and the system as a whole has 228 regression coefficients. VARs with m as low as six seem to be subject to substantial biases (Abadir *et al.* 1998), but for capturing the main interactions in most economic systems, six is a small number of variables. KPSW consider a closed-economy model and do not analyse unemployment, government expenditure or taxation; which limits the use of their model for policy analysis. Even very small traditional macro models could easily contain more than a dozen behavioural equations. Thus the VAR approach quickly runs into the difficulty faced by traditional macro modellers, that the implicit reduced form cannot be estimated. Therefore, if *a priori* information from economics or other sources can be used to reduce the dimensionality of the problem, the number of free parameters estimated, there will be improvements in efficiency and in the power of the tests.

One of the early solutions to the over-parameterization problem was in fact suggested by Sims and his colleagues. They followed a Bayesian route and applied priors, known as the 'Minnesota priors', to the short-run coefficients, treating all the variables in the VAR as random walks with drift. This approach seemed to work reasonably well for forecasting, but lacked a theoretical basis making them unreliable for policy analysis. In the case of cointegrating VARs, the major problem is how to restrict the short-run dynamics; applying economic theory to identify and restrict the long-run effects seems much more straightforward and less subject to controversy. On this also see Garratt *et al.* (1998).

There are two types of model which give rise to *a priori* restrictions on the short run dynamics. Here we mention them briefly for completeness, but will not discuss them in detail, since they are well covered in the literature. The first type is linear rational expectations models. These give rise to decision rules that take the form of a VAR, but are subject to a variety of cross-equation restrictions, which if accepted can substantially reduce the number of parameters that need to be estimated. Of course, testing such cross-equation restrictions will still confront the researcher with the curse of the dimensionality. The second type is Real Business Cycle (RBC) models. These are non-linear models derived from basic economic theory where there are a few deep parameters of technology and taste, which come from the assumed production and utility functions of the representative agent. To solve these models, the standard procedure is to compute the non-stochastic steady state values of the variables of the system and then log-linearise the first order conditions around these non-stochastic steady state values. This approximation can then be written as a VAR, where the large number of parameters in the VAR are functions of the few deep parameters of technology and tastes; again the theoretical restrictions substantially reduce the number of parameters to be estimated. While these two approaches may be promising in the future, at the moment there are severe difficulties with their application. In the case of RBC models, or more generally non-linear rational expectations models, there are difficulties with the solution procedures they use for the theoretical model and the conventional empirical implementations of RE and RBC models tend to be rejected by the data on a number of different statistical criteria. It is likely that advances in computing techniques and incorporation of learning in these models could help bring their predictions closer to the data.

In some cases the dimensions of the VAR can be reduced by using linear transformations of the variables. Such transformations are common in the literature either where the hypothesised cointegrating vector is believed to be known *a priori* or there are natural homogeneity restrictions, e.g. using the single variable real per-capita income rather than the three variables nominal income, prices and population. For instance, tests of Purchasing Power Parity (PPP) have been carried out in a three-variable VAR model with $y_t = (s_t, p_t, p_t^*)'$, where s_t is the logarithm of the spot exchange rate, p_t is the logarithm of the domestic price index, and p_t^* is the logarithm of the foreign price index; in a two-variable VAR model with $y_t = (s_t, p_t - p_t^*)'$; and in a univariate framework using the real exchange rate $y_t = (s_t - (p_t - p_t^*))$. Such transformations not only reduce the dimension of the system, but can be particularly useful when there are doubts concerning the order of the integration of the individual price variables. For example, it is often unclear from unit root tests whether domestic and foreign prices are $I(1)$ or $I(2)$, but there is more evidence that s_t and $p_t - p_t^*$ are $I(1)$. Boyd and Smith (1998) test the restrictions in moving from the two variable system in the spot rate and price differential to the univariate system in the real exchange rate. As another example, Alogoskoufis and Smith (1991) examine a five-variable VAR with $y_t = (q_t, e_t, w_t, p_t, l_t)'$ where q_t is the logarithm of real output, e_t is employment, w_t is wages, p_t is prices, and l_t is labour force; a three-variable VAR with $y_t = (q_t - e_t, w_t - p_t, l_t - e_t)'$ where $q_t - e_t$ is the logarithm of labour productivity, $w_t - p_t$ is the logarithm of real wages and $l_t - e_t$ is the logarithm of the unemployment rate; and finally a univariate model in logarithm of the share of wages $(w_t + e_t, - q_t - p_t)$, with different inferences in each case.[27]

In the case of the KPSW application, reduction in the dimension of the VAR can be achieved by focusing on the two great ratios, $cs_t = c_t - q_t$ and $is_t = i_t - q_t$ rather than on output, consumption and investment separately. ADF tests on cs_t and is_t give more support for two cointegrating vectors than do the VAR based cointegration tests discussed above. Using $p = 6$ with intercept and trend over the 1949:1–1988:4 sample, the ADF for the consumption share is −4.2 and the ADF for the investment share is −4.0. To see the restrictions involved in the use of such transformations, start from a second order cointegrating VAR with $m = 3$ and $r = 2$:

$$\Delta c_t = \alpha_{11}(c_{t-1} - q_{t-1}) + \alpha_{12}(i_{t-1} - q_{t-1}) + \gamma_{11}\Delta c_{t-1} + \gamma_{12}\Delta i_{t-1} + \gamma_{13}\Delta q_{t-1} + u_{1t},$$

$$\Delta i_t = \alpha_{21}(c_{t-1} - q_{t-1}) + \alpha_{22}(i_{t-1} - q_{t-1}) + \gamma_{21}\Delta c_{t-1} + \gamma_{22}\Delta i_{t-1} + \gamma_{23}\Delta q_{t-1} + u_{2t},$$

$$\Delta q_t = \alpha_{31}(c_{t-1} - q_{t-1}) + \alpha_{32}(i_{t-1} - q_{t-1}) \\ + \gamma_{31}\Delta c_{t-1} + \gamma_{32}\Delta i_{t-1} + \gamma_{33}\Delta q_{t-1} + u_{3t},$$

This can be written in terms of the great ratios, by subtracting the third equation from the other two, giving

$$\Delta(c_t - q_t) = (\alpha_{11} - \alpha_{31})(c_{t-1} - q_{t-1}) + (\alpha_{12} - \alpha_{32})(i_{t-1} - q_{t-1}) \\ + (\gamma_{11} - \gamma_{31})\Delta(c_{t-1} - q_{t-1}) + (\gamma_{12} - \gamma_{32})\Delta(i_{t-1} - q_{t-1}) \\ + [(\gamma_{13} - \gamma_{33}) + (\gamma_{11} - \gamma_{31}) + (\gamma_{12} - \gamma_{32})]\Delta q_{t-1} + (u_{1t} - u_{3t}),$$

and

$$\Delta(i_t - q_t) = (\alpha_{21} - \alpha_{31})(c_{t-1} - q_{t-1}) + (\alpha_{22} - \alpha_{32})(i_{t-1} - q_{t-1}) \\ + (\gamma_{21} - \gamma_{31})\Delta(c_{t-1} - q_{t-1}) + (\gamma_{22} - \gamma_{32})\Delta(i_{t-1} - q_{t-1}) \\ + [(\gamma_{23} - \gamma_{33}) + (\gamma_{21} - \gamma_{31}) + (\gamma_{22} - \gamma_{32})]\Delta q_{t-1} + (u_{2t} - u_{3t}),$$

This can only be written as a VAR in the two great ratios, if $\gamma_{11} + \gamma_{12} + \gamma_{13} = \gamma_{31} + \gamma_{32} + \gamma_{33}$ so that Δq_{t-1} drops out of the consumption share equation and $\gamma_{21} + \gamma_{22} + \gamma_{23} = \gamma_{31} + \gamma_{32} + \gamma_{33}$ so that Δq_{t-1} drops out of the investment share equation. To be able to write the equations as two separate autoregressions in the great ratios, requires in addition that $\alpha_{12} = \alpha_{32}$ and $\gamma_{12} = \gamma_{32}$ so the lagged investment share terms do not appear in the consumption share equation and $\alpha_{21} = \alpha_{31}$ and $\gamma_{21} = \gamma_{31}$ so the lagged consumption share terms do not appear in the investment share equation. There seems little economic justification for such symmetry in the short-run dynamics. In the KPSW example the restrictions required to give the ADF equations for the consumption and investment shares are rejected by Likelihood Ratio tests but in both cases the SBC chooses the restricted ADF equation.

To examine the more general case, consider the cointegrating VAR:

$$\Delta \mathrm{y}_t = -\alpha\beta'\mathrm{y}_{t-1} + \sum_{i=1}^{p-1} \Gamma_i \Delta \mathrm{y}_{t-i} + \mathrm{u}_t, \tag{4.1}$$

which can be written as

$$\Gamma(\mathrm{L})\Delta \mathrm{y}_t = -\alpha\beta'\mathrm{y}_{t-1} + \mathrm{u}_t,$$

where $\Gamma(\mathrm{L}) = \mathrm{I} - \sum_{i=1}^{p-1} \Gamma_i \mathrm{L}^i$ and

$$\Delta \mathrm{y}_t = \Gamma(\mathrm{L})^{-1}(-\alpha\beta'\mathrm{y}_{t-1} + \mathrm{u}_t).$$

Premultiplying by β' gives:

$$\Delta\xi_t = \beta'\Gamma(\mathrm{L})^{-1}(-\alpha\xi_{t-1} + \mathrm{u}_t), \tag{4.2}$$

where $\xi_t = \beta'\mathrm{y}_t$. Thus the cointegrating relations, ξ_t, will in general have an infinite order VARMA representation and cannot be written as a finite-order VAR model.[28] The important exception is where $p = 1$ and all the $\Gamma_i = 0$, and therefore $\Gamma(\mathrm{L})_{-1} = \mathrm{I}_m$. In this special case the cointegrating relations, ξ_t, can be represented as a first order VAR. In other cases, analysing the dynamics of ξ_t using finite order VARs will impose restrictions on (4.2). To see the restrictions, premultiply (4.1) by β'

$$\Delta\xi_t = -(\beta'\alpha)\xi_{t-1} + \sum_{i=1}^{p-1} \beta'\Gamma_i \Delta y_{t-i} + \beta' u_t.$$

If this can be rewritten in terms of a VAR which just involves the cointegrating relations, ξ_t, then the equations in ξ_t will take the form:

$$\Delta\xi_t = -(\beta'\alpha)\xi_{t-1} + \sum_{i=1}^{p-1} F_i \Delta\xi_{t-i} + \beta' u_t, \tag{4.3}$$

where the $r \times r$ matrices F_i are defined such that

$$\beta'\Gamma_i = F_i\beta'. \tag{4.4}$$

Post-multiplying both sides of this relation by β we have $\beta'\Gamma_i\beta = F_i\beta'\beta$, and noting that $\beta'\beta$ is a full rank $r \times r$ matrix we also have $F_i = \beta'\Gamma_i\beta(\beta'\beta)^{-1}$ Substituting this expression back in (4.4), we obtain the following restrictions:

$$\beta'\Gamma_i(I_m - \beta(\beta'\beta)^{-1}\beta') = 0, \qquad \text{for } i = 1, 2, \ldots, p-1.$$

Furthermore since F_i are $r \times r$ matrices and Γ_i are $m \times m$ matrices rewriting the model as a VAR in the cointegrating relations imposes $r(p-1)(m-r)$ restrictions. As the example above indicated, it is straightforward to test these restrictions, by adding $m-r$ elements of Δy_{t-i} that are not linear functions of the r cointegrating relations, to each equation of the VAR in the cointegrating relations, (4.3). Again as the example above shows, it may be difficult to give these restrictions an economic interpretation, other than that the adjustment is in terms of economically meaningful combinations of variables, rather than the original variables. When the potential dimension of the VAR is large there may be no alternative to using such transformations, e.g. cointegrating vectors, but it requires that the correct transformation or cointegrating vector be known and imposes strong restrictions on the short-run dynamics.

5. Cointegrating VARs with exogenous variables

The KPSW model is very special. Only for the U.S. would one even consider constructing a closed economy macro-model, in which the rest of the world is ignored. For almost every other country in the world foreign variables are important and largely exogenous to each country, so open macroeconomy models are the appropriate framework. Thus contrary to the impression given by small U.S. macro models there are a natural set of exogenous variables such as world prices, including the prices of commodities like oil, world output and world interest rates. Imposition of such exogeneity restrictions is also likely to result in substantial reductions in the number of freely estimated parameters. Exclusion restrictions on exogenous variables can aid the identification of A_0, the coefficient matrix of the current endogenous variables. The shocks can be directly measured as the effects of the exogenous variables rather than having to be indirectly inferred from the residuals.

As an example, consider the structural VAR model of the UK described in Garratt *et al.* (1998). This has eight variables: domestic and foreign output, domestic and foreign prices both measured relative to the price of oil, domestic and foreign interest rates, the exchange rate and real money balances. The theory suggests five cointegrating relationships amongst these variables. These are a modified Purchasing Power Parity condition, Interest Rate Parity, an output gap equation, a solvency or balance of payments constraint equation and a real money balances equation. Apart from the money demand function they all reflect international arbitrage and solvency constraints. Although consumption and investment are not included in the core structural VARDL, they can be explained by satellite models driven from variables in the core. Foreign prices relative to the oil price are treated as exogenous. The five cointegrating relations and the over-identifying restrictions suggested by the theory are not rejected by the data. Thus the long-run theory can be incorporated in a coherent and transparent way while allowing for flexible short-run dynamics which can be investigated using impulse response functions and persistence profiles.

To examine the implications of allowing for exogenous variables, we shall reintroduce the distinction between an $m_y \times 1$ vector of the endogenous variables, y_t and an $m_x \times 1$ vector of exogenous variables, x_t, and write the system as a partitioned VAR:[29]

$$\begin{aligned} \Delta \mathrm{y}_t &= \Pi_{yy}\mathrm{y}_{t-1} + \Pi_{yx}\mathrm{x}_{t-1} \\ &\quad + \sum_{i=1}^{p-1} \Gamma_{iyy}\Delta \mathrm{y}_{t-i} + \sum_{i=1}^{p-1} \Gamma_{iyx}\Delta \mathrm{x}_{t-i} + \mathrm{u}_t, \\ \Delta \mathrm{x}_t &= \Pi_{xy}\mathrm{y}_{t-1} + \Pi_{xx}\mathrm{x}_{t-1} \\ &\quad + \sum_{i=1}^{p-1} \Gamma_{ixy}\Delta \mathrm{y}_{t-i} + \sum_{i=1}^{p-1} \Gamma_{ixx}\Delta \mathrm{x}_{t-i} + \mathrm{v}_t, \end{aligned} \tag{5.5}$$

where the covariance matrix of the reduced form disturbances is given by:

$$\Sigma = \begin{pmatrix} \Sigma_{uu} & \Sigma_{uv} \\ \Sigma_{vu} & \Sigma_{vv} \end{pmatrix}.$$

This partition does not impose any restrictions in itself, but provides a framework for examining how exogenous variables relate to the structure of the VAR.

To condition y_t on current values of x_t, define

$$E(\mathrm{u}_t \mid \mathrm{v}_t) = \Sigma_{uv}\Sigma_{vv}^{-1}\mathrm{v}_t = \Theta \mathrm{v}_t,$$

then the system for y_t can be written as

$$\Delta y_t = (\Pi_{yy} - \Theta\Pi_{xy})y_{t-1} + (\Pi_{yx} - \Theta\Pi_{xx})x_{t-1} + \Theta\Delta x_t + \sum_{i=1}^{p-1}(\Gamma_{iyy} - \Theta\Gamma_{ixy})\Delta y_{t-i} + \sum_{i=1}^{p-1}(\Gamma_{iyx} - \Theta\Gamma_{ixx})\Delta x_{t-i} + \eta_t, \quad (5.6)$$

where[30]

$$\eta_t = u_t - \Theta v_t.$$

By construction $E(\eta_t|\Delta x_t) = 0$, and the parameters of (5.6) can be estimated efficiently by OLS. Also denoting the (conditional) variance of η_t by $\Sigma_{\eta\eta}$, it is easily seen that

$$\Sigma_{\eta\eta} - \Sigma_{uu} = -\Sigma_{uv}\Sigma_{vv}^{-1}\Sigma_{vu} \leqslant 0.$$

Therefore, in general the variance of η_t will be smaller than that of u_t, and the parameters in the conditional model, namely $(\Pi_{yy} - \Theta\Pi_{xy})$, $(\Pi_{yx} - \Theta\Pi_{xx})$, Θ, $(\Gamma_{iyy} - \Theta\Gamma_{ixy})$ and $(\Gamma_{iyx} - \Theta\Gamma_{ixx})$ are likely to be estimated more precisely than the parameters of the unconditional model (5.5). Whether this is an advantage depends on what the economic parameters of interest are. If the parameters of interest are $\Pi_y = (\Pi_{yy}, \Pi_{yx})$, it is clear from equation (5.6) that Δx_t will be weakly exogenous for Π_y only if either $\Sigma_{uv} = 0$, so that $\Theta = 0$, or if $\Pi_x = (\Pi_{xy}, \Pi_{xx}) = 0$.[31] In either of these cases the coefficient matrix on (y_{t-1}, x_{t-1}) in the conditional model (5.6) will provide an estimate of Π_y, otherwise it will not. In other cases, the economic parameters of interest may be the long-run effects of x_t on y_t so one might be interested in $(\Pi_y - \Theta\Pi_x)$ directly, in which case the model conditional on x_t is appropriate whether or not $\Pi_x = 0$. The special case of this system where y_t is a scalar gives the ARDL model discussed in more detail in Pesaran and Shin (1998a) and Pesaran, Shin and R. J. Smith (1996).

While adding exogenous variables does not in itself identify the short run parameters, identification of the contemporaneous coefficient matrix, A_0, could be much easier with exogenous variables. *A priori* restrictions that certain foreign variables do not appear in particular domestic equations may be much more plausible than *a priori* restrictions that certain unobserved structural shocks are orthogonal. Of course, foreign economic variables are determined by economic processes, but since they are not influenced by domestic economic variables they can be used as predetermined variables in small open-economies.

But it is important to recognize that the introduction of exogenous variables in the cointegrating VAR models also present the investigator with the additional problem of determining the order of integration and cointegration of the exogenous variables. Pesaran, Shin and R. J. Smith (1997) consider the case where all the exogenous variables, x_t, are $I(1)$ and are not cointegrated. They derive the relevant asymptotic theory and provide critical values for cointegration tests; distinguishing between models with restricted and unrestricted intercept/trend coefficients. In the case of these models the long run relations are given by $\beta' z_{t-1}$, where $z_t = (y_t', x_t')'$ and $\Pi_y = (\Pi_{yy}, \Pi_{yx}) = \alpha_y\beta'$. It is now possible for the endogenous variables to be cointegrated among themselves as well as being cointegrated jointly with the exogenous variables. Impulse responses can also be computed with respect to shocks to the exogenous variables. For this purpose a complete specification of the model generating the exogenous variables will be required. This will fully identify the impulse responses and no additional identifying restrictions will be needed. A prominent example is the impulse responses of shocks to foreign prices on domestic output and inflation.[32]

6. Concluding comments

Any empirical analysis involves balancing considerations of purpose (the relevance of the model to its intended use), theory (consistency with prior knowledge) and statistical adequacy (itself a function of fit and parsimony). In the case of a cointegrating VAR, this balancing act is particularly difficult because not only are there a large number of choices required to establish a specification but also because statistical criteria may not be very informative about these choices. In the case of the choice of just identifying restrictions statistical criteria are completely uninformative and observationally equivalent models can have widely different interpretations depending on the choice of just identifying restrictions. Thus considerations of purpose and theory have to be used to inform the choices. Of course, if imposing the theory leads to a large reduction in fit, the theory should be reconsidered, though often this is not done. One important choice is the size of the VAR. Using economic theory to impose structure on the VAR can reduce the dimensionality of the estimation problem substantially and increase the efficiency of the estimates and the power of the tests. Given the importance of systems properties, the theory has to be used to impose some structure on the system rather than to impose *ad hoc* restrictions on individual (dynamic) coefficients.

One important use of *a priori* information is in the characterisation of particular variables as exogenous. The closed economy focus of much U.S. empirical research in macroeconomics has been an unfortunate example to the world, since it gives the impression that exogenous variables are difficult to find. For the rest of the world, foreign variables provide natural candidates and international arbitrage and solvency conditions natural long-run relationships which are relatively easy to identify. For most microeconomic studies there are also natural exogenous variables, such as the weather for agriculture or aggregate variables for particular sectors of the economy. Thus a structural VARDL framework is much more natural than a VAR which treats all variables as endogenous. U.S. economists' concern with unobservable demand and supply shocks has also been unfortunate. For most countries, the important shocks — to world raw material prices or to world real interest rates — are not only exogenous but observable. Thus it is less difficult to measure their impact on the economy. However, it is more difficult to characterise them as either demand shocks or supply shocks, since they influence both. This indicates that there is no reason to believe that exogenous structural shocks are orthogonal.

Given the limited data available, there are difficult trade-offs between the weight one gives to the various elements: purpose, theory, fit. While sensitivity analysis can illuminate those trade-offs — for instance the marginal rate of substitution between the statistical and economic criteria — it cannot determine the optimum; that will inevitably be a matter of judgement.

Acknowledgements

The first author wishes to gratefully acknowledge partial financial support from the ESRC (grant no. L116251016) and from the Isaac Newton Trust of Trinity College Cambridge. We are grateful to Michael Binder and the editors for helpful comments on an earlier version of this paper.

Notes

1. The paper draws on Pesaran (1997); Pesaran and Shin (1996, 1997, 1998a, 1998b); Pesaran, Shin and R. J. Smith (1996, 1997).
2. More technical detail, further references and discussion of applications can be found in Pesaran and Pesaran (1997).
3. The role of economic theory is also discussed in Pesaran and Smith (1995).
4. We are grateful to Mark Watson for providing us with the data set used in KPSW. The data set is also available in a *Microfit 4.0* tutorial file. See Lesson 16.6 in Pesaran and Pesaran (1997).
5. Pesaran and Smith (1985) examine Keynes' attack on econometrics.
6. A time series is said to be integrated of order d, $I(d)$, if it must be differenced d times to make it stationary.
7. Smith (1997) discusses the history in more detail.
8. The problem of spurious regression in the case of stationary but *highly* serially correlated regressors was demonstrated earlier by Champernowne (1960), also using Monte Carlo techniques.
9. See Engle and Granger (1987).
10. In general, different orders can be assumed for the distributed lag functions associated with the endogenous and exogenous variables. Alternatively, p can be viewed as the maximum lag order of the distributed lag functions on y_t and x_t.
11. The interaction of logarithmic behavioural equations with linear identities made the systems non-linear creating further difficulties in estimating the reduced form.
12. Since A_0 is non-singular and the roots of $|A_0 - A_1\lambda - A_2\lambda^2 - \cdots - A_p\lambda^p| = 0$ are assumed to fall outside the unit circle, it also follows that the roots of $|I_{m_y} - \Phi_1\lambda - \Phi_2\lambda^2 - \cdots - \Phi_p\lambda^p| = 0$ will also fall outside the unit circle.
13. This would not, of course, be the case if x_t was only weakly exogenous.
14. This result also holds in non-Gaussian but linear settings where the conditional expectations $E(\varepsilon_t \mid \varepsilon_{it} = \sqrt{\omega_{ii}})$ can be assumed to be linear.
15. At a micro level, in the text book demand and supply example of a just identified system, there is no assumption that shocks to the demand and supply equations should be uncorrelated. At the macro level it is even less plausible. Suppose there was a large unexpected supply shock caused by bad weather. There would also almost certainly be corresponding contemporaneous demand shocks through monetary and fiscal policy innovations (unpredicted by past values of the observables) to offset the effects of the supply shocks.
16. Here to simplify the notation we denote the dimension of y_t by m.
17. A review of the econometric analysis of $I(2)$ variables is provided in Haldrup (1998).

18. A similar consideration also arises with respect to the intercepts in VAR models with unit roots but without linear deterministic trends.
19. This 'first-difference MA representation' was originally given in Engle and Granger (1987) for VAR models without linear trends.
20. It is also worth noting that $C_j^* = \Sigma_{i=0}^{j} C_i - C(1)$.
21. This decomposition of the stochastic part of y_t into permanent and transitory components is not unique and raises a number of identification problems discussed by Levtchenkova *et al.* (1998).
22. Notice that since $C(L)\Phi(L) = (1 - L)I_m$, then $C(1)\Phi(1) = -C(1)\Pi = 0$.
23. In deriving this result we have made use of the fact that $C(1) + C_n^* = \Sigma_{j=0}^{n} C_j$, which can be obtained from (2.8) and (2.17).
24. All the computations reported here were carried out using *Microfit for Windows* (see Pesaran and Pesaran, 1997).
25. When determining the lag length in an autoregression, if the correct model is in the set being considered the AIC is inconsistent, namely as T goes to infinity it will not necessarily choose the correct lag length; whereas the SBC is consistent. It is not clear how relevant this result is to practical problems where the correct model may not be in the set under consideration.
26. We saw no point in including VAR models without intercepts and trends in our analysis. Given the trended nature of the time series data on output, consumption and investment, only cases III, IV and V are likely to be relevant.
27. The Alogoskoufis and Smith data are available in the tutorial file of *Microfit 4.0*.
28. Exactly the same issues arise when the cointegrating relations are scalar residuals from the first-step in the two-step estimation procedure of Engle and Granger (1987).
29. To simplify the exposition we are abstracting from the deterministic terms. See Pesaran, Shin and Smith (1997) for alternative formulations of intercepts and linear trends in cointegrating VAR models with $I(1)$ exogenous variables, and Garratt *et al.* (1998) for an application to the U.K. economy.
30. Notice that this conditional model has the same form as the error correction representation of the reduced form of the VARDL model (2.4).
31. When the restrictions $\Pi_x = (\Pi_{xy}, \Pi_{xx}) = 0$ hold, x_t is referred to as 'long-run forcing' for y_t. This differs from the concept of 'Granger non-causality'. Recall that y_t is said to be Granger non-causal with respect to x_t (or loosely speaking x_t is causal for y_t) if $\Pi_{xy} = 0$, and $\Gamma_{ixy} = 0$ for $i = 1, 2, \ldots, p$. Also notice that under $\Pi_x = 0$, x_t can not themselves be cointegrated.
32. For an empirical application see Garratt *et al.* (1998).

References

Abadir, K., Hardi, K. and Tzavalis, E. (1998) The influence of VAR dimensions on estimator biases. *Econometrica* (forthcoming).

Alogoskoufis, G. and Smith, R. P. (1991) On error correction models: specification, interpretation and estimation. *Journal of Economic Surveys*, 5, 97–127. Reprinted as Chap. 6 in L. Oxley *et al.* (eds) (1994) *Survey in Econometrics*, Oxford: Blackwell, 139–170.

Bernanke, B. (1986) Alternative explanations of the money–income correlation. *Carnegie-Rochester Conference Series on Public Policy*, 25, 49–99.

Blanchard, O. and Watson, M. (1986) *Are all Business Cycles Alike?*. In R. J. Gordon (ed.) *The American Business Cycle*, 123–56, Chicago: University of Chicago Press.

Blanchard, O. and Quah, D. (1989) The aggregate effect of demand and supply disturbances. *American Economic Review*, 79, 655–673.

Boyd, D., and Smith, R. P. (1998) Testing for purchasing power parity: econometric issues and an application to developing countries. *Manchester School.* (forthcoming).

Champernowne, D. G. (1960) An experimental investigation of the robustness of certain procedures for estimating means and regression coefficients. *Journal of the Royal Statistical Society*, Series A, 123, 398–412.

Cooley, T. F. and LeRoy, S. F. (1985) A theoretical macroeconomics: a critique. *Journal of Monetary Economics*, 16, 283–308.

Dickey, D. and Fuller, W. (1979) Distribution of the estimators for autoregressive time series with a unit root. *Journal of the American Statistical Association*, 74, 427–431.

Diebold, F. X. and Senhadji, A. S. (1996) The uncertain unit root in real GNP: comment. *American Economic Review*, 86, 1291–1298.

Engle, R. F. and Granger, C. W. J. (1987) Cointegration and error correction representation: estimation and testing. *Econometrica*, 55, 251–276.

Garratt, A., Lee, K., Pesaran, M. H. and Shin, Y. (1998) A long run structural macroeconometric model of the UK. Unpublished manuscript, Cambridge University, available on http://www.econ.cam.ac.uk/faculty/pesaran.

Geary, R. C. (1948) Studies in the relations between economic time series, *Journal of the Royal Statistical Society*, Series B, 10, 140–158.

Granger, C. W. J. and Newbold, P. (1974) Spurious regressions in econometrics. *Journal of Econometrics*, 2, 111–120.

Haldrup, N. (1998), A review of the econometric analysis of $I(2)$ variables. *Journal of Economic Surveys*, **5**, 595–650.

Hendry, D. F., Pagan, A. R. and Sargan, J. D. (1984) *Dynamic Specification*. In Z. Griliches and M. D. Intriligator (eds) *Handbook of Econometrics*, Vol. II, Amsterdam: Elsevier, 1023–1100.

Johansen, S. (1988) Statistical analysis of cointegrating vectors. *Journal of Economic Dynamics and Control*, 12, 231–254.

Johansen, S. (1991) Estimation and hypothesis testing of cointegrating vectors in Gaussian vector autoregressive models. *Econometrica*, 59, 1551–80.

King, R. G., Plosser, C. I., Stock, J. H. and Watson, M. W. (1991) Stochastic trends and economic fluctuations, *American Economic Review*, 81, 819–840.

Koop, G., Pesaran, M. H. and Potter, S. M. (1996) Impulse response analysis in nonlinear multivariate models. *Journal of Econometrics*, 74, 119–147.

Lee, K. and Pesaran, N. H. (1993) Persistence profiles and business cycle fluctuations in a disaggregated model of UK output growth. *Richerche Economiche*, 47, 293–322.

Levtchenkova, S., Pagan, A. R. and Robertson, J. C. (1998) Shocking stories, *Journal of Economic Surveys*, **5**, 507–532.

Mann, H. B. and Wald, A. (1943) On the statistical treatment of linear stochastic difference equations. *Econometrica*, 11, 173–220.

Michael, P., Nobay, A. R. and Peel, D. A. (1997) Transactions costs and non-linear adjustment in real exchange rates: an empirical investigation. *Journal of Political Economy*, 105, 862–879.

Morgan, M. S. (1990) *The History of Econometric Ideas*, Cambridge: Cambridge University Press.

Nelson, C. R. and Plosser, C. I. (1982) Trends and random walks in macroeconomic time series: some evidence and implications. *Journal of Monetary Economics*, 10, 139–62.

Orcutt, G. H. (1948) A study of autoregressive nature of the time series used for Tinbergen's model of the economic system of the United States. *Journal of the Royal Statistical Society*, Series B, 1–45.

Perron, P. (1989) The great crash, the oil price shock and the unit root hypothesis. *Econometrica*, 57, 1361–1401.

Pesaran, M. H. (1997) The role of economic theory in modelling the long-run. *Economic Journal*, 107, 178–191.

Pesaran, M. H. and Pesaran, B. (1997) *Working with Microfit 4.0: Interactive Econometric Analysis*. Oxford: Oxford University Press.

Pesaran, M. H. and Shin, Y. (1996) Cointegration and the speed of convergence to equilibrium. *Journal of Econometrics*, 71, 117–143.
Pesaran, M. H. and Shin, Y. (1997) Long-run Structural Modelling, *University of Cambridge DAE Working Paper* No.9419. Revised July 1997.
Pesaran, M. H. and Shin, Y. (1998a) Generalised impulse response analysis in linear multivariate models. *Economics Letters*, 58, pp. 17–29.
Pesaran, M. H. and Shin, Y. (1998b), *An Autoregressive Distributed Lag Modelling Approach to Cointegration Analysis*. In S. Strom, A. Holly and P. Diamond (eds) *Centennial Volume of Ragnar Frisch*, Cambridge: Cambridge University Press, (forthcoming).
Pesaran, M. H., Shin, Y. and Smith, R. J. (1996) Testing for the Existence of a Long-run Relationship. Unpublished manuscript, *University of Cambridge*.
Pesaran, M. H., Shin, Y. and Smith, R. J. (1997) Structural Analysis of Vector Error Correction Models with Exogenous I(1) Variables. University of Cambridge DAE Working Paper No. 9706. January 1997.
Pesaran, M. H. and Smith, R. P. (1985) *Keynes on Econometrics*. In A. Lawson and M. H. Pesaran, *Keynes's Economics: Methodological Issues* (eds) Croom Helm, 134–150.
Pesaran, M. H. and Smith, R. P. (1995) The role of theory in econometrics. *Journal of Econometrics*, 67, 61–80.
Phillips, P. C. B. (1986) Understanding spurious regression in econometrics. *Journal of Econometrics*, 33, 311–340.
Shapiro, M. D. and Watson, M. (1988) Sources of business cycle fluctuations. *NBER Macroeconomics Annual*, Boston: National Bureau of Economic Research.
Sims, C. (1980) Macroeconomics and reality. *Econometrica*, 48, 1–48.
Sims, C. (1986) Are forecasting models usable for policy analysis? *Quarterly Review*, Federal Reserve Bank of Minneapolis, 10, 2–16.
Sims, C. (1996) Macroeconomics methodology. *Journal of Economic Perspectives*, 10, 105–120.
Smith, R. P. (1997) *The Development of Econometric Methods at the DAE*. In I. Begg and S. G. B. Henry (eds) *Applied Economics and Public Policy*, 88–103. Cambridge: Cambridge University Press.
Yule, G. U. (1926) Why do we sometimes get nonsense correlations between time-Series? A study in sampling and the nature of time series. *Journal of the Royal Statistical Society*, 60, 812–54.

SHOCKING STORIES

S. Levtchenkova and A. R. Pagan
Australian National University

J. C. Robertson
Federal Reserve Bank of Atlanta and Australian National University

Abstract. The paper provides a survey of methods that decompose multivariate series into permanent and transitory components by using ideas drawn from the co-integration literature. We adopt a two stage procedure to effect the decomposition. In the first stage a basic set of permanent and transitory components is formed by using standard definitions of the shocks which they are constituted from. The resulting measurements are not unique and further information needs to be employed to get uniqueness. Such information can come in many forms but a particularly important one involves the values of the long-run multipliers for permanent shocks that are available from many calibrated models. A comparison of the methods of effecting the decomposition is performed using a well known data set.

Keywords. Permanent shock; Transitory shock; Co-integration; Calibrated model; Structural VAR.

1. Introduction

Many see quantitative economic research as the construction of stories that rationalize observations. The plausibility of the recounted stories frequently depends upon their coherence with some theoretical framework. When the 'cointegration revolution' began it was often said that one of its attractions was its ability to provide a way of incorporating ideas about the 'long-run', gained from theoretical models, into quantitative models. That contention has manifested itself primarily by the examination of the implications of long-run behaviour for the cointegrating vectors. But such a focus seems to be too narrow. Theoretical models provide more information than this, as can be seen from studies which feature 'long-run' relations in systems composed of variables that are not even cointegrated, e.g. Lastrapes and Selgin (1995). This less studied branch of the literature emphasizes the effects of permanent and transitory shocks upon variables rather than cointegration *per se*. One advantage of this different perspective is that a good deal of modern macroeconomics involves studying such shocks. Results concerning the impact of shocks are many and varied, ranging from general statements such as 'supply shocks have a permanent effect upon output whereas demand shocks do not' to the specific numerical values assigned by 'calibrated' models. The latter are a rich source of information, encompassing results from both stochastic general equilibrium models, such as those in the Real Business Cycle class, and other models with a strong theoretical base that are frequently used in policy analyses. One example of a calibrated model, to which we shall frequently refer, is the MSG2 model of the global economy set out in McKibbin and Sachs (1991) and McKibbin (1997).

The presence of a common language might lead one to expect a close connection between the cointegration and shock analysis literatures. But, in fact, the relationship is a little hazy. Part of the problem lies in the fact that there are many papers in the econometric literature that use the cointegration properties of the data to provide a decomposition into permanent and transitory components with seemingly no reference to any economic story at all, e.g. Gonzalo and Granger (1995), and certainly not one associated with any theoretical model. Moreover, there are also 'reverse engineering' papers in which a story is told but the theoretical model is designed to be compatible with the cointegration properties of the data. Examples of the latter would be King, Plosser, Stock and Watson (1991) (KPSW) and the papers inspired by it, such as Mellander, Vredin and Warne (1992). Because of this loose connection, there seems a good case for a paper that places the literature into a framework that enables one to see more clearly how the stories (theory) enter into the picture, and what stories are being told with each solution. To do this we focus upon the way in which information is brought to bear upon methods of estimating the impulse responses with respect to permanent and transitory shocks. This information is of a diverse kind and can be used in many ways. In a decomposition such as that by Gonzalo and Granger it is very general, while in the KPSW variant it is much more specific. Moreover, there is a tendency for it to become increasingly specific as one gets closer to replicating any chosen theoretical model. As we will make clear there is a hierarchy of steps that can be followed when imposing the available information. On the top level it is possible to provide a split into temporary and permanent components that uses the minimal amount of information to discriminate between the two. Extra information can then be used to refine this division by combining the 'basic' set of permanent and transitory shocks into a new set which is consistent with the expanded information. As the information becomes more specific the stories become more recognizable.

In the following section we begin by looking at the case when all shocks are transitory. It may seem odd to do this but the analysis is formally the same as when all shocks are permanent, the situation considered in the first part of section 3. Things become more complex when both permanent and transitory shocks are allowed to co-exist and a study of the issues raised by the joint presence of both types of shocks constitutes the remaining parts of the section. Section 4 completes the analysis by discussing systems that have a combination of integrated and non-integrated variables. Section 5 gives a comparison of the different methods of isolating permanent and transitory components using a data set from KPSW, and section 6 concludes.

2. Stationary systems

Let y_t be an $n \times 1$ vector of $I(0)$ variables. Two tasks need to be performed. The first is to provide a convenient way to *summarize* the data while the second is to *interpret* it in an informative way. Regarding the first we will assume that the second moment properties of the data are summarized by a pth order VAR,

$$A(L)y_t = e_t, \tag{1}$$

where $A(L) = I_n - A_1L - \cdots - A_pL^p$ and $e_t \sim i.d.(0, \Omega)$.[1] For the second issue one notes that modern macroeconomics tends to focus upon the effects of 'shocks' with names given to them such as 'money demand', 'supply', 'real', etc. It is in ascribing names to the shocks that one constructs a story about them. Once one has defined the nature of the shocks in some way it is possible to interpret the data.

There are two general approaches that lead to a naming of shocks. In the first, the shocks are regarded as being the disturbances terms in n structural equations that are given names such as 'money supply function', 'aggregate supply function' etc. Then it is differences in the specification of these equations which defines the nature of the shocks. These relations may be written as

$$B(L)y_t = \varepsilon_t,$$

where $B(L) = B_0 - B_1L \cdots -B_pL^p$, and $B_0e_t = \varepsilon_t \sim i.d.(0, \Sigma)$. Although the shocks are differentiated by $\{B_j\}_{j=0}^p$ and Σ *in toto*, attention typically focuses upon the nature of B_0 and Σ. Some of the elements of these matrices are fixed through normalizations and restrictions and some will need to be estimated. In doing the latter a constraint that will be enforced is that the chosen structural representation exactly reproduces the statistical characteristics of the data summarized by the estimated parameters of (1), $\{\tilde{A}_j\}_{j=1}^p$ and $\tilde{\Omega}$. The question which then arises is whether it is possible to uniquely determine $\{B_j\}_{1=0}^p$ and Σ from the implied relationships

$$B_0A_j = B_j, \qquad j = 1, \ldots, p \tag{2}$$

$$B_0\Omega B_0' = \Sigma, \tag{3}$$

where A_j and Ω are fixed at their estimates $\tilde{A}_j$ and $\tilde{\Omega}$.[2] It is clear from counting the number of equations that it is impossible to identify B_0 if one maintains the assumption that all elements in $\{B_j\}_{j=0}^p$ are unknown, since that means (2) has no information in it. Accordingly, attention has focused upon (3), with Sims (1980) making B_0 triangular and $\Sigma = I_n$. The triangularity of B_0 imposes $n(n-1)/2$ exclusion restrictions while the requirement that $\Omega = B_0^{-1}(B_0')^{-1}$ imposes $n(n+1)/2$ non-linear restrictions on B_0. Later Sims and others allowed B_0 to have patterns of zeros other than the triangular one, provided their number did not exceed that in the triangular form.[3] This latter development is sometimes described as a 'structural VAR' approach, but is really a misnomer since it simply provides another way of describing B_0, i.e. it tells a different story to that implied by a particular recursive model. Although the interpretation offered in support of restrictions on B_0 ostensibly arises from some prior economic theory, in practice most ideas concerning the restrictions on B_0 come from past empirical work or introspection. A short hand way of describing the above would be as a *structural VAR methodology* (SVM).

To measure the responses of variables to particular shocks one needs to know the time paths of the y_t as a function of current and past shocks. This is given by the vector MA representation

$$y_t = C(L)\varepsilon_t. \tag{4}$$

where $C(L) = C_0 + C_1L + C_2L^2 + \cdots$. The representation in (4) gives rise to the second approach in which the information used to characterize the shocks stems primarily from the nature of the multipliers C_j. We will refer to this generically as the *structural MA methodology* (SMM). A great variety of information is subsumed under this heading. For example, it is possible that the impact responses of y_t to selected shocks, i.e. elements of C_0, are known. Alternatively, functions of C_j such as $\Sigma_{j=1}^{q} C_j$ may be prescribed. 'Calibrated models' are particularly good at providing the latter type of information but are not the only sources of it.[4] For example, a calibrated RBC model would produce impulse responses to an unanticipated shock to technical progress, while a model such as MSG2 details responses to unanticipated money and productivity shocks. Consequently, there is a lot of information produced by calibrated models pertaining to $C(L)$ and the major challenge is to make it tractable enough to be used for the purpose of measuring the impact of shocks from the data.

Regardless of whether one is working within the SVM or SMM, the symbol ε_t will be used to denote their respective 'economic shocks', reflecting the fact that the shocks in both approaches share common names, like 'money', and it is only through the process of definition that they differ. In the SMM tradition one still has to have a way of relating the shocks ε_t to the data via the VAR errors ε_t, and this is accomplished by taking the VAR errors to be some non-singular transformation of the economic shocks i.e. $T\varepsilon_t = e_t$. With such an assumption the estimation problem becomes one of how to convert the relations $C(L) = A(L)^{-1}T$ and $T\Sigma T' = \Omega$ into a method for determining the weights T. In the SVM it is the VAR errors that are combined to define the economic shocks as $B_0e_t = \varepsilon_t$, and the estimation problem involves converting the relations $B(L) = B_0A(L)$ and $\Sigma = B_0\Omega B_0'$ into methods for determining B_0.

The distinction between the methodologies should not be pushed too far, however, since B_0^{-1} can always be interpreted as T in the SMM, and vice versa. Also, as we will discuss below, it is sometimes easy to convert restrictions upon $C(L)$ into restrictions upon $B(L)$ and this can lead to some useful insights which would not be available if one was not within the SVM. Nevertheless, we believe that the dichotomy does capture general differences in attitudes towards where information comes from and how it is to be used to distinguish between shocks. It certainly seems to be the case that those working within the SVM emphasize the determination of B_0 as the way of identifying shocks and do not think primarily in terms of restrictions on $C(L)$.

Because y_t is assumed stationary, the shocks to them will be *transitory*; any such shock will be defined as one whose associated column of C_∞ is zero, where C_∞ shows the 'long-run' impact of the shocks. When all shocks are transitory it follows that $C_\infty = 0$, i.e. the impact of a transitory shock upon the level of all the $I(0)$ variables is zero 'in the long-run'. Clearly, when the variables are stationary, one can not use this outcome to differentiate between shocks. But it may be possible to do so based on some other features of $C(L)$, such as restrictions on the partial sums of the C_j or the 'mean lag' of $C(L)$. As a precursor to the discussion of nonstationary systems it will be useful to pay particular attention to $C(1) = \sum_{j=0}^{\infty} C_j$.[5]

Retaining the requirement that the data, as summarized by the fitted VAR, is to be exactly represented, means that the estimate of T (in the SMM) or B_0^{-1} (in the SVM) has to obey

$$C(1) = A(1)^{-1}T = A(1)^{-1}B_0^{-1}. \tag{5}$$

In fact there are many ways of re-expressing (5). Which one of these is most useful depends a good deal upon the type of information available. If rows of $C(1)$ are known then the relation $A(1)^{-1} = C(1)B_0 = C(1)T^{-1}$ produces linear restrictions upon the corresponding rows of B_0 (or T^{-1}), whereas (5) might be preferred if one knows columns of $C(1)$, which tends to be the information provided by calibrated models. For example, McKibbin *et al.* (1998) give an application in which the columns of $C(1)$ are computed from selected shocks applied to the MSG2 model of the world economy. Versions like (5) are also very useful if information is also available about the contemporaneous impact of shocks, e.g. that money has no immediate impact upon output, since that imposes exclusion restrictions directly on T.

In general, linear restrictions imposed upon $C(L)$ translate into non-linear constraints on $B(L) = C(L)^{-1}$, and vice versa. One exception is the case of triangular exclusion restrictions. For example, when C_0 is assumed lower triangular B_0 is also lower triangular. Similarly, when $C(1)$ is lower triangular so is $B(1) = \sum_{j=0}^{p} B_j$. Consequently, it is not surprising that the triangularity of C_0 or $C(1)$ has seen widespread use by those working in both the SVM and SMM. The case when C_0 is triangular is fairly straightforward. To explore the impact of triangularity of $C(1)$ in a little more detail let $n = 2$, and partition $B(L)$, $C(L)$ accordingly. From the relation $C(1)B(1) = I_n$ one has a system of four equations

$$C_{11}(1)B_{11}(1) + C_{12}(1)B_{21}(1) = 1$$

$$C_{11}(1)B_{12}(1) + C_{12}(1)B_{22}(1) = 0$$

$$C_{21}(1)B_{11}(1) + C_{22}(1)B_{21}(1) = 0$$

$$C_{21}(1)B_{12}(1) + C_{22}(1)B_{22}(1) = 1.$$

With $C_{12}(1) = 0$, and as long as $C_{11}(1) \neq 0$, it follows from the second equation that $B_{12}(1) = 0$. Thus, the restriction $C_{12}(1) = 0$ is equivalent to a homogeneity restriction on the first structural relation in $B(L)y_t = \varepsilon_t$. Making $p = 1$ and defining the elements of matrices as

$$B_0 = \begin{bmatrix} 1 & b_{12}^0 \\ b_{21}^0 & 1 \end{bmatrix}, \quad B_1 = \begin{bmatrix} b_{11}^1 & b_{12}^1 \\ b_{21}^1 & b_{22}^1 \end{bmatrix},$$

we have $B_{12}(1) = b_{12}^0 - b_{12}^1 = 0$. Imposing the latter restriction results in an estimable system of the form

$$y_{1t} + b_{12}^0(y_{2t} - y_{2t-1}) = b_{11}^1 y_{1t-1} + \varepsilon_{1t}$$
$$y_{2t} + b_{21}^0 y_{1t} = b_{21}^1 y_{1t-1} + b_{22}^1 y_{2t-1} + \varepsilon_{2t},$$

showing that a linear constraint has been imposed upon the coefficients of $B(L)$. In particular, this constraint means that y_{2t-1} can be used as an instrument for Δy_{2t} to estimate b_{12}^0, and this clearly defines the shock ε_{1t}. The assumption that ε_{2t} is uncorrelated with ε_{1t} then frees up ε_{1t} for use as an instrument in estimating the coefficients in the second equation. This instrumental variables approach to estimation was used in Shapiro and Watson (1988), and its properties are studied in Pagan and Robertson (1998).

The analysis above is also useful for looking at one criticism that has been made in the literature regarding the utility of restrictions based upon $C(1)$. Faust and Leeper (1997) argue that the resulting estimator of B_0 (or T) is hopelessly imprecise. Suppose that we modify the previous example by adding the assumption that $b_{21}^0 = 0$, and, in order to ensure that the structural model is observationally equivalent to the VAR, Σ is no longer required to be diagonal. From the relation $B_0A(1) = B(1)$, and with $B_{12}(1) = 0$, we have

$$\begin{bmatrix} 1 & b_{12}^0 \\ 0 & 1 \end{bmatrix} \begin{bmatrix} A_{11}(1) & A_{12}(1) \\ A_{21}(1) & A_{22}(1) \end{bmatrix} = \begin{bmatrix} B_{11}(1) & 0 \\ B_{21}(1) & B_{22}(1) \end{bmatrix}$$

from which it follows that

$$b_{12}^0 = -A_{12}(1)/A_{22}(1).$$

Clearly the distribution of the estimator of $A_{ij}(1)$ is central to the statistical behaviour of the estimator of b_{12}^0. If the order of the VAR is finite we would expect the maximum likelihood estimator $\tilde{A}_{22}(1)$ to be consistent and for $N^{1/2}\tilde{A}_{12}(1)$ to satisfy a central limit theorem, yielding standard asymptotic properties for the implied estimate of b_{12}^0. But, if the true order of the VAR is infinite, so that the fitted one is only an approximation, the situation is more complex. The literature on this allows $p \to \infty$ but in such a way that $p^3/N \to 0$ as $N \to \infty$, and also requires that the difference between the approximation and the true infinite order VAR be $0(N^{1/2})$. Under these restrictions the $\tilde{A}_j$ are consistent and $N^{1/2}\tilde{A}_j$ have a limiting normal distribution, but their sum $\tilde{A}(1) = \sum_{j=1}^{p} \tilde{A}_j$ has a variance that diverges as $N \to \infty$, see Lütkepohl (1990). It is hard to know what to make of the practical relevance of this point other than to say that the specification of the order of the VAR is not innocuous when utilising restrictions on $B(1)$ or $C(1)$. A similar point is made by Cooley and Dwyer (1998).

We can also use this simple bivariate framework to look at another issue that has received some attention in the literature. In particular, is there a connection between the assumption that $C(1)$ is triangular, and the standard approach where B_0 is made triangular? Suppose one modified the previous example by making B_0 lower triangular instead of upper triangular. Then the relation $B_0A(1)=B(1)$ has the form

$$\begin{bmatrix} 1 & 0 \\ b^0_{12} & 1 \end{bmatrix} \begin{bmatrix} A_{11}(1) & A_{12}(1) \\ A_{21}(1) & A_{22}(1) \end{bmatrix} = \begin{bmatrix} B_{11}(1) & 0 \\ B_{21}(1) & B_{22}(1) \end{bmatrix}.$$

Clearly, this can only hold when $A_{12}(1)=\Sigma^p_{i=1}\, a^i_{12}=0$, which implies that either only lagged *changes* of x_{2t} enter into the VAR equation for x_{1t}, or lags of x_{2t} are excluded entirely. Given this form for $A(1)$, the lower triangularity of B_0 and $C(1)$ are not independent restrictions. Consequently, an additional restriction is still required in order to uniquely determine b^0_{21}; Σ being diagonal would suffice.

3. Non-stationary I(1) systems

When variables are allowed to be $I(1)$ a new distinction between shocks can be made, namely whether they are *permanent* or transitory. Thus one needs to make a division in the analysis according to this feature. Given the way permanent shocks will be defined, a system of $I(1)$ variables will have $n-r$ of them, where r is the number of cointegrating vectors. Consequently, any analysis is naturally done by distinguishing between the situations when there is and is not cointegration. Permanent shocks may be of interest not only for their dynamic impact upon variables, but also because they are the building blocks of the common trends that are taken to drive $I(1)$ variables. If one is interested in this aspect, a trio of questions becomes relevant — how does one *determine* the number of common trends, how does one *find* the common trends and how should one *interpret* the common trends? The first of these relates to the number of co-integrating vectors in the system and, as it has been well covered in many papers, will be ignored here. Answers are provided to the other two.

3.1. *I(1) Variables are not cointegrated*

Let $y_t=\Delta x_t$ be such that x_t consists of n $I(1)$ variables that are not cointegrated. In this case the relevant VAR is in terms of the first differences

$$A(L)\Delta x_t = e_t, \tag{6}$$

while the relation between Δx_t and the economic shocks is given by

$$\Delta x_t = C(L)\varepsilon_t,$$

and impact of the shocks upon the *levels* of x_t is given by the elements of $\Psi(L)=(1-L)^{-1}C(L)$. A permanent shock will be defined as one whose associated column of Ψ_∞ has rank one. This means that not all the elements of that column are zero. This contrasts with the case of transitory shocks in which the relevant columns of Ψ_∞ will be zero. A key relationship in the analysis to follow is that $C(1) = \Psi_\infty$, and therefore the cumulative response of Δx_t to the shocks has the interpretation of showing the long run impact of the same shocks upon the level of the variables x_t. Apart from this modification, the analysis proceeds in exactly the same way as in the preceding section, simply by a re-definition of the variables (y_t) from the original levels into differenced ones. Studies by Ahmed, Ickes, Wang and Yoo (1993), Rogers and Wang (1993), Lastrapes and Selgin (1994, 1995), Tallman and Wang (1995), and Bullard and Keating (1995), *inter alia*, all proceed in this way. Of course, this specification relies on an assumption that the series are $I(1)$ and that there is no cointegration. The implied restrictions on the VAR representation of x_t can be tested.

To illustrate the basic ideas when restrictions on $C(1)$ are applied consider the example in Lastrapes and Selgin (1995). This has $n = 4$ variables given by the nominal interest rate r_t, the log of the level of output o_t, the log of the real money stock $m - p_t$, and the log of the nominal money stock m_t. There are four shocks. which are referred to as an IS shock, an aggregate supply shock. a money demand shock and a money supply shock. They adopt what is a very popular specification in this literature viz that $C(1)$ is triangular, with the form

$$C(1)_{LS} = \begin{bmatrix} * & 0 & 0 & 0 \\ * & * & 0 & 0 \\ * & * & * & 0 \\ * & * & * & * \end{bmatrix},$$

where an asterisk indicates that the value in that cell is unknown, but assumed non-zero. Thus, $C(1)_{LS}$ contains $n(n-1)/2$ restrictions, and combined with the assumption that the economic shocks are uncorrelated with $\Sigma = I_n$, one then has enough restrictions to be able to uniquely determine T.

This approach can be contrasted with what one might do when complete information about $C(1)$ is available. To illustrate this we simulated the long run response of the four variables above to four permanent shocks in the MSG2 model documented in McKibbin (1997).[6] The shocks chosen were to consumption, labour augmenting technical change, money demand and money supply, with each involving a 1% increase. These seem to correspond to what Lastrapes and Selgin envisage their shocks to be. The resulting $C(1)$ is

$$C(1)_{MSG2S} = \begin{bmatrix} 0.19 & 0 & 0 & 0 \\ -0.44 & 0.85 & 0 & 0 \\ 0.82 & 0.80 & 1 & 0 \\ 0 & 0 & 0 & 1 \end{bmatrix}.$$

Compared to the Lastrapes and Selgin solution, the MSG2 model provides all the elements of $C(1)$. Some of the elements in it clearly reflect the nature of MSG2; the final row for example arises because the first three shocks are 'pure', in the sense that the money supply is not allowed to increase. If the MSG2 model had a money rule in it that responded to output and price changes we would expect to see some non-zero values in this row replacing those elements that are zero.

It is interesting to now ask what the consequences would be of adopting $C(1)_{MSG2}$ as the set of restrictions for determining T from (5). First, because $C(1)_{MSG2}$ is non-singular, T follows immediately from (5) as $A(1)C(1)_{MSG2}$. Second, the triangularity of $C(1)_{MSG2}$ suggests that it is a special case of Lastrapes and Selgin's formulation. However, there is a difference: when using the MSG2 information no assumption was made concerning the correlation between the ε_t over any particular period of history, unlike the Lastrapes and Selgin set-up which maintains they are uncorrelated. In fact it would be inadvisable to impose orthogonal shocks in the 'MSG2 case' unless that restriction was supported by the data. If it is felt to be desirable to impose some zero correlations between the shocks, it would be possible to use the MSG2 information selectively. For example, if only the first two columns of $C(1)_{MSG2}$ are assumed known one needs eight further restrictions to recover ε_t. Six of these are potentially provided by the assumption of zero correlations between the ε_t. Obviously, a lot hinges on whether the assumption that the economic shocks are uncorrelated is reasonable, a matter that has often been debated.

Using the data set corresponding to Lastrapes and Selgin — see Pagan and Robertson (1995) — we looked at the correlation between shocks that the MSG2 model would infer i.e. the knowledge of $C(1)$ and the estimated VAR is used to estimate T and $\Sigma = T^{-1}\Omega(T')^{-1}$. The most striking was the high negative correlation between the IS and money demand shocks of -0.95. Money demand and money supply shocks had a much smaller correlation of 0.34. Thus, if one uses results from a model like MSG2 to determine shocks, it is not very likely that they can be taken as uncorrelated. Of course, this fact does not have any direct implications for the Lastrapes–Selgin shocks; since the VAR's of both models are identical one is just telling two different stories about the nature of the shocks that are needed to explain the data. It might be possible to discriminate between the models on other grounds than goodness of fit to the data: in the past this has meant using prior information about the signs and sizes of the impulse responses.

3.2. *I(1) variables are cointegrated*

Now let the x_t be a vector of n $I(1)$ series with r cointegrating vectors, $0<r<n$. In that case x_t can be represented as the vector ECM (VECM)

$$A^*(L)\Delta x_t = \alpha\beta' x_{t-1} + e_t,$$

where α and β are $n \times r$ matrices of rank r. Here β is the co-integrating vector and $\beta' x_t$ are the $I(0)$ cointegrating relations. Engle and Granger (1987) show that Δx_t can be represented as

$$\Delta x_t = D(L)e_t, \tag{7}$$

where $D(L) = I + D_1 L + \cdots$, and $D(1)$ is a singular matrix of rank $n-r$. They give the following expression for $D(1)$

$$D(1) = \beta_\perp(\alpha_\perp' A^*(1)\beta_\perp)^{-1}\alpha_\perp',$$

where $\alpha_\perp$ and $\beta_\perp$ are $n \times (n-r)$ matrices of rank $(n-r)$ such that $\alpha'\alpha_\perp = 0$, $\beta'\beta_\perp = 0$, and $\alpha_\perp' A^*(1)\beta_\perp$ has full rank of $n-r$.

One difference between this case and that of a stationary system arises from the selection of estimates of $\{A_j^*\}$, $\{\alpha, \beta\}$ and Ω to summarize the data. To get these one needs to estimate a VECM, but what VECM? In the stationary case many theoretical models could be constructed to produce the same VAR, but the set of models that would produce identical VECM's is circumscribed by the need for them to have the same number of permanent shocks and to also exhibit the same values for β. As will be seen later this issue raises problems when it comes to imposing long-run restrictions from theoretical models. We note that both the choice of $n-r$ and the values ascribed to β can be cast as testable restrictions on the VECM.

3.2.1. *A basic permanent–transitory decomposition*

Cointegration produces systems that are influenced by both permanent and transitory shocks. Stock and Watson (1988) showed that a co-integrated system would be driven by $n-r$ common trends and the shocks driving these common trends could be regarded as permanent. This leaves r shocks to make up the full complement of n and these are naturally defined as *transitory*. It is useful then to define the vector of permanent and transitory shocks as the $n \times 1$ vector $v_t = He_t$, where the $n \times n$ non-singular matrix H is chosen so that the last r elements in v_t are transitory. With such a relation (7) will become

$$\begin{aligned} \Delta x_t &= \mathrm{D}(L)H^{-1}He_t \\ &= \mathrm{F}(L)v_t, \end{aligned} \tag{8}$$

where the covariance of v_t is $V = H\Omega H'$.

From the definition of permanent and transitory shocks, it is clear that the last r columns of

$$F(1) = D(1)H^{-1}$$

must equal zero. In this context, we define a basic permanent–transitory decomposition by choosing H to have the form

$$H = \begin{bmatrix} \alpha_\perp' \\ \rho' \end{bmatrix},$$

for any $n \times r$ matrix ρ that makes H invertible. To see why this assumption is sufficient, observe that $H^{-1} = [\rho_\perp(\alpha_\perp'\rho_\perp)^{-1} \quad \alpha(\rho'\alpha)^{-1}]$ and $D(1)\alpha = 0$. Two choices for H that have appeared in the literature are

$$H_W = \begin{bmatrix} \alpha'_\perp \\ \alpha' \end{bmatrix}$$

(Warne (1993)), and

$$H_G = \begin{bmatrix} \alpha'_\perp \\ \beta' \end{bmatrix}$$

(Gonzalo and Granger (1995)).[7]

Which choice for H should be used? When producing estimates of the common trends in data a standard approach, due to Stock and Watson (1988), is to decompose $D(1)$ as $\delta\gamma'$, where δ and γ are $n \times (n-r)$ full rank matrices, and to then define the common trend as the random walk $\tau_t = \tau_{t-1} + \gamma' e_t$, with $x_t^p = \delta\tau_t$ giving the permanent components of the elements of x_t, formed by combining together the $n - \tau$ common trends. From the definition of $D(1)$, setting $\delta = \beta_\perp(\alpha'_\perp A(1)^* \beta_\perp)^{-1}$ and $\gamma = \alpha_\perp$ produces the requisite factorization. In the basic decomposition the permanent shocks will be

$$\nu_t^p = \alpha'_\perp e_t,$$

while δ is equal to the first $n - r$ columns of $F(1)$. One potential difficulty that might decide between H_W and H_G is that, although H_W must be non-singular, this is not so for H_G. Indeed, there may be instances in which $\beta = \alpha_\perp$. A simple example occurs in a two variable system when $\beta' = [1 \;\; -1]$ and $a' = [\alpha_1 \;\; \alpha_1]$, i.e. the coefficients on the ECM terms are the same in both equations. Under this scenario $\alpha'_\perp = [1 \;\; -1] = \beta'$.[8]

The basic decomposition uses knowledge of r and the VECM coefficients to isolate a group of permanent, and a group of transitory shocks. However, each type of shock is unique only up to a non-singular transformation. In order that the individual shocks can be given an economic interpretation one needs to incorporate some extra information about the system.

3.2.2. *Informative permanent–transitory decompositions*

To incorporate any extra information we consider a new set of shocks ε_t such that $\nu_t = T\varepsilon_t$. The non-singular $n \times n$ matrix T is chosen so as to impose the desired characteristics for these shocks. To highlight the ε_t we re-write (8) as

$$\begin{aligned} \Delta x_t &= \mathrm{F}(L)TT^{-1}\nu_t \\ &= \mathrm{C}(L)\varepsilon_t, \end{aligned}$$

where the covariance of ε_t is $\Sigma = T^{-1}V(T^{-1})'$, and

$$C(1) = F(1)T \tag{9}$$

gives the long-run impacts of the ε_t shocks upon the level of x_t. Now, assuming that the first $n - r$ elements of ε_t are permanent shocks, $C(1)$, like $F(1)$, must also have its last r columns equal to zero. Such a requirement constrains the nature of T and, to see how, partition $C(1)$ and $F(1)$ conformably with the permanent and transitory shocks to get

$$\begin{bmatrix} C_{11}(1) & 0 \\ C_{21}(1) & 0 \end{bmatrix} = \begin{bmatrix} F_{11}(1) & 0 \\ F_{21}(1) & 0 \end{bmatrix} \begin{bmatrix} T_{11} & T_{12} \\ T_{21} & T_{22} \end{bmatrix}$$

where T_{11} is $(n-r)\times(n-r)$, T_{21} is $r\times(n-r)$ etc. Using the notation that $F_p(L)$ collects together the first $n-r$ columns of $F(L)$, and $F_s(L)$ collects the last r columns, we have $F_s(1)=0$ and $F_p(1)T_{12}=0$, implying that $T_{12}=0$. Thus recombination of the permanent shocks in v_t is the only permissible operation when defining the permanent shocks in ε_t, and the latter are therefore $\varepsilon_t^p = T_{11}^{-1}v_t^p$, for any non-singular T_{11}. The covariance of ε_t^p, Σ_{11}, can then be solved from the expression

$$T_{11}\Sigma_{11}T_{11}' = V_{11} \tag{10}$$

where V_{11} is the covariance of v_t^p.

The specific characteristics of the permanent shocks are determined by the choice of T_{11}, and this choice may be guided, inter alia, by knowledge about the long run multiplier matrix $C_p(1)$. There are three cases to examine, depending on whether all, some, or none of $C_p(1)$ is assumed known.

(a) *Finding permanent shocks, all of* $C_p(1)$ *known*

To utilize such knowledge concatenate (9) and the fact that $T_{12}=0$ to deduce

$$C_p(1) = F_p(1)T_{11}. \tag{11}$$

Because $F_p(1)$ has full column rank one can then solve for T_{11} as

$$T_{11} = (F_p(1)'F_p(1))^{-1}F_p(1)'C_p(1). \tag{12}$$

Since $C(1) = [F_p(1)T_{11}\ \ 0]$, the implied trend component of x_t can then be expressed as $x_t^p = C_p(1)\phi_t$, with $\phi_t = \phi_{t-1} + \varepsilon_t^p$.

The dynamic response of Δx_t to changes in ε_t^p can be obtained by decomposing (8) into the separate effects of permanent and transitory elements to give

$$\Delta x_t = \mathrm{F}_p(L)v_t^p + F_s(L)v_t^s \tag{13}$$

$$= \mathrm{F}_p(L)T_{11}\varepsilon_t^p + F_s(L)(T_{21}\varepsilon_t^p + T_{22}\varepsilon_t^s). \tag{14}$$

Evidently there are two channels through which ε_t^p can influence Δx_t; a direct one through $F_p(L)T_{11}$, and an indirect one which comes via the fact that, in the data, v_t^s may be correlated with ε_t^p. The obvious way to capture this indirect effect is by regressing v_t^s on ε_t^p. The net contribution of the permanent shocks is then captured by the dynamic multipliers

$$F_p(L)T_{11} + F_s(L)\theta, \tag{15}$$

where $\theta = \mathrm{cov}(v_t^s, \varepsilon_t^p)\Sigma_{11}^{-1} = T_{21} + T_{22}\Sigma_{21}\Sigma_{11}^{-1}$ is the regression coefficient, and Σ_{21}

is the covariance between ε_t^s and ε_t^p. This choice for θ ensures that the linear combination $\nu_t^s - \theta\varepsilon_t^p$ is uncorrelated with ν_t^s.[9] Notice that the quantity being computed in (15) gives the impact of changes in ε_t^p upon Δx_t regardless of the assumed correlation between ε_t^p and ε_t^s. One might wish to consider the impacts of changing ε_t^p while keeping ε_t^s constant, i.e. setting $\Sigma_{21} = 0$. This has the immediate implication that θ is equal to T_{21}. But zero correlation itself has no implications for the computation of the dynamic responses, since θ is always obtained via the regression of ν_t^s on ε_t^p.

It is also important to realize that $F_p(1)$ in (12) has to be derived from a VECM which sets β to the vectors that are compatible with $\beta'C(1) = 0$. Many estimators of β exist that do not use any information regarding the form of $C(1)$ other than the number of permanent shocks. For example, if one uses Johansen's (1988) estimator to produce a $\tilde{\beta}$ there is no guarantee that $\tilde{\beta}'C(1) = 0$. If $\tilde{\beta}'C(1) \neq 0$ one cannot use the VECM that underlies Johansen's approach to construct the quantities in (12). Of course it is possible to test if a known β is compatible with the estimate $\tilde{\beta}$. But, if these $r(n-r)$ restrictions are rejected, one is left to ponder the validity of the choice of $C(1)$ used.

(b) *Finding permanent shocks, some of* $C_p(1)$ *known*

The most prominent paper dealing with this case is King *et al.* (1991) (KPSW). Several papers have since appeared using their technology; a short listing being Mellander *et al.* (1992), Fisher, Fackler and Orden (1995), and Fisher (1996). KPSW assume that $C_p(1) = S\Lambda$, where S is a known full rank $n \times (n-r)$ matrix with the property that $\beta'S = 0$, and Λ is some full rank $(n-r) \times (n-r)$ lower triangular matrix. From expression (12) we have that $T_{11} = (F_p(1)'F_p(1))^{-1}F_p(1)'S\Lambda = R\Lambda$, say, showing that the $(n-r)^2$ unknown elements in T_{11} have been reduced to the $(n-r)(n-r+1)/2$ unknown elements in Λ. This is exactly the number of independent elements in V_{11}. Assuming additionally that $\Sigma_{11} = I_{n-r}$, and making the substitution of $T_{11} = R\Lambda$ into equation (10), shows that Λ can be found by performing a Cholesky decomposition upon $R^{-1}V_{11}(R')^{-1}$. Once T_{11} is determined the multipliers can be computed from (15). KPSW interpret these multipliers as measuring the effect of changes in ε_t^p when the transitory shocks are held fixed, and this is achieved by assuming $\Sigma_{21} = 0$. As we noted, this has no implications for the computation of the multipliers.

One important qualification needs to be made about the KPSW procedure. Some action has to be taken to ensure that $\beta'C_p(1) = 0$. If one sets β to $\tilde{\beta}$, say Johansen's estimator, this would mean that $\tilde{\beta}'S = 0$. This constraint is enforced by KPSW in the way that S is chosen. Thus $C(1)$ is not really specified independently of the data but is constructed, in part, from it. In particular, S is only known after a VECM is estimated, and hence the constraint $\tilde{\beta}'S = 0$ is specific to the estimator of β employed. Whether such 'reverse engineering' produces an estimated $C(1)$ which makes economic sense, particularly given the triangular assumption for Λ, is problematic. KPSW tell a story about this in their paper but it is frequently a lot harder to do in other contexts. Moreover, as we will note later in the context of their empirical work, the story can get rather muddied, since it needs to be about $C(1)$ and that is a product of two items, S and Λ, and their interaction makes interpretation much more difficult. Certainly, it does not represent a solution that is easy to generalize.

(c) *Finding permanent shocks, none of* $C_p(1)$ *known*

If no elements of $C_p(1)$ are known the extra information to determine T_{11} must come from some other source. For example, restrictions might be imposed directly upon the structure of T_{11} as well as that of Σ_{11}. When T_{11} is made triangular and $\Sigma_{11} = I_{n-r}$, (10) shows that T_{11} can be found by performing a Cholesky decomposition on V_{11}. This method is proposed in Gonzalo and Ng (1996), and is described in a more general context by Yang (1998).[10] One advantage of this approach is that it can be done with standard packages; a disadvantage may be that it uses little economic information.

(d) *Finding transitory shocks*

In the discussion above the emphasis has been upon the isolation of permanent shocks. In order to identify the transitory shocks $\varepsilon_t^s = T_{22}^{-1}(v_t^s - T_{21}\varepsilon_\tau^p)$ some further assumptions are required. From the covariance relations $T\Sigma T' = V$, it follows that making the transitory and permanent shocks uncorrelated, i.e., setting $\Sigma_{21} = 0$, produces

$$T_{21}\Sigma_{11}T'_{11} = V_{21}. \tag{16}$$

Once T_{11} and Σ_{11} are known it is clear that T_{21} can be determined from (16) as $T_{21} = V_{21}\Sigma_{11}^{-1}(T'_{11})^{-1}$.[11] With this information the set of transitory 'economic' shocks are identified up to a normalization factor for any non-singular T_{22}. To find T_{22} turn to the last of the equations available from partitioning $T\Sigma T' = V$, namely

$$T_{21}\Sigma_{11}T'_{21} + T_{22}\Sigma_{22}T'_{22} = V_{22}. \tag{17}$$

Combining an assumption that the covariance of the transitory shocks, Σ_{22}, equals I_r with the symmetry of V_{22}, (17) points to the need for an additional $r(r-1)/2$ restrictions. When T_{22} is made triangular, the unknown elements can be found by performing a Cholesky decomposition of $V_{22} - T_{21}\Sigma_{11}T'_{21}$, as in Gonzalo and Ng (1996), but it is again unclear what the economic meaning of such a constraint is.

An alternative approach is to try to exploit information about $C(L)$, specifically the impact multipliers C_0. Defining $F_0 = H^{-1}$, and partitioning it conformably with ε_t^p and ε_t^p, allows us to write the impact responses to the permanent and transitory shocks as

$$C_0 = F_0T = [F_{p,0}T_{11} + F_{s,0}T_{21} \quad F_{s,0}T_{22}].$$

In general, a set of restrictions on T_{22} do not translate into the same restrictions on the impact responses $C_{s,0} = F_{s,0}T_{22}$, because the elements of $F_{s,0}$ are involved. This is clear from the fact that $T_{22} = (F'_{s,0}F_{s,0})^{-1}F'_{s,0}C_{s,0}$. Similarly, imposing restrictions directly upon $C_{s,0}$ is complicated by the presence of $F_{s,0}$. Thus, for example, restricting $C_{s,0}$ to be lower triangular need not correspond to the same restriction on T_{22}. This point has been made before by Englund, Vredin and Warne (1994) and the complexities it raises probably accounts for the fact that few studies have attempted to isolate the impact of the transitory shocks through information about $C(L)$.

So far the emphasis in this section has been upon obtaining shocks that have specific implications for the long-run properties of impulse response functions. But, as section 2 detailed, there is another history in which the shocks are treated as the error terms of structural equations. The impulse responses are then determined by estimating these structural relations and solving for the MA representation. KPSW did use the language of structural and reduced form shocks but did not formally write out any structural relations to be estimated. Most of those following in their footsteps have also adopted the language but have been suitably vague about what the structure was.[12] As is evident from the above derivations there is really no specific connection with a structural relation in the KPSW treatment.

If one wanted to proceed in the latter direction how would one adapt the solution in the stationary case to handle cointegrated variables? One simple solution is always available. The VECM is a VAR that imposes the cointegrating restrictions and so its errors remain as $e_t = B_0^{-1}\varepsilon_t$. Therefore, the determination of B_0 can be done through the usual process of exclusion restrictions on B_0 and Σ, except that the VAR parameters are now obtained from the VECM. There is no necessary connection with permanent or transitory shocks in this solution however, and it is likely that all shocks will have permanent components.

Suppose instead that the shocks associated with structural equations can be partitioned into permanent and transitory. Specifically, take the first $n-r$ structural equation shocks as being permanent and the remaining r as transitory. Then, after performing the same sequence of transformations as previously, one obtains the representation

$$\Delta x_t = F(L)HB_0^{-1}\varepsilon_t.$$

In order for this to be written as $\Delta x_t = F(L)T\varepsilon_t$ it must be the case that $HB_0^{-1} = T$ and so T becomes a non-singular transformation of B_0^{-1}. Because H is also involved, there seems no general way to ensure that a particular set of restrictions on B_0 will give a T that preserves the requisite lower block triangular form. However, the case when B_0 and H are both lower triangular has received some attention in the literature — see for example, Cochrane (1994), Gonzalo and Ng (1996), and Ribba (1997). In that case an assumption that B_0 is lower triangular ensures that T is lower triangular. For $n=2$, the necessary exclusion restriction on H is easily testable from the VECM since it amounts to excluding the error correction term from the first equation so as to eliminate any levels effect.

3.3. *Deriving the impulse responses*

In most instances the objective of the analysis is to find impulse responses with respect to shocks. This task can be performed in two steps. In the first, $D(L)$ is computed i.e. the impulse responses of Δx_t to the errors e_t. In the second, these are recombined as $D(L)TH^{-1}$ in order to produce the responses to the permanent and transitory shocks. When x_t are either stationary or not cointegrated, $D(L)$ is easily found by inverting $A(L)$, but, with cointegration, $A(L)$ can not be directly inverted. There have been a number of methods advanced to solve this problem. A useful one is that in Mellander, Vredin and Warne (1992), and it is adopted here.

Define M as an $n \times n$ non-singular matrix

$$\begin{bmatrix} \Gamma \\ \beta' \end{bmatrix},$$

where Γ is an $(n-r) \times n$ selection matrix,

$$\Phi_{\perp}(L) = \begin{bmatrix} (1-L)I_{n-r} & 0 \\ 0 & I_r \end{bmatrix} \quad \text{and} \quad \Phi(L) = \begin{bmatrix} I_{n-r} & 0 \\ 0 & (1-L)I_r \end{bmatrix}.$$ [13]

Then set $w_t = \Phi_{\perp}(L)Mx_t$, where the variables w_t will be $I(0)$, since the first $(n-r)$ components represent linear combinations of Δx_t, and the last r constitute the cointegrating errors $\beta' x_t$. This representation is a generalization of Campbell and Shiller (1988). Because w_t is $I(0)$ it will be represented as a stationary VAR of the form

$$E(L)w_t = Me_t, \tag{18}$$

and will have an associated MA representation

$$\begin{aligned} w_t &= \mathrm{E}^{-1}(L)Me_t = E^{-1}(L)MH^{-1}v_t \\ &= \mathrm{E}^{-1}(L)MH^{-1}T\varepsilon_t \\ &= \mathrm{Q}(L)\varepsilon_t. \end{aligned}$$

The following relationships between $E(L)$, $A(L)$ and $D(L)$ can then be established:

$$\begin{aligned} E(L) &= \mathrm{M}[A^*(L)M^{-1}\Phi(L) + \gamma^* L] \\ D(L) &= M^{-1}\Phi(L)E(L)^{-1}M, \end{aligned}$$

where $\gamma^* = [0 \;\; \alpha]$. Using these formulae $Q(L)$ can be constructed from M, $A^*(L)$ and T.

4. Mixtures of I(1) and I(0) variables

Cases arise when there are a mixture of $I(1)$ and $I(0)$ variables within a system. An example would be Gali (1992) in which there are two $I(1)$ variables, the log of output and the nominal interest rate, and two $I(0)$ variables, the real interest rate and the rate of growth of real money balances. One way to handle this complication is to act as if all variables are $I(1)$ but with the $I(0)$ variables cointegrating with themselves. Thus any cointegrating vectors among the $I(1)$ variables are augmented with the artificial vectors effecting this. In terms of Gali's model let the $I(0)$ variables be the third and fourth, in which case the artificial vectors are

$$\begin{bmatrix} 0 & 0 & 1 & 0 \\ 0 & 0 & 0 & 1 \end{bmatrix}.$$

With this re-definition it would be possible to do the analysis as described in the section on co-integration. However, in doing so one may have lost some information. To see this most clearly assume that the first n_1 variables in x_t are $I(1)$, the last n_2 are $I(0)$, so that $n = n_1 + n_2$, and there is no cointegration among the $I(1)$ variables. Designate the $I(1)$ variables by x_{1t} and the $I(0)$ by x_{2t}. In the section on co-integration the analysis worked with a MA representation of Δx_t, but it is more natural to define one in terms of Δx_{1t} and x_{2t}, viz.

$$\begin{pmatrix} \Delta x_{1t} \\ x_{2t} \end{pmatrix} = \begin{pmatrix} C_{11}(L) & C_{12}(L) \\ C_{21}(L) & C_{22}(L) \end{pmatrix} \begin{pmatrix} \varepsilon_t^p \\ \varepsilon_t^s \end{pmatrix} \tag{19}$$

Now, if there is some knowledge about $C_{21}(L)$, i.e. the impulse responses showing the effect of permanent shocks upon the $I(0)$ variables, it should presumably be used. Working with the representation above allows that to happen. If, instead, one proceeded as in the cointegrated case, the system will involve Δx_{2t} rather than x_{2t}. This has the effect of preserving only the information contained in $C_{11}(1)$, since $\Delta x_{2t} = (1-L)C_{21}(L)\varepsilon_t^p$ and, when $L=1$, any information about $C_{21}(1)$ would disappear from such a system. Values for $C_{21}(1)$ may well be available from calibrated models. For example, in Gali's system, it seems reasonable to treat one of the permanent shocks of the system as being to the money growth rate (given that he assumes that the growth rate in nominal money is $I(1)$). Then, simulations of a permanent shock to money growth in MSG2 allows one to calculate the effect of such a shock upon the real interest rate at different time horizons. Summing the latter gives a value of -1.6, and hence one of the elements of $C_{21}(1)$. It might be noted that such information is also available about the impact of a permanent shock upon cointegrating errors, since these would just be $\beta'\Psi(L)$, and one might wish to use it as well when extracting estimates of shocks. In the presentation of section 3.2 only values of Ψ_∞ were used. Obviously the appropriate way to incorporate this extra information would be to use the system given as (18). Another example of this framework is the two variable system of Blanchard and Quah (1989), where $n_1 = 1$. Their restriction is that $C(1)$ in (19) is triangular with the shocks $\varepsilon_t = T^{-1}e_t$ being uncorrelated, and where e_t are the errors in a VAR involving Δx_{1t} and x_{2t}. Crowder (1995) observes that this model can be represented using cointegration language by making $\beta = (0,1)'$.

5. An application

In this section we provide a small empirical illustration of the differences amongst the various techniques described above. The quarterly data are the same as used in KPSW and span the period 1954:Q1 to 1988:Q4 for six variables — the logs of private sector output (o_t), consumption (c_t), investment (i_t), and the real money stock ($m-p_t$), together with the nominal interest rate (r_t) and the annualized rate of inflation (dp_t). All variables are treated as being $I(1)$ with $r=3$, and the fitted VAR includes a constant and 6 lags.[14]

Since one is dealing with a theoretical model it is necessary to decide on what the three permanent shocks to the system are. From their discussion, labour augmenting technical change and money growth are suitable candidates; the latter because of their treatment of the inflation rate as being $I(1)$. The third is more difficult to decide upon. KPSW treat it as a source of permanent shifts in the real interest rate and there are many candidates for that. One that has been important over the sample period would be oil price shocks, so that we use this for illustrative purposes. The effects of permanent increases in these shocks upon the six nominated variables were then simulated in the MSG2 model; the magnitude of the shocks were one percentage point increases for the first two and a 100% rise in oil prices for the last. Below we give the first three columns of $C(1)$ coming from such a simulation – the remaining three are all zero. Variables and shocks are arranged in the order described above. Thus the first column shows the effects of an unanticipated one percentage point increase in the rate of labour augmenting technical change upon the six variables, with the third row of this column giving its impact upon the level of investment. For flow variables these impacts are percent changes, whereas for inflation and the interest rate they would need to be multiplied by a factor of one hundred to produce annualized basis point increases.

$$C_p(1)_{MSG2} = \begin{bmatrix} 0.82 & 0 & -1.16 \\ 0.85 & 0 & -4.12 \\ 1 & 0 & -5.33 \\ 0.79 & 4 & -1.50 \\ 0 & 1 & 0.32 \\ 0 & 1 & 0 \end{bmatrix} \tag{20}$$

Perhaps the result that is most curious is that a rise in the money growth rate leads to a rise in real balances in the long run. The reason for this is that prices are measured by the GDP deflator in KPSW's work. If, instead, money had been deflated by the CPI this effect would be absent as the CPI rises virtually one for one with the money supply in MSG2. Also, notice that a productivity shock does not raise consumption, output and investment by the same amount in the long run because of the open economy aspects of MSG2 — see Mellander et al (1992) for a discussion of this issue.

It is interesting to compare $C_p(1)_{MSG2}$ with that found using the KPSW approach. KPSW have $C_p(1)_{KPSW} = S\Lambda$ and construct the S matrix from the estimated β reported in their Table 2 (p. 828). We have normalised on the diagonal of Λ so that $C_p(1)_{KPSW}$ gives the long-run responses to 1 unit shocks.

$$C_p(1)_{KPSW} = \begin{bmatrix} 1 & 0 & 0 \\ 1 & 0 & 0.0033 \\ 1 & 0 & -0.0028 \\ 1.197 & -0.0134 & -0.0134 \\ 0 & 1 & 1 \\ 0 & 1 & 0 \end{bmatrix} \begin{bmatrix} 1 & 0 & 0 \\ \Lambda_{21} & 1 & 0 \\ \Lambda_{31} & \Lambda_{32} & 1 \end{bmatrix}$$
$$= \begin{bmatrix} 1 & 0 & 0 \\ 0.947 & -0.002 & 0.0033 \\ 1.045 & 0.002 & -0.0028 \\ 1.357 & -0.004 & -0.0134 \\ -11.891 & 0.294 & 1 \\ 4.033 & 1 & 0 \end{bmatrix} \tag{21}$$

The interpretation of the shocks defined in KPSW is given in terms of the matrix S (p. 831). But, as can be seen from (21), the long-run responses are measured by $C_p(1)_{KPSW}$ and not S; the two will differ whenever $n-r>1$ and the permanent shocks are constructed so as to be uncorrelated. Without the latter requirement one could proceed by setting $C(1) = [S \ 0]$. Consequently, the story told by KPSW about the nature of their permanent shocks, whilst consistent with S, does not actually hold in their empirical model, as it is not consistent with $C_p(1)_{KPSW}$.

Because $C_p(1)_{MSG2}$ is taken as known it is possible to estimate what the correlation between the 'MSG2 type' permanent shocks would need to be in order to replicate the data. The highest correlation amongst the permanent shocks is 0.51 between the productivity and oil price shocks, while the money growth shock is almost orthogonal to the oil price shock and negatively correlated with the productivity shock. Specification of $C_p(1)_{MSG2}$ and $C_p(1)_{KPSW}$ also imply certain cointegration properties. To examine these we proceed by partitioning $C(1)$ as before to give $\beta' C_p(1) = 0$, resulting in $r \times (n-r)$ equations in $n-r$ unknowns. Accordingly, r^2 elements in β have to be prescribed in order to find a unique set of cointegrating vectors. This is the same condition as derived by Pesaran and Shin (1997) through a different route, and is the foundation of the 'structural cointegration' literature. A simple solution is to adopt some normalization, for example $\beta' = [-I_r \ \beta_2']$, as that enables one to solve for β_2' as $C_{11}(1)C_{21}(1)^{-1}$. Assuming that the normalization is upon consumption, investment and real money balances, the cointegrating vectors underlying the MSG2 model are then found to be

$$\begin{aligned} c_t &= 1.04o_t - 0.09(r_t - dp_t) \\ i_t &= 1.22o_t - 0.12(r_t - dp_t) \\ m_t - p_t &= 0.96o_t - 0.012r_t + 0.052dp_t, \end{aligned} \tag{22}$$

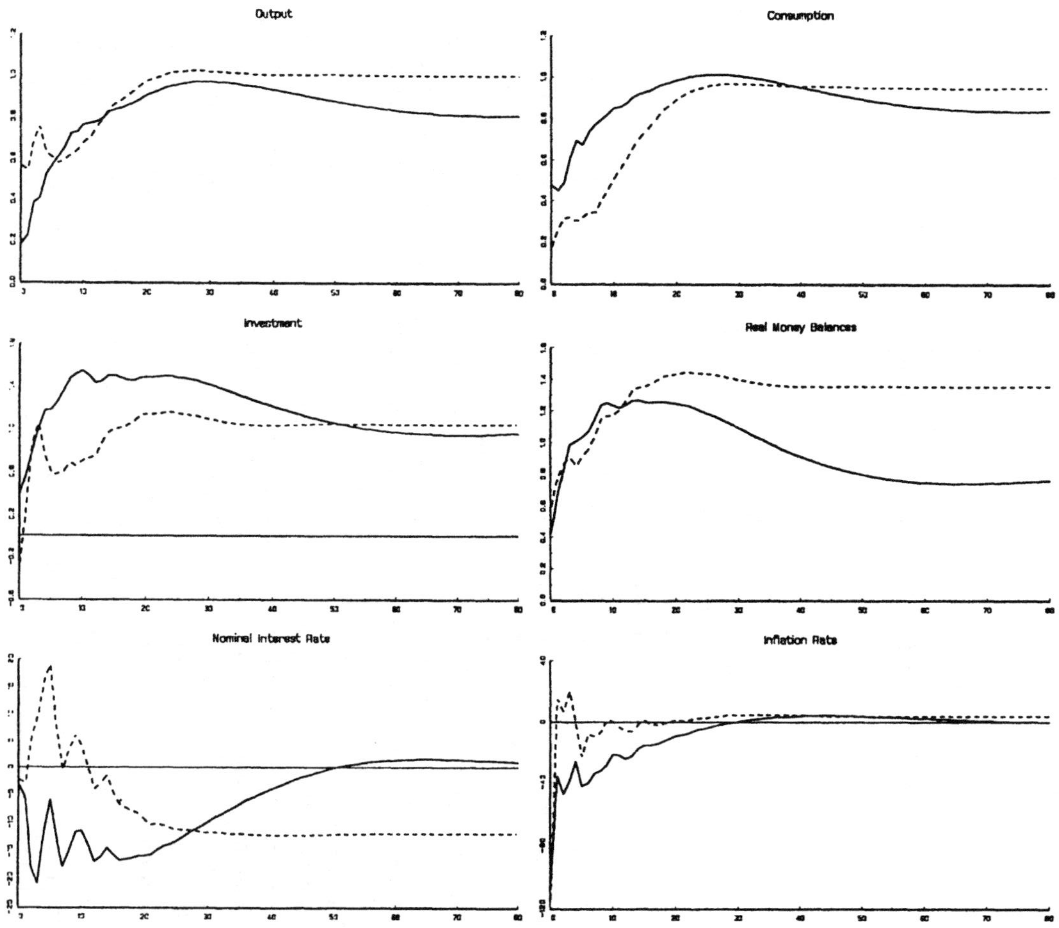

Figure 1. Responses to productivity shock: MSG2 (——) and KPSW (--)

which can be contrasted with those used by KPSW

$$\begin{aligned} c_t &= o_t + 0.0033(r_t - dp_t) \\ i_t &= o_t - 0.0028(r_t - dp_t) \\ m_t - p_t &= 1.197o_t - 0.013r_t. \end{aligned} \tag{23}$$

Unlike the MSG2 formulation KPSW impose unit output coefficients and work with smaller real interest rate effects in the consumption and investment relations. Also, KPSW have a larger output coefficient in the relation for real money balances, while the inflation coefficient is set to zero.[15]

The first columns of $C_p(1)_{MSG2}$ and $C_p(1)_{KPSW}$ give the long run responses to a positive permanent shock to the level of productivity in the two models. Figure 1 plots the set of impulse responses to this shock, as computed from (15). Probably the main differences lie in the behaviour of the nominal interest rate and the inflation rate. Using the KPSW story interest rates would be expected to increase after a favourable productivity shock. This seems unusual but might be explained by the fact that the VAR equations will tend to represent interest rates over this historical period with a 'Taylor rule', whereby a rise in output would induce a rise in nominal interest rates. Of course the rise in output in this case should be disregarded by the monetary authorities, as it comes from a positive supply side response rather than from demand.

The second column of $C_p(1)_{MSG2}$ and $C_p(1)_{KPSW}$ give the long run responses to a permanent shift in the rate of money growth. Figure 2 plots the set of impulse responses to this shock. Again, there are marked differences in interest rate responses from each model, although this time it is in magnitudes rather than in signs. Since money growth has risen by 1% per annum the MSG2 story has inflation and the nominal interest rate both rising eventually by 100 basis points. Under the KPSW story however, although the inflation rate rises by that amount, the nominal interest rate does not, i.e. a permanent shift in the money growth rate in their model actually permanently lowers the real interest rate.

Figure 3 plots the log output series together with the trend components implied by (21) and (20). There are some differences between the two trend components but the most striking features relate to the recessions. One can decompose the permanent part of a series into the contributions from each type of shock and, for both KPSW and MSG2, the permanent part of output turns out to be overwhelmingly due to productivity. This feature suggests that neither MSG2 nor KPSW see productivity variations as being the 'cause' of recessions, although Figure 3 does indicate that the MSG2 story would be compatible with it having some role in the mid 1970's recession.

6. Conclusion

The paper has tried to present a systematic approach to the literature dealing with the decomposition of multivariate time series into their permanent and transitory components. Because the shocks underlying such components frequently occur in

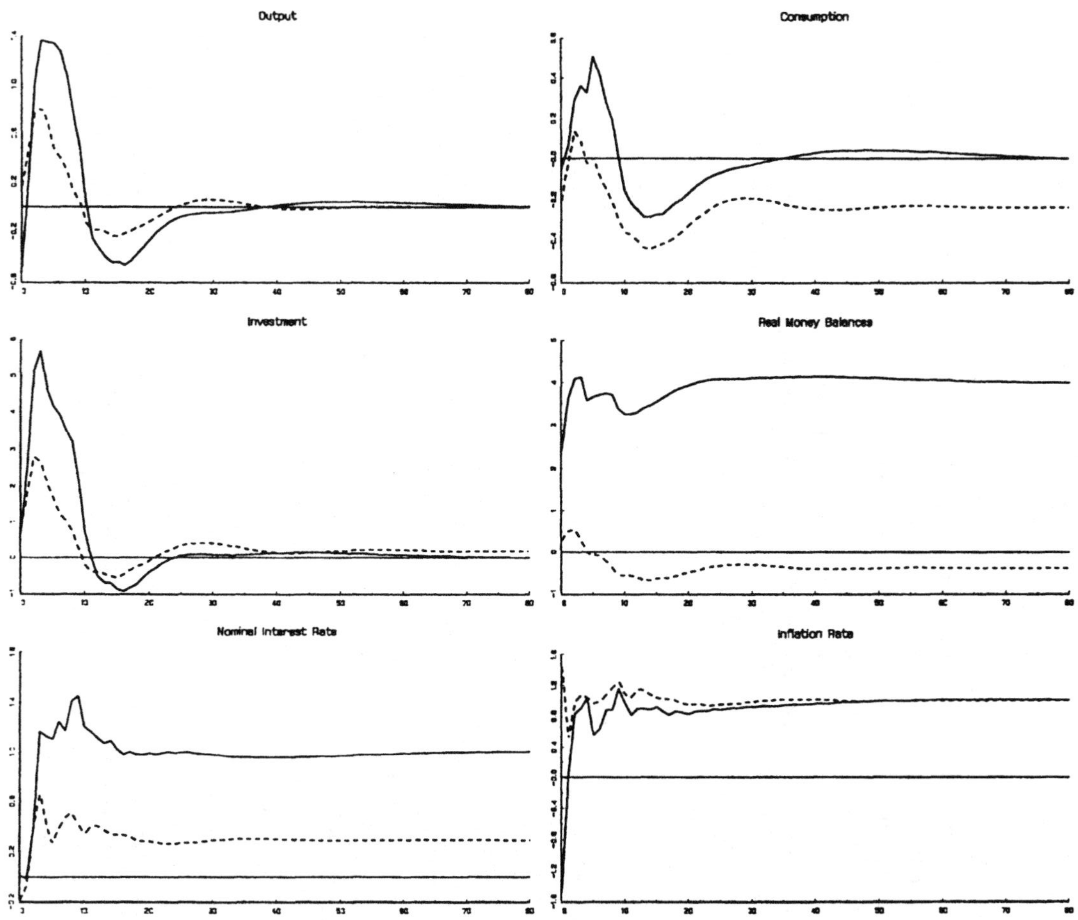

Figure 2. Responses to money growth shock: MSG2 (——) and KPSW (--)

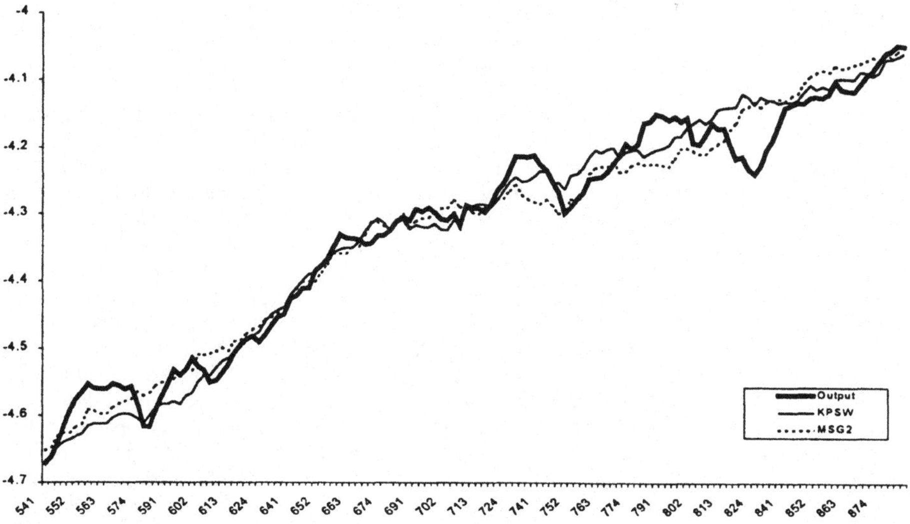

Figure 3. Estimated trend component of log output

the construction of theoretical models we have tried to emphasise how the information from such models might be brought to bear upon the task of separation. The central thrust of our paper was that theoretical models can be regarded as producing information about the magnitude of impulse responses, particularly the size of cumulated responses. This information is rarely fully exploited in much of the existing literature, which has tended to focus upon a subset of the implications, most notably those relating to co-integration.

Acknowledgements

Our thanks for comments on earlier versions of this paper go to Trevor Breusch and Mark Dwyer. We did not use Trevor's suggested title of *The Shocking Truth*, although it was certainly tempting to do so. We are also grateful to Warwick McKibbin for performing many simulations on the MSG2 model for us. The views expressed here are those of the authors and do not necessarily reflect those of the Federal Reserve System or the Federal Reserve Bank of Atlanta.

Notes

1. We have excluded discussion of the role of intercepts, deterministic trends and initial conditions here and in what follows. For $I(1)$ series these are important factors that can influence the testing for and estimation of cointegrating relations. But, conditional on their specification, they are of little consequence for impulse response analysis. A discussion of the role of deterministic terms and exogenous variables in VAR modelling is provided by Pesaran and Smith (1998).
2. With A_j and Ω *fixed at some estimated values* the estimates of the 'structural'

coefficients are obtained as the solution to the implied systems of equations, and the solution will vary with the specific identifying restrictions used.

3. Of course, this order condition is not sufficient by itself to ensure the shocks are uniquely determined.
4. Although we use the term 'calibrated model' somewhat loosely it would be expected that such a model has the dual characteristics of being based on a coherent theoretical framework and of providing some quantitative measures of the impacts of shocks.
5. In a stationary system $C(1)$ is simply a summary of information about the lag distribution and does not say anything about the level of y_t in the 'long-run' *per se*.
6. The MSG2 model is a multi-country dynamic intertemporal general equilibrium model of the world economy. It has a well determined long run being driven by a Solow–Swan–Ramsey neoclassical growth model, with exogenous technical progress and population growth. In the short run, however, the dynamics of the global economy towards this growth path are determined by a number of Keynesian style rigidities in the goods and labor markets. Households and firms are assumed to maximize intertemporal utility and profit functions subject to intertemporal budget constraints. In the short run some proportion of firms and households use optimal rules of thumb rather than recalculating the entire intertemporal equilibrium of the model. Wages are assumed to adjust slowly to clear labor markets subject to the institutional characteristics of labor markets in different economies. Intertemporal budget constraints are imposed so that all outstanding stocks of assets must be ultimately serviced, and asset markets are efficient, in the sense that asset prices are determined by a combination of intertemporal arbitrage conditions and rational expectations.
7. A choice suggested by Kasa (1992) has $H_K = [\beta_\perp, \beta]'$. This is unsatisfactory since $H_K^{-1} = [\beta_\perp(\beta_\perp'\beta_\perp)^{-1} \quad \beta(\beta'\beta)^{-1}]$ and $D(1)\beta \neq 0$.
8. Trevor Breusch has pointed out that this case could arise if the variables were from a system of demand relations subject to an adding up condition. This restriction normally forces the serial correlation in the equations to be of the same type — see Berndt and Savin (1975).
9. When doing policy analysis one could make a case for simply using $F_p(L)T_{11}$ as the impulse responses to a permanent shock as that assumes that the correlation between ε_t^p and ν_t^s is zero, which may be a better assumption in the policy period. McKibbin *et al.* (1998) use this particular variant.
10. We saw Yang's paper just as the final re-write of this paper was taking place. It follows a similar approach to ours. For instance, his N matrix is our T_{11}^{-1}.
11. Recall, T_{21} is the coefficient matrix in a regression of ν_t^s on ε_t^p when $\Sigma_{21} = 0$.
12. Although Englund *et al.* (1994, p. 144) say 'By structural shocks we mean innovations which — in contrast to the VAR residuals — are independent'.
13. They indicate that Γ can always be set to $\beta_\perp'$. However, if β was known, $\Gamma = [I_{n-r} \quad 0]$ would be available since β' can then always be re-written in the form $\beta' = [\beta_1' \quad I_r]$ by normalization.
14. A description of the construction of the data and the data's summary time series properties is presented in KPSW. The data set and various programs necessary to replicate their results are available at Mark Watson's Princeton University home page: http://www.wws.princeton.edu/~mwatson/.
15. The $\hat{\beta}$ used in KPSW and reported in (23) is not actually estimated by Johansen's maximum likelihood method. In particular, KPSW use an estimator that explicitly utilizes the normalization of β as $[-I_r \; \beta_2']'$. The LR statistic for a test of the $r(n-r) = 9$ restrictions on the VECM implied by the choice of β used in (23) is 20.49 (p-value = 0.02). An LR test of the 9 restrictions implied by the choice of β in (22) gives a value of 51.67 (p-value = 0.00). Thus, it seems that both the KPSW and MSG2 cointegrating vectors are rejected in the context of a VECM representation estimated by Johansen's method. This conclusion is invariant to the lag length used.

References

Ahmed, S., Ickes, B. W., Wang, P. and Yoo, B. S. (1993) International business cycles, *American Economic Review*, 83, 335–359.

Berndt, E. R. and Savin, N. E. (1975) Estimation and hypothesis testing in singular equation systems with autoregressive disturbances, *Econometrica*, 43, 937–58.

Blanchard, O. J. and Quah, D. (1989) The dynamic effects of aggregate demand and supply disturbances, *American Economic Review*, 79, 655–673.

Bullard, J. and Keating, J. W. (1995) The long-run relationship between inflation and output in postwar economies, *Journal of Monetary Economics*, 36, 477–496.

Campbell, J. and Shiller, R. (1987) Cointegration and tests of present value models, *Journal of Political Economy*, 95, 1062–1087.

Cochrane, J. H. (1994) Permanent and transitory components of GNP and stock prices, *Quarterly Journal of Economics*, 109, 241–265.

Cooley, T. F. and Dwyer. M. (1998) Business cycle analysis without much theory: A look at structural VARs, *Journal of Econometrics*, 83, 57–88.

Crowder, W. J. (1995) The dynamic effects of aggregate demand and supply disturbances: Another look, *Economic Letters*, 49, 231–237.

Crowder, W. J. (1997) The liquidity effect: Identifying permanent and transitory components of money growth, (mimeo, University of Texas at Arlington).

Engle, R. F. and Granger, C. W. J. (1987) Co-integration and error correction: Representation, estimation and testing, *Econometrica*, 55, 251–276.

Englund, P, Vredin, A. and Warne, A. (1994) Macroeconomic shocks in an open economy: A common-trends representation of Swedish data 1871–1990, In V. Bergstrom and Vredin, A. (eds) *Measuring and Interpreting Business Cycles*. Oxford: Clarendon Press.

Faust, J. and Leeper, E. M. (1997) When do long-run identifying restrictions give reliable results, *Journal of Business and Economic Statistics*, 15, 345–353.

Fisher, L. A. (1996) Sources of exchange rate and price level fluctuations in two commodity exporting countries: Australia and New Zealand, *The Economic Record*, 72, 345–358.

Fisher, L. A., P. L. Fackler and Orden, D. (1995) Long-run identifying restrictions for an error-correction model of New Zealand money, prices and output, *Journal of International Money and Finance*, 14, 127–147.

Gali, J. (1992) How well does the ISLM model fit postwar U.S. data?', *Quarterly Journal of Economics*, 107, 709–735.

Gonzalo, J. and Granger, C. W. J. (1995) Estimation of common long-memory components in cointegrated systems, *Journal of Business and Economic Statistics*, 13, 27–35.

Gonzalo, J. and Ng, S. (1996) A systematic framework for analyzing the dynamic effects of permanent and transitory shocks (mimeo, University of Montreal).

Johansen, S. (1988) Statistical analysis of cointegration vectors *Journal of Economic Dynamics and Control*, 12, 231–254.

King, R. G., Plosser, C. I., Stock, J. H. and Watson, M. W. (1991) Stochastic trends and economic fluctuations, *American Economic Review*, 81, 819–840.

Lastrapes, W. D. and Selgin, G. (1994) Buffer-stock money: Interpreting short-run dynamics using long-run restrictions, *Journal of Money, Credit, and Banking*, 26, 34–55.

Lastrapes, W. D. and Selgin, G. (1995) The liquidity effect: Identifying short-run interest rate dynamics using long-run restrictions, *Journal of Macroeconomics*, 17, 387–404.

Leeper, E., Sims, C. A. and Zha, T. (1996) What does monetary policy do?, *Brookings Papers in Economic Activity*, 1996/2, 1–78.

Lütkepohl. H. (1991) *Introduction to Multiple Time Series Analysis*. Berlin: Springer-Verlag.

McKibbin, W. J. (1997) *The MSG2 Multicountry Model, Version 431*, Virginia, Arlington: McKibbin Software Group.

McKibbin W. J. and Sachs, J. (1991) *Global Linkages: Macroeconomic Interdependence and Co-operation in the World Economy*, Washington: Brookings Institution.

McKibbin, W. J., Pagan, A. R. and Robertson, J. C. (1998) Some experiments in constructing a hybrid model for macroeconomic analysis, *Carnegie-Rochester Series on Public Policy* (forthcoming).

Mellander, E., Vredin, A. and Warne, A. (1992) Stochastic trends and economic fluctuations in a small open economy, *Journal of Applied Econometrics*, 7, 369–411.

Pagan, A. R. and Robertson, J. C. (1995) Resolving the liquidity effect, *Federal Reserve Bank of St Louis Review*, 77 (May/June), 33–54.

Pagan, A. R. and Robertson, J. C. (1998) Structural models of the liquidity effect, *Review of Economics and Statistics*, 80, 202–217.

Pesaran, M. H. and Shin, Y. (1997) Long-run structural modelling (mimeo, University of Cambridge).

Pesaran, M. H. and Smith, R. P. (1998) Structural analysis of cointegrating VARs' *Journal of Economic Surveys*, 5, 471–505.

Ribba, A. (1997) A note on the equivalence of long-run and short-run identifying restrictions in cointegrated systems, *Economics Letters*, 56, 273–276.

Rogers, J. H. and Wang. P. (1993) Sources of fluctuations in relative prices: Evidence from high inflation countries, *Review of Economics and Statistics*, 74, 589–605.

Sims, C. A. (1980) Macroeconomics and reality, *Econometrica*, 48, 1–48.

Shapiro, M. D. and Watson, M. (1988) Sources of business cycle fluctuation, In *NBER Macroeconomics Annual*, Boston: National Bureau of Economic Research.

Stock, J. and Watson, M. (1988) Testing for common trends, *Journal of the American Statistical Association*. 83, 1097–1107.

Tallman. E. and Wang, P. (1995) Money demand and the relative price of capital goods in hyperinflations, *Journal of Monetary Economics*, 36, 375–404.

Warne, A. (1993) A common trends model: Identification, estimation and asymptotics, mimeo, Institute for International Studies, Stockholm University.

Yang, M. (1998) On identifying permanent and transitory shocks in VAR models, *Economics Letters*, 58, 171–175.

INFERENCE IN COINTEGRATING MODELS: UK M1 REVISITED

Jurgen A. Doornik
David F. Hendry
Bent Nielsen
Nuffield College, Oxford

Abstract. The paper addresses the practical determination of cointegration rank. This is difficult for many reasons: deterministic terms play a crucial role in limiting distributions, and systems may not be formulated to ensure similarity to nuisance parameters; finite-sample critical values may differ from asymptotic equivalents; dummy variables alter critical values, often greatly; multiple cointegration vectors must be identified to allow inference; the data may be I(2) rather than I(1), altering distributions; and conditioning must be done with care. These issues are illustrated by an empirical application of multivariate cointegration analysis to a small model of narrow money, prices, output and interest rates in the UK.

Keywords. Cointegration; Deterministic terms; Indicator variables; Weak exogeneity; Identification; UK M1.

1. Introduction

The literature on the formulation, estimation, and testing of models for potentially cointegrated economic time series is truly vast, bordering on a complete discipline in its own right. Even texts which summarize the material comprise many hundreds of pages: see, *inter alia*, Banerjee, Dolado, Galbraith and Hendry (1993), Hamilton (1994), Hendry (1995), Johansen (1995b) (double that length when the companion workbook, Hansen and Johansen, 1998, is added), and Hatanaka (1996). Since, we could only consider a small fraction of the topic, we will focus on one salient problem: determining the cointegration rank of a linear dynamic system for economic time series.

Determining cointegration rank is difficult in practice for many reasons, including:

- the presence or absence of deterministic terms (such as constants and trends) in the generating process and/or the model can greatly alter limiting distributions;
- the system may have beeen formulated in such a way that the (asymptotic) similarity of key test statistics to nuisance parameters is lost;
- alternative choices of test statistics may deliver apparently conflicting inferences;
- finite-sample critical values can differ notably from asymptotic equivalents;

- the latter are usually approximations, obtained by simulation perhaps summarized by response surfaces;
- indicator variables for 'blips' can alter the outcome of the analysis;
- the lag length selected may not remove all residual autocorrelation, or may be too long;
- multiple cointegration vectors must be identifiable to allow coherent inference;
- the data may be I(2), or near I(2), rather than I(1), again altering the relevant limiting distributions;

  and:

- there may be non-modelled variables, and conditioning to create 'partial' systems must be done with care, even under weak exogeneity.

This paper addresses many of these important issues of inference in the empirical application of multivariate cointegration analysis, illustrating the analysis by a (much studied) four-equation model of narrow money (M1), prices, aggregate expenditure, and interest rates in the UK. These data have been the subject of extensive analysis: see, *inter alia*, Hendry (1979), Hendry (1985), Ericsson, Campos and Tran (1990), Hendry and Ericsson (1991), Boswijk (1992), Hendry and Mizon (1993), Hendry and Doornik (1994), and Harris (1995) as well as Johansen (1992b), Paroulo (1996) and Rahbek, Kongsted and Jørgensen (1998) who suggest they are I(2). Different investigators have also found varying numbers of cointegrating vectors, though all agree on at least one connecting these four variables.

Part of the difficulty in the empirical analysis is the important role played by structural breaks, including financial liberalization, and both external and domestic shocks. The first of these induced rapid growth in money holdings relative to nominal income, perhaps part of the explanation for the I(2) hypothesis, and is modelled here by using an appropriate measure of the opportunity cost of holding money. The treatment of the last two (oil shocks and major government budget changes) is problematic, and we consider below how indicator variables affect the empirical analysis. Consequently, the data modelling raises the typical problems empirical researchers regularly confront, and illustrates many of the aspects of the theoretical analysis of cointegration.

The structure of the paper is as follows. To set the scene on the roles of the various forms of non-stationarity, Section 2.1 discusses the effects of near unit roots in a scalar example, and Section 2.2 looks at the impacts of blip dummies. Section 3 discusses the statistical problem, beginning with a description of the time-series data we will analyse (Section 3.1), the economic analysis (Section 3.2), the notation and formulation of linear dynamic systems (Section 3.3), and the associated preliminary empirical analysis (Section 3.4): empirical illustrations occur throughout the text, and are not concentrated in one section. Then Section 3.5 introduces the cointegration representation, followed by the empirical unrestricted cointegration analysis in Section 3.6. Next, the impacts of various formulations of intercepts and linear deterministic trends are considered in

Section 4. New Monte Carlo simulation evidence illustrating the importance of the formulation of deterministic effects is presented in Section 5. Section 6 considers the impacts of impulse dummy variables (indicators) in cointegrated systems. Section 7 reviews other issues arising in determining the cointegration rank of a closed system, so briefly discusses recursive estimation, finite-sample critical values, and approximations to the asymptotic distributions of the tests. This is followed by a discussion of identification issues in Section 8.1, and the estimation of the restricted empirical cointegration relations. The problems when an I(2) analysis is needed are noted in Section 9. Then, Section 10 turns to the analysis of long-run weak exogeneity and conditional systems, where new problems in determining cointegration rank appear. Finally, Section 11 concludes. The Appendix gives relevant analytical results.

2. Background

This section first illustrates the problems arising when roots of the dynamics are close to unity, as often happens for empirical economic data; the ideas generalize to testing for cointegration in systems. Secondly, since our model of UK M1 includes two indicator variables to remove the impacts of interventions, we consider that issue in Section 2.2.

2.1. *Unit roots*

Consider the scalar, mean-zero, first-order autoregressive process:

$$y_t = \rho y_{t-1} + \nu_t \text{ where } \nu_t \sim \mathsf{IN}[0, \sigma_\nu^2]. \tag{1}$$

The ν_t are independent and normally distributed with mean zero and variance σ_ν^2. When $|\rho| < 1$, the least-squares estimator $\hat{\rho}$ is asymptotically distributed as:

$$\sqrt{T}(\hat{\rho} - \rho) \xrightarrow{\mathcal{D}} \mathsf{N}[0, (1 - \rho^2)]. \tag{2}$$

When $\rho \simeq 1$, but still lies in the stationarity region, then (2) suggests that in large samples, $\hat{\rho}$ will have a negligibly small variance. This transpires to be a poor approximation in small samples, and not very good in large. Figure 1a reports Monte Carlo sampling standard deviations (MCSDs, which estimate the actual variability in $\hat{\rho}$) and estimated standard errors (MCSEs, based on the usual regression formula) when $\rho = 0.9999$, together with their theoretical values $s = \sqrt{T^{-1}(1 - \rho^2)}$ from (2).[1] The ratios of the MCSDs and MCSEs to s are shown in panel c and reveal departures as large as 20-fold when $T \simeq 50$; even for $T = 350$, the MCSD overestimates s by 10-fold. However, when $\rho = 0.8$, the theory and practice are much closer, as panels b and d show: the maximum departures are about 10%, with the ratios converging on unity.[2]

Approximation (2) works poorly because the form of the limiting distribution changes as $\rho \rightarrow 1$ and a reformulation is required when $\rho = 1$. Write (1) as:

$$\Delta y_t = \gamma y_{t-1} + \nu_t \tag{3}$$

where $y_0 = 0$ and $\gamma = \rho - 1$. When $\gamma = 0$, then $\Delta y_t = \nu_t$. Now the estimate $\hat{\gamma}$ of γ

needs to be normalized by T (rather than $\sqrt{T}$ as in (2)), and does not converge on a normal distribution asymptotically, but to a functional of Brownian motion with a non-zero variance, and a substantial negative bias. This makes discrimination between I(1) and I(0) difficult (see, *inter alia*, Hendry, 1995, Ch.4). Economic data are certainly not stationary, and even if exact unit roots were not present in economics, many of the following results would be more useful as approximations to practical behaviour than assuming stationarity.

2.2. *Indicator variables*

Indicators are often added to remove the impacts of 'outliers' and thereby obtain a better estimate of the innovation variance (we construe outliers as residuals exceeding about three equation standard errors in absolute value). For example, Hillmer (1984) and Ledolter (1989) consider the impact of additive outliers (i.e., large measurement errors) on time-series models, and the latter shows that although parameter estimates are not greatly affected, forecast confidence intervals can increase markedly if the effect of an oulier is not removed. As Section 6 below shows, introducing dummy variables into cointegration analyses raises many issues, even when their existence is based on good historical grounds. This section first illustrates the potential problems in a stationary dynamic model. Let:

$$y_t = \rho y_{t-1} + \psi z_t + \nu_t \text{ where } \nu_t \sim \mathsf{IN}[0, \sigma_\nu^2] \tag{4}$$

when $|\rho| < 1$. In (4), $z_t = 1_{\{t=T_b\}}$ is a zero-one indicator ($1_{\{t=T_b\}} = 0$ except for

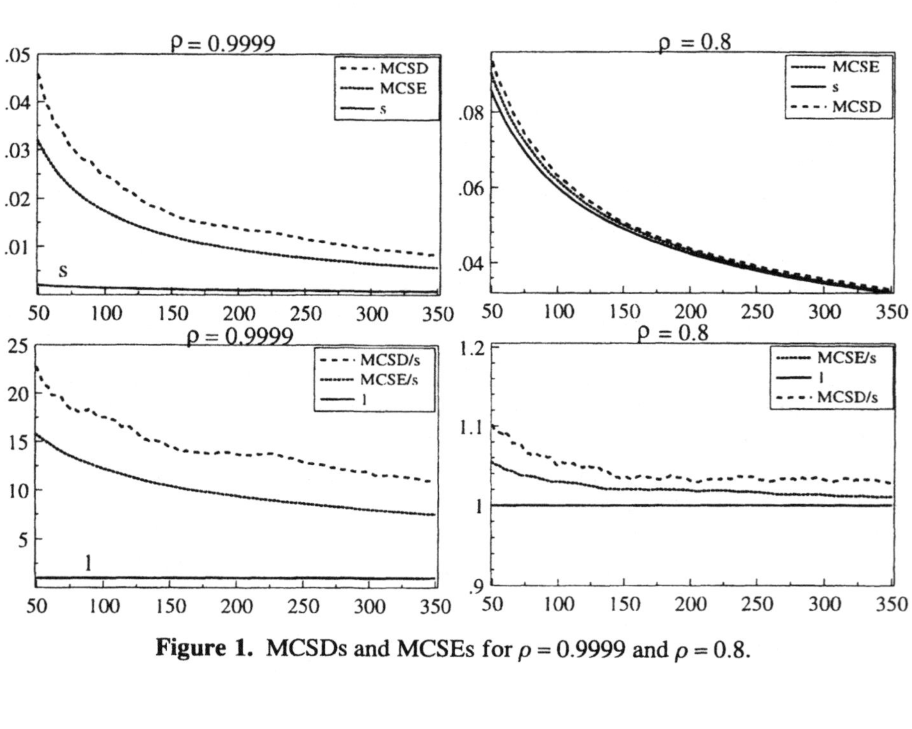

Figure 1. MCSDs and MCSEs for $\rho = 0.9999$ and $\rho = 0.8$.

$t = T_b$). In a static setting, including z_t is equivalent to dropping the T_b^{th} observation. Since:

$$y_t = \sum_{i=0}^{\infty} (\rho^i \psi z_{t-i} + \rho^i \nu_{t-i}),$$

then, letting $\sigma_u^2 = \sigma_\nu^2/(1-\rho^2)$:

$$T^{-1} \sum_{t=1}^{T} \mathsf{E}[y_t^2] \simeq \sigma_u^2 + \frac{T^{-1}\psi^2}{1-\rho^2}. \tag{5}$$

When ψ is a fixed number, its effect on (5) is negligible for large T, and hence it has no influence on the limiting distribution. Indeed, least-squares estimation of (4) yields:

$$\begin{pmatrix} \sqrt{T}(\hat{\rho} - \rho) \\ \hat{\psi} - \psi \end{pmatrix} \xrightarrow{\mathcal{D}} \mathsf{N}_2\left[0, \begin{pmatrix} 1-\rho^2 & 0 \\ 0 & \sigma_\nu^2 \end{pmatrix}\right].$$

The limiting distribution of $\sqrt{T}(\hat{\rho} - \rho)$ is unaffected by the inclusion of the dummy, and does not depend on the value of ψ. The residual variance remains a consistent estimator of σ_ν^2. However, since different scalings are needed on the two estimators to obtain non-degenerate limiting distributions, $\hat{\psi}$ is inconsistent for ψ. Omitting the indicator from the estimated model does not affect the limiting distribution, but would bias estimators of ρ and σ_ν^2 in finite samples.

When the impulse is large in terms of the error relative to the available sample, approximated by $\psi = \sqrt{T}\delta\sigma_\nu$, then:

$$T^{-1} \sum_{t=1}^{T} \mathsf{E}[y_t^2] \simeq \sigma_u^2 (1 + \delta^2). \tag{6}$$

As $y_{T_b - 1}$ does not depend on ψ:

$$\begin{pmatrix} \hat{\rho} - \rho \\ \hat{\delta} - \delta \end{pmatrix} \underset{app}{\sim} \mathsf{N}_2\left[0, T^{-1} \begin{pmatrix} (1-\rho^2)(1+\delta^2)^{-1} & 0 \\ 0 & 1 \end{pmatrix}\right]. \tag{7}$$

Thus, the approximate distribution of $\hat{\rho}$ in (7) is affected by the size of the break, but is little affected by the inclusion or exclusion of the dummy. This is unlike a static model, where including the indicator would completely remove the effect of the 'blip'. Again the residual variance is unbiased, but is biased if z_t is omitted. Finally, the appropriately-scaled dummy δ has a variance of $O(T^{-1})$: for example, if $\sigma_\nu = 0.01$ (1%) and $T = 100$, then $\psi = 0.05$ corresponds to $\delta = 0.5$ (SE $= 0.1$).

3. Formulation of the statistical problem

The analysis commences from an unrestricted Gaussian vector autoregression, such as that in (10) below. The objective is to find an empirically well-behaved specification as the starting point for cointegration analysis. But first we discuss the data and the economic analysis.

3.1. *Data*

The data used to illustrate issues in cointegration inference are quarterly, seasonally-adjusted, time series over 1963(1)–1989(2) on M, I, P and R_n for the United Kingdom.[3]

M	nominal M_1,
I	real total final expenditure (*TFE*) at 1985 prices,
P	the *TFE* deflator,
R_a	the three-month local authority interest rate,
R_m	learning-adjusted own interest rate,
R_n	$R_a - R_m$.

R_m is the learning-adjusted interest rate on interest-bearing checking accounts at commercial banks. This type of account was introduced in 1984(3), see Hendry and Ericsson (1991) for details. Money and expenditure are in £ million, the deflator is unity in 1985, and the interest rates are annual, in fractions. Lower-case letters denote logs of the corresponding capitals. After allowing for lags, estimation is usually over 1964(3)–1989(2), which yields 100 observations. We focus on the seasonally adjusted data: also see Hendry and Mizon (1993), and Hendry and Doornik (1994). Ericsson, Hendry and Tran (1994) analyse both the adjusted and the corresponding raw data. They find the same cointegrating vector for money demand, but different feedbacks. We treat the seasonal adjustment as having been effective, in order to concentrate on the remaining aspects of rank determination.

The lower-right panel in Figure 2 shows the time series of the observations for $m - p$, i, Δp, R_n (standardized to facilitate comparison).

3.2. *The economic background*

The theoretical formulation entails relationships to determine the demand for money, aggregate expenditure, inflation, and the opportunity cost of holding money. We consider these in turn.

Despite being primarily used for transactions, narrow money is also part of financial portfolios, and is held as a liquid reserve for contingencies. Thus, the quantity of nominal money demanded (M^d) depends on the price level (P), the volume of real transactions to be financed (I), the opportunity cost of intertemporal holding, measured by inflation ($\dot{p}$), and on both the own rate of interest and competing rates of return on alternative liquid assets.[4] Since money demand should be unit free, the relation is usually assumed to be homogeneous of degree one in P (i.e., real money is demanded), increasing in I (sometimes homogeneously as well), decreasing in both inflation and R_a and increasing in R_m. Frequently, a log-linear form is assumed linking M, P, and I, with interest rates entering in levels, and we write this schematically, in steady state, as:

$$m^d - p = \tau_0 + \tau_1 i - \tau_2 \dot{p} - \tau_3 R_a + \tau_4 R_m. \qquad (8)$$

The coefficients $\tau_1 \dots \tau_4$ are anticipated to be positive as written, probably with $\tau_1 = 1$, and $\tau_3 = \tau_4$. Equation (8) defines the anticipated cointegration relation. However, dynamics are central to many theories of money demand: here economic agents are assumed to have upper and lower targets for their desired real-money holdings, and adjust balances back towards the mean when these bands are exceeded.[5] While the observed money stock also depends on the supply, on the basis of institutional knowledge, we assume that the monetary authority controls the shortest interest rate, and manipulates that to achieve its policy objectives.

Total real expenditure is very schematically modelled here in terms of a trend, approximating growth in human and physical capital, both of which embody technical progress, and demand determinants, represented by the real interest rate $R_a - 4\dot{p}$ (inflation is re-scaled to annual units), leading to:

$$i = \rho_0 + \rho_1 t - \rho_2 (R_a - 4\dot{p}). \tag{9}$$

Again, dynamic adjustments to the path in (9) need to be modelled empirically. In both (8) and (9), the log form is adopted in the expectation of relatively constant proportional errors. The lack of data on R_m for most of the sample led us to replace $-\tau_3 R_a + \tau_4 R_m$ in (8) by $-\tau_3 R_n$, and $-\rho_2(R_a - 4\dot{p})$ in (9) by $-\rho_2 R_n + \rho_3 \dot{p}$. Large policy changes (such as major budget changes) are handled using an indicator variable, called *dout* (see Section 3.4).

Inflation is a complex phenomenon, and the model lacks many of the variables that might be expected to account for its behaviour, including exchange rates and world prices, government deficits, factor-market conditions, and commodity prices. Thus, the most likely long-run determinants here are the excess demands for money and goods embodied in deviations from (8) and (9). We also introduce a non-modelled indicator for special effects from price shocks (such as the oil crises).

Finally, despite being a net interest rate, R_n is sufficiently short term to be treated here as being set by the monetary authority, perhaps to stabilize the excess demands in (8) and (9), or achieve a target for inflation.

3.3. *Linear dynamic systems*

We consider a closed, linear dynamic system for n variables x_t, with a maximum lag length of s periods, and assume normality, thereby postulating a vector autoregression (VAR) with m deterministic variables q_t, over a sample $t = 1, \dots, T$ expressed as:

$$\Delta \mathrm{x}_t = \sum_{j=1}^{s-1} \Pi_j \Delta \mathrm{x}_{t-j} + \pi \mathrm{x}_{t-1} + \Phi \mathrm{q}_t + \nu_t \quad \text{where} \quad \nu_t \sim \mathsf{IN}_n[0, \Omega], \tag{10}$$

when $\mathsf{IN}_n[0, \Omega]$ denotes an n-dimensional independent, normal density with mean zero and covariance matrix Ω (symmetric, positive definite). In (10), the parameters $(\Pi_1 \dots \Pi_{s-1}, \pi, \Phi, \Omega)$ are assumed to be constant and variation free, with sufficient observations to sustain estimation and inference ($T - s \gg n(s + m + 2)$). To allow interpretation of the results, none of the roots of the companion-form polynomial should lie inside the unit circle (see e.g., Banerjee *et al.*, 1993, Ch. 5). We focus on $s = 2$ for exposition, and denote Π_1 by Π. Note that (10) is isomorphic to a VAR in levels.

3.4. *Preliminary empirical analysis*

For coherent inference, it is important that the empirical model satisfies the assumptions of the statistical analysis. We begin by analysing $m - p$, i, Δp, and R_n thereby imposing long-run price homogeneity; we return in Section 9 to consider the properties of the levels m and p. The four series analysed are treated as potentially I(1) over this sample. The initial VAR in (10) for $\{(m - p)_t, i_t, \Delta p_t, R_{n,t}\}$ has 2 lags and includes an intercept unrestrictedly, and a trend. Earlier research suggests that longer lags are not needed. We base our specification closely on Hendry and Doornik (1994), who provide modelling details, so include their dummy variables. These are *dout* for output shifts, zero except for unity in 1972(4), 1973(1), 1979(2), and *doil* for price shocks (such as the oil crises and VAT changes), equal to unity in 1973(3), 1973(4), and 1979(3). These indicators adjust for the largest residuals in the Hendry and Mizon (1993) model. The sample period (after creating lags) is 1964(3)–1989(2), so that $T = 100$. Computations and graphics were produced with GiveWin and PcFiml (see Doornik and Hendry, 1996, 1997); simulations were done in Ox (Doornik, 1998b).

Table 1 reports summary evaluation statistics for the estimated VAR: $\hat{\sigma}$ denotes the standard deviation of the residuals. The diagnostic tests comprise 5th-order residual vector serial correlation ($\mathsf{F}^{\mathsf{v}}_{\mathsf{ar5}}$: a multivariate version of Breusch, 1978, Godfrey, 1978, see Doornik, 1995b) and vector heteroscedasticity ($\mathsf{F}^{\mathsf{v}}_{\mathsf{het}}$: a multivariate version of White, 1980, see Doornik, 1995b), as well as a chi-square test for joint normality ($\chi^{2\mathsf{v}}_{\mathsf{nd}}(8)$: see Doornik and Hansen, 1994). Significance at the 5% and 1% levels is denoted by * and ** respectively; p-values are given in square brackets.

Apart from the non-normality due to some remaining outliers in the inflation equation, the results are consistent with a congruent system (i.e. matching the available evidence, see Hendry, 1995, p.365). All first lags and the indicators are

Table 1. System evaluation.

	$m - p$	i	$\Delta p R_n$
$\hat{\sigma}$	1.65%	1.04%	0.68% 1.31

statistic	value	p-value
$\mathsf{F}^{\mathsf{v}}_{\mathsf{ar5}}(80, 258)$	1.21	[0.13]
$\mathsf{F}^{\mathsf{v}}_{\mathsf{het}}(180, 548)$	0.97	[0.59]
$\chi^{2\mathsf{v}}_{\mathsf{nd}}(8)$	19.4*	[0.013]

significant, but the second lags and the trend appear insignificant (on $\mathsf{F}(4, 85)$, at 5% or less). The equations for Δp and R_n show some non-constancy, although the system break-point Chow (1960) test nowhere exceeds the 1% critical value within sample.

Following this preliminary analysis, it is of interest to determine the dynamic properties of the system. The eigenvalues of the long-run matrix π in (10) are -0.39, -0.17, and $-0.05 \pm 0.05\mathrm{i}$ (using i to denote $\sqrt{-1}$), so the rank seems non-zero, and is unlikely to be greater than two. The eigenvalues λ of the companion form (the inverses of the roots) are shown in Table 2.

Two roots are close to unity, two have moduli near 0.7, and the remainder are small, so overall, this representation appears to be $\mathsf{I}(1)$, probably with two cointegrating vectors, and two unit roots. We now formalize the cointegration analysis.

3.5. *Cointegration formulation*

Equation (10) shows that the matrix π determines how the levels of the process x enter the system: for example, when $\pi = 0$, the dynamic evolution does not depend on the levels. This indicates the importance of the rank of π in the analysis. The statistical hypothesis of cointegration is:

$$\mathsf{H}(r)\colon \operatorname{rank}(\pi) \leqslant r.$$

Under this hypothesis, π can be written as the product of two matrices:

$$\pi = \alpha\beta',$$

where α and β have dimension $n \times r$, and vary freely. As suggested by Johansen (1988, 1995b), such a restriction can be analysed by maximum likelihood methods. The idea is to find the canonical correlations between the first differences $\Delta \mathrm{x}_t$ and the lagged levels x_{t-1}, having corrected both of these for the other components in (10). It is then possible to test that the $n - r$ smallest canonical correlations are zero.

Keeping the lag length at two ($s = 2$), and restricting (10) by the hypothesis $\mathsf{H}(r)$, we obtain:

$$\Delta \mathrm{x}_t = \Pi \Delta \mathrm{x}_{t-1} + \alpha(\beta' \mathrm{x}_{t-1}) + \Phi \mathrm{q}_t + \nu_t. \tag{11}$$

In applications, it is of interest to estimate the rank rather than just finding an upper bound of the form $\operatorname{rank}(\pi) \leqslant r$. When the rank equals r, the properties of the system can be interpreted using the Granger representation theorem (see Engle and Granger, 1987, and Johansen, 1995b, Theorem 4.2).

Table 2. System dynamics.

λ	$0.96 ¢ 0.02\mathrm{i}$	$0.68 \pm 0.03\mathrm{i}$	-0.34	0.32	$-0.21 \pm 0.10\mathrm{i}$
$\lvert\lambda\rvert$	0.96, 0.96	0.68, 0.68	0.34	0.32	0.24, 0.24

When x_t is I(1), then the first differences Δx_t and the r cointegrating relations $\beta' x_t$ are I(0). To ensure that x_t is I(1) and not I(2), we require $\text{rank}(\alpha_\perp' \Gamma \beta_\perp) = n - r$. Here $\Gamma = -(I_n - \Pi + \pi)$ is the mean-lag matrix, $\alpha_\perp$ and $\beta_\perp$ are $n \times (n-r)$ matrices such that $\alpha_\perp' \alpha = 0$, $\beta_\perp' \beta = 0$ with $(\alpha : \alpha_\perp)$ and $(\beta : \beta_\perp)$ being rank-n matrices. The issue of I(2)-ness is discussed in Section 9.

3.6. *Unrestricted cointegration analysis*

Prior to a theoretical analysis of the deterministic terms, our I(1) cointegration analysis restricts the trend to the cointegration space (coefficients denoted by ρ), and enters the constant (ϕ) and dummies (d_t) unrestrictedly. Equation (11) then becomes:

$$\Delta x_t = \Pi \Delta x_{t-1} + \alpha \begin{pmatrix} \beta \\ \rho \end{pmatrix}' \begin{pmatrix} x_{t-1} \\ t \end{pmatrix} + \phi + \Upsilon d_t + \nu_t. \tag{12}$$

The first part of Table 3 reports the log-likelihood values (ℓ), and eigenvalues (μ). The latter are the squared canonical correlations between first differences and lagged levels with trend (corrected for lagged differences, constant and dummies). The remainder of Table 3 reports the trace and maximum eigenvalue (Max) statistics together with the first two estimated cointegrating vectors, and the p-values for the trace test. Table 4 records the feedback coefficients ($\hat{\alpha}$) and their standard errors when $r = 2$.

Table 3. Cointegration analysis.

r	0	1	2	3	4
ℓ	1799.7	1838.3	1845.5	1849.8	1852.9
μ		0.55	0.13	0.08	0.06

H(r)	$r=0$	$r \leqslant 1$	$r \leqslant 2$	$r \leqslant 3$
Trace	108.5**	29.3	14.8	6.2
	[0.00]	[0.55]	[0.60]	[0.45]
Max	79.3**	14.5	8.6	6.2

$\hat{\beta}'$	$m-p$	i	Δp	R_n	t
1	1	−1.00	7.34	7.65	−0.0005
2	−0.06	1	−3.38	0.86	−0.0059

Table 4. Feedback coefficients for rank 2.

$\hat{\alpha}$	1	2	SE[$\hat{\alpha}$]	1	2
$m-p$	−0.09	−0.01	$m-p$	0.012	0.074
i	−0.02	−0.10	i	0.007	0.047
Δp	−0.00	0.08	Δp	0.005	0.031
R_n	−0.00	−0.06	R_n	0.009	0.060

Before discussing the interpretation of these results, we consider the roles of the constant and trend.

4. Intercepts and linear deterministic trends

Deterministic terms, such as the intercept, linear trend, and indicator variables, play a crucial role in both data behaviour and limiting distributions of estimators and tests in integrated processes: see, for example, Johansen (1994). Depending on their presence or absence, the system may manifest drift, linear trends in cointegration vectors, or even quadratic trends (although the last seems unlikely in economics). Appropriate formulation of the model is important to ensure that cointegrating-rank tests are not too dependent on 'nuisance parameters' related to the deterministic terms. Here we consider the intercept and trend; Section 6 considers dummies.

The impact on the process x_t of q_t with parameter Φ in (11) can be described using Granger's representation theorem as:

$$C\Phi \sum_{i=0}^{t} q_i + \sum_{i=0}^{t} C_i \Phi q_{t-i}, \tag{13}$$

where $C = \beta_\perp(\alpha_\perp' \Gamma \beta_\perp)^{-1}\alpha_\perp'$. Two distinct effects are apparent: a cumulative influence through $C\Phi$, and a distributed lag with coefficients $C_i\Phi$. When $\Phi = \alpha R$ (say) the former vanishes since $C\alpha = 0$. It is no surprise that this affects the distributions of test statistics, which we now consider in detail.

4.1. *Statistical analysis*

When determining rank, three models merit consideration. These can be described by the dependence of the expected values of x and β'x on functions of t:

Hypothesis	x	β'x
$H_l(r)$	linear	linear
$H_c(r)$	constant	constant
$H_z(r)$	zero	zero

In these models, the process x and the cointegrating relations exhibit the same deterministic pattern. At a later stage, when the rank has been determined, it will be possible to consider further models of the trending behaviour. Note that, under $H_z(r)$, it is necessary that $E[x_0] = E[\Delta x_0] = 0$ to ensure that the non-stationary components have zero expectation. Likewise, for the other models, the conditions on the initial values must be such that they preserve the postulated behaviour.

The hypotheses are formalized in Table 5 in terms of the parameters of (11). The parameters $\alpha, \beta \in \mathbb{R}^{n \times r}$, $\phi \in \mathbb{R}^n$, and $\rho_c, \rho_l \in \mathbb{R}^r$ vary freely when present.

Table 5. Models for rank and deterministic trend.

$\mathsf{H}_l(r)$:	$\pi = \alpha\beta'$	and	$\Phi \mathrm{q}_t = \phi + \alpha\rho_l t$,
$\mathsf{H}_c(r)$:	$\pi = \alpha\beta'$	and	$\Phi \mathrm{q}_t = \alpha\rho_c$,
$\mathsf{H}_z(r)$:	$\pi = \alpha\beta'$	and	$\Phi \mathrm{q}_t = 0$.

Let $\mathsf{H}(r)$ be one of $\mathsf{H}_l(r)$, $\mathsf{H}_c(r)$, and $\mathsf{H}_z(r)$. The hypotheses are nested as follows:

$$\mathsf{H}(0) \subset \cdots \subset \mathsf{H}(r) \subset \cdots \subset \mathsf{H}(n). \tag{14}$$

The rank can be determined consistently by adopting the procedure given by Johansen (1995b, Section 12.3). Start by testing $\mathsf{H}(0)$ against the general alternative $\mathsf{H}(n)$. If $\mathsf{H}(0)$ is rejected, test $\mathsf{H}(1)$ against $\mathsf{H}(n)$, and so on. The rank is estimated as r if $\mathsf{H}(r)$ is the first hypothesis which cannot be rejected. The test statistic which is used in this procedure is the trace test. As pointed out by Nielsen and Rahbek (1998), these tests are asymptotically similar with respect to the parameters related to the deterministic components (provided that the $\mathsf{I}(1)$ conditions are satisfied).

The maximum eigenvalue test is the likelihood ratio test of $\mathsf{H}(r-1)$ against $\mathsf{H}(r)$. While this test is sometimes used in practice, a corresponding result of consistency has not been established.

4.2. *Test results*

There may be economic grounds for preferring one specification over another. In particular, for our model, we prefer $\mathsf{H}_l(r)$ based on the following economic considerations:

a) While inflation and R_n should not drift, real *TFE* has grown at an annual rate of about 2.5%, precluding a zero intercept. A long-run unit income elasticity of demand for real money then restricts its intercept to equal that for *TFE*.

b) A linear trend in the cointegration space approximates growth in *TFE* from cumulative human and physical capital; its coefficient must therefore match that in a).

c) When the analysis uses dummies, as with *doil* and *dout* in our case, similar considerations apply. We return to this issue in Section 6.

Referring to Table 3, and noting that it corresponds to $\mathsf{H}_l(r)$, we can now interpret the results of the test statistics. Following the rank selection procedure described in the previous section, the null of no cointegration is strongly rejected. Although the second cointegrating vector is not significant, we retain it following Hendry and Mizon (1993). The interpretation of the coefficients in relation to the economic issues in Section 3.2 will be considered in Section 8 after imposing further restrictions.

4.3. *Further models*

From Table 5, let $\phi_c = \alpha\rho_c$ and $\phi_l = \alpha\rho_l$. Two additional models arise when ϕ_c and ϕ_l are allowed to vary freely, and we embed these in an extension of that table:

Hypothesis	x	β'x
$\mathsf{H}_{ql}(r)$: $\pi = \alpha\beta'$, $\Phi q_t = \phi_c + \phi_l t$	quadratic	linear
$\mathsf{H}_{l}(r)$: $\pi = \alpha\beta'$, $\Phi q_t = \phi_c + \alpha\rho_l t$	linear	linear
$\mathsf{H}_{lc}(r)$: $\pi = \alpha\beta'$, $\Phi q_t = \phi_c$	linear	constant
$\mathsf{H}_{c}(r)$: $\pi = \alpha\beta'$, $\Phi q_t = \alpha\rho_c$	constant	constant
$\mathsf{H}_{z}(r)$: $\pi = \alpha\beta'$, $\Phi q_t = 0$	zero	zero

In terms of the notation used in PcFiml, the hypotheses are:

Hypothesis	trend	constant
$\mathsf{H}_{ql}(r)$	unrestricted	unrestricted
$\mathsf{H}_{l}(r)$	restricted	unrestricted
$\mathsf{H}_{lc}(r)$	absent	unrestricted
$\mathsf{H}_{c}(r)$	absent	restricted
$\mathsf{H}_{z}(r)$	absent	absent

Likelihood-ratio test statistics for the two additional models have also been derived by Johansen (1995b). The asymptotic distribution under $\mathsf{H}_{ql}(r)$ depends on whether or not $\alpha_\perp'\phi_l = 0$, and this complicates the rank determination considerably (*op. cit.*, Theorem 6.2). To develop a consistent test procedure, the idea is to only test $\mathsf{H}_{ql}(r)$ if $\mathsf{H}_{l}(r)$ has been rejected (*op. cit.*, Ch. 12). In that case, we rule out the possibility that the rank is at most r as well as $\alpha_\perp'\phi_l = 0$, and therefore the assumptions of the asymptotic theory are satisfied. The relevant hypotheses are nested as:

$$\begin{array}{ccccc} \mathsf{H}_{ql}(0) \subset \cdots \subset & \mathsf{H}_{ql}(r) & \subset \cdots \subset & \mathsf{H}_{ql}(n) \\ \cup & \cup & & \| \\ \mathsf{H}_{l}(0) \subset \cdots \subset & \mathsf{H}_{l}(r) & \subset \cdots \subset & \mathsf{H}_{l}(n). \end{array} \qquad (15)$$

By testing the hypotheses

$$\mathsf{H}_{l}(0), \mathsf{H}_{ql}(0), \mathsf{H}_{l}(1), \mathsf{H}_{ql}(1), \ldots, \mathsf{H}_{l}(n-1), \mathsf{H}_{ql}(n-1),$$

sequentially against the unrestricted alternative and stopping whenever the hypothesis is accepted, a consistent procedure is obtained.

A corresponding complication arises with $\mathsf{H}_{lc}(r)$. The test procedure is then based on:

$$\begin{matrix} \mathsf{H}_{lc}(0) \subset \cdots \subset \mathsf{H}_{lc}(r) \subset \cdots \subset \mathsf{H}_{lc}(n) \\ \cup \qquad\qquad \cup \qquad\qquad \| \\ \mathsf{H}_{c}(0) \subset \cdots \subset \mathsf{H}_{c}(r) \subset \cdots \subset \mathsf{H}_{c}(n). \end{matrix} \tag{16}$$

When we allow for a quadratic trend in the UK-M1 model we find for the trace test:

	$r=0$	$r \leqslant 1$	$r \leqslant 2$	$r \leqslant 3$
$\mathsf{H}_{ql}(r)$	97.4**	22.4	8.1	1.2 .
$\mathsf{H}_{l}(r)$	108.5**	29.3	14.8	6.2

We encounter 108.5**, 97.4**, 29.3, so that the first hypothesis to be accepted is $\mathsf{H}_l(1)$. Therefore the quadratic trend is rejected, and the conclusion is as before.

It is possible, but not very likely, that an insignificant value is followed by a significant statistic. An example would be: reject $\mathsf{H}_l(0)$, accept $\mathsf{H}_l(1)$, and reject $\mathsf{H}_l(2)$. This could be indicative of more general model mis-specification.

5. Illustrating the models of trend behaviour

The practical problem of estimating the cointegrating rank for an appropriate treatment of the deterministic terms can be done by the various sequential testing strategies just discussed. We now illustrate this using an artificial DGP based on the empirical model in this paper. The data exhibit a linear trend, apparent in fig. 2d, so we adopt the model with a restricted trend and two cointegrating vectors to generate the data.

5.1. *The artificial DGP*

The artificial DGP satisfies $\mathsf{H}_l(2)$. The design of the DGP closely mimics the UK-M1 empirical model, and uses the observations for 1964(1)–(2) as its initial conditions.

$$\Delta \mathrm{x}_t = \begin{pmatrix} -0.102 & 0 \\ 0 & -0.149 \\ 0 & 0.036 \\ 0 & -0.04 \end{pmatrix} \begin{pmatrix} 1 & -1 & 6.41 & 7.16 & 0 & -0.209 \\ 0 & 1 & -2.13 & 1.48 & -0.0063 & -11.186 \end{pmatrix} \begin{pmatrix} \mathrm{x}_{t-1} \\ t \\ 1 \end{pmatrix}$$
$$+ \begin{pmatrix} 0.0063 \\ 0.0063 \\ 0 \\ 0 \end{pmatrix} + \begin{pmatrix} -0.3 & 0 & 0 & -0.06 \\ 0 & 0 & 0 & 0 \\ 0.068 & 0 & -0.26 & 0 \\ 0 & 0 & 0 & 0.17 \end{pmatrix} \Delta \mathrm{x}_{t-1} + \nu_t, \tag{17}$$

when:

$$\nu_t \sim \mathsf{IN}_4[0, \Sigma], \quad \text{where} \quad \Sigma^* = \begin{pmatrix} 1.6\% & & & \\ -0.08 & 1\% & & \\ -0.51 & 0.03 & 0.69\% & \\ -0.49 & 0.09 & 0.31 & 1.3\% \end{pmatrix},$$

using the lower triangle of Σ^* to show the cross correlations of the errors, and:

$$\begin{pmatrix} \mathrm{x}'_{-1} \\ \mathrm{x}'_0 \end{pmatrix} = \begin{pmatrix} 10.9445 & 11.1169 & 0.000779 & 0.048967 \\ 10.9369 & 11.1306 & 0.013567 & 0.050 \end{pmatrix}.$$

Figure 2 records the data generated in three randomly-selected trials, together with the actual empirical outcomes in the fourth panel (all variables are standardized). The outcomes seem representative of the actual data.

5.2. *Monte Carlo analysis*

We now simulate the rejection frequencies of the tests $\mathsf{H}_{ql}(r)$, $\mathsf{H}_l(r)$, $\mathsf{H}_{lc}(r)$, and $\mathsf{H}_c(r)$ when using data generated by (17). We do not consider H_z, because it is too far removed from our DGP. The first cointegrating vector is very well determined, with $\mathsf{H}(0)$ rejected virtually 100% of the time at all the sample sizes considered, so we omit this from the graphs.

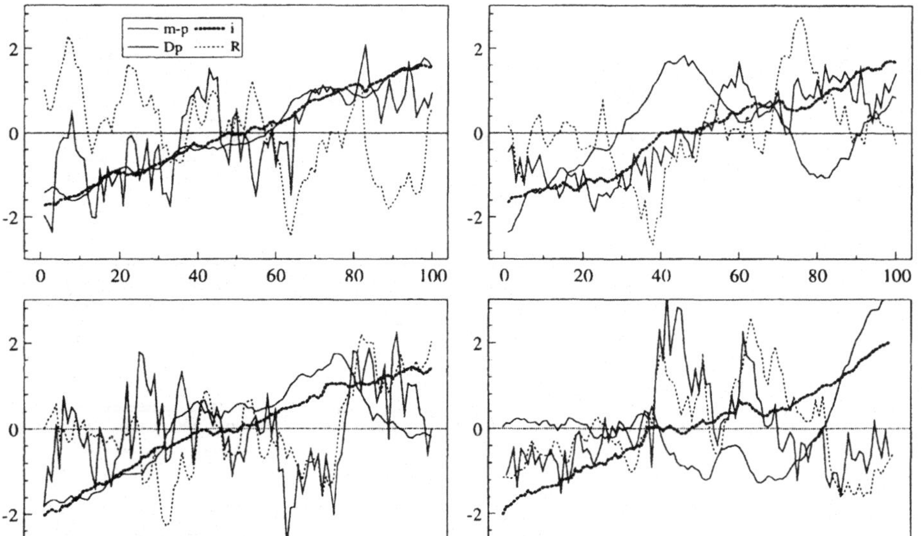

Figure 2. Data generated in three replications, with the actual outcomes.

The results are presented in fig. 3 as a 4×3 matrix of graphs. The graphs give recursive Monte Carlo results for sample sizes $T = 50$, 75, 100, 125, 150, 200, 250, 500. In all cases, common random numbers were used, so that all graphs were based on the same data, and within each replication, a subset of the 500 data points was analysed. Each row corresponds to one of the four models for testing the rank hypothesis. Each column corresponds to a different rank specification. Rejection frequencies are given at 10% and 5% level based on asymptotic critical values. For example, the graph for $\mathsf{H}_l(1)$ in the second row, (which also formed the basis for the DGP) shows a high probability for rejecting $r \leqslant 1$, which is satisfactory because the actual rank is two.

The second row outcomes for H_l correspond to our recommended treatment of deterministic factors: high rejection frequency of the null of no second cointegration vector, and somewhat oversized in rejecting the third. So adopting the procedure in (14) to determine the rank, we usually arrive at the correct conclusion. At $T = 100$, there is still some uncertainty about the second vector, but this problem gradually vanishes. The probability of rejecting $r \leqslant 3$ is virtually zero, as might be hoped when the rank is only two (and is expected from asymptotic theory).

The first row shows that serious problems arise when rank determination is solely based on H_{ql}. The rejection frequencies for $r \leqslant 2$ are considerably higher than 5% and 10% respectively, with even worse results for $r \leqslant 3$. However, when adopting the procedure (15), we reject $\mathsf{H}_l(1)$, $\mathsf{H}_{ql}(1)$ and accept $\mathsf{H}_l(2)$.

In the remaining two rows, the models are mis-specified relative to the DGP.

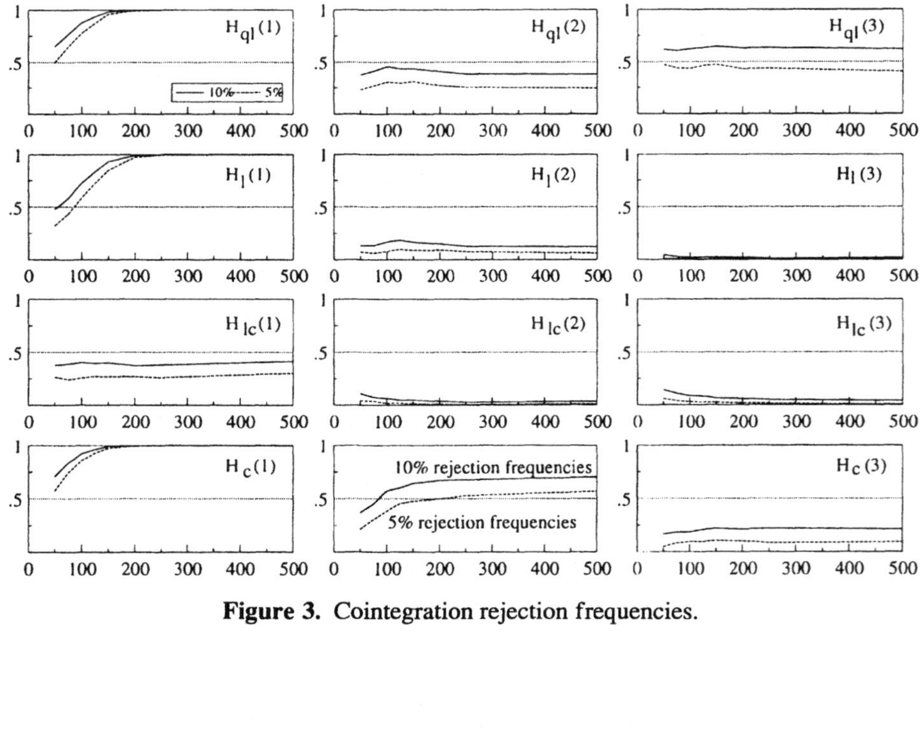

Figure 3. Cointegration rejection frequencies.

The fourth row (H_c) is certainly unrealistic, in that it enforces no growth on the system. This highlights the severe drawbacks of inappropriate treatment of the deterministic terms: now it is quite possible to accept 3 cointegrating vectors when using the procedure (14).

When the deterministic trend is erroneously omitted as in the third row, there is a tendency to replace it by a stochastic trend. Of course, the correct procedure to use here is (16), but the mis-specification prevents us from reaching the right rank.

5.3. *Over-specified trend*

It is interesting to consider what happens when H_l is used to analyze data that do not in fact have a deterministic trend. To investigate this, we used two versions of the DGP. The first omitted the trend from the cointegrating vector (so was a member of $\mathsf{H}_{lc}(2)$) and the second only maintained the intercept in the cointegrating vectors (i.e., all three values 0.0063 were replaced with zero, placing it in $\mathsf{H}_c(2)$).

The resulting graphs were visually impossible to distinguish from the second row of fig. 3. This is explained by the (asymptotic) invariance to the value of the trend coefficient in the model H_l. Thus, adopting a model that includes a trend in the cointegration space has low cost even when the DGP does not have one. Such a beneficial outcome contrasts markedly with the costs of adding an unnecessary unrestricted trend.

5.4. *Asymptotic analysis*

The asymptotic background for the results reported in fig. 3 is now discussed. Further details are given in the appendix.

Test for $\mathsf{H}_l(r)$ *against* $\mathsf{H}_l(n)$ *when the DGP is* $\mathsf{H}_l(s)$

This is the standard case (second row), and the results correspond to the asymptotic analysis.

Test for $\mathsf{H}_{ql}(r)$ *against* $\mathsf{H}_{ql}(n)$ *when the DGP is* $\mathsf{H}_l(s)$

The first row of fig. 3 shows oversized tests, as expected from the asymptotic analysis.

Two asymptotic distributions are of relevance in the analysis of $\mathsf{H}_{ql}(r)$. The standard distribution applies when the condition $\alpha_\perp'\phi_l \neq 0$ is satisfied. However, when the DGP, as here, satisfies $\mathsf{H}_l(r)$ the condition is not satisfied since $\alpha_\perp'\phi_l = 0$ and a different asymptotic distribution is relevant. The latter distribution is not tabulated in the literature. Simulations indicate that it dominates the standard distribution, and consequently the considered test is oversized.

In fig. 3, the test for $\mathsf{H}_{ql}(2)$ is based on the critical values 15.9 and 18.2, the 10% and 5% quantiles when $\alpha_\perp'\phi_l \neq 0$. The asymptotic p-values for these values are approximately 35% and 22% respectively when the rank is two as specified, but $\alpha_\perp'\phi_l=0$. Similarly, the asymptotic p-values for the test for $\mathsf{H}_{ql}(3)$ are approximately 60% and 38% when $\alpha_\perp'\phi_l=0$ and the rank is two.

Test for $\mathsf{H}_{lc}(r)$ *against* $\mathsf{H}_{lc}(n)$ *when the DGP is* $\mathsf{H}_l(s)$
The first panels of the first two rows of fig. 3 show that the power of a test for $\text{rank}(\pi) \leqslant (r-1)$ tends to one when $\text{rank}(\pi)=r$ in a well-specified model. This is not necessarily the case for a mis-specified model, as indicated by the first panel of the third row. Actually, the rejection frequency convergences to a constant less than unity when testing $\mathsf{H}_{lc}(1)$ using the DGP. This convergence is illustrated analytically in the Appendix.

Test for $\mathsf{H}_c(r)$ *against* $\mathsf{H}_c(n)$ *when the DGP is* $\mathsf{H}_l(s)$
For this test, the rejection frequency converges to one when testing that the rank is at most r and $r<\text{rank}(\pi)$. However, the rejection frequency of the test for $\mathsf{H}_c(\text{rank}(\pi))$ converges to a constant less than unity, explaining the excess rejections in the second panel of row four. Again, the Appendix provides an analytic derivation.

6. Dummy variables

Two impulse dummies were included unrestrictedly in the analysis. Since the inclusion of dummies can greatly alter the distribution approximating the rank test, we consider the empirical and economic background to the *dout* and *doil* dummies in more detail, noting some specific problems related to the UK M1 analysis. The effects of dummies are studied using a Monte Carlo experiment; analytical results are presented in the Appendix.

6.1. *Dummies in the UK M1 model*

The indicators *dout* and *doil* serve two purposes. The first is to improve the fit of the model. The graphs of output i, and inflation Δp, indicate two transient shocks to the economy around 1973 and 1979 — see fig. 2. Also, the residuals of a VAR fitted without dummies have large outliers in these periods. This problem is removed by the inclusion of dummies. Initially, six separate impulse dummies were included, but, as a special feature of this data set, it was found that they could be collected into just two dummies as discussed by Hendry and Mizon (1993). The second feature of the dummies is that they describe shocks to the economy which can be attributed to specific events in the UK's economic history: the 'Heath-Barber' boom and the first effects of the Thatcher government for output, and the two oil crises for inflation.

There are several possible strategies for handling impulse dummies: they could be ignored, entered unrestrictedly, restricted to the cointegration space, or a mixture of the last two. It transpires that the size of their effect matters, potentially even asymptotically. We now discuss the impact on the asymptotic distribution of the rank test of including small (really 'not too big') and large impulse dummies.

6.2. *The rank test in the presence of small dummies*

The impact of q_t on x_t was described in (13) above. The usual asymptotic results concerning the rank test hold as long as for all t:

$$\frac{1}{\sqrt{T}}\Phi\sum_{i=0}^{t} q_i \longrightarrow 0 \quad \text{for} \quad T \longrightarrow \infty,$$

so that the effect of the dummy is negligible as compared with a random walk (see Johansen, 1995a, Section 5.8). A break in the slope of a linear trend, corresponding to a change in the growth rate, would lead to new asymptotic tables. New tables also apply when a level shift is included in the cointegrating vector. These different asymptotic distribution could be simulated using the program DisCo (Johansen and Nielsen, 1993).

A dummy which is unity at a few points and zero otherwise may give a persistent shock to the non-stationary components of the process, but is usually asymptotically negligible. However, if the parameter of such a dummy is big in relation to $\sqrt{T}$, then this is not necessarily the case.

6.3. *Distribution of the rank test in the presence of large dummies*

In the analysis of Hendry and Doornik (1994), the impact of the dummies is quite dramatic. When the dummy for the output shocks, *dout*, was entered unrestrictedly in the model, one cointegration relation was found, whereas two were found when *dout* was restricted to the cointegrating vector. In this particular example, the estimated coefficient for the dummy is large, so the standard asymptotic distribution — which is derived by ignoring the dummies — is misleading. In their final model (Table 5), the coefficient for the *dout* dummy is 0.046. The dummy is unity for three out of 100 observations, and zero otherwise, hence, the cumulated effect of the dummy is 0.138. This number is approximately 10, or $\sqrt{100}$, times the standard deviation of the innovations, which is of order 0.014. The impact of such a big dummy is illustrated by the following example, related to that in Section 2.2; details are given in the Appendix.

Consider a data generating process given by:

$$\Delta x_t = \rho\sqrt{T}1_{\{t=T_b\}} + \nu_t \text{ where } \nu_t \sim \mathsf{IN}[0,1], \tag{18}$$

and $1 < T_b < T$. This is a unit-root process with a broken constant level. Assuming $x_0 = 0$, then:

$$x_t = \rho\sqrt{T}1_{\{t \geq T_b\}} + \sum_{i=1}^{t} \nu_i.$$

When these data are analysed using a univariate, first-order model, where the dummy is entered unrestrictedly as in Table 3 of Hendry and Doornik (1994), then the likelihood-ratio test for a unit root converges to a distribution which depends on the nuisance parameter ρ. However, when a univariate first-order model with a dummy restricted to the cointegration space is applied, as in Table 4 of Hendry and Doornik (1994), the eigenvalue converges to a non-zero distribution. Accordingly, the size of the likelihood-ratio test for a unit root converges to unity, leading to the conclusion that the process may be stationary. Thus, the two results for the UK money data could be explained by a DGP with one cointegrating vector and a shock generated by unrestricted dummies.

6.4. *A Monte Carlo study of impulse dummies*

To investigate the impact of dummies, we use the artificial DGP from Section 5.1. We start by investigating the impact of adding dummies to the model when they are not present in the DGP. So the baseline is a DGP under $\mathsf{H}_l(2)$ as in (17). In the experiments we restrict ourselves to two dummy variables. Let s_{49} and s_{55} denote step dummies with value zero before $T = 49, 55$ respectively, and unity after. The impulse dummies are $d_{49} = \Delta s_{49}$ and $d_{55} = \Delta s_{55}$. Estimation (after allowing for lags) was from $T = 3$ onwards.

In the first experiment there were no breaks in that DGP, but impulses were included in the statistical models (i.e., small dummies). Concerning trend and intercept, the model conforms to H_l. Four specifications were considered for the dummy variables:

M_1: d_{49} and d_{55} unrestricted
M_2: d_{49} and d_{55} restricted
M_3: d_{49} and d_{55} restricted, Δd_{49} and Δd_{55} unrestricted
M_4: s_{49} and s_{55} restricted, d_{49} and d_{55} unrestricted

Figure 4 shows the rejection frequencies for $\mathsf{H}_l(1)$ and $\mathsf{H}_l(2)$ for the four models. The graphs reveal that the specifications of the dummies had little impact on the test for $r \leqslant 1$, but could dramatically alter the outcome of testing $r = 2$ when $\text{rank}(\pi) = 2$. Now only M_1 produces reasonable sizes, which are essentially unchanged from fig. 3 (the first two graphs in the second row).

Changing the DGP to $\mathsf{H}_c(2)$ hardly alters the outcomes from fig. 4. However, changing the coefficients of the impulses in the DGP from zero can significantly alter the results. We consider two further versions of (17) under $\mathsf{H}_l(2)$, where we add the two dummies unrestrictedly to the DGP:

DGP_1: small break: $0.05d_{49}$ in x_2, $0.02d_{55}$ in x_3,
DGP_2: large break: $0.5d_{49}$ in x_2, $0.2d_{55}$ in x_3.

The two new DGPs are analyzed by M_0 (no dummies in model), and M_1–M_3 from the previous experiment. This generates the eight graphs shown in fig. 5. The two columns correspond to small and large dummies, the four rows to the models. Panel a reveals that there is little problem in simply omitting the impulses when they are small, and b shows this finding extends approximately to large dummies.

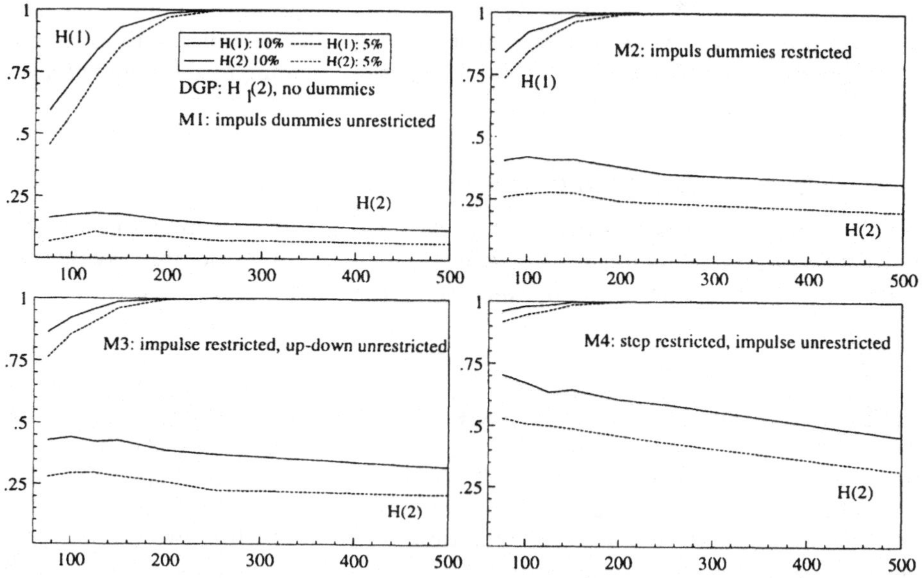

Figure 4. Impacts of impulse dummies on cointegration-rank test.

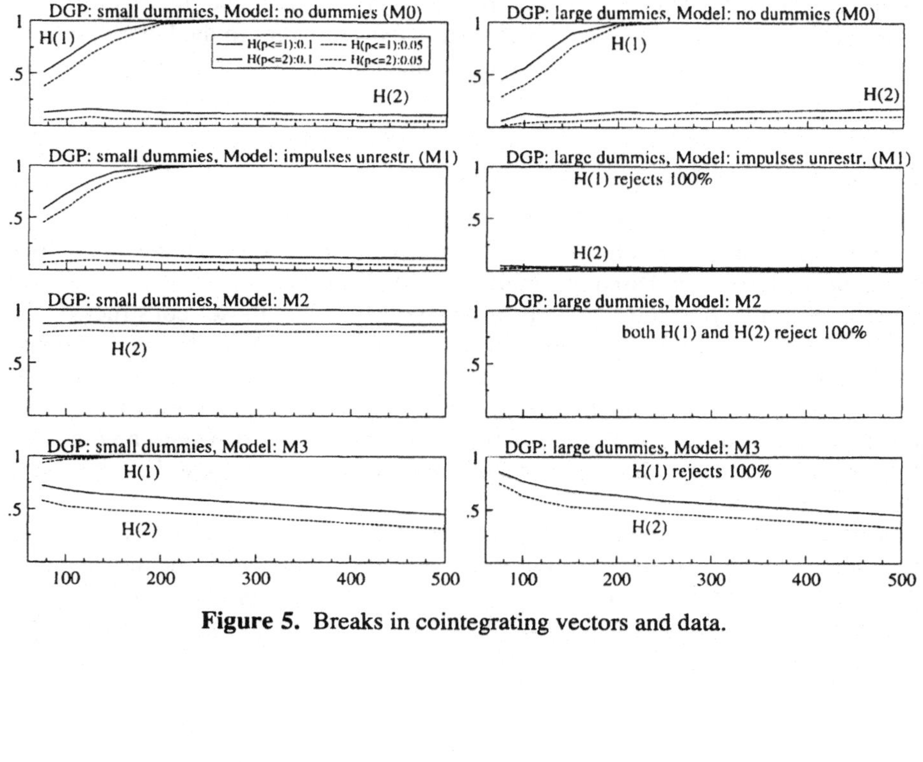

Figure 5. Breaks in cointegrating vectors and data.

Panel c confirms the results in fig. 4a, and d shows that large dummies entered unrestrictedly, if anything, enhance that finding. The remaining four panels emphasise the disastrous nature of restricting the dummies to the cointegration space and adopting conventional critical values.

7. Further issues in determining cointegration rank

Three further issues are noted in this section: recursive estimation of the eigenvalues μ_i; computationally convenient approximations to the asymptotic distribution of the rank test; and the small-sample properties of the trace test.

7.1. *Recursive estimation*

Graphs of the recursive estimates of the eigenvalues may be of help in revealing which eigenvalues stay systematically away from zero (see Hansen and Johansen, 1992, and Hansen and Johansen, 1998). It must be remembered that the eigenvalues are ordered at each sample size, and hence cannot 'cross over' by construction. Figure 6 below records the time series of the first two recursively-computed eigenvalues in panels b and d. They are shown for models with unrestricted dummies and with no impulses included. Both sets of eigenvalues are relatively constantly estimated, and the omission of the dummies has not worsened the constancy.

When plotting the recursive eigenvalues, there is a choice between re-estimating the complete cointegration analysis for every sample size, or estimating the short-run only once for the full sample, and then doing the cointegration analysis conditional on the estimated short-run. In the latter case, the distributions of the eigenvalues are more concentrated, and those of μ_3 and μ_4 collapse on zero more rapidly.

7.2. *Approximating the asymptotic distribution*

The asymptotic distributions of tests for cointegration rank involve integrals of Brownian motions for which no closed form expressions are available. To allow testing, tables have been based on simulation experiments.

Until recently, the most widely used tables were those constructed by Osterwald-Lenum (1992). Updated versions of these tables are in Johansen (1995b), computed with the DisCo program (Johansen and Nielsen, 1993). However, a sample size of 400, on which these tables are based, is not so accurate for higher dimensions. These approaches are inconvenient for use in a computer program, either because they only list a few quantiles, or because they require a large amount of data.

Doornik (1998a) approximates the asymptotic distribution of cointegration tests using the Gamma distribution. Formulae for the parameters of the Gamma distributions are derived from response surfaces involving terms of $O(T^{-1})$ (although this remains an asymptotic and not a finite-sample approximation). The resulting approximation works sufficiently well to replace the standard tables, and can provide quantiles as well as p-values. It is also easy to implement, requiring only 150 numbers to summarize the distributions for all test statistics (both for the I(1) and the I(2) model). All rejection frequencies and p-values in this paper are based on this approximation. Ox code implementing I(1) and I(2) cointegration tests and their p-values is available from the first author's web page.

7.3. *Small-sample properties of the trace test*

Whereas the previous section dealt with tabulating the asymptotic distribution, there has been some concern in the literature about the appropriateness of the asymptotic distribution in small samples. Figure 3 showed that in simulations the asymptotic distributions worked well in samples $\geqslant 150$, although there is some lack of power to find the second vector for the sample size we use ($T \leqslant 100$).

Somewhat ad hoc small-sample corrections have been suggested by Reinsel and Ahn (1992) and Reimers (1992). This involves a so-called degrees-of-freedom correction, which entails scaling the test statistic by $(1 - ns/T)$ where n is the dimension of the time series and s is the lag length. The effect of such a correction is that the acceptance region for the hypothesis $\mathsf{H}(r)$ is enlarged and therefore more cointegrating relations are found than when the correction is not used.

The degrees-of-freedom correction is not theoretically founded, and sometimes misleading. This is, for instance, the case for the very simplest situation: testing for a unit root in a univariate first-order autoregressive model. The exact distribution of the trace statistic is indistinguishable from the asymptotic distribution whenever the sample has more than seven observations, see Nielsen (1997a). In this situation the degrees of freedom correction $(1 - 1/T)$ introduces a size distortion. When testing the hypothesis of no cointegration, H(0), in a first-order model, the degrees-of-freedom correction is similarly over-correcting (Nielsen, 1997b).

In most practical situations, nuisance parameters are involved in the asymptotic distribution of the trace test. If the rank of π is r and the I(1) conditions are satisfied, then only one asymptotic distribution applies when testing $\mathsf{H}(r)$. However, this does not ensure asymptotic similarity. On the boundary of the set given by these restrictions, different distributions apply whenever the process has extra unit roots. The simplest example is the test for 'no cointegration', H(0), in a univariate second-order model, $n = 1$, $s = 2$. Under H(0), the time series is given by:

$$\Delta x_t = \pi_1^* \Delta x_{t-1} + \varepsilon_t.$$

The I(1) conditions are satisfied if the first difference of the process is I(0), that is $|\pi_1^*| < 1$. However, if $\pi_1^* = 1$, the first difference is I(1) and the process itself is I(2). In this case, a different asymptotic distribution applies (see Pantula, 1989). Asymptotically, this is obviously not a problem; however, the small-sample distribution is close to a weighted average of the various asymptotic distributions. Nielsen (1997b) suggests a new asymptotic theory which includes the nuisance parameters continuously. This would give rather accurate approximations to the exact distribution at the expense of a more complicated asymptotic distribution.

8. Cointegration in the UK M1 model

8.1. *Identification*

When $r>1$, as $\alpha\beta' = \alpha\mathrm{HH}^{-1}\beta'$ for all $r \times r$ non-singular matrices H, the cointegration vectors and feedback coefficients are not uniquely determined. One cannot compute standard errors of $\hat{\beta}$ until it is identified, although by fixing $\hat{\beta}$, standard errors of $\hat{\alpha}$ can be obtained, as shown in Table 4 for a fixed rank of two. Consequently, we next consider the use of restricted estimation of the parameters of $\alpha\beta'$; this allows us to test over-identification and obtain standard errors for the over-identified parameters. The number of restrictions imposed in doing so may not match the degrees of freedom of the resulting tests as some restrictions are not binding, or can be 'absorbed' by changes elsewhere. Johansen (1995a) and Boswijk (1994) consider the identification conditions applicable to cointegration vectors and tests thereof. Doornik (1995a) considers identification under general, possibly non-linear, restrictions on the cointegration space.

8.2. *Restricted cointegration analysis*

To uniquely determine the two cointegration vectors, given their possible interpretations as excess demands for money and goods respectively as discussed in Section 3.2, we removed the trend from the first, and $m-p$ from the second. Then we restricted the income coefficient to -1 in the first vector (converting it to an inverse-velocity relation), and the trend coefficient in the second to the mean value of Δi (namely, 0.0063, approximately 2.5% p.a.). Finally, we set the feedbacks to zero for the second vector on the first equation, and the first on the last three equations (related to long-run weak exogeneity) which yields the results shown in Table 6, with the test of the restrictions being $\chi^2(6) = 5.36$ [p = 0.5].

The first cointegration vector relates the ratio of money to expenditure $(m-p-i)$ negatively to inflation and interest rates, corresponding to an excess

Table 6. Restricted cointegration analysis.

$\hat{\alpha}$	1	2
$m-p$	−0.102 (0.011)	0 (−)
i	0 (−)	−0.149 (0.038)
Δp	0 (−)	0.036 (0.023)
R_n	0 (−)	−0.040 (0.043)

$\hat{\beta}'$	$m-p$	i	Δp	R_n	t
1	1 (−)	−1 (−)	6.41 (1.37)	7.16 (0.53)	0 (−)
2	0 (−)	1 (−)	−2.13 (0.69)	1.48 (0.27)	−0.0063 (−)

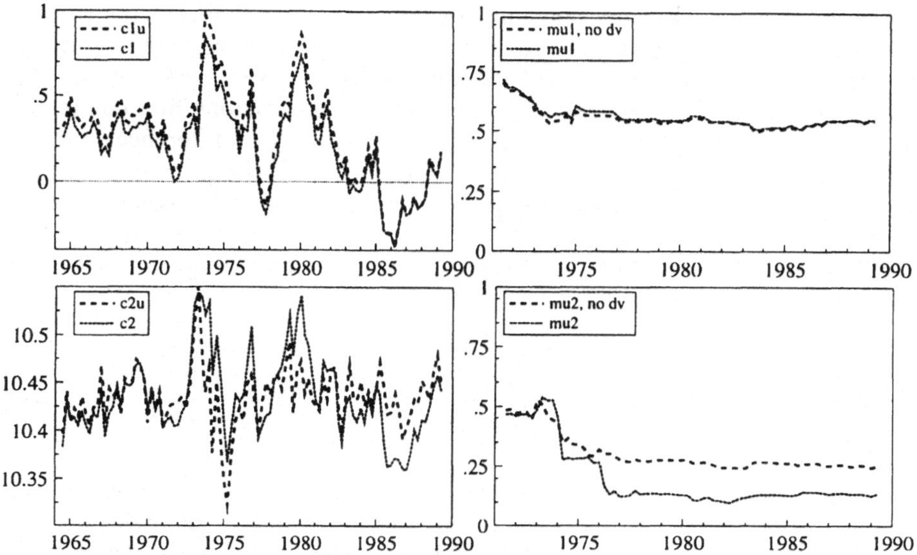

Figure 6. Cointegration vectors and recursively-computed eigenvalues.

demand for transactions money. The second cointegration vector is interpretable as the excess demand for goods and services, being the deviation of expenditure from trend, negatively related to interest rates and positively to inflation; as its main influence is onto the i equation, we retain these two long-run relations.

Figure 6 records the time series of the two unrestricted (ciu) and restricted (ci) cointegration vectors, and the associated recursively-computed eigenvalues discussed above. The unrestricted and restricted vectors for money are similar, whereas the restrictions have somewhat altered the second. Thus, subtracting their in-sample means, the two, zero-mean, I(0) linear combinations defining the equilibrium-correction mechanisms (EqCMs) are:

$$c_{1,t} = m_t - p_t - i_t + 6.41\Delta p_t + 7.16R_{n,t} - 0.209 \quad (19)$$

and:

$$c_{2,t} = (i_t - 0.0063t) - 2.13\Delta p_t + 1.48R_{n,t} - 11.186. \quad (20)$$

The definitions in (19) and (20) are required for multi-step forecasts when formulating the model in terms of the differences $(\Delta(m-p)_t, \Delta i_t, \Delta^2 p_t, \Delta R_{n,t})$ of the original variables.

9. I(2) analysis

The UK money data have been analysed in I(2) models by Johansen (1992a), Paroulo (1996) and Rahbek *et al.* (1998). The data m, p, i, R_n were analysed in levels using a fifth-order VAR. The last two papers conclude that there are two

I(2) trends and one stationary polynomial cointegrating relation. To compare that result with the I(1) analysis reported above, we now return to analyse the original measures, m, p, i, and R_n Should the analysis commence in I(2) space, then $\alpha_{\perp}'\Gamma\beta_{\perp}=\gamma\delta'$ is also reduced rank, so some linear combinations first cointegrate from I(2) to I(1) and then r others (perhaps with I(1) differences of I(2) variables) cointegrate to I(0). Thus, both I(2) and I(1) impose reduced rank restrictions on the initial formulation in (10), and the former imposes restrictions on (11).

Empirically, Rahbek *et al.* (1998) find that the cointegration relation has the form:

$$C_1^* = C_1 + 11.63\Delta(m-p), \tag{21}$$

where:

$$C_1 = m - p - i + 6.13\Delta p + 7.01R.$$

Thus, the change in real money is needed to establish cointegration in their analysis, so real money is I(2). Hence, either the nominal magnitudes are one degree of integration higher, or nominal money and prices do not cointegrate. Neither implication is very palatable, nor can we interpret (21) easily in terms of the possible plans of economic agents. Conversely, adding $11.63\Delta(m-p)$ to C_1 makes it look considerably more stationary as fig. 7b shows. Note that the cointegrating relations found in Hendry and Ericsson (1991), Hendry and

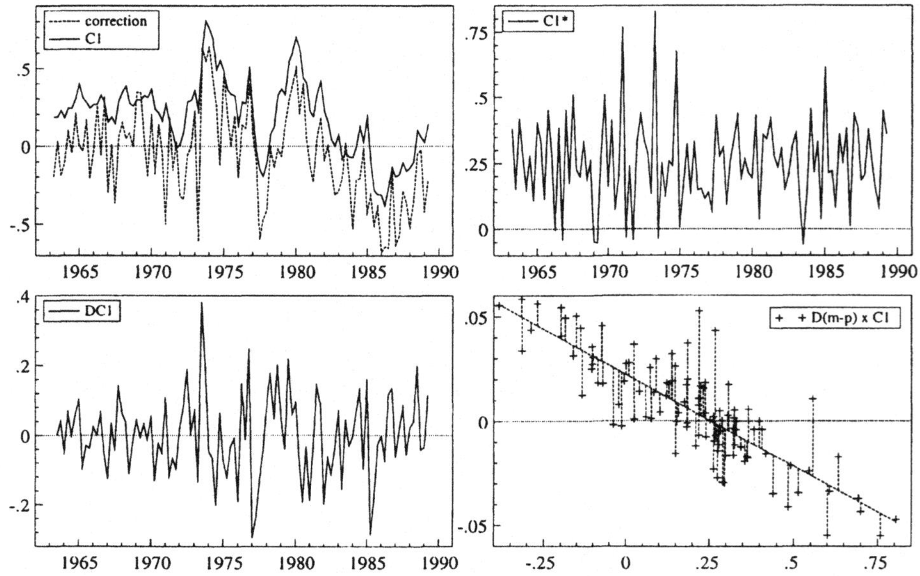

Figure 7. Comparisons of alternative cointegration measures.

Doornik (1994), C_1, and c_1 in (19), are all very similar. Figure 7a records the original and the negative of the additional correction (without any graphical matching), and fig. 7d records the cross plot: as can be seen, there is an almost perfect offset. Figure 7c shows the first difference of C_1, which would be I(0) if the original was I(1).

The coefficient of 11.63 times a feedback of 0.093 is almost precisely unity, hence in equation (6) of Hendry and Ericsson (1991):

$$\Delta(m-p)_t = -0.17\Delta(m-p)_{t-1} - 0.093C_{1,t-1} + \dots, \tag{22}$$

or:

$$\begin{aligned}\Delta^2(m-p)_t &= -1.17\Delta(m-p)_{t-1} - 0.093C_{1,t-1} + \dots \\ &= -0.09\Delta(m-p)_{t-1} - 0.093C^*_{1,t-1} + \dots,\end{aligned} \tag{23}$$

so the I(1) versus I(2) decision turns on the significance of $\Delta(m-p)_{t-1}$. Estimating (23) by OLS reveals a very small effect, even though it was significant in (22). Interestingly, on ADF tests $\Delta(m-p)_t$, $\Delta R_{n,t}$ and $\Delta^2 p_t$ are all I(0) (i.e., the tests reject unit roots at 1% or better), but do not reject for $C_{1,t}$. As (23) shows, if ones keeps $C_{1,t}$, then the coefficient on $\Delta(m-p)_{t-1}$ is less than -1, and if $\Delta(m-p)_t$ is I(0), then $\Delta^2(m-p)_t$ is I(-1), so $\Delta(m-p)_t$ cannot matter for cointegration.

In the I(2) analysis, there is also some evidence for a second cointegrating relation. Rahbek *et al.* (1998) find that the asymptotic probability of rejecting the hypothesis of at most one cointegrating relation, and thereby accepting two such relations, is around 15%. Their second relation has the form:

$$C^*_2 = C_2 + 0.38\Delta(m-p),$$

where the coefficients of C_2 are very similar to those reported in (20). The coefficient of the (possibly) I(1) component, the first differences of real money, is very small as compared with that in the money relation (21): however, the second relation, C_2, appears to be more stable than the first, C_1,

The economic analysis in Section 3.2 suggested that it was more convenient to base an econometric analysis on the variables $m-p$, Δp, i, and R_n. An I(2) analysis of these data confirms this. There is one I(2) trend and one (possibly two) cointegrating relations. The p-values and coefficients are hardly changed from the I(1) analysis. When dummies are included, as discussed in Section 6, the conclusions are similar to those in Hendry and Doornik (1994). This analysis was based on the extension by Jørgensen (1996) to the program CATS by Hansen and Juselius (1994), and also using an Ox routine for testing I(2)-ness (Doornik, 1998b).

10. Long-run weak exogeneity and conditional systems

In a conditional analysis, namely of a system with unmodelled variables, there is a tendency to find more cointegrating relations than in the corresponding closed-system analysis. For the UK money data, this was found in the analysis of Harbo, Johansen, Nielsen and Rahbek (1998).

The joint likelihood of $x_t = (y_t, z_t)$ can always be factorised into the product of the conditional likelihood of y_t given z_t, and the marginal likelihood of z_t. When the parameters of the two likelihood functions vary freely, z_t is said to be weakly exogeneous for the parameters of the conditional likelihood, and, in particular, it is equivalent to maximize the two likelihood functions jointly or separately (see Engle, Hendry and Richard, 1983). For cointegration analysis, Johansen (1995b, Ch. 8) finds that z_t is weakly exogeneous for the cointegration parameter if the adjustment parameter has the form $\alpha' = (\alpha_y', 0)$.

The conditional likelihood can be analysed for cointegration using the 'partial' systems approach of Harbo *et al.* (1998). They consider an analysis of $m-p$ conditional on $(i, \Delta p, R_n)$ assuming the rank is at most unity, as well as $(m-p, \Delta p)$ conditional on (i, R_n) when the rank is at most 2. The dummies are omitted in their analysis, and a lag length of five is chosen. The results are therefore slightly different from those of this paper and Hendry and Doornik (1994).

To test for long-run weak exogeneity in the two-variable conditional model requires testing if α is of the form:

$$\begin{matrix} m-p \\ i \\ \Delta p \\ R_n \end{matrix} \quad \begin{pmatrix} * & * \\ 0 & 0 \\ * & * \\ 0 & 0 \end{pmatrix}.$$

Referring back to Table 6, we see a highly significant feedback coefficient for the second cointegrating vector in the i equation, rejecting this hypothesis in the restricted model. In the unrestricted rank-two model of Tables 3–4, we also reject this form of long-run weak exogeneity: $\chi^2(4) = 10.9^*$ [0.03]. The same result (to the reported accuracy) is obtained when we apply the mis-specification test suggested in Harbo *et al.* (1998). In that case, the significance of the cointegration vectors is tested in a regression of Δi_t and ΔR_{nt} on $\Delta(m-p)_{t-1}$, $\Delta^2 p_{t-1}$, Δi_{t-1}, $\Delta R_{n,t-1}$, $c_{1,t-1}$, $c_{2,t-1}$, 1, t, *doil*, *dout*. When using five lags and without dummies (as in Harbo *et al.*, 1998), the p-value of the test increases to about 30%, and the hypothesis is not rejected.

Table 7. Cointegration analysis, conditional on R_n.

r	0	1	2	3
ℓ	1363.0	1401.7	1408.6	1412.7
μ		0.55	0.13	0.08
$\mathsf{H}_l(r)$		$r=0$	$r\leqslant 1$	$r\leqslant 2$
Trace		101.4**	22.2	8.4
		[0.00]	[0.35]	[0.43]

Long-run weak exogeneity is easily accepted for R_n. The results for the model conditional on R_n are given in Table 7. Now the critical values are changed (the p-values are derived using the Gamma approximation of Doornik, 1998a), and there is slightly stronger support for the hypothesis of two cointegrating vectors.

A valid conditional cointegration analysis should give higher power in determining the cointegration rank. A power analysis can explain this finding. To simplify the argument, consider a three-dimensional DGP such that:

$$\Delta x_{1,t} = -\frac{b}{T} x_{1,t-1} + \nu_{1,t},$$

$$\Delta x_{i,t} = \nu_{i,t} \quad \text{for } i = 2, 3.$$

The asymptotic power of the test for no cointegration in the full system is derived by Johansen (1995b, Chapter 14). The power for the conditional analysis of the first component, given the last two, can be derived correspondingly: also see Phillips (1988). Figure 8 shows that the asymptotic power of the test in a conditional system is considerably higher than for the closed-system test, which explains the tendency to find more cointegrating relations. Table 6 gives the adjustment coefficient for the first cointegrating vector as approximately 0.1. The corresponding value of b is 10 when $T = 100$.

11. Conclusions

The determination of cointegration rank remains a subtle task, dependent on a number of modelling considerations. The introduction listed many of these, and the paper concentrated on seven issues.

First, the treatment of the constant and a deterministic trend in the cointegration formulation. A range of possible models was evaluated analytically and by Monte Carlo simulation. We found that including an unrestricted trend was problematic, and could lead to excess rejection for ranks above that in the DGP. However, a restricted trend in the cointegration space with an unrestricted constant produced

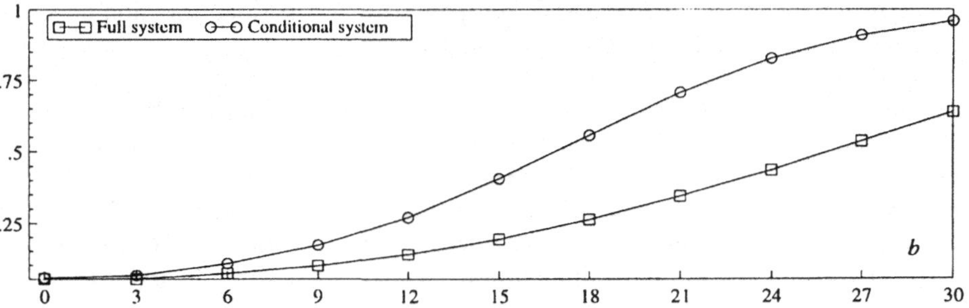

Figure 8. Asymptotic power functions of the test for no cointegration at 5% in a closed and conditional system, $T = 400$, $M = 10\ 000$.

good power, and reasonable size. Moreover, the known asymptotic similarity of this case extended to finite samples in our Monte Carlo, and the same formulation worked well even when the DGP was a special case with no trend, and even no drift. Thus, we recommend commencing the analysis with a linear trend restricted to the cointegration space and an unrestricted constant to ensure (asymptotic) similarity to the nuisance parameters of these effects.

Next, concerning the choice of test statistic, there is a consistent rank-selection procedure for the trace test, even for the extended set of models in Section 4.3. However, for the maximum eigenvalue test, the consistency of the rank-selection procedure has not been established. For the model formulations $\mathsf{H}_l(r)$ in Table 5, trace tests are asymptotically similar with respect to the values taken by the parameters of the deterministic components (assuming the $\mathsf{I}(1)$ conditions are satisfied): see Nielsen and Rahbek (1998). As this does not apply to the extended models, we recommend the sequential trace test based on $\mathsf{H}_l(r)$.

Third, the asymptotic distributions of the test statistics under the null can be well approximated by response surfaces for most case of practical concern. However, their adequacy as a guide to finite samples depends on the unknown values of various nuisance parameters, particularly the presence of roots close to making the process $\mathsf{I}(2)$. Existing finite-sample corrections based on degrees of freedom need not work well, and often over-correct.

Concerning the treatment of impulse indicator variables, we strongly recommend that these be entered unrestrictedly if they are used to establish an estimate of the innovation variance. We certainly advise against their restriction to the cointegration space, and the Appendix suggested an explanation for the results in Hendry and Doornik (1994). However, our analysis is incomplete, and requires extension to other forms of dummy (such as step changes). Also, further analysis is needed of including the integral of a dummy in the cointegration space with the original unrestricted, as some forms of invariance, or similarity, may be present, although new critical values will be needed.

We did not address the selection of lag length in this paper.

Restricted cointegration analysis to estimate identified cointegration relations is straightforward to implement, and yielded interpretable results for our empirical example of UK M1. This allowed standard errors of the cointegration and the feedback coefficients to be calculated. Nevertheless, formal identification depends on having an adequate number of restrictions to impose.

Considerable doubt remains as to whether the UK M1 data are $\mathsf{I}(1)$ or $\mathsf{I}(2)$. We first analyzed them as $\mathsf{I}(1)$ in the space of real money, real expenditure, inflation and nominal net interest rates, and in earlier research developed a congruent model of the four series. However, when (m, p, i, R_n) are treated as $\mathsf{I}(2)$, two $\mathsf{I}(2)$ components have been found, and consistent with that result, when $(m-p, \Delta p, i, R_n)$ are treated as $\mathsf{I}(2)$, one $\mathsf{I}(2)$ component remains. Thus, reduction to $\mathsf{I}(0)$ involves polynomial cointegration, with double differencing of $m-p$. Nevertheless, the resulting model is essentially isomorphic to the earlier specification — a plus for focusing on developing congruent representations.

Finally, we considered recent research on modelling conditional, or 'partial' systems, and noted the care needed to ensure coherent inference. If possible, it seems advisable to first model the complete system, test for long-run weak exogeneity, and only model the conditional system if long-run weak exogeneity is not rejected. This may increase the power of the trace test.

Acknowledgements

Financial support from the UK Economic and Social Research Council under grant R000234954 is gratefully acknowledged. We are grateful to Hans-Martin Krolzig for helpful discussions on the topic. The authors' web pages are respectively: www.nuff.ox.ac.uk/users/doornik/, www.nuff.ox.ac.uk/economics/people/hendry.htm www.nuff.ox.ac.uk/users/nielsen/.

Notes

1. 1000 replications were used in PcNaive: see Hendry, Neale and Ericsson (1991). In figures, 2×2 panels of graphs are notionally labelled a, b; c, d, such that $[^{a\,b}_{c\,d}]$ denotes the location; 3×3 panels as a, b, c; d, e, f; g, h, i; and so on.
2. There remained considerable sampling uncertainty in the MCSD at 1000 replications, so 10,000 were used in panels b and d; that the MCSE underestimates the MCSD may be due to averaging estimated standard errors, rather than variances.
3. The data are supplied with the demo version of PcGive, available from Doornik's web page.
4. A measure of the volatility of income might reflect precautionary demands, but is omitted here: see e.g., Tobin (1958).
5. See e.g., Miller and Orr (1966), Akerlof (1973), Milbourne (1983), and Smith (1986).

References

Akerlof, G. A. (1973) The demand for money: A general equilibrium inventory-theoretic approach. *Review of Economic Studies*, 40, 115–130.

Banerjee, A., Dolado, J. J., Galbraith, J. W., and Hendry, D. F. (1993) *Co-integration, Error Correction and the Econometric Analysis of Non-Stationary Data*. Oxford: Oxford University Press.

Boswijk, H. P. (1992) *Cointegration, Identification and Exogeneity*, Vol. 37 of *Tinbergen Institute Research Series*. Amsterdam: Thesis Publishers.

Boswijk, H. P. (1994) Identifiability of cointegrated systems. Mimeo, Department of Actuarial Sciences and Econometrics, University of Amsterdam.

Breusch, T. S. (1978) Testing for autocorrelation in dynamic linear models. *Australian Economic Papers*, 17, 334–355.

Chow, G. C. (1960) Tests of equality between sets of coefficients in two linear regressions. *Econometrica*, 28, 591–605.

Doornik, J. A. (1995a) Testing general restrictions on the cointegrating space. Mimeo, Nuffield College.

Doornik, J. A. (1995b) Testing vector autocorrelation and heteroscedasticity in dynamic models. Mimeo, Nuffield College.

Doornik, J. A. (1998a) Approximations to the asymptotic distribution of cointegration tests. *Journal of Economic Surveys*, 5, 573–593.

Doornik, J. A. (1998b) *Object-Oriented Matrix Programming using Ox 2.0*. London: Timberlake Consultants Press.

Doornik, J. A., and Hansen, H. (1994) A practical test for univariate and multivariate normality. Discussion paper, Nuffield College.

Doornik, J. A., and Hendry, D. F. (1996) *GiveWin: An Interactive Empirical Modelling Program*. London: Timberlake Consultants Press.

Doornik, J. A., and Hendry, D. F. (1997) *Modelling Dynamic Systems using PcFiml 9 for Windows*. London: Timberlake Consultants Press.

Engle, R. F., and Granger, C. W. J. (1987) Cointegration and error correction: Representation, estimation and testing. *Econometrica*, 55, 251–276.

Engle, R. F., Hendry, D. F., and Richard, J.-F. (1983) Exogeneity. *Econometrica*, 51, 277–304. Reprinted in Hendry, D. F. (1993), *Econometrics: Alchemy or Science?* Oxford: Blackwell Publishers.

Ericsson, N. R., Campos, J., and Tran, H.-A. (1990) PC-GIVE and David Hendry's econometric methodology. *Revista De Econometria*, 10, 7–117.

Ericsson, N. R., Hendry, D. F., and Tran, H.-A. (1994) Cointegration, seasonality, encompassing and the demand for money in the United Kingdom. In Hargreaves, C. (ed.), *Non-stationary Time-series Analysis and Cointegration*, pp. 179–224. Oxford: Oxford University Press.

Godfrey, L. G. (1978) Testing for higher order serial correlation in regression equations when the regressors include lagged dependent variables. *Econometrica*, 46, 1303–1313.

Hamilton, J. D. (1994) *Time Series Analysis*. Princeton: Princeton University Press.

Hansen, H., and Johansen, S. (1992) Recursive estimation in cointegrated VAR-models. Discussion paper, Institute of Mathematical Statistics, University of Copenhagen.

Hansen, H., and Johansen, S. (1998) Some tests for parameter constancy in cointegrated VAR-models. Mimeo, Economics Department, European University Institute.

Hansen, H., and Juselius, K. (1994) Manual to cointegration analysis of time series CATS in RATS. Discussion paper, Estima, Evanston, IL.

Hansen, P. R., and Johansen, S. (1998) *Workbook on Cointegration*. Oxford: Oxford University Press.

Harbo, I., Johansen, S., Nielsen, B., and Rahbek, A. (1998) Asymptotic inference on cointegrating rank in partial systems. Forthcoming, *Journal of Business and Economic Statistics*.

Harris, R. I. D. (1995) *Using Cointegration Analysis in Econometric Modelling*. London: Prentice Hall.

Hatanaka, M. (1996) *Time-Series-Based Econometrics: Unit Roots and Cointegration*. Oxford: Oxford University Press.

Hendry, D. F. (1979) Predictive failure and econometric modelling in macro-economics: The transactions demand for money. In Ormerod, P. (ed.), *Economic Modelling*, pp. 217–242. London: Heinemann. Reprinted in Hendry, D. F. (1993), *Econometrics: Alchemy or Science?* Oxford: Blackwell Publishers.

Hendry, D. F. (1985) Monetary economic myth and econometric reality. *Oxford Review of Economic Policy*, 1, 72–84. Reprinted in Hendry, D. F. (1993), *Econometrics: Alchemy or Science?* Oxford: Blackwell Publishers.

Hendry, D. F. (1995) *Dynamic Econometrics*. Oxford: Oxford University Press.

Hendry, D. F., and Doornik, J. A. (1994) Modelling linear dynamic econometric systems. *Scottish Journal of Political Economy*, 41, 1–33.

Hendry, D. F., and Ericsson, N. R. (1991) Modeling the demand for narrow money in the United Kingdom and the United States. *European Economic Review*, 35, 833–886.

Hendry, D. F., and Mizon, G. E. (1993) Evaluating dynamic econometric models by encompassing the VAR. In Phillips, P. C. B. (ed.), *Models, Methods and Applications of Econometrics*, pp. 272–300. Oxford: Basil Blackwell.

Hendry, D. F., Neale, A. J., and Ericsson, N. R. (1991) *PC-NAIVE, An Interactive Program for Monte Carlo Experimentation in Econometrics. Version 6.0*. Oxford: Institute of Economics and Statistics, University of Oxford.

Hillmer, S. (1984). Monitoring and adjusting forecasts in the presence of additive outliers. *Journal of Forecasting*, 3, 205–215.

Johansen, S. (1988) Statistical analysis of cointegration vectors. *Journal of Economic Dynamics and Control*, 12, 231–254.

Johansen, S. (1992a) A representation of vector autoregressive processes integrated of order 2. *Econometric Theory*, 8, 188–202.

Johansen, S. (1992b) Testing weak exogeneity and the order of cointegration in UK money demand. *Journal of Policy Modeling*, 14, 313–334.

Johansen, S. (1994) The role of the constant and linear terms in cointegration analysis of nonstationary variables. *Econometric Reviews*, 13, 205–229.

Johansen, S. (1995a) Identifying restrictions of linear equations with applications to simultaneous equations and cointegration. *Journal of Econometrics*, 69, 111–132.

Johansen, S. (1995b) *Likelihood-based Inference in Cointegrated Vector Autoregressive Models*. Oxford: Oxford University Press.

Johansen, S., and Nielsen, B. (1993) Asymptotics for cointegration rank tests in the presence of intervention dummies — manual for the simulation program DisCo. http://www.math.ku.dk/~sjo, University of Copenhagen, Institute of Mathematical Statistics, Copenhagen.

Jørgensen, C. (1996) I(2) cointegration procedure for CATS. http://www.estima.com/procs/ i2index.htm, University of Copenhagen, Institute of Mathematical Statistics, Copenhagen.

Ledolter, J. (1989) The effect of additive outliers on the forecasts from ARIMA models. *International Journal of Forecasting*, 5, 231–240.

Milbourne, R. (1983) Optimal money holding under uncertainty. *International Economic Review*, 24, 685–698.

Miller, M. H., and Orr, D. (1966) A model of the demand for money by firms. *Quarterly Journal of Economics*, 80, 735–759.

Nielsen, B. (1997a) Bartlett correction of the unit root test in autoregressive models. *Biometrika*, 84, 500–504.

Nielsen, B. (1997b) On the distribution of tests for cointegration rank. Discussion paper, Nuffield College, Oxford.

Nielsen, B., and Rahbek, A. (1998) Similarity issues in cointegration analysis. Mimeo, Nuffield College, Oxford.

Osterwald-Lenum, M. (1992) A note with quantiles of the asymptotic distribution of the ML cointegration rank test statistics. *Oxford Bulletin of Economics and Statistics*, 54, 461–472.

Pantula, S. G. (1989) Testing for unit roots in time series data. *Econometric Theory*, 5, 256–271.

Paroulo, P. (1996) On the determination of integration indices in I(2) systems. *Journal of Econometrics*, 72, 313–356.

Phillips, P. C. B. (1988) Regression theory for near-integrated time series. *Econometrica*, 56, 1021–1043.

Phillips, P. C. B., and Solo, V. (1992) Asymptotics of linear processes. *Annals of Statistics*, 20, 971–1001.

Rahbek, A., Kongsted, H. C., and Jørgensen, C. (1998) Trend-stationarity in the I(2) cointegration model. Forthcoming, *Journal of Econometrics*.

Rahbek, A., and Mosconi, R. (1998) The role of stationary regressors in the cointegration test. Mimeo 1998, University of Copenhagen, Institute of Mathematical Statistics, Copenhagen.

Reimers, H.-E. (1992) Comparisons of tests for multivariate cointegration. *Statistical Papers*, 33, 335–359.

Reinsel, G. C., and Ahn, S. K. (1992) Vector autoregressive models with unit roots and reduced rank structure, estimation, likelihood ratio tests, and forecasting. *Journal of Time Series Analysis*, 13, 353–375.

Smith, G. W. (1986) A dynamic Baumol-Tobin model of money demand. *Review of Economic Studies*, 53, 465–469.
Tobin, J. (1958) Liquidity preference as behavior toward risk. *Review of Economic Studies*, 25, 65–86.
White, H. (1980) A heteroskedastic-consistent covariance matrix estimator and a direct test for heteroskedasticity. *Econometrica*, 48, 817–838.

12. Appendix: Some analytical results

12.1. *Illustration of the models of trend behaviour*

Test for $\mathsf{H}_{ql}(r)$ *against* $\mathsf{H}_{ql}(n)$ *when the DGP is* $\mathsf{H}_l(s)$
When $\alpha_\perp'\phi = 0$, so the assumption $\alpha_\perp'\phi \neq 0$ is not satisfied, the standard asymptotic distribution does not apply. Instead, if $r < \text{rank}(\pi)$, then the power converges to unity; otherwise $(r \geqslant \text{rank}(\pi))$, the limit distribution of the trace test is given by the distribution of the sum of the $n - r$ smallest eigenvalues of:

$$\int_0^1 \mathrm{dB}_u \mathrm{F}_u' \left(\int_0^1 \mathrm{F}_u \mathrm{F}_u' \mathrm{d}u \right)^{-1} \int_0^1 \mathrm{F}_u \mathrm{dB}_u'. \tag{24}$$

Here B_u is an n-rank(π) dimensional standard Brownian motion, and F_u is B_u corrected for a linear trend and a constant.

Simulations indicate that when $r = \text{rank}(\pi)$, the distribution in (24) is stochastically larger than that for $\alpha_\perp'\phi \neq 0$ (given in Johansen, 1995b, Theorem 11.1 and Table 15.5). On the other hand, the distribution is smaller than that which applies when testing $\mathsf{H}_l(r)$ in $\mathsf{H}_l(n)$ (*op. cit.*, Table 15.4).

Test for $\mathsf{H}_{lc}(r)$ *against* $\mathsf{H}_{lc}(n)$ *when the DGP is* $\mathsf{H}_l(s)$
The power of this mis-specified test converges to unity if $r < \text{rank}(\pi) - 1$, and to a constant less than unity if $r \geqslant \text{rank}(\pi) - 1$, provided the $\mathsf{I}(1)$ conditions are satisfied. The constant depends on a number of nuisance parameters, which we illustrate for a bivariate case.

Consider a bivariate DGP with one cointegrating vector and a restricted trend:

$$\Delta \mathrm{x}_t = \begin{pmatrix} 0 & 0 \\ 0 & -1 \end{pmatrix} \mathrm{x}_{t-1} + \begin{pmatrix} \phi \\ 0 \end{pmatrix} + \begin{pmatrix} 0 \\ \rho \end{pmatrix} t + \nu_t \quad \text{where} \quad \nu_t \sim \mathsf{IN}_2[0, \mathrm{I}].$$

The model H_{lc} is analysed by a two-step procedure. First, $\Delta \mathrm{x}_t$ and x_{t-1} are corrected for the intercept, giving the residuals R_0 and R_1:

$$\mathrm{R}_0 = \Delta \mathrm{x}_t | 1 = \begin{cases} \nu_{1t} - \bar{\nu}_{1t}, \\ \Delta\nu_{2t} - \Delta\bar{\nu}_{2t}, \end{cases}$$

$$\mathrm{R}_1 = \mathrm{x}_{t-1} | 1 = \begin{cases} \phi(t - \bar{t}) + \varsigma_{t-1} - \bar{\varsigma}, \\ \rho(t - \bar{t}) + \nu_{2t} - \bar{\nu}_{2t}, \end{cases}$$

where $\varsigma_t = \sum_{i=1}^t \nu_{1t}$. Next, the empirical canonical correlations of R_0 and R_1 are found as the solutions to the eigenvalue problem:

$$|\lambda \mathrm{S}_{00} - \mathrm{S}_{01}\mathrm{S}_{11}^{-1}\mathrm{S}_{10}| = 0, \tag{25}$$

where $\mathrm{S}_{ij} = T^{-1}\mathrm{R}_i'\mathrm{R}_j$ (the product-moment matrices of the residuals).

For the asymptotic analysis, let B_u be a univariate standard Brownian motion and let:

$$\bar{B} = \int_0^1 B_u \mathrm{d}u.$$

Further, for $\rho \neq 0$, define:

$$\mathrm{A} = \begin{pmatrix} (\phi^2+\rho^2)\sqrt{T} & 0 \\ 0 & -\rho \end{pmatrix}^{-1} \begin{pmatrix} \phi & \rho \\ -\rho & \phi \end{pmatrix},$$

so that:

$$\mathrm{AR}_1 = \begin{cases} \dfrac{1}{\sqrt{T}}(t-\bar{t}) + \dfrac{\phi}{\sqrt{T}(\phi^2+\rho^2)}(\varsigma_{t-1}-\bar{\varsigma}) + \dfrac{\rho}{\sqrt{T}(\phi^2+\rho^2)}(\nu_{2t}-\bar{\nu}_{2t}), \\ (\varsigma_{t-1}-\bar{\varsigma}) - \dfrac{\phi}{\rho}(\nu_{2t}-\bar{\nu}_{2t}), \end{cases}$$

and similarly for AR_0.

Then, by the analysis of linear processes in Phillips and Solo (1992):

$$T^{-1}\mathrm{AS}_{11}\mathrm{A}' \xrightarrow{\mathcal{D}} \int_0^1 \begin{pmatrix} (u-\frac{1}{2}) \\ (B_u-\bar{B}) \end{pmatrix} \begin{pmatrix} (u-\frac{1}{2}) \\ (B_u-\bar{B}) \end{pmatrix}' \mathrm{d}u,$$

$$\mathrm{AS}_{10} \xrightarrow{\mathcal{D}} \begin{pmatrix} \int_0^1 (u-\frac{1}{2})\mathrm{d}B_u & 0 \\ \int_0^1 (B_u-\bar{B})\mathrm{d}B_u & \phi/\rho \end{pmatrix},$$

$$\mathrm{S}_{00} \xrightarrow{\mathcal{P}} \begin{pmatrix} 1 & 0 \\ 0 & 2 \end{pmatrix},$$

since:

$$T^{-3}\sum(t-\bar{t})^2 \to \int(u-\tfrac{1}{2})^2\mathrm{d}u, \qquad \sum(t-\bar{t})(\nu_{2t}-\bar{\nu}_{2t}) = O_p(T^{3/2}),$$
$$T^{-5/2}\sum(t-\bar{t})(\varsigma_{t-1}-\bar{\varsigma}) \to \int(u-\tfrac{1}{2})(B_u-\bar{B})\mathrm{d}u, \qquad \sum(\varsigma_{t-1}-\bar{\varsigma})(\nu_{2t}-\bar{\nu}_{2t}) = O_p(T),$$
$$T^{-2}\sum(\varsigma_{t-1}-\bar{\varsigma})^2 \to \int(B_u-\bar{B})^2\mathrm{d}u, \qquad \sum(\nu_{2t}-\bar{\nu}_{2t})^2 = O_p(T),$$

and

$$T^{-3/2}\sum(t-\bar{t})\nu_{1t} \to \int(u-\tfrac{1}{2})\mathrm{d}B_{\mathrm{u}}, \qquad \sum(t-\bar{t})\Delta\nu_{2t} = O_p(T),$$
$$T^{-1}\sum(\varsigma_{t-1}-\bar{\varsigma})\nu_{1t} \to \int(B_u-\bar{B})\mathrm{d}B_{\mathrm{u}}, \qquad \sum(\varsigma_{t-1}-\bar{\varsigma})\Delta\nu_{2t} = O_p(T^{1/2}),$$
$$\sum(\nu_{2t}-\bar{\nu}_{2t})\nu_{1t} = O_p(T^{1/2}), \qquad \sum(\nu_{2t}-\bar{\nu}_{2t})\Delta\nu_{2t} = -T + O_p(T^{1/2}).$$

By substituting these asymptotic results into the eigenvalue problem (25), it can be shown that both eigenvalues converge to zero at a rate of $1/T$. So when testing $\mathsf{H}_{lc}(0)$, the power does not converge to unity, but to a constant which is smaller than unity: compare with the power function for the test of $\mathsf{H}_{lc}(1)$ in fig. 3. Moreover, the asymptotic distribution of $T\lambda_1, T\lambda_2$ depends on the ratio ϕ/ρ.

Figure 3 illustrates that, for certain values of ϕ, the rejection frequency of the test of $\mathsf{H}_{lc}(\text{rank}\pi - 1)$ could converge to a level which is larger than the nominal size. This is not generally the case for all values of ϕ. If actually $\phi = 0$ and $\rho \neq 0$, then the rejection frequency for the test of $\mathsf{H}_{lc}(0)$ against $\mathsf{H}_{lc}(2)$ converges to zero. The reason is that the smallest eigenvalue converges to zero at rate $1/T^2$, and the largest eigenvalue, normalized by T, converges to the asymptotic distribution of the test for $\mathsf{H}_c(0)$ against $\mathsf{H}_c(1)$ in a well-specified model. So, the test for $\mathsf{H}_{lc}(0)$ against $\mathsf{H}_{lc}(2)$ for the above DGP has the same asymptotic distribution, which is tabulated as the entry for one degree of freedom in Johansen (1995b, Table 15.1). The postulated result is then found by comparison of this distribution with the standard asymptotic distribution for the test for $\mathsf{H}_{lc}(0)$ against $\mathsf{H}_{lc}(2)$ (*op. cit.*, Table 15.3).

Test for $\mathsf{H}_c(r)$ *against* $\mathsf{H}_c(n)$ *when the DGP is* $\mathsf{H}_l(s)$

The first asymptotic observation concerning this test is that the power converges to unity if $r < \text{rank}(\pi)$ and to a constant less than unity otherwise, provided that the $\mathsf{I}(1)$ conditions are satisfied. However, for certain values of the nuisance parameter, the convergence of the test for $\mathsf{H}_c(\text{rank}\pi)$ is rather slow. This feature is seen in fig. 3 for the test of $\mathsf{H}_c(1)$. The DGP of the previous argument is considered again.

The statistical analysis is based on the squared empirical canonical correlations of $\Delta \mathrm{x}_t$ and the vector of x_{t-1} and 1. Because of invariance, the latter vector can be replaced by that of x_{t-1} corrected for 1, and 1. The new residual matrices are denoted S^*_{ij}. Now, define s_0 as:

$$\mathrm{s}_0 = \frac{1}{T}\sum_{t=1}^{T} \Delta \mathrm{x}_t = \begin{pmatrix} \phi \\ \rho \end{pmatrix} + \frac{1}{T}\sum_{t=1}^{T} \begin{pmatrix} \nu_{1,t} \\ \Delta \nu_{2,t} \end{pmatrix} = \begin{pmatrix} \phi \\ \rho \end{pmatrix} + O_p(1/\sqrt{T}),$$

then:

$$\mathrm{S}^*_{11} = \begin{pmatrix} \mathrm{S}_{11} & 0 \\ 0 & 1 \end{pmatrix}, \quad \mathrm{S}^*_{10} = \begin{pmatrix} \mathrm{S}_{10} \\ \mathrm{s}_0' \end{pmatrix}, \quad \mathrm{S}^*_{00} = \mathrm{S}_{00} + \mathrm{s}_0\mathrm{s}_0',$$

so the eigenvalue problem is given by:

$$\begin{aligned} 0 &= |\lambda \mathrm{S}^*_{00} - \mathrm{S}^*_{01}\mathrm{S}^{*-1}_{11}\mathrm{S}^*_{10}| \\ &= |(\lambda - 1)\mathrm{s}_0\mathrm{s}_0' + \lambda \mathrm{S}_{00} - \mathrm{S}_{01}\mathrm{S}_{11}^{-1}\mathrm{S}_{10}|. \end{aligned}$$

Thus, one eigenvalue converges to a non-zero constant, whereas the smallest, normalized by T, converges to a distribution involving various nuisance parameters. It also follows that, if $\mathrm{s}_0\mathrm{s}_0'$ is small relative to S_{00}, then the convergence of the largest eigenvalue could be rather slow.

A corresponding result holds for general processes as in (10). A more detailed representation of the process than that given by Johansen (1995b, Theorem 4.2) yields:

$$s_0 \xrightarrow{\mathcal{P}} C\phi - (C\Gamma + I_r)\beta(\beta'\beta)^{-1}\rho,$$

where $C = \beta_{\perp}(\alpha_{\perp}'\Gamma\beta_{\perp})^{-1}\alpha_{\perp}'$, and, for a process with two lags, $\Gamma = -(I_n - \Pi + \pi)$: see Appendix A of Rahbek and Mosconi (1998). For the DGP (17), both ρ_l and $\alpha_{\perp}'\phi_c$ are rather small.

12.2. *Dummies*

12.2.1. *Unit-root test in a model with an unrestricted dummy*

It is of interest to find out whether the distribution of the test depends on the parameter of the dummy. From the following analysis, it is concluded that the asymptotic distribution does not depend on a nuisance parameter unless this parameter is of a size proportional to the square root of the sample size. Since dummies are often used in connection with big outliers, this indicates that the finite-sample distribution would be affected.

Consider the univariate DGP:

$$\Delta x_t = \psi 1_{\{t=T_b\}} + \nu_t \quad \text{where } \nu_t \sim \mathsf{IN}[0, \sigma_\nu^2] \tag{26}$$

when $t = 1, \ldots, T$ and $1 < T_b < T$. The unit-root test is based on the squared correlation of Δx_t and x_{t-1} where both are corrected for $1_{\{t=T_b\}}$. We set $\sigma_\nu^2 = 1$.

The case of large dummies is considered first. Introduce the scaled parameter $\delta = \psi/\sqrt{T}$ and the univariate Brownian motion B_u. Then the asymptotic behaviour of the residual matrix, for fixed δ, is given by:

$$\begin{aligned}
S_{00} &= \frac{1}{T}\sum_{t \neq T_b} (\Delta x_t)^2 \quad \xrightarrow{\mathcal{P}} 1 \\
S_{10} &= \frac{1}{T}\sum_{t \neq T_b} x_{t-1}\Delta x_t \xrightarrow{\mathcal{D}} \int_0^1 B_u \mathrm{d}B_u + \delta(B_1 - B_b) = G \text{ (say)}, \\
S_{11} &= \frac{1}{T^2}\sum_{t \neq T_b} x_{t-1}^2 \quad \xrightarrow{\mathcal{D}} \int_0^1 (B_u + \delta 1_{\{u \geq b\}})^2 \mathrm{d}u = H \text{ (say)}.
\end{aligned} \tag{27}$$

In (27), B_1 and B_b are the values at full sample and the proportion b. Therefore the distribution of the unit-root test is asymptotically equivalent to

$$T\lambda = TS_{00}^{-1}S_{01}S_{11}^{-1}S_{10} \xrightarrow{\mathcal{D}} \frac{G^2}{H}.$$

This also indicates that for small dummies, for fixed ψ, the usual asymptotic distribution without nuisance parameters applies.

12.2.2. *Unit-root test in a model with a restricted dummy*

A well-specified model of this type may lead to similar tests, although these are based on non-standard distributions. A general model to consider in this case is given by:

$$\Delta x_t = \pi' \begin{pmatrix} x_{t-1} \\ 1 \\ 1_{\{t=T_b\}} \end{pmatrix} + \psi \Delta 1_{\{t=T_b\}} + \nu_t.$$

This would allow for processes with a 'blip' in all components at time T_b. However, to simplify the algebra, we consider a simpler situation, where the conclusion is basically the same.

Consider the DGP:

$$\Delta x_t = \nu_t.$$

This will be analysed using the squared multiple correlation, λ, of Δx_t and the vector $(x_{t-1}, 1_{\{t=T_b\}})$. Due to invariance, x_{t-1} can be replaced by x_{t-1} corrected for the dummy. The residual matrices are:

$$S_{00} = \frac{1}{T} \sum_{t \neq T_b} (\Delta x_t)^2 \xrightarrow{\mathcal{P}} 1,$$

$$\begin{pmatrix} 1 & 0 \\ 1 & T \end{pmatrix} S_{10} = \begin{pmatrix} \frac{1}{T} \sum_{t \neq T_b} x_{t-1} \Delta x_t \\ \Delta x_{T_b} \end{pmatrix} \xrightarrow{\mathcal{D}} \begin{pmatrix} \int_0^1 B_u \mathrm{d}B_u \\ \nu_{T_b} \end{pmatrix},$$

$$\frac{1}{T} \begin{pmatrix} 1 & 0 \\ 1 & T \end{pmatrix} S_{11} \begin{pmatrix} 1 & 0 \\ 1 & T \end{pmatrix} = \begin{pmatrix} \frac{1}{T^2} \sum_{t \neq T_b} x_{t-1}^2 & 0 \\ 0 & 1 \end{pmatrix} \xrightarrow{\mathcal{D}} \begin{pmatrix} \int_0^1 B_u^2 \mathrm{d}u & 0 \\ 0 & 1 \end{pmatrix},$$

Consequently:

$$T\lambda \xrightarrow{\mathcal{D}} \frac{\left(\int_0^1 B_u \mathrm{d}B_u \right)^2}{\int_0^1 B_u^2 \mathrm{d}u} + \nu_{T_b}^2. \tag{28}$$

This is the usual asymptotic unit-root statistic plus an extra term, which has an expected value of unity. There are three points to be made.

First, the two asymptotic terms in (28) are independent. This is seen by noting that $x_t = \sum_{i=1}^{t} \nu_i$ and introducing $x_t^* = x_t - \nu_{T_b} 1_{\{t > T_b\}}$. Then:

$$\frac{1}{T} \sum_{t \neq T_b} x_{t-1} \Delta x_t = \frac{1}{T} \sum_{t \neq T_b} x_{t-1}^* \Delta x_t + \frac{\nu_{T_b}}{\sqrt{T}} T^{-1/2} \sum_{t > T_b} \nu_t.$$

The first term is independent of ν_{T_b}, whereas the second term is asymptotically negligible. Correspondingly:

$$\frac{1}{T^2}\sum_{t\neq T_b} x_{t-1}^2 = \frac{1}{T^2}\sum_{t\neq T_b} x_{t-1}^{*2} + \frac{2\nu_{T_b}}{\sqrt{T}}\, T^{-3/2}\sum_{t>T_b} x_{t-1} + \frac{\nu_{T_b}^2}{T}\, T^{-1}\sum_{t>T_b} 1.$$

Again the first term is independent of ν_{T_b}, and the last two terms are asymptotically negligible.

Secondly, a model with (say) two dummies would result in the addition of an extra independent term in (28), again with an expectation of unity. We checked this result using the Monte Carlo in Section 6.4 when there were no breaks in the DGP. Figure 9 shows the rejection frequencies when restricting dummies to the cointegration space, and increasing the number of impulses added to the model. The size of the test of $r = 2$ when $\text{rank}(\pi) = 2$ grows towards unity in this four-variable system. Indeed, the means of the test statistics increased essentially linearly in $n - r$ as Table 8 shows. The columns correspond roughly to n, $n - 1$ and $n - 2$, as anticipated from (28).

Finally, the asymptotic distribution does not depend on the location in the sample of the dummy.

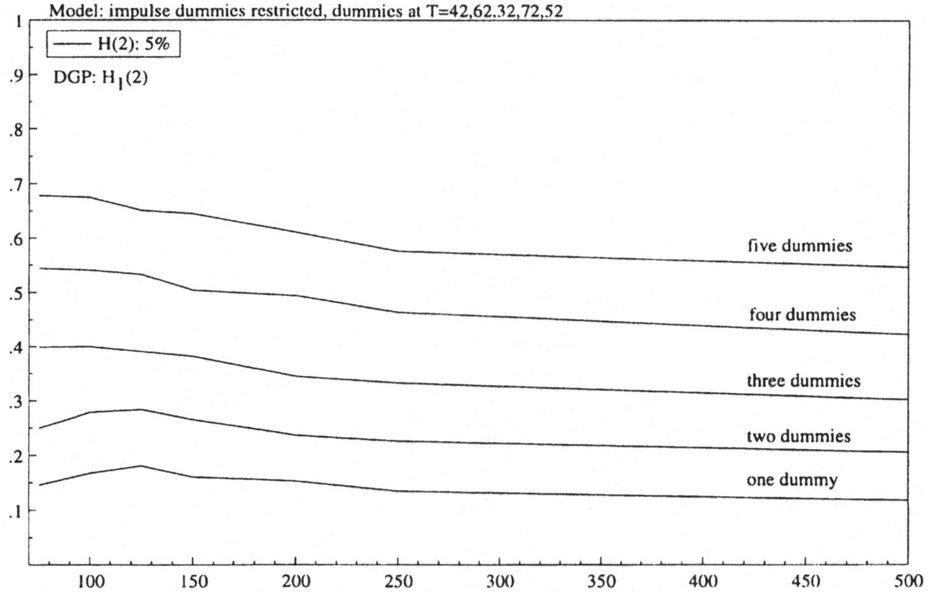

Figure 9. Rejection frequencies with restricted dummies in the model but none in the DGP.

Table 8. Increments in means of test statistics.

dummies	$\mathsf{H}_l(0)$	$\mathsf{H}_l(1)$	$\mathsf{H}_l(2)$
0	0.00	0.00	0.00
1	4.24	3.18	2.08
2	4.03	3.04	1.96
3	4.07	2.95	1.92
4	4.18	3.17	2.06
5	4.03	3.05	1.99

12.2.3. *Unit-root test in a model with a mis-specified restricted dummy*

This example illustrates a possible explanation for the results reported in Hendry and Doornik (1994, Table 4): a dummy in the non-stationary component is modelled using a dummy which only occurs in the cointegration space. The conclusion from the analysis below is quite dramatic. The asymptotic distribution of the test depends on nuisance parameters, and in case of large dummies, the test is not consistent.

Consider the DGP (26). This is analyzed using the squared multiple correlation, λ, of Δx_t and of the vector $(x_{t-1}, 1_{\{t=T_b\}})$. The results of Section 12.2.1 are therefore of relevance again. The residual matrices are given by:

$$S^*_{00} = \frac{1}{T}\sum_{t=T_b}(\Delta x_t)^2 \overset{\mathcal{P}}{\longrightarrow} 1+\rho^2, \quad \mathsf{S}^*_{10} = \begin{pmatrix} S_{10} \\ \Delta x_{T_b}/T \end{pmatrix}, \quad \mathsf{S}^*_{11} = \begin{pmatrix} S_{11} & 0 \\ 0 & 1 \end{pmatrix}.$$

Using the scaling matrix:

$$\mathsf{M}_T = \begin{pmatrix} 1/\sqrt{T} & 0 \\ 0 & \sqrt{T} \end{pmatrix},$$

for large values of ψ, i.e., fixed values of $\delta = \psi/\sqrt{T}$:

$$\begin{aligned} \lambda &= S^{*-1}_{00}\mathsf{S}^*_{01}\mathsf{S}^{*-1}_{00}\mathsf{S}^*_{10} \\ &= S^{*-1}_{00}\mathsf{S}^*_{01}\mathsf{M}_T(\mathsf{M}_T\mathsf{S}^*_{11}\mathsf{M}_T)^{-1}\mathsf{M}_T\mathsf{S}^*_{10} \\ &\overset{\mathcal{P}}{\longrightarrow} (1+\delta^2)^{-1}\begin{pmatrix} 0 \\ \delta \end{pmatrix}'\begin{pmatrix} G & 0 \\ 0 & 1 \end{pmatrix}^{-1}\begin{pmatrix} 0 \\ \delta \end{pmatrix} = \frac{\delta^2}{1+\delta^2}, \end{aligned}$$

so that the test statistic, which is asymptotically equivalent to $T\lambda$, diverges to infinity.

It can be seen that for small values of the dummy parameter, the asymptotic distribution of the test involves a nuisance parameter.

APPROXIMATIONS TO THE ASYMPTOTIC DISTRIBUTIONS OF COINTEGRATION TESTS

Jurgen A. Doornik

Nuffield College, Oxford

Abstract. The asymptotic distributions of cointegration tests are approximated using the Gamma distribution. The tests considered are for the I(1), the conditional I(1), as well as the I(2) model. Formulae for the parameters of the Gamma distributions are derived from response surfaces. The resulting approximation is flexible, easy to implement and more accurate than the standard tables previously published.

Keywords. Cointegration tests; Conditional model; Gamma distribution; I(1); I(2); Partial system; Trend stationarity.

1. Introduction

Cointegration analysis is now a standard tool for the applied econometrician. A commonly used procedure is to test the rank of the long-run matrix using the maximum likelihood procedure of Johansen (1988, 1995a). The distributions of the test statistics involve integrals of Brownian motions, for which no closed-form expressions are available (but see Abadir, 1995, on the univariate Dickey-Fuller distribution). Consequently, tables have been published for specific quantiles, based on simulation experiments. Current regression packages do not report p-values, but usually list the 95% quantile, based on the published tables (or perhaps on a response surface fitted to the tables, as in PcFiml, see Doornik and Hendry, 1997). However, for Monte Carlo experiments, as well as for applied modellers, it would be useful to be able to compute p-values and quantiles easily. This paper addresses that need.

There is an increasing awareness that non-standard distributions need to be approximated in a form which can be readily implemented on a computer, as shown by, for example, MacKinnon (1991, 1996) and Hansen (1997). However, the approximations in the last two papers involve 21 000 and 9 000 coefficients respectively. In comparison, the approximations in this paper use fewer than 150 coefficients, and only a few lines of additional computer code. This makes it especially suitable for econometric computer programs.

Johansen (1988, p. 239) noted that a 'surprisingly accurate description' of the distribution of the likelihood ratio test (without deterministic variables) is obtained by a scaled χ^2 distribution. Subsequently, Nielsen (1997a) found that, in a single equation model, a Gamma distribution is a remarkably good approximation to the asymptotic distribution (at least for quantiles $\geqslant 0.5$). In that case, the distribution being approximated corresponds to the squared Dickey-Fuller distribution. Since the Dickey-Fuller is close to a t-distribution with bias, the square resembles a non-central χ^2 distribution. This, in turn, can be closely approximated by a Gamma distribution. The χ^2 distribution, which arises for the likelihood-ratio test in a standard setting, is a special case of the Gamma distribution.

In this paper we confirm that the Gamma distribution works very well as an approximation to the tests for cointegration rank. We proceed to derive formulae to compute the two parameters of the Gamma distribution, based on a response surface analysis of Monte Carlo experiments. The fitted Gamma distributions can be used to compute p-values and quantiles of the cointegration tests. It is shown that the proposed approximate procedure is easily used in practice, and more accurate than previously published tables. It is important to note that this paper is not concerned with the small-sample distribution of the cointegration tests (although it is discussed), but primarily considers the asymptotic distributions. Indeed, the asymptotic distribution may not be very reliable in small samples, see, e.g. Nielsen (1997b).

The next section introduces the I(1) tests, and discusses the tables available to date. The usefulness of the Gamma distribution to approximate the asymptotic distribution is illustrated in Section 3. Sections 4–5 introduce the design of the simulation experiments and discuss the trade-off between the number of replications and the sample size. The main result for the I(1) models is presented in Section 6; the effect of sample size on the asymptotic distributions is modelled in Section 7. Then Section 8 treats the test statistics in the I(2) case; Section 9 applies the procedure to conditional ('partial') systems. Finally, Section 10 gives some examples. The core tables are presented in the Appendix.

2. The I(1) analysis

Two test forms are considered in the I(1) case: the trace and maximum-eigenvalue (also called λ-max) statistics for testing the rank of the cointegrating space. In the simplest case, the former is a test for $\Pi = 0$ in:

$$\Delta X_t = \Pi X_{t-1} + \Phi q_t + \varepsilon_t, \qquad t = 1, \ldots, T, \tag{1}$$

where X_t is an n-dimensional vector, X_0 fixed, and ε_t IID multivariate normal, see Johansen (1988, 1995a). The deterministic components are contained in q_t.

The maximum likelihood method proposed by Johansen (1988) writes $\Pi = \alpha\beta'$, where α and β are $n \times p$ matrices. At this stage I(2)-ness is ruled out. If there are additional lagged differences (and non-modelled variables, see Section 9) in (1), these are partialled out from ΔX_t and X_{t-1}, giving r_{0t} and r_{1t}. In stacked notation: $R_0' = r_{01} \ldots r_{0T}$.

The likelihood is maximized by solving the generalized eigenvalue problem:

$$|\lambda S_{11} - S_{10} S_{00}^{-1} S_{01}| = 0,$$

writing $S_{ij} = R_i' R_j$, for $i, j = 0, 1$. This gives n eigenvalues $1 > \hat{\lambda}_1 > \ldots > \hat{\lambda}_n > 0$. The trace statistic $\mathsf{T}(p)$ tests whether Π has rank $\leqslant p$, given that it has rank n or less: $\mathsf{H}(p)|\mathsf{H}(n)$. The maximum-eigenvalue statistic $\mathsf{M}(p)$ tests for rank $\leqslant p$ given that the rank is $p+1$ or less: $\mathsf{H}(p)|\mathsf{H}(p+1)$. The trace and maximum-eigenvalue test statistics are:

$$\begin{aligned} \mathsf{T}(p) &= -T\sum_{i=p+1}^{n}\log(1-\hat{\lambda}_i), \\ \mathsf{M}(p) &= -T\log(1-\hat{\lambda}_{p+1}). \end{aligned} \tag{2}$$

The asymptotic distributions are unaffected by the presence of $\mathsf{I}(0)$ components, so the distribution of $\mathsf{H}(p)|\mathsf{H}(n)$ equals that of $\mathsf{H}(0)|\mathsf{H}(n-p)$. The implication is that, to simulate the distributions, we only need to consider $\mathsf{H}(0)|\mathsf{H}(n)$ and $\mathsf{H}(0)|\mathsf{H}(1)$, corresponding to:

$$\begin{aligned} \mathsf{T}(0) &= -T\sum_{i=1}^{n}\log(1-\hat{\lambda}_i), \\ \mathsf{M}(0) &= -T\log(1-\hat{\lambda}_1). \end{aligned}$$

Therefore, when discussing the simulation experiments we shall use n, but in practical settings and in the tables this will be replaced by $n-p$. Johansen (1995a, Theorem 11.1) gives the limit distribution of the trace test as:

$$\mathrm{tr}\left\{\int (dB)F'\left[\int FF'\,\mathrm{d}u\right]^{-1}\int F(dB)'\right\}. \tag{3}$$

Here, B is a Brownian motion, and F depends on B and the adopted model for deterministic terms.

We consider five models for the deterministic variables Φq_t. Using the notation of Doornik, Hendry and Nielsen (1998):

	Constant	Trend	Model: $\Pi = \alpha\beta'$ and $\Delta X_t =$
H_{ql}	unrestricted	unrestricted	$\Pi X_{t-1} + \mu + \tau t + \varepsilon_t$
H_l	unrestricted	restricted	$\Pi X_{t-1} + \mu + \alpha\tau_p t + \varepsilon_t$
H_{lc}	unrestricted	none	$\Pi X_{t-1} + \mu + \varepsilon_t$
H_c	restricted	none	$\Pi X_{t-1} + \alpha\mu_p + \varepsilon_t$
H_z	none	none	$\Pi X_{t-1} + \varepsilon_t$

In practice, the main interest is in H_l (see Doornik *et al.*, 1998 and the references therein). When the constant or trend is unrestricted, these are partialled out together with the lagged differences. Any restricted variable is appended to X_{t-1}, increasing the number of rows in β by one (and adding an eigenvalue of zero in the analysis). Combined with the models of trending behaviour, there are 10 test statistics to tabulate: $\mathsf{T}_x(0)$ and $\mathsf{M}_x(0)$ for $x = ql, l, lc, c, z$.

The first tables were published in Johansen (1988) and Johansen and Juselius (1990). Until recently, the most widely used tables were those constructed by Osterwald-Lenum (1992). Updated versions are in Johansen (1995a), computed with Bent Nielsen's disco program (Johansen and Nielsen, 1993). These tables are restricted to just a few quantiles. Sections 4 and 5 will also show that these tables are not so accurate for higher dimensions (in particular for $n \geqslant 5$). Very accurate tables for some cases are given in MacKinnon, Haug and Michelis (1998), who make available Fortran code to obtain p-values of the tests. This uses simulated quantiles at 221 points (with interpolation to obtain intermediate values), thus using a large amount of data as input.

3. Using the Gamma distribution

The Gamma distribution, $\Gamma(z; r, a)$, is defined here as:

$$\Gamma(z; r, a) = \int_0^z \frac{a^r}{\Gamma(r)} x^{r-1} e^{-ax}\, dx, \qquad z > 0, r > 0, a > 0. \tag{4}$$

If a stochastic variable Z has a Gamma distribution:

$$\mathsf{E}Z = \mu = \frac{r}{a}, \qquad \mathsf{V}Z = \sigma^2 = \frac{r}{a^2}.$$

The Gamma distribution is related to the χ^2 distribution (allowing for non-integer degrees of freedom): $2aZ \sim \chi^2(2r)$. Johnson, Kotz and Balakrishnan (1994, Section 17.3) state that using the Gamma distribution to approximate quadratic forms is well established.

Given a sample mean $\hat{m}$ and variance $\hat{v}$ of a test statistic, the parameters for the approximating Gamma distribution can be found by matching the first two moments:

$$\hat{r} = \hat{m}^2/\hat{v}, \qquad \hat{a} = \hat{m}/\hat{v}.$$

This procedure yields a fitted distribution, which can be used to compute p-values or quantiles. Maximum likelihood estimation (see Pearson and Hartley, 1972, p. 88) was also tried, but worked less well at low dimensions, at least for the more interesting right tail.

The tables by Osterwald-Lenum (1992) contain means and variances of the tests. Applying the procedure for the trace test under H_l, we can compare the tabulated quantiles to those from the approximating Gamma distribution (the latter are in italic). Table 1 shows a very close match.

Another way of assessing the accuracy, which will be used in the remainder, is to use the fitted Gamma distribution to compute the p-values of the tabulated critical values. When applied to the previous table (but for $n = 1, \ldots, 10$), the absolute error count is presented in Table 2. The maximum in each cell is 10, since the errors for all dimensions are added together. For example, for the trace

Table 1. Tabulated quantiles compared to those from Gamma approximation (Osterwald-Lenum tables).

	$n-p=1$	2	3	4	6	9
90% (Gamma)	*10.48*	*22.83*	*39.07*	*59.13*	*110.3*	*215.1*
90% (table)	10.49	22.76	39.06	59.14	110.4	215.2
95% (Gamma)	*12.20*	*25.18*	*42.06*	*62.81*	*115.2*	*221.8*
95% (table)	12.25	25.32	42.44	62.99	114.9	222.2
99% (Gamma)	*15.88*	*30.00*	*48.06*	*70.12*	*124.7*	*234.7*
99% (table)	16.26	30.45	48.45	70.05	124.7	234.4

Table 2. Discrepancies (out of 10) of Gamma approximation when applied to Osterwald-Lenum tables

	Trace test			Max. Eigenvalue		
	p-value: 0.90	0.95	0.99	0.90	0.95	0.99
>0.001 error	7	10	7	7	8	10
>0.0025 error	3	1	1	1	6	5
>0.005 error	0	0	0	0	6	0
>0.0075 error	0	0	0	0	0	0

test there are only 3 instances out of 10 at the 90% level where the (left-sided) p-value is outside the 0.8975–0.9025 range, and 7 outside 0.899 – 0.901 (this includes the earlier three). This is a remarkably good fit, much more accurate than what is really necessary for practical use (especially for the sample sizes normally used; a similar point is made by Elliot, 1998).

While the trace test behaves like a gamma-distributed variable, the maximum-eigenvalue test resembles the smallest order statistic, and is therefore differently distributed. This is borne out by the worse fit, although this may be quite acceptable in practical situations.

4. Experimental procedure

We now turn to the design of the experiments. The simulation procedure starts by constructing E^*, which consists of $T \times n$ drawings from a standard normal distribution. E is the standardized version of E^* (using the Choleski decomposition) such that $E'E = TI_n$. A zero mean cannot be imposed on E (at least not for models H_c and H_z), because the tests are not similar with respect to the treatment of the mean. E approximates dB in (3).

Next, S is constructed as the lagged sum of E. Writing E' as $(e_1, \dots, e_T)$, and S similarly, then $s_l = 0$, $s_t = \Sigma_{i=1}^{t-1} e_i$. R, which approximates F in (3), is based on S

in the following way:

H_{ql}	H_{l}	H_{lc}	H_{c}	H_{z}
$S_{n-1}, t^2 \| t, 1$	$S, t \| 1$	$S_{n-1}, t \| 1$	$S, 1$	S

where S_{n-l} is S with the last column dropped. For H_{ql}, the last column of S is replaced by an integrated trend $(0, 1, 3, 6, \ldots)$, the resulting matrix is then regressed on a constant and a trend. In H_l a trend $(0, 1, \ldots, T-1)$ is appended to S, and each column is given a zero mean. The remainder can be interpreted similarly.

There are three ways of computing the trace statistic, all of which are asymptotically equivalent:

(a) using

$$\mathrm{tr}\{E^{*\prime}R^*(R^{*\prime}R^*)^{-1}R^{*\prime}E^*\}, \tag{5}$$

where the asterisk indicates that these are based on the unstandardized drawings, so $E^{*\prime}E^* \neq TI_n$ (but, of course, asymptotically it is).

(b) using the drawings with standardized variance-covariance:

$$\mathrm{tr}\{E'R(R'R)^{-1}R'E\}. \tag{6}$$

(c) using the same procedure as in the statistical analysis (2):

$$-T\sum_{i=1}^{n}\log(1-\hat{\lambda}_i), \tag{7}$$

with λ_i denoting the eigenvalues of:[1]

$$T^{-1}E'R(R'R)^{-1}R'E.$$

These three forms of the test statistics are compared in Nielsen (1997a) for $n = 1$. Nielsen finds that method (7) converges much faster to the asymptotic distribution than the other two statistics.

As an (extreme) illustration we simulated the three forms of the trace statistic for $n = 12$ using $M = 5000$ replication.[2] The results for the 95% quantiles under model H_l (all cases behave in a similar way) are in Table 3. Not only does (7)

Table 3. The role of sample size on the various methods of approximating $\mathsf{T}_l(0)$, $n = 12$.

using eqn.	$T = 100$	$T = 200$	$T = 400$	$T = \infty$
(5)	326.75	347.43	361.81	374.84
(6)	320.06	345.22	360.82	374.84
(7)	401.80	386.59	382.07	374.84

approximate the asympotic statistic better, it also approaches it from above, where the others approach it from below. The value for $T=\infty$ is based on the results in this paper.

5. Simulating the asymptotic distribution

The simulations considered here approximate a continuous Brownian motion with a discrete random walk. Therefore, it is to be expected that the choice of sample size (i.e. the number of discrete steps) plays a role in the quality of the approximation. This is borne out by Table 3, where $T=400$ is still far away from the asymptotic critical value. The tables in Johansen (1995a) use method (5) with $T=400$ and $M=100\,000$. The 95% critical value reported there for H_l is 361.07. This is very close to the 361.81 reported in Table 3 above (which had $M=5000$), suggesting that the number of replications is much less important than the choice of sample size. In the remainder all experiments use method (7).

Figure 1 illustrates the effect of sample size. We did 20 repetitions of the Monte Carlo experiment under H_z for the trace test, using $M=500$ in each repetition, and sample sizes $T=50, 100, 250, 500, 1000, 2500, 5000$. This gave 20 simulated means and variances of the test statistic for each sample size. The plotted lines are based on the average of these (now using 10 000 replications), while the error bars are twice the standard deviations within the 20 experiments. The figure shows that, as the dimension grows, the mean and variance become more dependent on

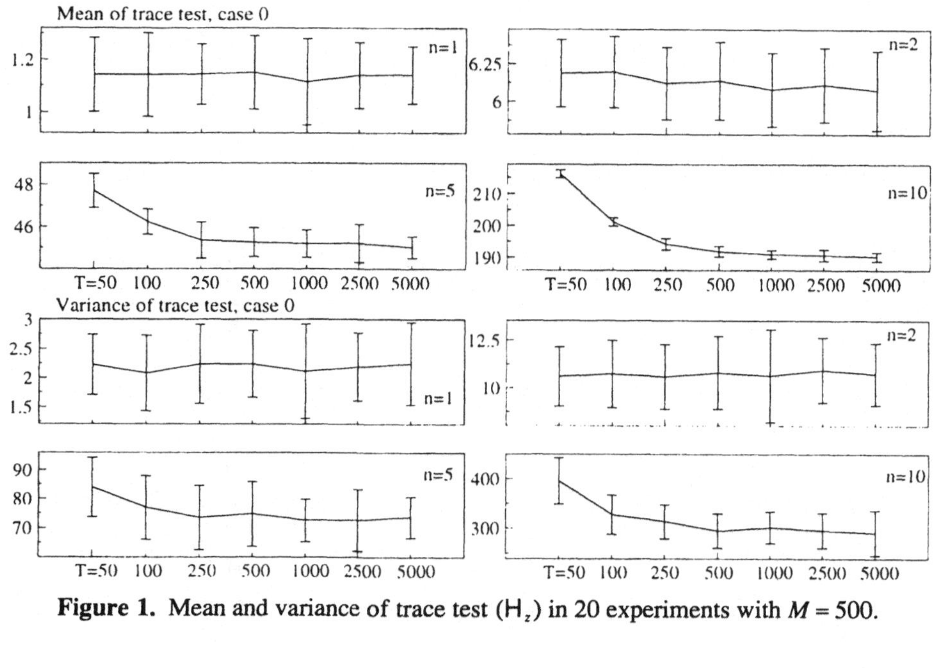

Figure 1. Mean and variance of trace test (H_z) in 20 experiments with $M=500$.

the sample size. It is interesting to see the low Monte Carlo variation of the estimate of the mean for $n = 10$ at small sample sizes, while this estimate is still far away from the mean of the asymptotic distribution.

The improvement in accuracy of estimates of the mean for growing dimension is explained by Fig. 2: as the dimension grows ($T = 100$ in all graphs), the distribution becomes more symmetric, with fewer outliers.

The approach of MacKinnon (1996), to estimate the statistics at various sample sizes and then fit a response surface, gives a better estimate of the asymptotic distribution. Consequently, the experimental design is as follows:

tests:	trace, maximum eigenvalue, computed as in (7),
models:	$\mathsf{H}_{ql}, \mathsf{H}_{l}, \mathsf{H}_{lc}, \mathsf{H}_{c}, \mathsf{H}_{z}$,
replications M:	100 000, (except: 20 000 for $T = 2500, 5000, n = 9, \ldots, 15$),
dimension n:	$1, \ldots, 15$,
sample size T:	$50, 75, 100, 150, 200, 250, 500, 1000, 2500, 5000$.

Then estimates of the mean of each test are obtained separately by an automated regression on a constant, $1/T, 1/T^2$. A dummy for $T = 50$ is included if significant. The $1/\mathrm{T}^2$ term is omitted if insignificant, in which case $1/T$ is also dropped if insignificant. These tests are done at a 5% level. The intercept in these 75 regressions (5 cases and 15 dimensions) of sample size 10 gives the asymptotic mean. The same procedure is used for the variances.

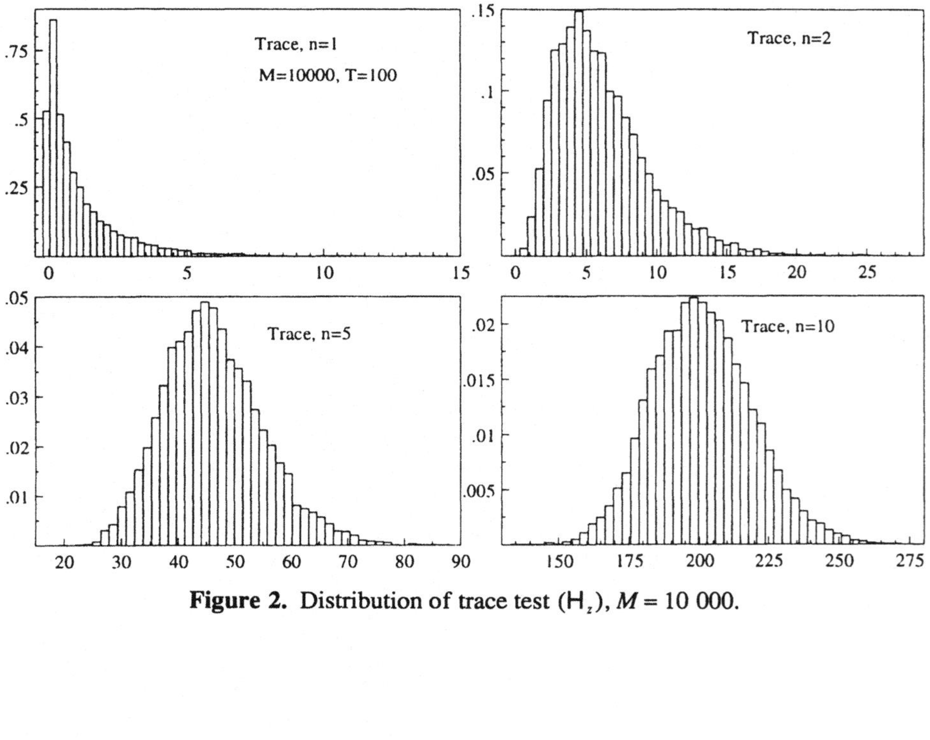

Figure 2. Distribution of trace test (H_z), $M = 10\,000$.

Table 4. Errors (out of 12) of Gamma approximation for H_l.

p-value:	0.01	0.05	0.1	0.2	0.4	0.5	0.6	0.8	0.9	0.95	0.99
>0.0025 error	4	7	6	3	8	9	8	3	1	2	0
>0.005 error	1	3	3	1	3	3	3	1	0	0	0
>0.01 error	1	1	1	0	0	0	1	0	0	0	0

6. A response surface for the mean and variance

Based on the simulations of the previous section, we proceed to derive a response surface for the mean and variance of the trace test, from which the parameters of the Gamma distributions can be derived.

First, it was noted that both the mean and variance are dominated by an n^2 term. The remainder is essentially linear in n (although for the mean of H_{ql} an $n^{1/2}$ term was still required to pick up the remaining curvature). The coefficients are given in Table 7 in the Appendix for the trace statistic. As the dimension grows, $m \longrightarrow 2n^2 + \alpha n$, and $v \longrightarrow 3n^2 + \beta n$.

To verify the result, we count the absolute errors for the trace test in model H_l when feeding separately computed quantiles (based on a regression on sample size as used for the mean and variance) into the Gamma approximation. Table 4 shows that the Gamma approximation based on the response surface works well for the whole distribution. The other cases work equally well.

A similar procedure is used for the maximum-eigenvalue statistic, see Table 8. As expected, the approximation for the maximum-eigenvalue test works somewhat less well.

MacKinnon *et al.* (1998) have very accurate 95% critical values for cases H_c, H_z and H_l. When applying the response-surface based Gamma approximation to these, all but one of the absolute errors of the trace test are less than 0.002. For the maximum-eigenvalue test, all are less than 0.005.

7. The role of sample size

Because the adopted procedure mimics the statistical analysis (apart from the presence of additional $\mathsf{I}(0)$ components, such as lagged differences), we also capture the effect of sample size on the Monte Carlo experiments. Figure 3 illustrates for H_z. It shows in the left panels m, v as found in the simulations, together with $\hat{m}$, $\hat{v}$ from the Gamma approximation to the asymptotic distribution. Each step is a new dimension. Within each dimension, the mean falls as the sample size grows; the fitted mean is for $T \longrightarrow \infty$, so independent of T. The right panels show the the fitted values to $\log(m/\hat{m})$ and $\log(v/\hat{v})$. The parameters for the sample size adjustment are given in Table 9 for the trace statistic.

It was shown before that the sample size has to be sufficiently large to approximate the asymptotic distribution. Indeed, the top half of Table 5 shows much larger errors when using the asymptotic approximations of Table 7 for the

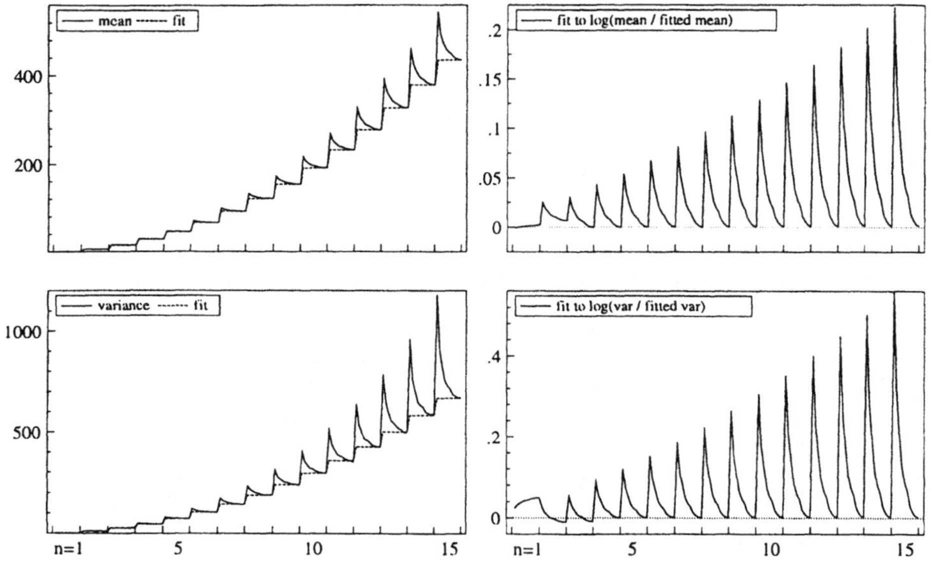

Figure 3. Effect of dimension and sample size on the trace test for H_z.

distribution of the trace statistics at $T = 100$. This is based on simulated critical values for $M = 20\ 000$, $T = 100$, and combining all cases for $n = 1, \ldots, 12$, giving 60 critical values per p-value. But, if the sample size correction is applied, the distribution is described much more accurately (bottom half of Table 5).

This section captures one aspect of the discrepancies between the asymptotic tables and the practical application of the test, namely the part which can be ascribed to using a small sample provided that there are no additional I(0) components. In practical situations, the additional I(0) components may well matter more to the small sample distribution. In Section 10 we return to this issue.

Table 5. Errors (out of 60) of Gamma approximation when applied to critical values obtained at $T = 100$.

p-value:	0.01	0.05	0.1	0.2	0.4	0.5	0.6	0.8	0.9	0.95	0.99
Trace test, asymptotic approximation applied to $T = 100$											
>0.005 error	57	58	59	57	53	52	54	50	51	47	36
>0.01 error	31	53	54	51	51	51	51	47	46	43	0
>0.02 error	21	37	44	47	46	45	44	43	40	33	0
Trace test, approximation with sample size correction											
>0.005 error	5	18	15	8	20	24	22	11	4	1	0
>0.01 error	2	3	3	1	1	7	9	0	0	0	0
>0.02 error	0	0	0	0	0	0	0	0	0	0	0

8. The I(2) case

Tests in I(2) models combine testing the rank of Π in:

$$\Delta^2 X_t = \Pi X_{t-1} - \Gamma \Delta X_{t-1} + \Phi q_t + \varepsilon_t, \qquad t = 1, \ldots, T, \tag{8}$$

with a reduced rank condition on Γ.

The arguments in the previous sections carry over to the I(2) case: again, the sample size is an important factor, with the test statistics behaving in a similar fashion. Here we first concentrate on the case discussed in Rahbek, Kongsted and Jørgensen (1998): the trend-stationary model which precludes a quadratic trend but allows for a linear trend in the levels.

$$\Delta^2 X_t = \Pi(X_{t-1} - \mu - \tau(t-1)) + \Gamma(\Delta X_{t-1} - \tau) + \varepsilon_t, \tag{9}$$

where X_t is again an n-dimensional vector.

In the I(2) model presented in (8) there are two reduced rank matrices. The first is $\Pi = \alpha\beta'$, where α and β are $n \times p$ matrices as before. Next, define the $n \times (n-p)$ matrix $\alpha_\perp$ so that $\alpha'_\perp \alpha_\perp = I_{n-p}$ and $\alpha'_\perp \alpha = 0$. The second reduced rank condition is: $\alpha'_\perp \Gamma \beta_\perp = \xi' \eta$, where ξ and η are $(n-p) \times s$ matrices.

The statistical analysis follows the two-step procedure proposed by Johansen (1995b):

(1) In the first step, ΔX_{t-1} and a constant enter unrestrictedly in an I(1) analysis of $\Delta^2 X_t$ on X_{t-l} with a restricted trend. This gives $\hat{\alpha}$ and $\hat{\beta}$ for each rank p, and corresponding orthogonal complements.

(2) The second step is a reduced rank analysis of $\hat{\alpha}'_\perp \Delta^2 X_t$ on $(\hat{\beta}'_\perp \hat{\beta}_\perp)^{-1} \hat{\beta}'_\perp \Delta X_{t-1}$ with restricted constant and the differenced linear combinations of I(2) variables from the first step entered unrestrictedly.

The first step of the procedure involves testing the rank of Π, leaving Γ unrestricted. The test statistic is denoted by $\mathsf{Q}(p)$. This step amounts to testing the number of I(2) components. The second step then tests for the number of I(1) components remaining, and is denoted by $\mathsf{Q}(p, s)$. The test statistic of interest is $\mathsf{S}(p, s) = \mathsf{Q}(p) + \mathsf{Q}(p, s)$.

The design of the Monte Carlo experiment again mimics the statistical analysis, and may be described as follows:

$$\begin{aligned} \mathsf{Q}(p) &= -T \sum_{i=p+1}^{n} \log(1 - \lambda_i), \\ \mathsf{Q}(p, s) &= -T \sum_{i=s+1}^{n-p} \log(1 - \mu_i), \\ \mathsf{S}(p, s) &= \mathsf{Q}(p) + \mathsf{Q}(p, s) \end{aligned} \tag{10}$$

The λ_i are the n eigenvalues from:

$$E' R (R' R)^{-1} R' E,$$

and μ_i are the $n-s$ eigenvalues from:

$$E'_{n-s}D(D'D)^{-1}D'E_{n-s}.$$

The matrices in the quadratic forms are obtained as follows. Let E^* be $T \times n$ drawings from the standard normal distribution, S^* the lagged cumulated sum of E^*, and Q^* the cumulated sum of S^*. Take S^*_s to be the first s columns of S^* and Q^*_{n-s} the last $n-s$ columns of Q^*. Finally, write E for the drawings after standardization using the Choleski decomposition such that $E'E = TI_n$, E_{n-s} for the last $n-s$ columns. R are the residuals from regressing $[t, S^*_s, Q^*_{n-s}]$ on D, where $D = [1, \Delta Q^*_{n-s}] = [1, S^*_{n-s}]$.

The hypotheses involved are:

(i) $\mathsf{Q}(p)$ tests whether rank(Π) $\leqslant p$ given that rank(Π) $\leqslant n$: $\mathsf{H}(p)|\mathsf{H}(n)$. When there are no $\mathsf{I}(2)$ relations: $n-p-s=0$, and $\mathsf{Q}(p)$ equals $\mathsf{T}(p)$, the trace test in the $\mathsf{I}(1)$ case.

(ii) $\mathsf{Q}(p, s)$ tests whether rank(Π) $\leqslant p$ and there are $\leqslant n-p-s$ $\mathsf{I}(2)$ components given that rank(Π) $\leqslant n$ and there are $\leqslant n-p$ components which are $\mathsf{I}(2)$.

(iii) $\mathsf{S}(p, s)$ tests whether rank(Π) $\leqslant p$ and there are $\leqslant n-p-s$ $\mathsf{I}(2)$ components given that rank(Π) $\leqslant n$. When there are no $\mathsf{I}(2)$ relations: $\mathsf{S}(p, n-p) = \mathsf{Q}(p) = \mathsf{T}(p)$.

As for the $\mathsf{I}(1)$ tests, 5 cases may be distinguished, although we rule out the cases without a constant term, and with a quadratic trend:

	Constant	Trend	Model, $\Delta^2 X_t =$
H_l	unrestricted	restricted	$\Pi(X_{t-1} - \mu - \tau(t-1)) + \Gamma(\Delta X_{t-1} - \tau) + \varepsilon_t$,
H_{lc}	unrestricted	none	$\Pi(X_{t-1} - \mu) + \Gamma(\Delta X_{t-1} - \tau) + \varepsilon_t$,
H_c	restricted	none	$\Pi(X_{t-1} - \mu) + \Gamma\Delta X_{t-1} + \varepsilon_t$.

The theory for H_l is developed in Rahbek *et al.* (1998), with tables based on $T = 400$ and $M = 10\,000$. H_{lc} and H_c are tabulated in Paruolo (1996) using $T = 400$ and $M = 6000$. Models H_z and H_{ql} are omitted here; the former is tabulated in Johansen (1995b), the latter in Paruolo (1996).

The new set of tables has an extra dimension, with s denoting the number of $\mathsf{I}(1)$ components, and n-p-s the number of $\mathsf{I}(2)$ components. In the simulation experiments there are no extra $\mathsf{I}(0)$ variables, and n-p-s in the tables corresponds to n-p in the simulations. The experimental design is as follows:

tests:	$\mathsf{Q}(p), \mathsf{S}(p, s)$
M for H_l:	100 000, (except: 20 000 for $T = 2500, 5000$)
M for $\mathsf{H}_{lc}, \mathsf{H}_c$:	10 000, (except: 2 000 for $T = 2500, 5000$)
dimension n:	$1, \ldots, 12$
sample size T:	50, 75, 100, 150, 200, 250, 250, 500, 1000, 2500, 5000.

Table 6. Errors (out of 156) of Gamma approximation for I(2) tests $\mathsf{Q}(p)$ and $\mathsf{S}(p, s)$, H_l.

p-value:	0.01	0.05	0.1	0.2	0.4	0.5	0.6	0.8	0.9	0.95	0.99
>0.005 error	3	5	5	0	22	34	28	3	1	0	0
>0.01 error	1	2	0	0	2	4	4	2	0	0	0
>0.02 error	0	0	0	0	0	0	0	0	0	0	0

The mean and variance of the test statistics is derived as in Section 5.[3] Again, a response surface is fitted to the mean and variance, with the final result given in Table 10, for $n - s > 0$. To assess the success, the approximation is applied to the asymptotic critical values for $\mathsf{Q}(p)$ and $\mathsf{S}(p, s)$ together, up to dimension 12. This gives 78 entries for each test (for $s = j \geqslant 0$: $n - s = 1, \ldots, 12 - j$; $n\text{-}s = 0$ is excluded). The critical values to which the Gamma distribution is applied were obtained separately at each left-sided p-value as the constant term in a regression against functions of the sample size. Table 6 shows that the Gamma approximation also works very well in the I(2) case. The lower number of replications used in H_{lc} and H_c are reflected in larger absolute errors.

9. Conditional systems

In a conditional (or 'partial') system, the I(1) analysis is done conditional on a subset of the variables in the full system. Harbo, Johansen, Nielsen and Rahbek (1998) show that this requires the conditioning variables to be weakly exogenous for the cointegration parameters (i.e. the cointegrating vectors do not enter the marginal model of the conditioning variables). In the conditional analysis, the dimensionality of the system (which is now not a VAR anymore) is reduced, and, when the conditioning is valid, the trace test may have more power.

Harbo *et al.* (1998) derive the trace test in the conditional system, which is again of the form (3), where F is as before, but B has lower dimension. They also provide tables for the new test in models H_l, H_c, and H_z. The Gamma approximation again works very well here. The tables in Harbo *et al.* (1998) report means and variances of the trace test, and this can be used to compute the Gamma parameters. Then, applying the Gamma distribution to the 95% quantiles in the tables, we find that all 52 are between 0.945 and 0.956; 24 out of 52 are between 0.949 and 0.951.

Under the assumption that the asymptotic distribution of the full system is known and fully described by the mean and variance, the distributions for the conditional system can be derived analytically, up to a covariance term. Given this term, no new tables are actually required.

In (2), $\mathsf{T}(p)$ denotes the trace test for rank p in the closed system of dimension n. Let $\mathsf{T}(p, n_l)$ denote the test for rank p in a system of dimension n_1, conditional on $n - n_1$ variables (so the corresponding closed system has dimension n).

As $T \rightarrow \infty$, the distribution of $\mathsf{T}(p, n_1)$ is represented by (6), but with $n - n_1$ columns dropped from E. Because each column is independent, the elements in the trace are exchangeable, and we find that:

$$\mathsf{E}[\mathrm{tr}\{E'R(R'R)^{-1}R'E\}] = \mathsf{E}\left[\sum_{i=1}^{n} e_i'R(R'R)^{-1}R'e_i\right] = \sum_{i=1}^{n} \mathsf{E}[\mathsf{T}_i],$$

where the subscript i denotes column i. T_i is the test using column i only: $\mathsf{T} = \Sigma_i \mathsf{T}_i$. The same argument can be applied to the variances, for example, for $n = 3$:

$$\mathsf{V}[\mathsf{T}] = \mathsf{V}[\mathsf{T}_1 + \mathsf{T}_2] + \mathsf{V}[\mathsf{T}_3] + 2\mathsf{cov}[\mathsf{T}_1 + \mathsf{T}_2, \mathsf{T}_3],$$

$$\mathsf{V}[\mathsf{T}] = \mathsf{V}[\mathsf{T}_1] + \mathsf{V}[\mathsf{T}_2] + \mathsf{V}[\mathsf{T}_3] + 2\mathsf{cov}[\mathsf{T}_1, \mathsf{T}_2] + 2\mathsf{cov}[\mathsf{T}_2, \mathsf{T}_3] + 2\mathsf{cov}[\mathsf{T}_1, \mathsf{T}_3].$$

Consequently, the mean and variance of the partial test statistics can be derived from the closed-system tests using:

$$\begin{aligned}
\mathsf{E}\left[\sum_{i=1}^{n_1-p} \mathsf{T}_i\right] &= \frac{n_1 - p}{n - p}\,\mathsf{E}[\mathsf{T}], \\
\mathsf{V}\left[\sum_{i=1}^{n_1-p} \mathsf{T}_i\right] &= \frac{n_1 - p}{n - p}\,\mathsf{V}[\mathsf{T}] - (n - n_1)(n_1 - p)\,\mathsf{cov}, \\
\mathsf{H}_l &: \mathsf{cov} = -1.35, \\
\mathsf{H}_c &: \mathsf{cov} = -1.066, \\
\mathsf{H}_z &: \mathsf{cov} = -1.270.
\end{aligned} \tag{11}$$

$\mathsf{E}[\mathsf{T}(p)]$ and $\mathsf{V}[\mathsf{T}(p)]$ have already been computed, and the only unknown term is cov. Simulating $\mathsf{V}[\Sigma_{i=1}^{n_1} \mathsf{T}_i]$ up to $n = 5$ using the method of Section 5, the cov term can be estimated. The reported numbers in (11) are the average, which assumes that the covariance term does not depend on n or n_1. The corresponding standard deviations are respectively: 0.01,0.001,0.001.

Harbo *et al.* (1998) show that the asymptotic distributions of the conditional-system tests for the models H_{ql} and H_{lc} depend on nuisance parameters. Therefore, procedure (11) does not work in these models. Indeed, attempting to estimate the covariance term gives 0.9 and 1.5, but with standard deviations 1.6, 3.2. In case the distribution is required for certain values of the nuisance parameters, it is recommended to simulate the mean and variance, and use that in the Gamma approximation.

10. Some applications

The Gamma approximation based on the fitted means and variances makes it very easy to obtain p-values and quantiles. This section illustrates in a few examples how the approximation can be used.

10.1 *I(1) analysis*

The first example takes the model in Table 7.1 of Johansen (1995a, Section 7.3.1), which is a 4-dimensional system using Danish data. The model has a restricted constant, making it model H_c, as well as centred seasonals. Two lags are used, and $T = 53$ after allowing for these lags. The approximation in Table 7 (see Appendix), can be applied. For $n - p = 4$:

$$\mathsf{E}[\mathsf{T}(4)] \approx 2 \times 16 + 2.01 \times 4 = 40.04,$$

$$\mathsf{V}[\mathsf{T}(4)] \approx 3 \times 16 + 3.6 \times 4 + 0.75 = 63.15.$$

The approximating distribution is $\Gamma(40.04^2/63.15 = 25.4, 40.04/63.15 = 0.634)$. The following table lists right-sided p-values and approximating Gamma distributions:

rank p	$n-p$	trace	distribution	p-value	tests
0	4	49.14	$\Gamma(25.4, 0.634)$	0.129	$\mathsf{H}_c(0) \mid \mathsf{H}_c(4)$
1	3	19.06	$\Gamma(14.9, 0.623)$	0.781	$\mathsf{H}_c(1) \mid \mathsf{H}_c(4)$
2	2	8.89	$\Gamma(7.41, 0.614)$	0.747	$\mathsf{H}_c(2) \mid \mathsf{H}_c(4)$
3	1	2.35	$\Gamma(2.38, 0.586)$	0.709	$\mathsf{H}_c(3) \mid \mathsf{H}_c(4)$

10.2. *Conditional I(1) analysis*

Both Harbo *et al.* (1998) and Doornik *et al.* (1998) consider a conditional I(1) analysis using the UK-M1 data set (see Hendry and Ericsson, 1991). The latter use H_l and condition on the interest rate, so that $n = 4$, $n_1 = 3$. The hypotheses of interest are for rank $\leqslant n_1 - p$, for $p = 0, 1, 2$.

The first step is to use Table 8 to obtain the means and variances for the closed system tests $\mathsf{H}_l(0) \mid \mathsf{H}_l(3), \mathsf{H}_l(1) \mid \mathsf{H}_l(3)$, and $\mathsf{H}_l(2) \mid \mathsf{H}_l(3)$. Next, these are adjusted using (11):

p	E[T]	V[T]	new mean	new variance	distribution
0	48.70	74.0	$3/4\mathsf{E}[\mathsf{T}] = 36.52$	$3/4\mathsf{V}[\mathsf{T}] + 3 \times 1.35 = 59.55$	$\Gamma(22.4, 0.613)$
1	30.65	47.3	$2/3\mathsf{E}[\mathsf{T}] = 20.43$	$2/3\mathsf{V}[\mathsf{T}] + 2 \times 1.35 = 34.23$	$\Gamma(12.2, 0.597)$
2	16.53	26.1	$1/2\mathsf{E}[\mathsf{T}] = 8.265$	$1/2\mathsf{V}[\mathsf{T}] + 1 \times 1.35 = 14.40$	$\Gamma(4.74, 0.574)$

10.3. *I(2) analysis*

The Gamma approximation for the I(2) case allows us to attach p-values to Table 5 in Rahbek *et al.* (1998), which uses the same UK M1 data. A VAR of four variables and five lags is used, under model H_l. The following table gives the observed test statistic, with the right-sided p-value in square brackets. The next line gives the appropriate Gamma distribution from which the p-value is obtained:

p	$\mathsf{S}(p,s)$				$\mathsf{T}(p)$
0	205.3[0.00]	154.8[0.00]	111.4[0.00]	101.1[0.00]	96.61[0.00]
	$\Gamma(90.4, 0.753)$	$\Gamma(69.9, 0.727)$	$\Gamma(53.2, 0.698)$	$\Gamma(40.5, 0.670)$	$\Gamma(32.1, 0.658)$
1		111.9[0.00]	62.08[0.18]	53.44[0.06]	49.07[0.01]
		$\Gamma(53.3, 0.740)$	$\Gamma(38.1, 0.704)$	$\Gamma(26.9, 0.667)$	$\Gamma(19.9, 0.648)$
2			37.69[0.39]	26.44[0.33]	22.67[0.12]
			$\Gamma(25.8, 0.714)$	$\Gamma(16.0, 0.661)$	$\Gamma(10.5, 0.633)$
3				14.82[0.24]	8.860[0.19]
				$\Gamma(7.85, 0.647)$	$\Gamma(3.78, 0.598)$
	$n-p-s=4$	3	2	1	0

10.4. *Further applications*

The approximations can also be useful in parametric bootstraps. As an example, we take the model in Section 10.1, with the DGP based on the fitted results for the VAR(2), assuming a rank of 0 or 1. Figure 4 plots the rejection frequencies of the trace test for $\mathsf{H}_c(0)|\mathsf{H}_c(4), \mathsf{H}_c(1)|\mathsf{H}_c(4)$, and $\mathsf{H}_c(2)|\mathsf{H}_c(4)$ as a function of sample size ($T = 50, 75, 100, 200$). These are based on the asymptotic distribu-

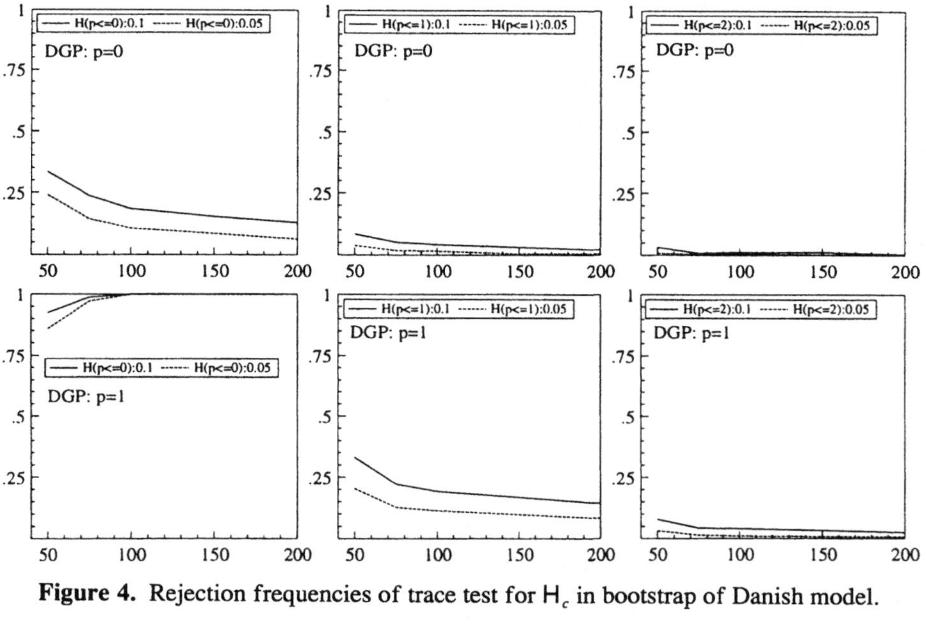

Figure 4. Rejection frequencies of trace test for H_c in bootstrap of Danish model.

tions, approximated by the Gamma distribution according to Table 7 (see Appendix).

The first row of graphs has rank zero in the DGP, the second has a rank of unity. The experiments were generated with PcNaive (see Doornik and Hendry, 1998), using 1000 replications, and conditional on the actual values of 1974 (1)–(2). The first panel of row 1, and the second of row 2 correspond to size experiments. Both show some over-rejection in small samples, which disappears as T grows:

		$T=53$	$T=200$	$T=1000$	$1-\mathsf{P}_T(c_{0.95})$	$1-\mathsf{P}_s(c_{0.95})$
H(0)	10%	0.33	0.13	0.12	0.16	0.34
H(0)	5%	0.21	0.06	0.06	0.09	0.22
		$T=53$	$T=200$	$T=1000$	$1-\mathsf{P}_T(c_{0.95})$	$1-\mathsf{P}_s(c_{0.95})$
H(1)	10%	0.31	0.14	0.11	0.13	0.32
H(1)	5%	0.31	0.08	0.06	0.07	0.20

The first two rows, testing H(0), have rank zero in the DGP, the last two correspond to one cointegrating vector. The column labelled $1-\mathsf{P}_T(c_{0.95})$ lists the probability of a value exceeding the 95% asymptotic critical value using the small sample adjustment of Table 9 (see Appendix) at $T=45$ (i.e. 53 allowing for 8 regressors). This is well short of the rejection frequencies found in the parametric bootstrap. The last column uses a Gamma approximation based on the mean and variance found in the simulation. Now the probability to exceed the asymptotic critical value is very close to that found in the experiment. Using this distribution for the results in Section 10.1 gives a p-value of 0.39 to 49.14; this indicates that the small sample correction to the asymptotic distribution of Table 9 (see Appendix) may not be so useful.

For a sample size of 150–200 or more, the asymptotic distribution works satisfactorily. A similar result was found by Doornik *et al.* (1998).

11. Conclusion

This paper derives an approximation to the asymptotic distributions of the cointegration tests using the Gamma distribution. Tables 7, 8 and 10 in the Appendix give the formulae for computing the parameters of the approximating Gamma distribution. Equation (11) extends the application to conditional (or 'partial') systems. The procedure gives reliable p-values and quantiles for the whole distribution. It is easily programmed, requiring only 150 numbers to summarize the distributions for both the I(1) and the I(2) test statistics. The actual Ox program, including data, takes less than 100 lines and is available from the author's web page.

The approach of this paper could be used in similar situations, thus avoiding the need for additional tables. As a minimum, all tables should include the mean and variance of the tabulated statistics, to allow application of the Gamma approximation.

Acknowledgements

I wish to thank Bent Nielsen for many invaluable comments and suggestions, and David Hendry and Tom Rothenberg for helpful discussions. Financial support from the UK Economic and Social Research Council under grant R000237500 is gratefully acknowledged.

Notes

1. Writing $S_{00} = T^{-1}E'E(=I_n), S_{01} = T^{-1}E'R$, etc it can be seen that the eigenvalues are the solution to $|\lambda S_{00} - S_{01}S_{11}^{-1}S_{10}| = 0$. This yields the same eigenvalues as $|\lambda S_{11} - S_{10}S_{00}^{-1}S_{01}| = 0$.
2. All simulations in this paper were done with Ox versions 1.11–2.00 (Doornik, 1998).
3. When $n - s$ is small, the distribution is shifting inwards as the sample size increases, in line with the I(1) tests. However, with more I(2) components, the opposite starts to happen.

References

Abadir, K. M. (1995) The limiting distribution of the t ratio under a unit root. *Econometric Theory* 11, 775–793.

Doornik, J. A. (1998) *Object-Oriented Matrix Programming using Ox 2.0.* London: Timberlake Consultants Press.

Doornik, J. A. and Hendry, D. F. (1997) *Modelling Dynamic Systems using PcFiml 9 for Windows.* London: Timberlake Consultants Press.

Doornik, J. A. and Hendry, D. F. (1998) Monte Carlo simulation using PcNaive for Windows. Unpublished typescript, Nuffield College, University of Oxford.

Doornik, J. A., Hendry, D. F. and Nielsen, B. (1998) Inference in cointegrated models: UK M1 revisited. *Journal of Economic Surveys*, this issue.

Elliot, G. (1998) Review of 'Time Series Analysis: Nonstationary and Noninvertible Distribution Theory' by Katsuko Tanaka. *Econometric Theory* 14, 511–516.

Hansen, B. E. (1997) Approximate asymptotic p-values for structural change tests. *Journal of Business and Economic Statistics* 15, 60–67.

Harbo, I., Johansen, S., Nielsen, B. and Rahbek, A. (1998) Asymptotic inference on cointegrating rank in partial systems. *Journal of Business and Economic Statistics.* Forthcoming.

Hendry, D. F. and Ericsson, N. R. (1991) Modeling the demand for narrow money in the United Kingdom and the United States. *European Economic Review* 35, 833–886.

Johansen, S. (1988) Statistical analysis of cointegration vectors. *Journal of Economic Dynamics and Control* 12, 231–254.

Johansen, S. (1995a) *Likelihood-based Inference in Cointegrated Vector Autoregressive Models.* Oxford: Oxford University Press.

Johansen, S. (1995b) A statistical analysis of cointegration for I(2) variables. Econometric Theory 11, 25–59.

Johansen, S. and Juselius, K. (1990) Maximum likelihood estimation and inference on cointegration – With application to the demand for money. *Oxford Bulletin of Economics and Statistics* 52, 169–210.

Johansen, S. and Nielsen, B. (1993) Asymptotics for cointegration rank tests in the presence of intervention dummies — manual for the simulation program DisCo. http://www.math.ku.dk/~sjo, University of Copenhagen, Institute of Mathematical Statistics, Copenhagen.

Johnson, N. L., Kotz, S. and Balakrishnan, N. (1994) *Continuous Univariate Distributions — 1* 2nd edn. New York: John Wiley.

MacKinnon, J. G. (1991) Critical values for cointegration tests. In Engle, R. F. and Granger, C. W. J. (eds.), *Long-Run Economic Relationships*, pp. 267–276. Oxford: Oxford University Press.

MacKinnon, J. G. (1996) Numerical distribution functions of likelihood ratio tests for cointegration. *Journal of Applied Econometrics* 11, 601–618.

MacKinnon, J. G., Haug, A. A. and Michelis, L. (1998) Numerical distribution functions of likelihood ratio tests for cointegration. Mimeo, Queens University, Canada.

Nielsen, B. (1997a) Bartlett correction of the unit root test in autoregressive models. *Biometrika* 84, 500–504.

Nielsen, B. (1997b) On the distribution of tests for cointegration rank. Discussion paper, Nuffield College, Oxford.

Osterwald-Lenum, M. (1992) A note with quantiles of the asymptotic distribution of the ML cointegration rank test statistics. *Oxford Bulletin of Economics and Statistics* 54, 461–472.

Paruolo, P. (1996) On the determination of integration indices in I(2) systems. *Journal of Econometrics* 72, 313–356.

Pearson, E. S. and Hartley, H. O. (1972) *Biometrika Tables for Statisticians*, Vol. II. Cambridge: Cambridge University Press.

Rahbek, A., Kongsted, H. C. and Jørgensen C. (1998) Trend-stationarity in the I(2) cointegration model. *Journal of Econometrics*, Forthcoming.

Appendix: tables with approximations

Table 7. Mean and variance of the I(1) trace statistic T.

$\mathsf{E}[\mathsf{T}(p)] \approx 2(n-p)^2 +$	H_z	H_c	H_{lc}	H_l	H_{ql}
$(n-p)$	-1	2.01	1.05	4.05	2.85
1	0.07	0	-1.55	0.50	-5.10
$n-p=1$	0.07	0.06	-0.50	-0.23	-0.10
$n-p=2$	0	0.05	-0.23	-0.07	-0.06
$(n-p)^{1/2}$	0	0	0	0	1.35
$\mathsf{V}[\mathsf{T}(p)] \approx 3(n-p)^2 +$	H_z	H_c	H_{lc}	H_l	H_{ql}
$(n-p)$	-0.33	3.60	1.80	5.70	4.00
1	0	-0.30	-1.10	-0.50	-2.66
$n-p=1$	-0.55	0.75	0	3.20	0.80
$n-p=2$	0	-0.40	-2.80	-1.30	-5.80

Table 8. Mean and variance of the I(1) maximum-eigenvalue statistic M.

$\mathsf{E}[\mathsf{M}(p)] \approx$	H_z	H_c	H_{lc}	H_l	H_{ql}
$(n-p)$	6.0019	5.9498	5.8271	5.8658	5.6364
1	−2.7558	0.43402	−1.6487	2.5595	−0.90531
$n-p=1$	0.67185	0.048360	−1.6118	−0.34443	−3.5166
$n-p=2$	0.11490	0.018198	−0.25949	−0.077991	−0.47966
$(n-p)^{1/2}$	−2.7764	−2.3669	−1.5666	−1.7552	−0.21447
$\mathsf{V}[\mathsf{M}(p)] \approx$	H_z	H_c	H_{lc}	H_l	H_{ql}
$(n-p)$	1.8806	2.2231	2.0785	1.9955	2.0899
1	−15.499	−7.9064	−9.7846	−5.5428	−5.3303
$n-p=1$	1.1136	0.58592	−3.3680	1.2425	−7.1523
$n-p=2$	0.070508	−0.034324	−0.24528	0.41949	−0.25260
$(n-p)^{1/2}$	14.714	12.058	13.074	12.841	12.393

Table 9. Sample size adjustment for the mean and standard deviation of the I(1) trace statistic T.

$\log(\mathsf{E}[\mathsf{T}_T(p)]/\mathsf{E}[\mathsf{T}(p)]) \approx$	H_z	H_c	H_{lc}	H_l	H_{ql}
$(n-p)^{1/2}/T$	−0.101	0	0.134	0.0252	−0.819
$(n-p)/T$	0.499	0.465	0.422	0.448	0.615
$(n-p)^2/T^2$	0.896	0.984	1.02	1.09	0.896
$(n-p=1)/T$	−0.562	−0.273	2.17	−0.353	2.43
$n-p=1$	0.00229	−0.00244	−0.00182	0	0.00149
$n-p=2$	0.00662	0	0	0	0
$n-p=3$	0	0	−0.00321	0	0
$\log(\mathsf{V}[\mathsf{T}_T(p)]/\mathsf{V}[\mathsf{T}(p)]) \approx$	H_z	H_c	H_{lc}	H_l	H_{ql}
$(n-p)^{1/2}/T$	−0.204	0.224	0.422	0	−1.29
$(n-p)/T$	0.98	0.863	0.734	0.836	1.01
$(n-p)^2/T^2$	3.11	3.38	3.76	3.99	3.92
$(n-p=1)/T$	−2.14	−0.807	4.32	−1.33	4.67
$n-p=1$	0.0499	0	−0.00606	−0.00298	0.00484
$n-p=2$	−0.0103	0	0	−0.00139	−0.00127
$n-p=3$	−0.00902	−0.0091	−0.00718	−0.00268	−0.0199

Table 10. Mean and variance for I(2) tests $Q(p)$ and $S(p, s)$, where s is the number of I(1), and $n-p-s>0$ the number of I(2) components.

$E[Q(p)] \approx c_1 +$	H_c	H_{lc}	H_l
$(n-p)(n-p-s)$	1.9998	1.9980	2.0043
$(n-p-s)^2$	0.017957	0.014504	0.010704
$n-p-s$	−0.20907	−2.1649	−0.21254
$s=0$	0	1.4170	0
$E[S(p,s)] \approx c_1 +$	H_c	H_{lc}	H_l
$(n-p)(n-p-s)$	1.9946	1.9929	2.0042
$(n-p-s)^2$	2.0112	2.0073	2.0091
$n-p-s$	−1.1079	−0.060440	1.8118
$s=0$	0	1.3392	0
$c_1 =$	H_c	H_{lc}	H_l
$(n-p)^2$	1.9906	1.9966	1.9954
$n-p$	2.1248	1.0758	4.1140
1	−0.42846	−1.7843	0.19778

$V[Q(p)] \approx c_2 +$	H_c	H_{lc}	H_l
$(n-p)(n-p-s)$	3.1351	3.2175	3.4897
$(n-p-s)^2$	0	0	−0.068124
$n-p-s$	0.76645	−2.9496	0
$s=0$	0	12.173	−1.0696
$V[S(p,s)] \approx c_2 +$	H_c	H_{lc}	H_l
$(n-p)(n-p-s)$	2.3807	2.2688	2.6055
$(n-p-s)^2$	2.0770	2.2175	1.9891
$n-p-s$	0	0	2.6848
$s=0$	0	9.8887	0
$c_2 =$	H_c	H_{lc}	H_l
$(n-p)^2$	3.1448	2.8999	2.9350
$n-p$	2.2065	4.1618	6.5371
1	4.9710	−5.6183	1.9913

AN ECONOMETRIC ANALYSIS OF I(2) VARIABLES

Niels Haldrup

Aarhus University

Abstract. This paper provides a selective survey of the recent literature dealing with I(2) variables in economic time series, that is, processes that require to be differenced twice in order to become stationary. With reference to particular economic models intuition is provided of why I(2)-and polynomial cointegration are features likely to occur in economics. The properties of I(2) series are discussed and I review topics such as: Testing for double unit roots, representations of I(2) cointegrated systems, and hypothesis testing in single equations as well as in systems of equations. Different data sets are used to illustrate the various econometric and statistical techniques.

Keywords. I(2) processes; Unit root tests; VAR models; Error correction models.

1. Introduction

The past decade has witnessed a veritable explosion of research on the analysis and implications of non-stationary time series with unit roots. By now there seems to be general consensus in the literature of how such time series can be characterized, represented, tested, and analyzed, both within univariate and multivariate settings. Moreover, many economic theories provide good arguments why time series may have such non-stationary features. There exist numerous recent contributions in the literature that survey this literature. A list of references which is far from being exhaustive includes Diebold and Nerlove (1990), Dolado and Jenkinson (1990), Muscatelli and Hurn (1992), Banerjee *et al.* (1993), Hamilton (1994), Stock (1994), and Watson (1994).

Notwithstanding, an extended class of non-stationary time series models has been attached only a minor interest in these surveys, that is, processes with double unit roots. Perhaps this is not too surprising since processes with a single unit root seems best at describing the behaviour of most economic time series. However, some time series like prices, wages, money balances, stock-variables etc., appear to be more smooth and more slowly changing than what is normally observed for variables integrated of order one, I(1). Such time series are potentially integrated of order 2 such that double differencing is needed to make the series stationary. If the series are log-transformed, the differenced series (i.e. the growth rates) will therefore be I(1). Since both levels and growth rates of economic time series are important for many economic theories the complicated interaction between I(2) and I(1) series is thus of great importance in the econometric analysis of such models. The purpose of this survey is to demonstrate why I(2) processes are a relevant class of models to consider in economics and I shall review different econometric tools that are presently available in the literature in the study of I(2) models.

In section 2 some introductory concepts are presented in order to discuss the cointegration possibilities in I(2) systems. The subsequent section presents various economic models justifying cointegration amongst doubly integrated time series and polynomial cointegration, that is, models where both the levels and the first differences of I(2) variables are needed in the equilibrium relations. In particular, I address models of intertemporal economic behaviour and stock-flow models of the inventory accelerator type. Following this motivation a selective survey of the econometric literature is given which includes: The basic properties of I(2) processes compared to I(1) processes and other classes of non-stationary time series models (section 4), testing for I(2)-ness (section 5), and single equation analysis in multivariate I(2) systems (section 6). In particular, section 6 addresses spurious regression problems in I(2) models and based on this analysis the natural extension is made to residual based testing for cointegration when I(2) and I(1) variables are present. The general properties of single equation cointegration models with stationary errors are characterized as well. In section 7 cointegration in systems is motivated from the triangular representation. Next, section 8 is dedicated to a review of the different ways cointegrated I(2) VAR systems can be represented. In practice most empirical analyses of I(2) systems are conducted within the context of the so-called Johansen maximum likelihood procedure so it is natural to emphasize this technique in particular. This is done in section 9. The next section briefly discusses other representation, estimation and testing procedures in multivariate systems and finally section 11 concludes. Throughout the paper the various techniques are demonstrated by empirical examples.

2. Introductory definitions and the cointegration possibilities amongst I(2) variables

Before discussing the different ways that I(2) variables may appear in economic models it will be useful to define formally what is meant by I(2) series and I discuss briefly, at an introductory level, how cointegration can occur amongst such series.

Following the initial benchmark description of Box and Jenkins (1970), a univariate variable x_t that needs to be differenced d times in order to have a stationary and invertible ARMA representation is said to be integrated of order d, ($x_t \sim \mathrm{I}(d)$). That is, an I(2) variable is one for which $\Delta^2 x_t$, can be given an ARMA representation with no unit roots in the AR or MA parts of the process. I use standard notation and hence let Δ and L signify difference and lag operators: $\Delta x_t = (1-L)x_t = x_t - x_{t-1}$. Initially it is assumed that x_t is free of deterministic components. The two series displayed in the first graph of figure 1 are examples of I(2) series.

Following Engle and Granger (1987), we can consider a $(p \times 1)$ vector time series x_t for which each component is integrated[1] of order d. More compactly we then write $x_t \sim I(d)$ and by construction this also implies that $\Delta x_t \sim I(d-1)$. Now the possibility exists that the levels of the series cointegrate, i.e. such that one can find a p-vector β satisfying that $\beta' x_t \sim I(d-b)$, $d \geqslant b > 0$, and where β is the so-called cointegration vector. In Engle and Granger's terminology we write $x_t \sim CI(d, b)$. Generally several linearly independent cointegration vectors may exist and in this case β becomes a matrix with rank less than p. How exactly the cointegration rank is given for systems where $d > 1$ is non-trivial (I return to this in sections 7 and 8) so to clarify the arguments in what follows it is assumed that β is just a vector.

In order to focus particularly on $I(2)$ systems we define the vector series $x_{2t} \sim I(2)$ and $x_{1t} \sim I(1)$, so that really we have a combination of $I(2)$ and $I(1)$ variables. The processes have dimension m_2 and m_1, respectively. The cointegration possibilities that may occur for $I(2)$ systems can now be described as the following three cases:

$$\beta_1' x_{2t} \sim I(0) \tag{1}$$

$$\beta_2' x_{2t} \sim I(1) \tag{2}$$

$$\beta_3' x_{2t} + \beta_4' x_{1t} + \beta_5' \Delta x_{2t} \sim I(0) \tag{3}$$

In the above expressions $\beta_i, i = 1, \ldots, 5$, are parameter vectors of matching dimensions. In (1) linear combinations exist between the $I(2)$ variables such that $x_{2t} \sim CI(2, 2)$; hence, in this situation no $I(1)$ variables are needed to induce stationarity amongst the $I(2)$ series. It is interesting to observe that for this particular case the *timing* of the variables will be of importance. For instance, consider two cointegrated $I(2)$ variables, $x_{21,t}$ and $x_{22,t}$, such that e.g. $x_{21,t} - x_{22,t}$ is stationary $I(0)$. Instead, if $x_{22,t}$ is lagged by one period and we focus on the relation $x_{21,t} - x_{22,t-1} = (x_{21,t} - x_{22,t}) + \Delta x_{22,t}$ this is seen to be $I(0) + I(1)$ which in sum is $I(1)$. The phenomenon that the timing of the variables will matter for the cointegration property to hold is something which does not apply to $I(1)$ systems.

The second type of cointegration that may arise is when variables are $CI(2, 1)$. This is the situation described in (2). If the relation $\beta_2' x_{2t}$, does not cointegrate with other $I(1)$ variables in the system, then the relation can be described alternatively as an $I(0)$ relation in the *differenced* series since $\beta_2' \Delta x_{2t}$ is stationary. If this is the only cointegration possibility present, then we can just model the series as an $I(1)$ system for the growth rates (given that the original variables are in logs) and the standard $I(1)$ analysis can be adopted.

The final cointegration possibility (3) is perhaps the most interesting because this is the one creating new insights compared to the $I(1)$ model. In this case[2] $\beta_3' x_{2t}$ is integrated of order one, ($x_{2t} \sim CI(2, 1)$), but with the further implication that there exist $I(1)$ variables in the system cointegrating with $\beta_3' x_{2t}$. This could be the variables x_{1t}, but as indicated in (3) it may also be necessary to include the differenced $I(2)$ variables, Δx_{2t}, which obviously will be integrated of order one as well. Sometimes the situation where first differences of the $I(2)$ variables are included in cointegration relations is referred to as *polynomial* cointegration,

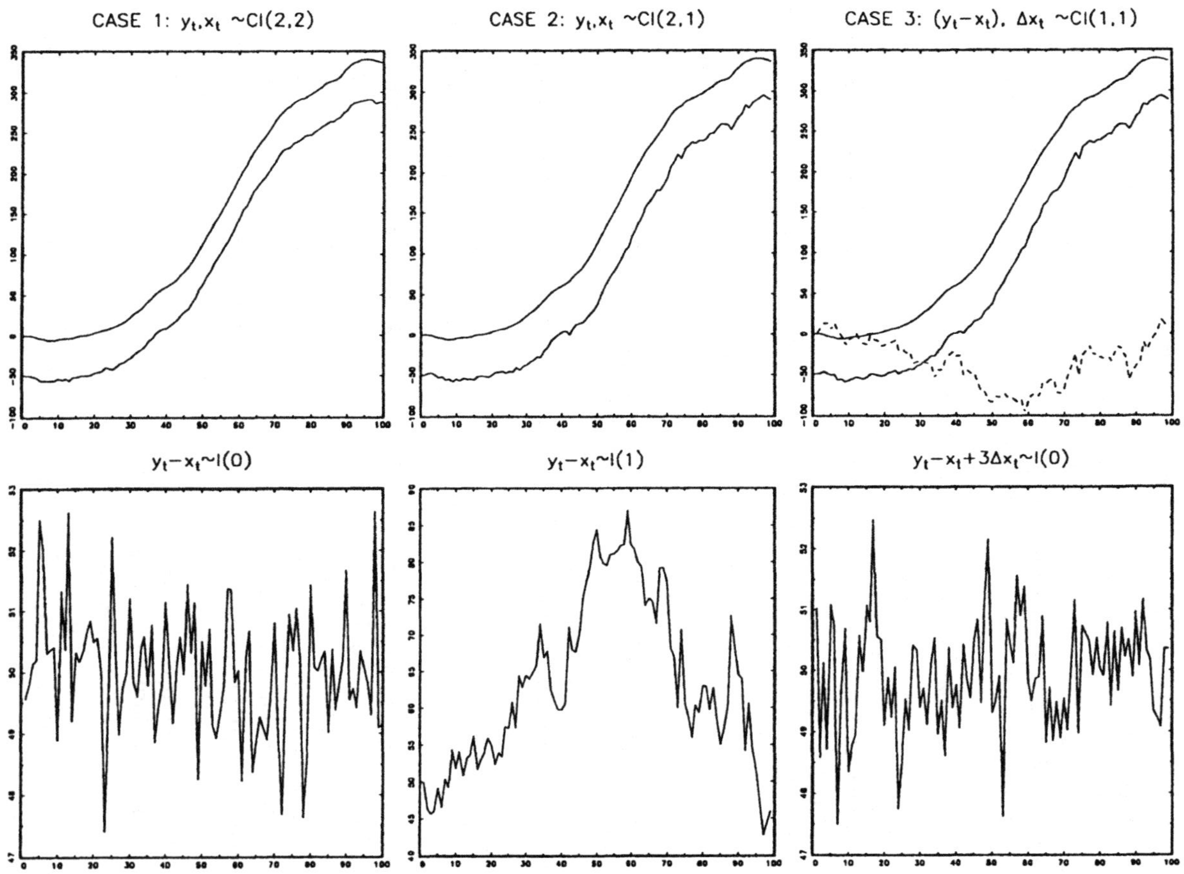

Figure 1. Examples of cointegrated I(2) series for $T = 100$ observations. Case 1: $y_t, x_t \sim \mathrm{CI}(2,2)$. Case 2: $y_t, x_t \sim \mathrm{CI}(2,1)$. Case 3: $y_t, x_t \sim \mathrm{CI}(2,1)$, and $(y_t - x_t)$, $\Delta x_t \sim \mathrm{CI}(1,1)$: *polynomial cointegration*. Note: Δx_t in case 3 has been scaled to ease comparison with $y_t - x_t$ in the second panel of case 2.

because the cointegration relation can be expressed in terms of a polynomial in the lag operator.

In figure 1 I have simulated different bivariate examples of two cointegrated I(2) series corresponding to the 3 cases outlined above.

3. Some motivation for economic models with I(2) variables

Recently cointegration amongst I(2) series and polynomial cointegration has been analyzed in a growing number of empirical studies. As I shall demonstrate in section 4 a dominating empirical regularity is that many nominal variables, price indices, and stock variables have characteristics that mimic those of I(2) processes, and hence models involving such variables may potentially be (polynomially) cointegrated according to the possibilities sketched in the previous section. Examples include models of money demand relations, see *inter alia*. King *et al.* (1991), Hallman *et al.* (1991), Johansen (1992a), Juselius and Hargreaves (1992), Stock and Watson (1993), Juselius (1994, 1996, 1998), Rahbek *et al.* (1998) and Haldrup (1994), and models of the Purchasing Power Parity (PPP), see, *inter alia*, Johansen and Juselius (1992), Juselius (1992, 1995a,b). Banerjee *et al.* (1998) presents an interesting I(2) analysis for inflation and the markup. In many of these studies the purpose has been to test empirically whether unit elasticity and homogeneity restrictions could be satisfied by the data, for instance whether money demand should be specified in real or in nominal terms. Consider also the PPP; if p_{1t}, p_{2t} are the logarithms of domestic and foreign prices, respectively, and $e_{12,t}$ is the logarithm of the domestic exchange rate in domestic currency per unit of the foreign currency, then the theory predicts that $p_{2t} - p_{1t} - e_{12t} = 0$ is an equilibrium relation. When the price series are I(2) and the exchange rate is I(1), as is frequently found in empirical studies, the theory suggests cointegration amongst the variables in a particular way.

Polynomial cointegration is not only a statistical property that can sometimes be found in the data but can be justified in many cases on theoretical grounds. In the following I shall describe some models where agent's intertemporal behaviour will lead to equilibrium relations with polynomial cointegration.

3.1. *Polynomial cointegration in models of intertemporal behaviour*

Cagan's model of hyperinflation. Cagan's model of hyperinflation, see Cagan (1956), has been investigated in numerous empirical studies, see e.g. Sargent (1977), Goodfriend (1982), Taylor (1991), and Engsted (1993, 1994). The model is derived under the assumption of rational expectations and instantaneous market clearing in the money market and dictates that

$$m_t - p_t = \alpha - \delta(\mathrm{E}_t p_{t+1} - p_t) + u_t \tag{4}$$

where m_t and p_t are the natural logarithms of the stock of money and the price level, respectively, and u_t is a variable capturing velocity and demand shocks. E_t is the mathematical expectations operator with respect the information available at time t, and α and δ are parameters to be estimated. Cagan's model predicts that if real balances tend to rise it indicates expected reductions in future inflation.

There are different ways of writing the cointegration implications that follow from this model. First, it is easy to see that (4) can be rewritten as

$$\Delta p_{t+1} - \alpha\delta^{-1} + \delta^{-1}(m_t - p_t) - \delta^{-1}u_t = \varepsilon_{t+1} \tag{5}$$

where $\varepsilon_{t+1} = p_{t+1} - \mathsf{E}_t p_{t+1}$ is the rational expectations forecast error at time $t+1$ and hence is a martingale difference. If the properties of the time series are such that the demand/velocity shock variable u_t is stationary $\mathsf{I}(0)$ whilst real balances and inflation variables are $\mathsf{I}(1)$ then $((m_t - p_t), \Delta p_{t+1})' \sim \mathsf{CI}(1,1)$. However, the theory also predicts then, that $(m_t, p_t) \sim \mathsf{CI}(2,1)$ with a cointegration vector given by $(1,-1)$. Hence $(m_t, p_t, \Delta p_t)$ constitutes an $\mathsf{I}(2)$ cointegrated system with polynomial cointegration.

Linear Quadratic Adjustment Cost models. The costs of adjusting economic policy instruments provides another important justification for considering polynomial cointegration. A class of intertemporal models having this feature is the Linear Quadratic Adjustment Cost (LQAC) model which has been extensively used in studies of e.g. labour and money demand, and models of price adjustment, see *inter alia* Sargent (1978), Kennan (1979), Dolado *et al.* (1991), Pesaran (1991), Price (1992), Gregory *et al.* (1993), West (1995), and Engsted and Haldrup (1994, 1997). In this model economic agents are assumed to choose some decision variable, y_t, in order to minimize the conditional expectation of an intertemporal loss function which in its most simple form is given as

$$L_t = \sum_{i=0}^{\infty} \delta^i [y_{t+i} - y^*_{t-i})^2 + (y_{t+i} - y_{t+i-1})^2]. \tag{6}$$

The variable y_t^* is the desired level of the decision variable and costs are incurred by discrepancies between this level and the actual level.[3] However, since adjustments are penalized through the presence of the term $(y_{t+i} - y_{t+i-1})$ in the loss function there is no instantaneous reaction towards the equilibrium. The parameter θ measures the relative cost of the two cost terms and δ is the subjective discount rate of the agents.

The first order condition of the problem which minimizes the conditional expectation of the loss function (6) yields an Euler equation which can be reparametrized as

$$\Delta^2 y_{t+1} = (\delta^{-1} - 1)\Delta y_t + \frac{\theta}{\delta}(y_t - y_t^*) + u_{t+1} \tag{7}$$

where $u_{t+1} = y_{t+1} - \mathsf{E}_t y_{t+1}$ is again an $\mathsf{I}(0)$ rational expectations prediction error. Equation (7) is deliberately formulated such that it facilitates analysis when y_t is an $\mathsf{I}(2)$ variable. In this situation, unless we are in the degenerate case with no discounting, $\delta = 1$, y_t and its target y_t^* will cointegrate into an $\mathsf{I}(1)$ relation which further cointegrates with Δy_t; hence y_t and the variables determining y_t^* are polynomially cointegrated. An important feature of this model is that due to adjustment costs the gap between y_t and y_t^* will not be closed completely.

The above examples of intertemporal models show that if certain variables can be considered I(2), then theory predicts variables to be polynomially cointegrated. It should be emphasized, however, that cointegration testing *per se* is *not* sufficient for rejection or non-rejection of this sort of economic theories. Theoretical models (and in particular intertemporal models based on Euler equations) provide many more (overidentifying) restrictions that need to be tested against the data; cointegration only delivers a necessary condition to be fullfilled for such models to be valid.[4]

3.2. *Multicointegration as defined by Granger and Lee (1989, 1990)*

It is normally the case that if one considers just two I(1) series, then only a single cointegration relation can exist between the variables. However, in some situations it may happen that more than one cointegration vector exists amongst the series because the cumulated equilibrium errors cointegrate with the basic economic variables. This property refers to *multicointegration*. As we shall see shortly it may be advisable in this situation to formulate the system in terms of an I(2) system which will facilitate the analysis although the original economic variables are really I(1).

The notion of multicointegration was initially introduced and defined by Granger and Lee (1989, 1990) and is also considered in Salmon (1988). They consider the case with a system of two I(1) variables, production, y_t, and sales, x_t, of some commodity and assume that these variables are cointegrated, $(y_t, x_t)' \sim \mathrm{CI}(1,1)$, with a cointegrating vector implying that $y_t - x_t$ is stationary. The variable $y_t - x_t$ has a nice interpretation as this is just the change of inventories, ΔI_t, and, assuming no depreciation, the inventory stock is then given as $I_t = \Delta^{-1}(y_t - x_t) = \sum_{i=1}^{t} \Delta I_i$, i.e. the cumulated equilibrium errors of the equilibrium relation between y_t and x_t. Naturally the inventory stock is I(1) by construction and hence it can happen that this variable cointegrates with y_t and/or x_t such that

$$I_t - \gamma_{11} y_t - \gamma_{12} x_t \sim \mathrm{I}(0). \tag{8}$$

This is the condition for multicointegration amongst just two variables.

In the literature polynomial cointegration, and multicointegration are frequently used as synonyms, simply because multicointegrated series can be rewritten in terms of polynomial cointegration amongst I(2) variables including their differences. Note that (8) can be written in the alternative way $\Delta^{-1}y_t - \Delta^{-1}x_t - \gamma_{11}y_t - \gamma_{12}x_t$ where e.g. $\Delta^{-1}y_t = \sum_{i=0}^{t} y_i \equiv Y_t$ and capital letters indicate cumulated series which then are I(2). In terms of the new series we can rewrite (8) as

$$Y_t - X_t - \gamma_{11}\Delta Y_t - \gamma_{12}\Delta X_t \sim \mathrm{I}(0), \tag{9}$$

and hence this indicates polynomial cointegration in the variables[5] (Y_t, X_t).

There are numerous examples of economic models that imply multi-cointegration[6] and in particular models which describe the interaction amongst stock and flow variables. Granger and Lee's inventory model is one such example, but one could also consider, for instance, a model of stock-adjustment in housing construction where y_t is housing units started, x_t is housing units completed, and $I_t = \sum_{i=0}^{t}(y_i - x_i)$ is the stock of housing units under construction, see Lee (1992, 1996) and Engsted and Haldrup (1998). Similarly, according to the life-cycle hypothesis of income another example is when y_t is income, x_t is consumption, and I_t measures wealth (cumulated savings), see e.g. Lee (1996), and Hendry and von-Ungern Sternberg (1981). In these papers many examples are given supporting that multicointegration is an empirically relevant concept in stock-flow models.

In the above examples it could seem as if the first level cointegration vector is always trivially given as $(1, -1)$. This is not the case, however. Sometimes it is an empirical problem to measure for instance durable goods and the corresponding service flows, see e.g. Campbell (1987). Similarly, in the housing example some housing starts may never be completed and hence the relationship between y_t and x_t is not given beforehand as the difference between the variables, but rather as the quasi-difference $y_t - \kappa x_t$ where κ is a parameter which needs to be estimated.

An interesting property of the multicointegration concept is that the implied decision rules that correspond to generalized error correction models can be derived from LQAC type of models with *proportional, integral, and derivative (PID)* control mechanisms, see e.g. Phillips (1954), Holt *et al.* (1960), and Hendry and von-Ungern Sternberg (1981). Granger and Lee (1990) provide this formal connection, see also Engsted and Haldrup (1998).

4. A comparison of some properties of univariate processes

In this section I describe some of the univariate features characterizing I(2) processes. To facilitate comparison with other time series models, possibly with maintained deterministic components, we consider the general data generating process (DGP)

$$x_t = \gamma' c_t + x_t^0, \qquad t = 1, 2, \ldots T. \tag{10}$$

The deterministic part of the time series is given by $\gamma' c_t$ whereas x_t^0 contains the stochastic part. For instance, c_t can be a polynomial trend vector $c_t = (1, t, t^2, \ldots, t^k)'$ such that $\gamma' c_t = \sum_{i=0}^{k} \gamma_i t^i$ is a general trend polynomial. In practice $c_t = (1, t, t^2)'$ is most common as the specification of the trend part, however, other (even non-polynomial) characterizations of the deterministic part may be considered.

Asymptotic behaviour of the processes. It is of interest to compare some of the asymptotic properties of I(0), I(1), and I(2) series, viewed as possible DGP's, and their relation to various sorts of deterministic components. To ease the comparison the following (stochastic) processes are addressed:

$$x_{0t}^0 = \varepsilon_t, \qquad \Delta x_{1t}^0 = \varepsilon_t, \qquad \Delta^2 x_{2t}^0 = \varepsilon_t \tag{11}$$

Notice that subscripts $i = 0, 1, 2$ indicate the order of integration of the series.

The assumptions I shall make about the errors driving the processes are quite general and certainly need not be just martingale difference sequences. In fact, the errors are only needed to be I(0) with a dependency that is not too long in memory. The regularity conditions of the errors are rather familiar in the literature and are discussed in detail by e.g. Phillips (1987).

For later reference we need to define $\sigma^2 = \lim_{T\to\infty} \mathrm{E}(T^{-1}(\sum_{i=1}^T \varepsilon_i)^2)$ which is frequently denoted the 'long run variance'. This can be written in the alternative way: $\sigma^2 = \sigma_\varepsilon^2 + 2\lambda$, where $\sigma_\varepsilon^2 = \mathrm{E}(\varepsilon_1^2)$ and $\lambda = \sum_{j=2}^\infty \mathrm{E}(\varepsilon_1 \varepsilon_j)$.

One of the basic properties of I(0) series is that certain functions of the sample values will converge to constants as the number of observations tends to infinity. For instance laws of large numbers guarantee that the sample mean converges in probability to its true mean for a wide range of processes, including stationary processes, see e.g. White (1984). However, one of the basic features of I(1) and I(2) processes is that this sort of convergence theorems will fail to hold. Instead, sample moments, suitably normalized, will converge (weakly) to random variables rather than to constants.

I(1) Processes. Initially, consider the I(1) series x_{1t}^0 and assume for convenience a zero initial condition, $x_{1,0}^0 = 0$. In levels the series can thus be written as the stochastic trend

$$x_{1t}^0 = \sum_{j=1}^t \varepsilon_j = \varepsilon_1 + \varepsilon_2 + \cdots + \varepsilon_t. \tag{12}$$

This demonstrates an important feature of I(1) series, namely, that a shock to the series occurring in the past will persist and hence will have an everlasting influence on the levels of the series.

Under weak regularity conditions the limiting behaviour of x_{1t}^0, after appropriate scaling, can be shown to be a Brownian motion. More specifically it holds that

$$T^{-1/2} x_{1,[Tr]}^0 = T^{-1/2} \sum_{j=1}^{[Tr]} \varepsilon_j + o_p(1) \Rightarrow B(r) \equiv \sigma W(r) \tag{13}$$

where '$\Rightarrow$' signifies weak convergence and $[\cdot]$ selects the integer value of its argument. $B(r)$ is a Brownian motion defined on the unit interval $r \in [0, 1]$ with long run variance σ^2. $W(r)$ is a standard Brownian motion.

In calculating the limiting behaviour of the sample mean and sample variance of x_{1t}^0 it can be shown that $\bar{x}_1^0 = O_p(T^{1/2})$ and $\widehat{\mathrm{Var}}(x_{1t}^0) = O_p(T)$. Hence the process will be without bound asymptotically and the empirical variance will increase with the sample size.

I(2) Processes. Turning to I(2) processes it is easy to see that by assuming $x^0_{2,-1} = x^0_{2,0} = 0$, the series can be written in levels as

$$x^0_{2t} = \sum_{k=1}^{t}\sum_{j=1}^{k} \varepsilon_j = t\varepsilon_1 + (t-1)\varepsilon_2 + \cdots + 3\varepsilon_{t-2} + 2\varepsilon_{t-1} + \varepsilon_t. \tag{14}$$

This is also a stochastic trend but it is better to denote it an I(2) trend to discriminate it from usual I(1) trends. It is obvious that since an I(2) trend is a double sum of errors such series will be very smooth by nature. Notice that Δx^0_{2t} is just the I(1) trend given in (12). As seen the influence from a shock that occurred in the past will have an amplifying impact on the levels of the series as the time goes. This may seem as an odd property and researchers have argued that this feature makes I(2) processes an inconvenient class of models to consider in reality, see e.g. Granger (1997, p. 173). However, one way of looking at the amplified persistency phenomenon is to consider a shock to the growth rate of an already persistent time series, e.g. inflation; of course, this will have an accumulating effect on the levels of the series since this is just how the price level, for instance, is defined.

It is important to make a brief side remark on explosive processes, i.e. processes with roots outside the unit circle. Such processes have characteristics that mimic I(2) processes, at least for sample sizes of moderate length. A simple example of an explosive process is $x^0_{\text{exp},t} = \alpha x^0_{\text{exp},t-1} + \varepsilon_t$, with $|\alpha| > 1$. With a zero initial condition the series can be given the levels representation

$$x^0_{exp,t} = \sum_{j=1}^{j} \alpha^{t-j}\varepsilon_j = \alpha^{t-1}\varepsilon_1 + \alpha^{t-2}\varepsilon_2 + \cdots + \alpha\varepsilon_{t-1} + \varepsilon_t. \tag{15}$$

Since $|\alpha| > 1$ a shock in the past will have an increasing effect on the series as t increases, just like I(2) processes. However, whilst the impact of shocks increases exponentially in (15) the rate is the slower linear rate for I(2) series as shown in (14). Asymptotically it is easy to discriminate I(2) series from explosive processes, but in finite samples it can be difficult, especially if α is not too large.

Returning to I(2) series, I proceed by describing their asymptotic behaviour. By suitable scaling it can be shown that the limiting process of an I(2) variable is an integrated Brownian motion. More precisely we have that

$$T^{-3/2}x^0_{2t} = T^{-3/2}\sum_{s=1}^{[Tr]}\sum_{j=1}^{[Ts]} \varepsilon_j + o_p(1) \Rightarrow \int_0^r B(s)\mathrm{d}s \equiv \sigma\int_0^r W(s)\mathrm{d}s. \tag{16}$$

The easier notation $\overline{W}(r) = \int_0^r W(s)\mathrm{d}s$ is used to indicate an integrated Brownian motion. For I(2) processes the limits of the sample mean and variance imply that $\bar{x}^0_1 = O_p(T^{3/2})$ and $\widehat{\mathrm{Var}}(x^0_{1t}) = O_p(T^3)$. Hence the scaling of these quantities needs to be increased in comparing I(1) and I(2) processes.

Deterministic Components. Deterministics are important because they appear in most time series in one form or another, for instance as a trend polynomial $\gamma' c_t$ as in (10). If not taking proper account of such components it may flaw and possibly invalidate the statistical analysis. Hence some insight of their behaviour is necessary. In Eq. (10), consider a single component of c_t, which I denote c_{it}. Since the Brownian motions previously discussed are defined on the unit interval $r \in [0, 1[$ we may want a scaling of the deterministics which facilitates comparison. Obviously, we can scale c_{it} and define $f_{Ti}(r)$ such that

$$f_{Ti}(r) = \frac{c_{it}}{T^i} = \frac{[Tr]^i}{T^i} + o(1) \longrightarrow r^i \text{ for } T \longrightarrow \infty$$

where $i = 0, 1, 2, \ldots$ In particular it is seen that a linear and a quadratic trend require normalizations T and T^2, respectively, for $f_{Ti}(r)$ to be bounded.

A time series x_t like in Eq. (10) is generally a mixture of deterministic and stochastic components; the latter possibly with components of different integration orders. With respect to the asymptotic behaviour of x_t it is therefore the component of the largest order which dominates the series in the limit. In finite samples the relative influence of the components will naturally depend on the parameters as well as the signal to noise ratio. If we let ' > ' signify 'dominance in variation', the following ranking can be made:

$$t^2 > \mathsf{I}(2) > t > \mathsf{I}(1) > \mathsf{I}(0). \tag{17}$$

This ordering becomes especially important with respect to hypothesis testing.

5. Determining the order of differencing

In the univariate time series literature following the Box and Jenkins tradition it is commonplace to difference the series an appropriate number of times until, by visual inspection, the autocorrelations of the transformed series exhibit fast decay. The idea about unit root testing is to use a more formal statistical testing procedure to identify the number of differences needed to render the time series stationary. However, in doing so it is quite important to be aware of the alternative hypothesis under consideration, i.e. whether I(2) is tested against I(1), I(0), or explosive processes, possibly with maintained deterministic components. A large number of tests for double unit roots exist in the literature, but their properties differ depending upon the actual alternative that power is wanted against.

In the following some of these tests are described. The discussion is separated into two types of tests: parametric tests which assume that the series can be given a finite order AR representation, and the semi-parametric equivalents of the tests which permit a more general class of processes. To simplify the discussion I assume that I(2) is the largest order of integration to consider; to my knowledge there are no examples of economic time series which have been found to be I(3) or of higher order.

5.1. *Parametric approaches to testing for I(2)*

Initially I shall assume that the time series x_t is free of deterministic components and can be given the finite order $\mathsf{AR}(p)$ representation

$$A(L)x_t = u_t \tag{18}$$

where u_t is a sequence of iid errors.

A joint test for double unit roots. $A(L)$ can be factorized as $A(L) = A(1)L + A^*(1)\Delta L + A^{**}(L)\Delta^2$ where $A^{**}(L)$ is a polynomial of order $p-2$ with $A(0) = 1$. By defining $A(1) = 1 - \alpha_1$ and $A^*(1) = 1 - \alpha_2$ the regression equivalent of (18) can be written in the generalized augmented Dickey-Fuller form

$$\Delta^2 x_t = (\hat{\alpha}_1 - 1)x_{t-1} + (\hat{\alpha}_2 - 1)\Delta x_{t-1} + \sum_{j=1}^{p-2} \hat{\varphi}_j \Delta^2 x_{t-j} + \hat{u}_t. \tag{19}$$

Hasza (1977) and Hasza and Fuller (1979) were the first to suggest using this auxiliary regression as the basis to test for double unit roots. They used the fact that when x_t is $\mathsf{I}(2)$, $\alpha_1 = \alpha_2 = 1$, and hence it is natural to test this joint hypothesis by a standard F-test, for instance. Observe that since the F-test is two-sided, the alternative hypothesis is quite general as it covers all the situations where x_t is either explosive, $\mathsf{I}(0)$, or $\mathsf{I}(1)$. In the paper by Hasza and Fuller the non-standard limiting distribution of the F-test statistic is derived; by using the notation previously given, the distribution reads

$$F_{\alpha_1, \alpha_2} \Rightarrow \frac{1}{2} \int_0^1 dWG(r)' \left(\int_0^1 G(r)G(r)'dr \right)^{-1} \int_0^1 G(r)dW \tag{20}$$

where $G(r) = (W(r), \overline{W}(r))'$.

Empirical critical values of this distribution are reported by Hasza and Fuller. As it is the case for the Dickey-Fuller test for integration of order 1, it is important that the correct augmentation is used in the regression (19): A too low order implies that the errors will not be iid and hence gives rise to size distortion of the test. On the other hand, including too many lags of the lagged second differences will give power loss. This trade-off is a difficult compromise in practical situations, especially when the errors contain moving average components.

An interesting property which follows from estimation of the parameters in (19) is that, given the true process is $\mathsf{I}(2)$, the parameters α_1 and α_2 converge to their true value 1 very rapidly. In fact, it can be shown that

$$T^2(\hat{\alpha}_1 - 1) = \mathrm{O}_{\mathrm{p}}(1) \tag{21}$$

$$T(\hat{\alpha}_2 - 1) = \mathrm{O}_{\mathrm{p}}(1). \tag{22}$$

So, the parameter α_1 is estimated at a more rapid rate than the usual super-consistent rate $O_p(T^{-1})$ applying for $\mathsf{I}(1)$ systems.

Despite the fast convergence rates of the least squares estimates the use of single t-tests of the hypotheses H_0: $\alpha_1 = 1$, and H_0: $\alpha_2 = 1$ based on the regression (19) is of little use in practice when testing for $\mathsf{I}(2)$. For instance, one may consider a sequential testing procedure where one first tests H_0: $\alpha_1 = 1$ and, given acceptance, proceeds to testing for a second unit root, H_0: $\alpha_2 = 1$. But this procedure is invalid as the first test will depend upon whether the second hypothesis is actually true or false. Observe that both when a single and double unit root exist in the process it will hold that $\alpha_1 = 1$. However, in the case of an I(2) process ($\alpha_2 = 1$) the distribution of t_{α_1} is given by a complicated functional of the stochastic integrals $W(r)$, and $\overline{W}(r)$, whereas when x_t is I(1)($|\alpha_2| < 1$), t_{α_1} will follow the usual Dickey-Fuller distribution,[7] see Fuller (1976), Dickey and Fuller (1979) and Phillips (1987):

$$t_{\alpha_1} \Rightarrow \left(\int_0^1 W(r)\mathrm{d}W\right)\left(\int_0^1 W^2(r)\mathrm{d}W\right)^{-1/2}. \tag{23}$$

Hence the t_{α_1} test of H_0: $\alpha_1 = 1$ is not invariant to the actual value of α_2. Dickey and Pantula (1987) conducted a simulation study to examine the empirical relevance of the size distortions that result from using the Dickey-Fuller test in the first step of the sequential procedure sketched above. They found that for a sample of length 50 the Dickey-Fuller test has an actual size against the stationary alternative which exceeds the nominal 5% level when, in fact, two unit roots are present. In other words, it is more likely that the sequential procedure gives the misleading inference that the series is stationary when the process is I(2) compared to when it is I(1); intuition says that we should strongly reject stationarity when two unit roots are present rather than just a single unit root.

A consistent sequential testing procedure for the number of unit roots. As an alternative strategy to the one outlined above Dickey and Pantula (1987) suggest to reverse the sequence of testing by starting with the highest possible integration order and then testing down the integration order of the model.[8] By using this sequence of testing the hypotheses a consistent α-level of the procedure is obtained. The test procedure is conditional[9] in the sense that first I(2)-ness is tested given at least the series is I(1) and, provided rejection, I(1)-ness is subsequently tested against the stationary I(0) alternative. In the first step of the procedure a unit root is present both under the null and the alternative hypothesis so the appropriate auxiliary regression to focus on is (19) with the restriction $\alpha_1 = 1$ imposed. Hence the auxiliary regression reads

$$\Delta^2 x_t = (\hat{\alpha}_2 - 1)\Delta x_{t-1} + \sum_{j=1}^{p-2} \hat{\varphi}_j \Delta^2 x_{t-j} + \hat{u}_t \tag{24}$$

where the t-ratio associated with the regressor Δx_{t-1} is used to test H_0: $\alpha_2 = 1$. Since this is nothing else than a standard I(1) problem for the first differenced data, the test statistic follows the usual Dickey-Fuller distribution[10] (23) which is tabulated in e.g. Fuller (1976) and McKinnon (1991). When the null hypothesis is rejected, I(1) is tested against I(0) using standard procedures, for instance a Dickey-Fuller test on the levels of the series. Of course this is equivalent to testing H_0: $\alpha_1 = 1$ in (19).

Dickey and Pantula's procedure seems to be the most dominant procedure in applied work and obviously has the advantage that in each step the null distributions is given by the well-known Dickey-Fuller distribution and with a size which is controllable by choice of the significance level. In terms of power against the I(1) alternative, Dickey and Pantula demonstrate that the sequential procedure is preferable compared to the joint test of Hasza and Fuller, because the imposition of a unit root in the first step will be correct, both under the null and the alternative hypothesis. They also argued that some power is gained as the joint test is two-sided in nature, whereas the alternative is one-sided by using the sequential t-test procedure.

Notwithstanding, it is important to note that if power is wanted against the *explosive* alternative the Dickey-Pantula testing strategy is inappropriate. As indicated in section (4) explosive processes are a relevant class of models to consider as their properties (at least in finite samples) mimic those of I(2) series. If the true underlying process is explosive, the prior imposition of a unit root in the first stage of Dickey and Pantula's procedure may give the misleading inference that the series is really I(2) because, in principle, an explosive process can be differenced infinitely many times without becoming stationary. In addition, wrongly differencing an explosive process may produce a noninvertible error term which may cause serious problems with respect to estimation and inference. A Monte Carlo study reported in Haldrup (1994a) shows that when $\alpha_1 > 1$ the power following from the Dickey-Pantula procedure tends rapidly to zero as α_1 and the sample size T increase.

If power against the explosive alternative is wanted the Hasza-Fuller I(2)-test should be used. When this test rejects the series can be either I(1), I(0) or explosive. Subsequently the usual Dickey-Fuller t-test for the I(1)-null can be performed on the levels of the series but with a two-sided alternative: the lower tail of the Dickey-Fuller distribution indicates rejection of I(1) in favour of the stationary alternative; the right tail of the distribution favours the explosive alternative. In most applications only the one-sided stationary alternative is considered but in the present case the upper tail is naturally of interest as well.

A symmetrized joint test for double unit roots. A different class of (non-sequential) tests is the so-called symmetric tests which, in an I(2) setting, were initially suggested by Sen (1986) and Sen and Dickey (1987). The test is a symmetric version of Hasza and Fuller's (1979) joint F-test. The motivation arises from the interesting property that if the difference equation defining the time series is given by

$$x_t = \phi_1 x_{t-1} + \phi_2 x_{t-2} + \cdots + \phi_p x_{t-p} + u_t \tag{25}$$

where u_t is white noise with variance σ_u^2, then the series with the same difference equation equal to

$$x_t = \phi_1 x_{t+1} + \phi_2 x_{t+2} + \cdots + \phi_p x_{t+p} + v_t \tag{26}$$

will also have white noise errors v_t with the same error variance as for u_t, see

Fuller (1976). The basic idea is thus to jointly estimate (25) and (26), in a symmetric fashion, and use it to test for double unit roots.

The symmetrized version of the Hasza-Fuller regression model (19) is given by the pair of regression equations

$$\begin{aligned}\Delta^2 x_t &= (\hat{\alpha}_1 - 1)x_{t-1} + (\hat{\alpha}_2 - 1)\Delta x_{t-1} + \sum_{j=1}^{p-2} \hat{\varphi}_j \Delta^2 x_{t-j} + \hat{u}_t,\ t = p+1, \ldots, n \\ \Delta^2 x_t &= (\hat{\alpha}_1 - 1)x_{t-1} - (\hat{\alpha}_2 - 1)\Delta x_t + \sum_{j=1}^{p-2} \hat{\varphi}_j \Delta^2 x_{t+j} + \hat{v}_t,\ t = 3, \ldots, n-p+2.\end{aligned} \tag{27}$$

In table 1 the regressand and the p columns of the independent variables are completely characterized. The above system corresponds to a SURE regression model with allowance made for the constraint that parameters are the same and hence this will provide more efficient estimates of the parameters of interest, α_1 and α_2.

From this 'extended' Hasza-Fuller regression the F-test of the hypothesis H_0: $\alpha_1 = \alpha_2 = 1$ can be constructed. Notice that using just the first $n-p-1$ rows of Table 1 (i.e. the first panel) corresponds to the usual Hasza-Fuller regression. Due to the symmetry of the regression model, the limiting distribution of the F-test statistic is somewhat simplified as cross terms appear to cancel. The distribution is still non-standard, of course. More specifically it reads

$$F_{\alpha_1,\alpha_2}^{Sym} \Longrightarrow \left(\int_0^1 \overline{W}^2(r)\mathrm{d}r\right)^{-1}\left(\int_0^1 \overline{W}(r)\mathrm{d}W\right)^2 + \frac{1}{4}\left(\int_0^1 W^2(r)\mathrm{d}r\right)^{-1}. \tag{28}$$

The empirical distributions are reported in Sen and Dickey's article.

The purpose of the symmetrized F-test is to gain power and simulations reported by Sen and Dickey support this intuition. They find that for a sample size of either 50 or 100 a wide range of parameters under the stationary alternative

Table 1. Regressand and regressors in the Sen and Dickey (1987) symmetric test.

Dependent variable	Independent variables				
$\Delta^2 x_{p+1}$	x_p	Δx_p	$\Delta^2 x_p$	$\cdots$	$\Delta^2 x_3$
$\Delta^2 x_{p+2}$	x_{p+1}	Δx_{p+1}	$\Delta^2 x_{p+1}$	$\cdots$	$\Delta^2 x_4$
$\Delta^2 x_{p+3}$	x_{p+2}	Δx_{p+2}	$\Delta^2 x_{p+2}$	$\cdots$	$\Delta^2 x_5$
$\vdots$	$\vdots$	$\vdots$	$\vdots$		$\vdots$
$\Delta^2 x_n$	x_{n-1}	Δx_{n-1}	$\Delta^2 x_{n-1}$	$\cdots$	$\Delta^2 x_{n-p+2}$
$\Delta^2 x_{n-p+2}$	x_{n-p+1}	$-\Delta x_{n-p+2}$	$\Delta^2 x_{n-p+3}$	$\cdots$	$\Delta^2 x_n$
$\Delta^2 x_{n-p+1}$	x_{n-p}	$-\Delta x_{n-p+1}$	$\Delta^2 x_{n-p+2}$	$\cdots$	$\Delta^2 x_{n-1}$
$\Delta^2 x_{n-p}$	x_{n-p-1}	$-\Delta x_{n-p}$	$\Delta^2 x_{n-p+1}$	$\cdots$	$\Delta^2 x_{n-2}$
$\vdots$	$\vdots$	$\vdots$	$\vdots$		$\vdots$
$\Delta^2 x_3$	x_2	$-\Delta x_3$	$\Delta^2 x_4$	$\cdots$	$\Delta^2 x_{p+1}$

leads to considerable power increases compared to the Hasza-Fuller non-symmetric test. For explosive alternatives (for a sample of 50 observations) power is found to be larger as well, but their study is more limited in this respect.

Obtaining power against deterministic trend alternatives. So far little has been said about the appropriate treatment of deterministic components. Notwithstanding, it is of crucial importance that deterministics be adequately dealt with since otherwise very misleading inference may result. A few examples will demonstrate this.

The difficulties are well-known from the I(1) analysis. Consider a trend stationary process $x_t = \gamma_0 + \gamma_1 t + x_t^0$ where $x_t^0 \sim \mathrm{I}(0)$ and $\gamma_1 \neq 0$. In testing for unit roots one may consider a Dickey-Fuller test; assume the analyst wrongly conducts the regression

$$\Delta x_t = \hat{\mu} + (\hat{\alpha} - 1)x_{t-1} + \sum_{j=1}^{p-1} \hat{\varphi}_j \Delta x_{t-j} + \hat{u}_t \tag{29}$$

without a trend. In this case it can be shown that although $|\alpha| < 1$, $\mathrm{plim}_{T\to\infty}\hat{\alpha} = 1$ (unit root) and $\mathrm{plim}_{T\to\infty}\hat{\mu} = \gamma_1$ (drift). The explanation is that the regression (29) does not accomodate a trend stationary process under the alternative. Hence the only way the trending feature of the process can be captured is to bias $\hat{\alpha}$ towards unity and letting $\hat{\mu}$ become an estimate of the trend slope, γ_1.

The problem carries over to the I(2) analysis. For instance, if the data generating mechanism is given by either of the processes

$$\begin{aligned} x_t &= \gamma_0 + \gamma_1 t + \gamma_2 t^2 + x_t^0, \qquad && \text{with } \gamma_2 \neq 0,\ x_t^0 \sim \mathrm{I}(0), \\ x_t &= \gamma_0 + \gamma_1 t + x_t^0, && \text{with } \gamma_1 \neq 0,\ x_t^0 \sim \mathrm{I}(1), \end{aligned} \tag{30}$$

then in both cases x_t is dominated by a deterministic trend. Consider the Hasza Fuller regression (19), possibly with an intercept added, but no linear or quadratic trend. In this situation it can be shown that for both processes sketched in (30) $\mathrm{plim}_{T\to\infty}\hat{\alpha}_1 = \mathrm{plim}_{T\to\infty}\hat{\alpha}_2 = 1$ and hence the test has zero asymptotic power and therefore erroneously indicates the series to be I(2). One way of getting power against the processes in (30) is to include also a quadratic trend in the auxiliary regression since in both cases the series have a quadratic trend when written in levels.

Essentially detrending can be undertaken in two different, though equivalent, ways. In accordance with the first route, the following Hasza-Fuller regressions may be conducted:

$$\Delta^2 x_t = \hat{m}_0 + (\hat{\alpha}_1 - 1)x_{t-1} + (\hat{\alpha}_2 - 1)\Delta x_{t-1} + \sum_{j=1}^{p-2} \hat{\varphi}_j \Delta^2 x_{t-j} + \hat{u}_t \tag{31}$$

$$\Delta^2 x_t = \tilde{m}_0 + \tilde{m}_t t + (\tilde{\alpha}_1 - 1)x_{t-1} + (\tilde{\alpha}_2 - 1)\Delta x_{t-1} + \sum_{j=1}^{p-2} \tilde{\varphi}_j \Delta^2 x_{t-j} + \tilde{u}_t \tag{32}$$

$$\Delta^2 x_t = \bar{m}_0 + \bar{m}_1 t + \bar{m}_2 t^2 + (\bar{\alpha}_1 - 1)x_{t-1} + (\bar{\alpha}_2 - 1)\Delta x_{t-1} + \sum_{j=1}^{p-2} \bar{\varphi}_j \Delta^2 x_{t-j} + \bar{u}_t. \tag{33}$$

In (33) the test of H_0: $\alpha_1 = \alpha_2 = 1$ has power against alternatives where the true series is $I(0)$ + quadratic trend or $I(1)$ + linear trend. Notice that in both cases the series in levels will have a quadratic trend and this is exactly why this regressor should be included in the regression. Turning to (32), the test based on this regression has power against $I(0)$ + linear trend and $I(1)$ + drift processes because in these cases the dominant feature of the series in levels is the linear trend. Finally (31) should be used when the series is suspected to have a non-zero mean.

It is important to realize that the reason for including a linear and quadratic trend in (33) is not because a cubic trend or a trend of order $O(T^4)$ is believed to characterize the series when two unit roots are present, but because the appropriate alternative should be accommodated to ensure a consistent test.

The above reflections apply equally to the symmetric test of Sen and Dickey and of course also to the sequential procedure of Dickey and Pantula. However, when using the sequential procedure the first step deterministic regressors are of order one less compared to the Hasza-Fuller procedure, since the assumption of one unit root increases the order of all deterministic regressors.

The second route to pursue in detrending time series is to consider

$$\begin{aligned} x_t &= \hat{\gamma}_0 + \hat{x}_t^0 \\ x_t &= \tilde{\gamma}_0 + \tilde{\gamma}_1 t + \tilde{x}_t^0 \\ x_t &= \bar{\gamma}_0 + \bar{\gamma}_1 t + \bar{\gamma}_2 t^2 + \bar{x}_t^0 \end{aligned} \tag{34}$$

and proceed with the same analysis as in the case with no deterministics, but by using as new series the detrended processes $\hat{x}_t^0$, $\tilde{x}_t^0$, and $\bar{x}_t^0$. The considerations of which deterministic regressors to use follows the discussion already given. This latter detrending procedure appears to be especially attractive when conducting semiparametric tests as I shall demonstrate later.

Both of the detrending procedures are going to deliver the same results. The way that detrending affects the asymptotic distributions is rather straightforward since in place of the Brownian motion expressions $W(r)$ and $\overline{W}(r)$ used in (20), (23) and (28) one substitutes by appropriately detrended Brownian motions, i.e. the limiting processes of $\hat{x}_t^0$, $\tilde{x}_t^0$ and $\bar{x}_t^0$. These are given by

$$W^i(r) = W(r) - f_i(r)'\left(\int_0^1 f_i(s) f_i(s)' \mathrm{d}s\right)^{-1} \int_0^1 f_i(s) W(s) \mathrm{d}s, \quad i = 0, 1, 2 \tag{35}$$

where, respectively, $f_0(r) = 1$, $f_1(r) = (1, r)'$, and $f_2(r) = (1, r, r^2)'$.

With respect to the repeated Brownian motions $\overline{W}(r) = \int_0^r W(s)\mathrm{d}s$ this is replaced by integrated equivalents of the above detrended Brownian motions.

The finite sample critical values relevant for the different tests are reported in

Table 2. Some references to critical values used in tests for double unit roots.

Detrending Test	None	Constant	Trend	Quadratic trend
Hasza-Fuller, F_{α_1,α_2}	Hasza and Fuller (1979),			Haldrup (1994a)
Dickey-Pantula*, t_{α_1}	Fuller (1976)			
Sen-Dickey, $F^{Sym}_{\alpha_1\alpha,2}$	n.a.	Sen and Dickey (1987)		Shin and Kim (1997)

* The Dickey-Pantula test is equivalent to the Dickey-Fuller test on the differenced data.

various articles. Table 2 provides a review of the appropriate references where the relevant fractiles can be found.

5.2. *Examples of parametric tests for I(2)*

Throughout the paper I will apply the various techniques presented to actual time series. The first data set is the money and price series (in logs) for the German hyperinflation episode 1920:1–1923:6. The period is the same as in other analyses of this data set, see e.g. Engsted (1993, 1994), and Casella (1989).

The next data set is used to analyze money demand in Denmark and has previously been examined by Juselius (1998). The sample is 1974:1–1993:4 and extends the sample period considered by Johansen and Juselius (1990). The series, except the bond rate i_{bt}, are in logs. Potentially, consumer prices, p_{ct}, the implicit GDP deflator, p_t, and nominal money, m_t will have I(2) features. The remaining series, real money, $m_t - p_t$, real GDP, y_t, and the effective bond rate, i_{bt} are more likely to be I(1), but naturally these are empirical questions to be tested.

The final data set is for housing construction in the US and covers the period 1968:1–1994:12. The series are new privately owned housing units started and completed, respectively. This data set is included to demonstrate the idea of multicointegration as we shall see later. The data set has previously been analyzed by Lee (1996) and Engsted and Haldrup (1998).

In table 3 (1st. panel) the money and price series during the German hyperinflation episode have been tested for the presence of double unit roots. All three tests described in the previous section have been conducted.[11] To account for the different deterministic alternatives the cases with constant, trend, and quadratic trend were considered. A quadratic trend was not considered in the Dickey-Pantula procedure since this implies the presence of at least a cubic trend in the levels of the series and power against this alternative does not seem reasonable. As seen, all tests favour the I(2) null.

In the second panel results for the price and money series from the Danish money demand data set are displayed. Both p_{ct} and m_t are accepted to be I(2). The GDP deflator series p_t is on the limit of being I(2) when the Dickey-Pantula procedure is considered. However, when models with trend and quadratic trends are addressed, both the joint F type tests accept the presence of two unit roots.

Table 3. Parametric tests for double unit roots.

		lags	constant	trend	quadratic trend
Germany 1920:1–1923:6 (T = 42)					
	HF-$F_{\alpha_1\alpha_2}$	4	6.72*	6.59	12.37
m_t	SD-$F^{sym}_{\alpha_1\alpha}$	4	6.94	7.78	6.45
	DP-t	4	−2.92*	−3.62*	—
	HF-$F_{\alpha_1\alpha_2}$	4	2.51	4.23	12.33
p_t	SD-$F^{sym}_{\alpha_1\alpha_2}$	4	0.94	1.18	1.81
	DP-t	4	−1.59	−2.92	—
Denmark 1974:1–1993:4 (T = 80)					
	HF-$F_{\alpha_1\alpha_2}$	7	5.14	4.97	6.49
p_{ct}	SD-$F^{sym}_{\alpha_1\alpha_2}$	7	0.46	7.53	9.95
	DP-t	7	−0.54	−3.06	—
	HF-$F_{\alpha_1\alpha_2}$	3	9.23**	8.81	12.91
p_t	SD-$F^{sym}_{\alpha_1\alpha_2}$	3	1.89	11.27	14.06
	DP-t	5	−2.77**	−3.56**	—
	HF-$F_{\alpha_1\alpha_2}$	3	3.41	5.83	6.02
m_t	SD-$F^{sym}_{\alpha_1\alpha_2}$	3	2.20	6.56	8.78
	DP-t	3	−2.41	−2.42	—

Note: The three different tests denote respectively the Hasza-Fuller F-test, the Sen-Dickey symmetric F-test, and the Dickey-Pantula t-test. 'lags' refers to the number of lags in the auxiliary regression. The deterministic components indicate whether these were included. '*', '**', and '***' refer to significance on 10,5, and 1% levels.

5.3. *Semiparametric approaches to testing for I(2)*

A major problem about the 'parametric' approach to test for double unit roots, as well as in testing for a single unit root, is that a finite order AR process is assumed to adequately describe the time series. This may be valid in many cases, at least as an approximation, but clearly the presence of moving average errors may yield poor finite order AR descriptions of the data and may invalidate the tests in the sense that their size may be hard to control without destroying the power. In testing for a single unit root Phillips (1987) and Phillips and Perron (1988) suggest semiparametric tests, known as the Phillips-Perron Z-tests, which are modifications of the standard Dickey-Fuller tests. The idea behind these tests is that when the distribution of the Dickey-Fuller t-ratio depends upon nuisance parameters under the null, the unknown population parameters can be consistently estimated, and the t-ratio subsequently be adjusted in a particular way to yield a distribution free of nuisance parameters. The problem about the semiparametric tests is that although in principle these are valid for MA errors they appear to have rather large size distortions when the root of the MA errors tends to minus one; Schwert (1989) reports these findings in a large simulation study. This criticism applies to any unit root test, since it may always be difficult for a finite stretch of data to identify a unit root when AR and MA roots are close to cancellation. However, size distortions appear to be particularly serious for semiparametric tests.

As an alternative to the Hasza-Fuller test described in the previous section, I (Haldrup (1994a)) develop a semi-parametric equivalent to the Hasza-Fuller joint F-test. The test is a straightforward generalization of the Phillips-Perron Z-tests developed for the I(1) case. The basic regression model to consider is

$$\Delta^2 x_t = (\hat{\alpha}_1 - 1)x_{t-1} + (\hat{\alpha}_2 - 1)\Delta x_{t-1} + \hat{\varepsilon}_t \tag{36}$$

which is just (19) but with no lags of $\Delta^2 x_t$ included in the regression. The error term captures all the short run dynamics which is reflected by the presence of nuisance parameters in the asymptotic distribution of the F-test of H_0: $\alpha_1 = \alpha_2 = 1$. The way the nuisance parameters enter the asymptotic distribution follows from the asymptotic expression

$$\begin{aligned} F_{\alpha_1, \alpha_2} \Rightarrow \frac{\sigma^2}{2\sigma_\varepsilon^2} D^{-1} \Bigg\{ & \left(\int_0^1 \overline{W}(r)\mathrm{d}W\right)^2 \int_0^1 W^2(r)\mathrm{d}r \\ & - 2\left(\int_0^1 W(r)\mathrm{d}W + \lambda'\right)\left(\int_0^1 \overline{W}(r)W(r)\mathrm{d}r\right)\left(\int_0^1 \overline{W}(r)\mathrm{d}W\right) \\ & + \left(\int_0^1 W(r)\mathrm{d}W' + \lambda'\right)^2 \left(\int_0^1 \overline{W}^2(r)\mathrm{d}r\right) \Bigg\} \end{aligned} \tag{37}$$

where $D = \int_0^1 \overline{W}^2(r)\mathrm{d}r \int_0^1 W^2(r)\mathrm{d}r - (\int_0^1 \overline{W}(r)W(r)\mathrm{d}r)^2$ and $\sigma^2, \sigma_\varepsilon^2$ have previously been defined. We also let $\lambda' = (\sigma^2 - \sigma_\varepsilon^2)/2\sigma^2$.

When errors are independent $\sigma^2 = \sigma_\varepsilon^2$ and the limiting distribution can be shown to simplify to (20). To adjust the F-ratio given above such that the subsequent test has the distribution (20), consistent estimates of σ^2 and σ_ε^2 are needed.

A consistent estimator of the long run variance σ^2 is given by

$$\hat{\sigma}^2 = T^{-1}\sum_1^T \hat{\varepsilon}_t^2 + 2T^{-1}\sum_{\tau=1}^{l} \omega_{\tau l} \sum_{t=\tau+l}^{T} \hat{\varepsilon}_t \hat{\varepsilon}_{t-\tau} \tag{38}$$

where $\hat{\varepsilon}_t$ are regression residuals from the regression (36), see Newey and West (1987). $\omega_{\tau l}$ is a weight function which corresponds to the lag window used for spectral smoothing in the frequency domain. Any lag window can be used, e.g. Parzen, Tukey, etc., but in the sequel I use the Bartlett window $\omega_{\tau l} = 1 - \tau/(l+1)$. Choosing the width l of the lag window is difficult in practice. My recommendation is to use different values but ensuring that l increases with the available sample size. Alternatively, an automatic kernal lag selection can be used, see e.g. Andrews (1991). A consistent estimate of the regression standard error $\hat{\sigma}_\varepsilon{}^2$ can be found as

$$\hat{\sigma}_\varepsilon^2 = T^{-1}\sum_1^T \hat{\varepsilon}_t^2. \tag{39}$$

From these estimates it follows trivially that λ and λ' can be estimated by $\hat{\lambda} = (\hat{\sigma}^2 - \hat{\sigma}_\varepsilon^2)/2$ and $\hat{\lambda}' = \hat{\lambda}/\hat{\sigma}^2$. Phillips (1987) described very carefully the moment and mixing conditions that are needed for the estimates $\hat{\sigma}^2$ and $\hat{\sigma}_\varepsilon^2$, and hence for the construction of the semiparametric statistics, to be valid.

In order to construct the semiparametric equivalent of Hasza and Fuller's test we need to define the following quantities:

$$\begin{aligned}
m_{xx} &= T^{-4}\sum_1^T x_t^2 & m_{x\Delta x} &= T^{-3}\sum_1^T x_{t-1}\Delta x_t \\
m_{x\Delta^2 x} &= T^{-2}\sum_1^T x_{t-1}\Delta^2 x_t & m_{\Delta x\Delta^2 x} &= T^{-1}\sum_1^T \Delta x_{t-1}\Delta^2 x_t \\
m_{\Delta x\Delta x} &= T^{-2}\sum_1^T \Delta x_t \Delta x_t & M &= m_{xx}m_{\Delta x\Delta x} - m_{x\Delta x}^2.
\end{aligned} \tag{40}$$

Let $F_{\alpha_1\alpha_2}$ be the F-statistic from the regression (36). The test is now given by

$$Z(F_{\alpha_1\alpha_2}) = F_{\alpha_1\alpha_2}\frac{\hat{\sigma}_\varepsilon^2}{\hat{\sigma}^2} - \frac{1}{2}M^{-1}\left[2\hat{\lambda}'(m_{\Delta x\Delta^2 x}m_{xx} - m_{x\Delta x}m_{x\Delta^2 x}) - \left(\frac{\hat{\lambda}}{\hat{\sigma}}\right)^2 m_{xx}\right] \tag{41}$$

which follows the Hasza-Fuller distribution (20).

If power is desired against deterministic alternatives the series should be detrended prior to the construction of the $Z(F_{\alpha_1\alpha_2})$ test. This can be done by the regressions (34) and subsequently use the regression residuals as the new (detrended) series.

The above test is found to suffer from the size distortions, which also characterize the Phillips-Perron tests, by the presence of a large negative MA root. However, in cases where the alternative is explosive there is evidence that the semiparametric test has favourable properties compared to the sequential procedure.

The paper by Shin and Kim (1997) is jointly motivated by the symmetric Sen and Dickey $F_{\alpha_1\alpha_2}^{Sym}$-test and the semiparametric $Z(F_{\alpha_1\alpha_2})$-test. A semiparametric version of the Sen-Dickey test is suggested and not surprisingly this test is found to have better (size-corrected) power compared to previously existing tests. More importantly, however, it is found that some of the size distortions of the $Z(F_{\alpha_1\alpha_2})$-test can be considerably reduced by symmetrizing the regression. The test is constructed in a manner like the test of Sen and Dickey but, again, no augmentation through lagged second differences is used. Hence the regressions estimated jointly are

$$\begin{aligned}
\Delta^2 x_t &= (\hat{\alpha}_1 - 1)x_{t-1} + (\hat{\alpha}_2 - 1)\Delta x_{t-1} + \hat{\varepsilon}_t, \quad t = 3, \ldots, n \\
\Delta^2 x_t &= (\hat{\alpha}_1 - 1)x_{t-1} - (\hat{\alpha}_2 - 1)\Delta x_t + \hat{\eta}_t, \quad t = n, \ldots, 3
\end{aligned} \tag{42}$$

where the dependent and independent variables in the joint estimation are given by

$$Y = (\Delta^2 x_3, \Delta^2 x_4, \ldots, \Delta^2 x_n, \Delta^2 x_n, \ldots, \Delta^2 x_4, \Delta^2 x_3)', \text{ and}$$

$$X = [(x_2, x_3, \ldots, x_{n-1}, x_{n-1}, \ldots, x_3, x_2)' \vdots \\ (\Delta x_2, \Delta x_3, \ldots, \Delta x_{n-1}, -\Delta x_n, \ldots, -\Delta x_4, -\Delta x_3)'].$$

Note that this corresponds to setting $p = 2$ in table 1. Based on this regression the F-test of the joint double unit root hypothesis follows the distribution

$$F^{Sym}_{\alpha_1, \alpha_2} \Rightarrow \frac{\hat{\sigma}^2}{\sigma_\varepsilon^2}\left(\int_0^1 \overline{W}^2(r)\mathrm{d}r\right)^{-1}\left(\int_0^1 \overline{W}(r)\mathrm{d}W\right)^2 + \frac{\sigma_\varepsilon^2}{4\sigma^2}\left(\int_0^1 W^2(r)\mathrm{d}r\right)^{-1} \quad (43)$$

which depends upon nuisance parameters σ_ε^2 and σ^2. These can be estimated exactly as in (38) and (39), that is, by using the first half of the data points.[12] Given these estimates the semiparametric test is defined as

$$Z(F^{Sym}_{\alpha_1\alpha_2}) = \frac{1}{2\hat{\sigma}_\varepsilon^2}\left(\frac{\hat{\sigma}_\varepsilon}{\hat{\sigma}}(\hat{\alpha}_1 - 1), \frac{\hat{\sigma}}{\hat{\sigma}_\varepsilon}(\hat{\alpha}_2 - 1)\right)(X'X)\left(\frac{\hat{\sigma}_\varepsilon}{\hat{\sigma}}(\hat{\alpha}_1 - 1), \frac{\hat{\sigma}}{\hat{\sigma}_\varepsilon}(\hat{\alpha}_2 - 1)\right)' \quad (44)$$

where $(\hat{\alpha}_1 - 1, \hat{\alpha}_2 - 1)' = (X'X)^{-1}X'Y$. The distribution of this test is given as in (43) with $\sigma_\varepsilon^2 = \sigma^2$, i.e. the Sen and Dickey distribution (28). The extension of this test to account for deterministic components follows the same procedure as for the $Z(F_{\alpha_1\alpha_2})$-test.

In a rather comprehensive Monte Carlo study Shin and Kim (1997) find their test to have rather good size properties compared to other semiparametric tests, especially in the situations where the other tests seem to perform rather poorly. They provide a reasonable intuitive argument why this is so. Note simply, that the non-symmetrized $Z(F_{\alpha_1\alpha_2})$-test is adjusting $F_{\alpha_1\alpha_2}$ both by scale (through $\sigma^2/\sigma_\varepsilon^2$) and by location (through λ'); compare the asymptotic formula (37). However, the $Z(F^{Sym}_{\alpha_1\alpha_2})$-test only requires a scale adjustment as some cross terms appear to cancel due to symmetry. Hence, less adjustments of the original statistic is needed in the symmetric test. Concerning the size adjusted powers Shin and Kim's simulation study also turned out to be rather favourable to their own test as powers were significantly higher compared to the $Z(F_{\alpha_1\alpha_2})$-test and the test based on the Dickey-Pantula procedure.

It is obvious that a semiparametric analogue of the Dickey-Pantula procedure can be easily adopted by use of Phillips-Perron tests.

5.4. *Examples of semi-parametric tests for I(2)*

I consider the same data series as in section 5.2, but now by focusing on the semi-parametric versions of the tests.[13] In calculating the long run variance used in the construction of the tests, the Bartlett kernal estimator was used. The truncation parameter was chosen to reflect both the frequency of the data and the number of observations. However, different values were tried and this did not have a significant impact on the test results.

The overall evidence from the semi-parametric tests reported in table 4 is quite different from the parametric tests displayed in table 3. Only in few cases can the I(2) null not be rejected. It seems likely that these results are due to the poor power that semi-parametric tests seem to have more generally. Note however that the Shin-Kim symmetric F test generally seems to be less significant than the other tests, just as their Monte Carlo results indicate.

6. Single equation analysis in multivariate I(2) systems

Determining the integration order of economic time series is not necessarily interesting *per se*, but it provides a valuable input to be used in the formulation of multivariate models. In the following sections various aspects of multivariate regression models will be analyzed. First I focus on single equation analysis and in section 8 the systems approach to multivariate analysis is addressed.

The set up of the analysis can be described as follows. Consider a model where y_t, is a scalar I(2) variable related to the time series x_t which consists of m_1 I(1) variables, x_{1t}, and m_2 I(2) variables, x_{2t}, as well as m_0 separate deterministic

Table 4. Semi-parametric tests for double unit roots.

		lags	constant	trend	quadratic trend
Germany 1921:1–1923:6 ($T=42$)					
	HF-$Z(F_{\alpha_1\alpha_1})$	8	2.41	1.12	5.71
m_t	SK-$Z(F^{Sym}_{\alpha_1\alpha_1})$	8	0.79	3.47	10.66
	DP-$Z(t)$	8	−0.99	−2.45	—
	HF-$Z(F_{\alpha_1\alpha_1})$	8	11.58***	6.52	22.80*
p_t	SK-$Z(F^{Sym}_{\alpha_1\alpha_1})$	8	2.62	5.59	38.45***
	DP-$Z(t)$	8	−3.71***	−5.27***	—
Denmark 1974:1–1993:4 ($T=80$)					
	HF-$Z(F_{\alpha_1\alpha_1})$	4	27.56***	12.66***	35.62***
p_{ct}	SK-$Z(F^{Sym}_{\alpha_1\alpha_1})$	4	1.95	7.47	37.81***
	DP-$Z(t)$	4	−4.99***	−7.89***	—
	HF-$Z(F_{\alpha_1\alpha_1})$	4	80.83***	57.40***	82.90***
p_t	SK-$Z(F^{Sym}_{\alpha_1\alpha_1})$	4	5.91	23.24***	74.25***
	DP-$Z(t)$	4	−10.51***	−12.55***	
	HF-$Z(F_{\alpha_1\alpha_1})$	4	108.98***	107.19***	115.27***
m_t	SK-$Z(F^{Sym}_{\alpha_1\alpha_1})$	4	28.14***	67.17***	75.24***
	DP-$Z(t)$	4	−14.51***	−15.04***	—

Notes: The three different tests denote respectively the semiparametric versions of the Hasza-Fuller F-test, the Shin-Kim symmetric F-test, and the Dickey-Pantula t-test. The latter test is just the Phillips-Perron test on the differenced data. 'lags' refers to the truncation parameter used in the Bartlett kernal estimate of σ^2. The deterministic components indicate whether these were included. '*', '**', and '***' refer to significance on 10,5, and 1% levels.

components of different orders. We let $m = m_0 + m_1 + m_2$ and specify the separate series as in (10):

$$\begin{aligned} y_t &= \gamma_0' c_t + y_t^0, \\ x_{1t} &= \gamma_1' c_t + x_{1t}^0, \qquad \Delta x_{1t}^0 = \varepsilon_{1t} \\ x_{2t} &= \gamma_2' c_t + x_{2t}^0, \qquad \Delta^2 x_{2t}^0 = \varepsilon_{2t} \\ x_t &= (c_t', x_{1t}', x_{2t}')'. \end{aligned} \tag{45}$$

For the subsequent analysis to be correct x_{1t} and x_{2t} are required to be individually non-cointegrated vector series, and furthermore x_{1t} and Δx_{2t} are assumed not to cointegrate.[14] The stochastic part of y_t denoted y_t^0 is integrated of order two and is related to x_{1t}^0 and $x^0{}_{2t}$ as follows

$$y_t^0 - \beta_1' x_{1t}^0 - \beta_2' x_{2t}^0 = u_t. \tag{46}$$

In terms of the original variables y_t and x_t we therefore have[15]

$$y_t = \beta_0' c_t + \beta_1' x_{1t} + \beta_2' x_{2t} + u_t = \beta' x_t + u_t \tag{47}$$

with $\beta_0' = (\gamma_0' - \beta_1'\gamma_1' - \beta_2'\gamma_2')$. With respect to the errors u_t these can be $\mathsf{I}(0)$, $\mathsf{I}(1)$ or $\mathsf{I}(2)$. We let $\Delta^d u_t = v_t, d = 0, 1, 2$, so depending upon the integration properties of u_t different situations with distinct cointegration features may arise.

Under rather weak conditions, known as the multivariate invariance principle, it can be shown that in defining the $p = 1 + m_1 + m_2$ dimensional error process $w_t = (v_t, \varepsilon_{1t}', \varepsilon_{2t}')'$, the scaled vector partial sum process

$$T^{-1/2} \sum_{1}^{[Tr]} w_t \Longrightarrow B(r) \quad \text{as } T \longrightarrow \infty, \tag{48}$$

where $B(r) = (B_0(r), B_1(r)', B_2(r)')'$ is a vector Brownian motion (partitioned conformably with w_t) with long-run covariance matrix $\Omega = \lim_{T\to\infty} T^{-1} \mathsf{E}((\Sigma_1^T w_t)(\Sigma_1^T w_t)')$. Alternatively we write $\Omega = \Sigma + \Lambda + \Lambda'$ where $\Sigma = \mathsf{E}(w_1 w_1')$ and $\Lambda = \Sigma_{k=2}^{\infty} \mathsf{E}(w_1 w_k')$. The covariance matrix can be partitioned conformably with w_t, and, in so doing, the sub-covariance matrices associated with x_{1t} and x_{2t} must be of full rank. This condition implies that the right hand side variables in (47) do not cointegrate. This is an important assumption, but I shall slack this in section (8).

Given the above assumptions we consider in the following the regression model

$$y_t = \hat{\beta}_0' c_t + \hat{\beta}_1' x_{1t} + \hat{\beta}_2' x_{2t} + \hat{u}_t = \hat{\beta}' x_t + \hat{u}_t. \tag{49}$$

The properties of statistics based on this model depend upon the integration order of u_t. When u_t is $\mathsf{I}(0)$, y_t, x_{1t}, and x_{2t} are cointegrated and hence constitute a long-run equilibrium relationship. As noted previously, this definition of cointegration is slightly different from Engle and Granger's (1987) definition. When $u_t \sim \mathsf{I}(1)$, y_t, $x_{2t} \sim \mathsf{CI}(2, 1)$, but do not cointegrate with x_{1t}. Finally, the case where $u_t \sim \mathsf{I}(2)$ refers to non-cointegration amongst the variables. Sometimes the cases where u_t is either $\mathsf{I}(1)$ or $\mathsf{I}(2)$ may lead to spurious regressions as we shall see below, and therefore these situations should be analyzed with care. However, spurious regressions are typically also the basis for residual based tests for (non) cointegration and hence are of separate interest to examine.

6.1. *Spurious regression*

In a much cited paper Granger and Newbold (1974) demonstrated how regressions that involved statistically independent random walks would lead to the incorrect inference that the series were related if standard statistical tools were used for analysis. Through simulations they also showed that 'spurious' regressions were accompanied with low values of the Durbin-Watson (*DW*) statistic, i.e. residuals were highly positively correlated, and the coefficient of determination, R^2, was found to be higher than expected and hence essentially indicating that a large proportion of the variation in data could be explained by artificial regressors. Phillips (1986) provided an analytical explanation of Granger and Newbold's findings: In regressing independent random walks on each other the t-ratio of a zero coefficient null diverges of order $O_p(T^{1/2})$, the regression coefficients of stochatic regressors are non-degenerate, the DW-statistic tends in probability to zero as $T \longrightarrow \infty$, and finally the R^2 statistic has a non-degenerate distribution.

In Haldrup (1994b) I extend Phillips' analytical results to the case where the regression model is (49) under the assumptions outlined above. These results, together with Phillips' findings, are reported in schematic form in Table 5. The regression errors in my own (Haldrup (1994b)) analysis are assumed to be integrated of either order one or two. In the table the $F(\hat{\beta})$-statistic refers to the general F-test of hypotheses H_0: $R\beta = r$, where R is a $q \times m$ restriction matrix and

Table 5. Orders in probability of regression coefficients and diagnostics. Index d refers to the integration order of u_t.

		I(1)-model of Phillips (1986)*	I(2) model based on the regression (49)	
		$d=1$	$d=1$	$d=2$
constant:	$\hat{\beta}^0_{0t}$	$O_p(T^{1/2})$	$O_p(T^{1/2})$	$O_p(T^{3/2})$
trend:	$\hat{\beta}^1_{0t}$	$O_p(T^{-1/2})$	$O_p(T^{-1/2})$	$O_p(T^{1/2})$
quadratic trend:	$\hat{\beta}^2_{0t}$	—	$O_p(T^{-3/2})$	$O_p(T^{-1/2})$
x_{1t}:	$\hat{\beta}_{1t}$	$O_p(1)$	$O_p(1)$	$O_p(T)$
x_{2t}:	$\hat{\beta}_{2t}$	—	$O_p(T^{-1})$	$O_p(1)$
Diagnostics:				
$F(\hat{\beta})$		$O_p(T)$	$O_p(T)$	$O_p(T)$
DW		$O_p(T^{-1})$	$O_p(T^{-1})$	$O_p(T^{-1})$
R^2		$O_p(1)$	$1+O_p(T^{-1/2})$	$O_p(1)$

*Note: The Phillips model is based on the regression $y_t = \hat{\beta}^0_0 + \hat{\beta}^1_0 t + \hat{\beta}'_1 x_{1t} + \hat{u}_t$, where y_t, x_{1t}, u_t are I(1) series.

r is a known q-dimensional vector.[16] Concerning the deterministic regressors it is assumed that $c_t = (1, t, t^2)'$ and with β_0^0, β_0^1 and β_0^2 being the associated coefficients.

When u_t is non-stationary, either I(1) or I(2), it is seen that many of the spurious regression results applying to the I(1) model of Granger and Newbold (1974) and Phillips (1986) carry over to the I(2) model; apart from R^2 all spurious regression results for $d = 1$ appear to be the same across the two different models. Generally, if the order of a particular regressor is less than $O_p(T^{d-1/2})$, it is seen that the least squares estimate is inconsistent and diverges at a rate which depends upon the order of the regressor. Consistency is only achieved when the order of the regressor exceeds $O_p(T^{d-1/2})$. F-tests diverge at the same rate $O_p(T)$ (t-ratios $= O_p(T^{1/2})$) regardless of the order d, and similarly the DW statistic tends to zero at the same rate.

The reason why $R^2 \rightarrow 1$ in the I(2) model when $T \rightarrow \infty$, even though $d = 1$, follows from the fact that in this case $y_t, x_{2t} \sim \mathrm{CI}(2, 1)$, and thus, because cointegration to I(1) level occurs, the residual variation will be of a lower order in probability than the dependent I(2) variable. Note however, that when $d = 2$ the distribution of R^2 is non-degenerate, but still bounded on $[0, 1]$ of course.

6.2. *Residual based test for (non) cointegration*

Spurious regression occurs when variables are not fully cointegrated and hence this can naturally be used as a basis for testing the hypothesis of no cointegration. Following the initial benchmark description of Engle and Granger's (1987) 2-step procedure, the idea is to test the integration order of residuals from a cointegration regression. A common class of tests adopted in the single equation I(1) analysis is the augmented Dickey-Fuller class of tests including their associated semiparametric analogues. This procedure can be straightforwardly extended to the I(2) case such that regression residuals from a regression like (49) can be tested for the order of integration.

In principle, any of the unit root tests previously discussed in section 5 may be considered in a cointegration framework. Hence the relevant hypotheses are

H_2: There is no cointegration amongst y_t, x_{1t}, x_{2t}, such that u_t is I(2)
H_1: The I(2) variables y_t and x_{2t} cointegrate to I(1) level, but no further cointegration occurs whereby u_t is I(1).

Tests for both types of hypotheses may be constructed. However, in most practical situations the I(2) variables cointegrate at least to an I(1) relation such that the hypothesis H_1 is the most relevant. This is the assumption made by Haldrup (1994b) who derives the properties of the augmented Dickey-Fuller class of tests when the hypothesis H_1 is tested using regression residuals $\hat{u}_t$ based on the regression (49). Since the single equation model depends upon both I(1) and I(2) variables, the asymptotic distributions and hence the critical values need to be modified.[17]

It can be shown that the limiting behaviour of $\hat{u}_t$ after appropriate scaling is a

Brownian motion process which depends upon a number of parameters. Hence the asymptotic distribution of the Dickey-Fuller t-ratio based on the regression

$$\Delta\hat{u}_t = (\hat{\alpha} - 1)\hat{u}_{t-1} + \sum_{j=1}^{q} \hat{\varphi}_j \Delta\hat{u}_{t-i} + \hat{\eta}_{qt} \tag{50}$$

is qualitatively similar to the distributions known from univariate unit root testing and cointegration testing in the I(1) case. Quantitatively, however, the distributions will depend upon m_1 and m_2, i.e. the number of I(1) and I(2) regressors in the regression. In addition, the distributions are affected by the deterministic components included in the first step auxiliary regression (49). Critical values for different values of m_1 and m_2 are reported in Haldrup (1994b) for the case with a constant and in Engsted *et al.* (1997) for the trend and quadratic trend cases. Interestingly, it appears that asymptotic critical values are rather similar to the asymptotic critical values reported in Phillips and Ouliaris (1990) for a given value of the sum $m_1 + m_2$. Hence there is indication that it is the total number of stochastic regressors in the auxiliary regression which matters for the asymptotic distributions. In finite samples, however, one has to discriminate between the number of I(1) and I(2) regressors.

Polynomial cointegration and multicointegration. The analysis above can be straightforwardly extended to the case of testing the null of non-polynomial cointegration by including in x_{1t} first differences of the I(2) variables x_{2t}. This will not affect the validity of the analysis.

In section (3.2) Granger and Lee's (1989,1990) notion of multicointegration was introduced, i.e. the idea that cumulated cointegration errors cointegrate with the original variables. Assume for a moment, that y_t is I(1) and cointegrates with the I(1) vector x_{1t}, such that the *first layer* of cointegration occurs when $y_t - \beta_1' x_{1t} = z_t$ is I(0). Multicointegration implies that $\sum_{j=1}^{t} z_j - \beta_1^{*\prime} x_{1t} - \beta_1^{**} y_t = u_t$ is also I(0); we denote this the *second layer* of cointegration. When β_1 is unknown there are essentially two ways of testing for multicointegration.

Granger and Lee suggest a two step procedure where the first layer of cointegration is tested by using standard procedures for I(1) models. Given cointegration this gives the estimate $\hat{\beta}_1$ and the generated series $\sum_{j=1}^{t} \hat{z}_j$ of regression residuals; note that this series is I(1) by construction. Subsequently $\sum_{j=1}^{t} \hat{z}_j$ is regressed on the remaining variables to see whether multicointegration occurs. In Engsted *et al.* (1997) we demonstrate that there are a number of important statistical problems about this procedure, one fundamental problem being that the null of no multicointegration in the second step of the procedure is invalidated when using standard residual based cointegration test procedures.

Instead, we suggest a single step procedure with favourable statistical properties, by exploiting the fact that a multicointegrated model can be written as an I(2) model. The idea is thus to use cumulated data series in the cointegration regression such that the model is formulated directly in terms of I(2) and I(1) variables. Note simply, that when u_t is stationary, the multicointegration relation can be written as

$$\sum_{j=1}^{t} y_j = \beta_1' \sum_{j=1}^{t} x_{1j} + \beta_1^{*\prime} x_{1t} + \beta_1^{**} y_t + u_t \tag{51}$$

where $\Sigma_{j=1}^{t} y_j$ and $\Sigma_{j=1}^{t} x_{1j}$ are the generated I(2) series. In practical situations deterministics may be included in (49) since the cumulated series may also generate a trend, for instance. As seen the residual based testing procedure described above naturally encompasses the single step procedure of testing for multicointegration.[18]

6.3. *Examples of residual based testing for I(2) cointegration and multicointegration*

By applying the ML procedure for I(2) models, which I return to in section 8, Juselius (1998) analyzed the Danish money demand data set previously described. In the specification of a (nominal) money demand relation she considers the variables: nominal money, m_t, real income, y_t, the GDP deflator, p_t, and the deposit and bond rates, i_{dt}, and i_{bt}. The parametric tests for double unit roots in section 5.2 indicated that m_t and p_t are I(2). Unit root tests (not reported) also indicated that y_t, i_{bt}, i_{dt}, are I(1). Also the real money stock, $m_t - p_t$, was found to be I(1), hence implying that $m_t, p_t \sim \mathrm{CI}(2, 1)$ with a cointegrating vector given by $(1, -1)$. The same cointegrating vector is naturally given for $\Delta m_t, \Delta p_t \sim \mathrm{CI}(1, 1)$. These results suggest that we may consider both a real specification of the money demand relation (in terms of I(1) variables) as well as a nominal specification in terms of mixed I(2) and I(1) variables. In both situations Δp_t or Δm_t are likely variables to appear amongst the cointegrating variables.[19]

We start by considering a nominal specification. The variables included in the first model are $[m_t, p_t, y_t]$. According to the residual based procedure outlined above m_t is regressed on p_t and y_t, and an augmented Dickey-Fuller test is subsequently applied to the residuals. A constant was also included in the cointegration regression. The ADF-t value with lags 2, 3, and 4 yields -3.01. The 10% critical value tabulated in Haldrup (1994b), table 1, is -3.55 for $m_1 = m_2 = 1$ (corresponding to the number of I(1) and I(2) regressors) so we cannot reject the null. Next we estimate a model with the bond rate included as well so the information set now consists of $[m_t, p_t, y_t, i_{bt}]$. In this case the ADF-t-value with lags 2 and 4 yields -5.80 which is strongly significant (the 1% critical value for $m_1 = 2$ and $m_2 = 1$ is -4.81). Hence a nominal specification with these 4 variables suggests cointegration. Observe that inflation Δp_t needs not to be included to ensure that the variables cointegrate.

The above results suggest that we may also consider a real specification which includes the data set $[m_t - p_t, y_t, i_{bt}]$. Note that this information set consists only of I(1) variables so the standard Engle-Granger two-step procedure can be conducted in this case. The ADF-t-value with lags 2 and 4 included yields -5.17 which is also strongly significant. Hence the data satisfies a specification where money and prices satisfy long run homogeneity.

To demonstrate testing for multicointegration I consider the US housing data set, 1968:1–1994:12 ($T = 324$), previously analyzed by Lee (1996) and Engsted and Haldrup (1998). Lee argued that if y_t is housing units completed and x_t is housing units started, then, given that these series are I(1), it is likely that $y_t, x_t \sim \mathrm{CI}(1,1)$. However, it is also likely that the stock of new housing units under construction, $Q_t = \sum_{j=1}^{t}(x_j - y_j)$, cointegrates with e.g. y_t such that $Q_t - ky_t$ is I(0). When this occurs the data series are multicointegrated. Actually Lee (1996) modified the Q_t variable as follows $Q_t = \sum_{j=1}^{t}(0.98x_j - y_j)$ since he was judging that 2% of all new housing starts are never completed. Using the US data set, he found rather strong evidence for the presence of multicointegration. However, rather than imposing the parameter 0.98 in the definition of the Q_t variable this can be estimated from the data by considering a regression of the form:

$$\sum_{j=1}^{t} y_j = \beta_1 \sum_{j=1}^{t} x_j + \beta_2 y_t + \gamma_0 + \gamma_1 t + u_t \tag{52}$$

where the trend is included to account for the fact that the cumulated series may produce a linear trend. Hence the idea of testing for multicointegration amounts to testing whether u_t is stationary. An augmented Dickey-Fuller test of $\hat{u}_t$ from the above regression yields a value of -4.82 which for $m_1 = m_2 = 1$ is significant at a 1% level. Note that the critical value should account for the presence of a linear trend in the cointegration regressions so the critical values of Engsted *et al.* (1997, table 1), should be used. Observe that the estimate $(1-\hat{\beta}_1)$ provides an estimate of the unknown percentage of housing units that are never completed. In the above case this estimate is 5.3%. As we shall see in section 6.4 this estimate is rather precise as the rate of consistency is $O_p(T^2)$.

6.4. *Properties of single equation cointegration regressions with I(1) and I(2) variables*

When the errors u_t in (47) appear to be stationary the time series $y_t, \mathrm{x}_{1t}, \mathrm{x}_{2t}$, are I(2) cointegrated[20] and in this case it is of interest to examine the properties of statistics based on the regression model (49) where, once again, c_t is assumed to be given by the vector $(1, t, t^2)'$. Haldrup (1994b) shows that from this regression $R^2 = 1 + O_p(T^{-3})$ and therefore an indication is given of a very good fit. Next we focus on the properties of least squares regression estimates. The following distribution result holds:[21]

$$\mathrm{D}_T\mathrm{G}(\hat{\beta} - \beta) \Rightarrow \left(\int_0^1 \mathrm{B}_*(r)\mathrm{B}_*'(r)\mathrm{d}r\right)^{-1}\left(\int_0^1 \mathrm{B}_*(r)\mathrm{d}B_0 + (0', \Delta_{10}', 0')'\right) \tag{53}$$

where $D_t = \text{diag}(T^{1/2}, T^{3/2}, T^{5/2}, T, T^2)$, $B_*(r) = (1, r, r^2, B_1(r)', \overline{B_2(r)}')'$, and

$$G = \begin{pmatrix} I_3 & \gamma_1 & \gamma_2 \\ 0 & I_{m_1} & 0 \\ 0 & 0 & I_{m_2} \end{pmatrix}. \tag{54}$$

The term Δ_{10} is the $(1, 1)$ vector element of $\Delta = \Sigma + \Lambda$.

In particular, it follows from (53) that

$$\begin{aligned} T^2(\hat{\beta}_2 - \beta_2) &= O_p(1) \\ T(\hat{\beta}_1 - \beta_1) &= O_p(1). \end{aligned} \tag{55}$$

Hence, in cointegration regressions with I(2) variables the least squares estimate $\hat{\beta}_2$, corresponding to the I(2) regressors, will tend to its true value β_2 at the rapid *super-super* consistent rate, $O_p(T^{-2})$. This rate is much faster than the usual *super* consistent rate, $O_p(T^{-1})$, found in I(1) cointegrating regressions. However, with respect to the I(1) regressors the associated estimate $\hat{\beta}_1$ is seen to be super consistent. In general, we cannot say what the orders of the deterministic regressors will be since this depends upon which (non-zero) deterministics are present in the time series.[22] The largest orders possible of the elements in $\hat{\beta}_0$ are given by $O_p(T^{-1/2})$, $O_p(T^{-3/2})$, and $O_p(T^{-5/2})$, respectively; a situation occurring, for instance, when the regressors have no deterministic components, $\gamma_1, \gamma_2 = 0$.

Generally, the distributions of the least squares estimates can be expressed in terms of the non-standard distributions given in (53) so standard gaussian inference cannot be undertaken in general, but only in special situations. One such special case is when x_{1t} and x_{2t} can be considered strictly exogenous regressors such that the single Brownian motions are uncorrelated. In this situation the distribution in (53) simplifies to a mixed gaussian distribution (i.e. a gaussian distribution conditional on information) of the form, see Park and Phillips (1989) and Haldrup (1994b),

$$D_T G(\hat{\beta} - \beta) \Rightarrow \int_V N(0, V) dP(V) \tag{56}$$

with $V = (\int_0^1 B_*(r) B_*'(r) dr)^{-1}$ being the mixing variate matrix. Hence hypothesis testing can be undertaken using standard procedures, for instance t-tests will follow the standard normal distribution.[23]

Strict exogeneity is a very restrictive property of the data and this has led Choi *et al.* (1997) to suggest a generalization of Park's (1992) canonical cointegration regression procedure which is based on transformation of the regressors and the regressand in the model (49) such that the resulting distribution of the least squares estimator becomes mixed gaussian as in (56). I will not go into a technical discussion of this procedure but refer to Choi *et al.* (1997).

An estimation method which is somewhat related to that of Choi *et al.* (1997) is the *residual-based fully modified ordinary least-squares* (RBFM-OLS) procedure suggested by Chang and Phillips (1995). However, the way the dependency of nuisance parameters is accounted for is different; mainly because no prior assumptions are made about the cointegration dimension and the mixture of I(0), I(1), and I(2) variables in the model.

6.5. *Examples of estimation of cointegration relations from single equations*

In section 6.3 I found for the Danish money demand data set that $[m_t, p_t, y_t, i_{bt}]$ is I(2) cointegrated. I also estimated a relation where the model included also a linear trend and this was found to constitute an equally significant relationship. Least squares estimation gave the following regression results:

$$m_t = 1.18p_t + 1.03y_t - 9.80i_{bt} + constant$$
$$R^2 = 0.994, DW = 1.54$$

$$m_t = 1.10p_t + 1.05y_t - 9.42i_{bt} + constant + trend$$
$$R^2 = 0.994, DW = 1.53$$

As seen, despite $O_p(T^2)$-consistency, the estimate of the coefficient associated with p_t seems to depend much upon the presence of a linear trend in the model. It could therefore be of interest to produce a confidence interval for this coefficient. However, simple OLS will not produce the correct standard errors in order to do standard inference, so instead the Choi *et al.* (1997) CCR estimator for I(2) systems was used to reestimate the relations.[24] This gave the following results where the numbers in parenthesis indicate standard errors:

$$m_t = \underset{(0.03)}{1.17}p_t + \underset{(0.12)}{1.04}y_t - \underset{(0.76)}{10.79}i_{bt} + constant$$

$$m_t = \underset{(0.08)}{1.19}p_t + \underset{(0.12)}{1.05}y_t - \underset{(0.85)}{10.74}i_{bt} + constant + trend$$

It can be seen that in both cases a standard confidence interval for the p_t coefficient does not include 1 which perhaps is a bit surprising given the fact that the real specification in section 6.3 was found to exhibit cointegration. Note however, that the coefficient of y_t cannot be rejected to equal unity.

7. Cointegrated models in systems: some motivation

In order to clarify the different cointegration possibilities that can occur in systems of variables it may be useful to introduce the so-called triangular I(2) representation.

For I(1) processes Phillips (1991) suggested a parametrization of cointegrated time series in terms of a so-called *triangular system.* He used this parametrization as a convenient framework for conducting optimal inference when the number of unit roots, and hence the number of cointegrating relations, are known a priori. Within the context of triangular systems, generalizations to I(2) processes have been introduced by, *inter alia*, Stock and Watson (1993) and Kitamura (1995), and are discussed in e.g. Chang and Phillips (1995), and Boswijk (1997). I will not go into a detailed discussion of all the different forms triangular representations may take; here I follow Stock and Watson's exposition for $d = 2$ (maximal order of integration) as it nicely demonstrates the main ideas and motivates how cointegration can occur.

In the triangularization of Stock and Watson a p-vector time series x_t can be partitioned (and possibly rearranged) as $x_t = (x_{0t}', x_{1t}', x_{2t}')$ where the single components are of dimension r, s, and $p - r - s$, which (rather importantly) are assumed to be known *a priori*. As we shall see these numbers will refer to the so-called integration indices to be defined in section (8.2). For ease of exposition I assume that the series are free of deterministic components. The triangular I(2) representation is now given by:

$$\begin{aligned} x_{0t} &= A_1 x_{1t} + A_2 x_{2t} + A_3 \Delta x_{2t} + u_{0t}, \\ \Delta x_{1t} &= A_4 \Delta x_{2t} + u_{1t}, \\ \Delta^2 x_{2t} &= u_{2t}, \end{aligned} \tag{57}$$

where $u_t = (u_{0t}, u_{1t}, u_{2t})$ is a general stationary process. This model is rather general and encompasses as a special case the vector autoregressive model.[25]

This representation shows that the single time series can be arranged such that $x_{2t} = \sum_{j=1}^{t} \sum_{i=1}^{j} u_{2i}$ with a total of $p - r - s$ (non-cointegrating) I(2) trends. In a similar fashion, s I(1) trends are given by $x_{1t} - A_4 x_{2t} = \sum_{i=1}^{t} u_{1i}$ such that x_{1t} and x_{2t} jointly determine the common I(1) and I(2) stochastic trends of the system. Lastly, the stationary components are given by the first expression in (57), that is, the linear combinations $x_{0t} - A_1 x_{1t} - A_2 x_{2t}$ are generally integrated of order 1 but cointegrates (polynomially) with Δx_{2t}. These are the stationary relations.

Note that if $A_3 = 0$ then no differences are needed in defining the stationary relations (no polynomial cointegration) since $x_t \sim CI(2, 2)$ in this case. Other special cases are encompassed in (57). For instance, all elements in x_t need not be I(2) since rows of A_4 can have zero elements. In fact, full blocks may be absent in (57).

In the following these different possibilities will be analyzed within the framework of a Gaussian vector autoregressive (VAR) model since this model appears to be especially well suited with respect to estimation and hypothesis testing.

8. System representations of cointegrated I(2) VAR models

It will be instructive to define the class of models we are now dealing with. Cointegrated I(1) and I(2) models can be characterized as restricted sub-models of the general p dimensional kth order VAR model, $A(L)x_t = \phi c_t + \varepsilon_t$. We will prefer to write it in the form[26]

$$x_t = \sum_{i=1}^{k} \Pi_i x_{t-i} + \Phi c_t + \varepsilon_t, \tag{58}$$

where it is assumed that ε_t is a sequence of *i.i.d.* zero mean errors with covariance matrix Ω. In most cases we also assume errors to be Gaussian so more compactly we have $\varepsilon_t \sim N_p(0, \Omega)$. The vector c_t, contains the possible deterministic components of the process, i.e. a constant and trend. Frequently the finite order Gaussian VAR model (58) is found to describe economic time series rather well.

The Gaussian VAR model (58) is the basis for a huge empirical literature analyzing cointegration in I(1) systems by using the so-called Johansen cointegration procedure, see Johansen (1988,1991,1995b). It is probably one of the most frequently adopted techniques in cointegration analysis and giving references to applied papers seems superfluous. Given the popularity of this technique it seems natural to extend its use to the case where variables are I(2), but before presenting results on this model, it will be instructive for comparative reasons to briefly report some important results when variables are I(1).

8.1. *Johansen's representation theorem for I(1) systems*

To simplify the analysis I will first abstract from the possible presence of deterministic components in (58). Johansen (1991) has characterized the Granger representation theorem, see Engle and Granger (1987), in terms of the Gaussian VAR described above. It is useful to reparametrize (58) as the *vector error correction model* (VECM)

$$\Delta x_t = \Pi x_{t-1} + \sum_{i=1}^{k-1} \Gamma_i \Delta x_{t-i} + \varepsilon_t, \tag{59}$$

with $\Pi = -I + \sum_{i=1}^{k} \Pi_i$, $\Gamma_i = \sum_{j=i+1}^{k} \Pi_j$. We also define the matrix $\Gamma = I - \sum_{i=1}^{k-1} \Gamma_i$.

If the x_t vector is cointegrated it means that $A(1) = -\Pi$ has reduced rank $r < p$, so that $\Pi = \alpha\beta'$ where α and β are both full rank matrices of dimension $p \times r$.

Johansen shows that the cointegrated VAR model can also be given the alternative *common stochastic trends representation*, see also Stock and Watson (1988),

$$x_t = C \sum_{i=1}^{t} \varepsilon_i + C(L)\varepsilon_t \tag{60}$$

where $C = \beta_\perp(\alpha'_\perp \Gamma \beta_\perp)^{-1}\alpha'_\perp$ and $\beta_\perp$ (and similarly with $\alpha_\perp$) is defined to be the orthogonal complement matrix of β with dimension $p \times (p - r)$ such that $\beta'_\perp\beta = 0$ and $\text{rank}(\beta_\perp, \beta) = p$. $C(L)$ is such that $C(L)\varepsilon_t$ corresponds to a p-dimensional I(0) component. It is now easy to see that although x_t is p-dimensional, the vector series is driven by just $p - r$ common stochastic I(1) trends $\alpha'_\perp \sum_{i=1}^{t} \varepsilon_i$. In terms of observable variables it is also possible to calculate the I(1) directions as $\beta'_\perp x_t$ which are just particular linear combinations of the stochastic trends. It is necessary though, that the matrix $\alpha'_\perp \Gamma \beta_\perp$ be invertible, i.e. has full rank $p - r$, (as it can be seen from the definition of C); otherwise the system is not an I(1) system, but a system integrated of order higher than one as we shall see.

It can be easily verified from (60) that r linear combinations of the series appear stationary. These are the I(0) directions and are given by

$$\beta' x_t = \beta' C(L)\varepsilon_t \tag{61}$$

and hence constitute the *r cointegrating relations* of the I(1) system.[27] The single cointegration vectors are not individually identified but the space they span is.

Note that when $r = p$ this corresponds to the Π matrix being of full rank and hence x_t is really a vector I(0) series. On the other hand, $r = 0$ corresponds to $\Pi = 0$ so that the number of variables is just the number of common stochastic trends.

8.2. *Johansen's representation theorem for I(2) systems*

In the I(1) model Π is of reduced rank and $\alpha_\perp' \Gamma \beta_\perp$ is of full rank. For the system to be I(2) it is additionally required that $\alpha_\perp' \Gamma \beta_\perp$ be of reduced rank $s < p - r$. To see this, it will be useful to follow Johansen (1992b, 1995a, 1997) and reparametrize the model (59) as

$$\Delta^2 x_t = \Pi x_{t-1} - \Gamma \Delta x_{t-1} + \sum_{i=1}^{k-2} \Psi_i \Delta^2 x_{t-i} + \varepsilon_t \tag{62}$$

which explicitly includes Γ as a parameter and where $\Psi_i = -\sum_{j=i+1}^{k-1} \Gamma_j$. Notice that this equation corresponds to a multivariate version of the univariate Hasza-Fuller regression previously presented in section 5.1, so when $\Pi = \Gamma = 0$, for instance, the system consists of p non-cointegrating double unit root processes. With $\alpha_\perp' \Gamma \beta_\perp$ being of rank s it is possible to define parameter matrices ξ and η, such that the joint pair of reduced rank conditions of the I(2) model can be written:[28]

$$\Pi = \alpha\beta', \quad \text{with } \alpha, \beta \text{ being } p \times r, \quad r < p \tag{63}$$

$$\alpha_\perp' \Gamma \beta_\perp = \xi\eta', \quad \text{with } \xi, \eta \text{ being } (p-r) \times s, \quad s < (p-r). \tag{64}$$

These reduced rank restrictions naturally have testable implications as we shall see in section 9. In order to characterize the stochastic trends driving the system and the cointegration relations, it is necessary to define parameters describing the I(0), I(1), and I(2) directions of the variables. As demonstrated below, matrices $(\beta, \beta_1, \beta_2)$ can be found such that they individually provide a basis of the I(0), I(1), and I(2) relations, respectively, of the p-dimensional system. The associated dimension of each sub-system is given by r, s, and $p - r - s$; Paruolo (1996) denote these numbers the *integration indices* of the VAR.

We use the notation $\bar{a} = a(a'a)^{-1}$ such that $a'\bar{a} = I$, and $P_a = \bar{a}a'$ defines the projection onto the space spanned by the columns of a. Then it can be shown that $\beta_1 = \bar{\beta}_\perp \eta$, $\beta_2 = \beta_\perp \eta_\perp$, and similarly $\alpha_1 = \bar{\alpha}_\perp \xi$, and $\alpha_2 = \alpha_\perp \xi_\perp$. It is easy to see from these definitions that $\beta_\perp = (\beta_1, \beta_2)$ and $(\beta, \beta_1)_\perp = \beta_2$ such that β, β_1 and β_2 are mutually orthogonal and thus jointly describe a basis for the p-dimensional space. The α's have a similar property.

The *common stochastic trends representation* (the I(2) equivalent of (60)) is now given by[29]

$$x_t = C_2 \sum_{j=1}^{t} \sum_{i=1}^{j} \varepsilon_i + C_1 \sum_{i=1}^{t} \varepsilon_i + C^*(L)\varepsilon_t \tag{65}$$

where

$$C_2 = \beta_2(\alpha_2'\Theta\beta_2)^{-1}\alpha_2'. \tag{66}$$

The matrix C_1 is rather complicated but it can be shown that it satisfies the restriction

$$\beta_1'C_1 = \bar{\alpha}_1'\Gamma C_2 \tag{67}$$

which will show useful later. $C^*(L)$ is a matrix polynomial with all roots strictly outside the unit circle. All these formulae may seem difficult but are useful in visualizing the cointegrating combinations of the variables.

Note first that in general x_t will have $p-r-s$ common stochastic I(2) trends given by $\alpha_2' \sum_{j=1}^{t} \sum_{i=1}^{j} \varepsilon_i$. A different way of looking at the I(2) trends is to consider $\beta_2'x_t$. Since $\beta_2'C_2 \neq 0$ it follows that $\beta_2'x_t$ by construction is a $p-r-s$ dimensional I(2) trend; indeed, these are just linear combinations of the stochastic trends $\alpha_2' \sum_{j=1}^{t} \sum_{i=1}^{j} \varepsilon_i$.

Consider now the combinations $\beta_{2\perp}'x_t = (\beta, \beta_1)'x_t$. Since in this case $(\beta, \beta_1)'C_2 = 0$ it follows from (65) that in general

$$(\beta, \beta_1)'x_t = (\beta, \beta_1)'C_1 \sum_{i=1}^{t} \varepsilon_i + (\beta, \beta_1)'C^*(L)\varepsilon_t \sim \mathrm{I}(1) \tag{68}$$

so (β, β_1) reduces the integration order from 2 to 1. However, this is not the end of the story because even in the I(2) model it makes sense to talk about β as the vectors defining the I(0) relations. It appears that the combinations $\beta'x_t$ can cointegrate to I(0) level and/or will have the property that they potentially cointegrate with $\beta_2'\Delta x_t$ such that *polynomial cointegration* results, see Johansen (1995a). Note that $\beta_2'\Delta x_t$ by construction is I(1) and non-cointegrated. These r relations read

$$\beta'x_t - \delta\beta_2'\Delta x_t \sim \mathrm{I}(0) \tag{69}$$

with $\delta = \bar{\alpha}'\Gamma\bar{\beta}_2$ of dimension $r \times (p-r-s)$ and hence define the I(0) directions.

Not all of the r stationary relations given in (69) need include the differenced I(2) component $\beta_2'\Delta x_t$. Consider the orthogonal complement matrix of δ denoted $\delta_\perp$ which is of dimension $r \times (r-(p-r-s))$ such that $\delta_\perp'\delta = 0$. Then it follows that

$$\delta_\perp'\beta'x_t \sim \mathrm{I}(0) \tag{70}$$

and hence these are not polynomially cointegrating relations. On the other hand, the $p-r-s$ relations

$$\delta'\beta'x_t - \delta'\delta\beta_2'\Delta x_t \sim \mathrm{I}(0) \tag{71}$$

are all polynomially cointegrating. Note that the number of polynomial cointegrating relations equals the number of I(2) trends which requires, of course, that $r \geqslant p - r - s$.

Table 6, which is motivated by Paruolo (1996), reviews the cointegration possibilities of I(2) and I(1) VAR models. As seen, the cointegration parameters of interest are given by β, β_1 and δ.

A different ay of writing the VAR is in ECM form by directly incorporating the cointegration parameters:

$$\Delta^2 x_t = \alpha(\beta' x_{t-1} - \delta\beta_2' \Delta x_{t-1}) - (\zeta_1, \zeta_2)(\beta, \beta_1)' \Delta x_{t-1} + \sum_{i=1}^{k-2} \Psi_i \Delta x_{t-i} + \varepsilon_i, \quad (72)$$

see Paruolo and Rahbek (1996). ζ_i are appropriately defined adjustment parameters. This way of writing the VAR is perhaps more intuitive since all the cointegration possibilities can be explicitly defined through error correction terms.

As for cointegrated I(1) models it must be emphasized that only the space spanned by the cointegrating vectors is identified; the single cointegration relations are unidentified. However, for I(2) systems this problem is more complex since β, β_1 and δ cannot be determined independently from each other. In section 9.4 I briefly discuss the identification problem.

Example: The Cagan model.
As a simple illustration consider calculating the integration indices of the Cagan (1956) hyper-inflation model discussed in section 3.1. It was shown that when (m_t, p_t) are I(2) series the theory predicts that the series are polynomially cointegrated. The polynomial cointegration relation is given by $m_t - p_t + \delta\Delta m_t$. As seen, in this model $p = 2$, $r = 1$, and $s = 0$: There is one I(2) trend and a single I(0) relation. Granger and Lee's multicointegration model which consists of just two series, i.e. production and sales of some commodity, can be shown to yield the same integration indices.

Table 6. Integration indices and the associated processes in VAR models. Note that the cointegration parameters are given by β, β_1 and δ.

	Dimension	Basis	Associated processes
I(1)-model			
I(0)-relations	r	β	$\beta' x_t$
I(1)-relations	$p - r$	$\beta_\perp$	$\beta_\perp' x_t$
I(2)-model			
I(0)-relations	r	β	$\beta' x_t - \delta\beta_2' \Delta x_t \quad \left\{ \begin{array}{ll} r - (p - r - s): & \delta_\perp' \beta' x_t \\ p - r - s: & \delta' \beta' x_t - \delta' \delta \beta_2' \Delta x_t \end{array} \right\}$
I(1)-relations	s	β_1	$\beta_1' x_t$
I(2)-relations	$p - r - s$	β_2	$\beta_2' x_t$

Source: Partially taken from Paruolo (1996).

8.3. *Deterministic components*

In the presentation given above I have abstracted from the possible presence of deterministic components in the processes. Without going too much into the details I briefly outline how deterministic trends may potentially enter the models. First we consider the case where the VAR model (62) is augmented with an intercept, μ, that is,

$$\Delta^2 x_t = \mu + \Pi x_{t-i} - \Gamma \Delta x_{t-1} + \sum_{i=1}^{k-2} \Psi_i \Delta^2 x_{t-i} + \varepsilon_t. \tag{73}$$

We want to understand the meaning of μ in this model. Paruolo (1996) considers the following factorization of the intercept:

$$\mu = \alpha\mu_0 + \alpha_1\mu_1 + \alpha_2\mu_2, \quad \text{with } \mu_d = \bar{\alpha}_d'\mu, \quad \text{for } d = 0, 1, 2. \tag{74}$$

Hence μ is projected onto the spaces spanned by α, α_1, and α_2, with the respective dimensions r, s, and $p - r - s$. The μ_d-terms will indicate the extent to which the intercept will influence the associated $\mathrm{I}(d)$ space. Generally, the I(2) space will have a quadratic trend, the I(1) space will have a linear trend, and the I(0) space will have no trend. To see this, consider the stochatic trends representation of the I(2)-VAR given in (65) where ε_i is replaced by $\varepsilon_i + \mu$:

$$x_t = \tau_2 t^2 + (\tau_2 + C_1\mu)t + C_2 \sum_{j=1}^{t}\sum_{i=1}^{j} \varepsilon_i + C_1 \sum_{i=1}^{t} \varepsilon_i + C^*(L)\varepsilon_t \tag{75}$$

$$\tau_2 = \tfrac{1}{2} C_2 \mu. \tag{76}$$

It follows that in general x_t will have quadratic trends but more can be said. Note simply from the decomposition (74), that $\tau_2 = \frac{1}{2}C_2\mu = \frac{1}{2}\beta_2(\alpha_2'\Theta\beta_2)^{-1}\alpha_2'\alpha_2\mu_2$ so it is the presence of $\mu_2 \neq 0$ that causes the quadratic trend. By focusing explicitly on the I(2) directions $\beta_2' x_t$ these are seen to have quadratic trends,[30] unless $\mu_2 = 0$.

Next we address the I(1) directions $\beta_1' x_t$. Naturally there will be no quadratic trend in these directions since $\beta_1'\tau_2 = 0$. The C_1 matrix is rather complicated, however, unless μ_1 and μ_2 are both equal to zero, $\beta_1' x_t$ will have a linear trend.

Finally, by using the fact that $\beta' C_1 = \bar{\alpha}'\Gamma C_2$ it can be shown that the stationary polynomially cointegrating relations $\beta' x_t - \delta\beta_2'\Delta x_t$ will be free of deterministic trends.

Rahbek *et al.* (1998) choose a different parametrization of the model corresponding to the factor representation $x_t = x_t^0 + \gamma_0 + \gamma_1 t$, where x_t^0 is the stochastic part of the process defined in (65), that is,

$$x_t = \gamma_0 + \gamma_1 t + C_2 \sum_{j=1}^{t}\sum_{i=1}^{j} \varepsilon_i + C_1 \sum_{i=1}^{t} \varepsilon_i + C^*(L)\varepsilon_t. \tag{77}$$

As in Paruolo (1996), who assumes $\mu_2 = 0$, it is seen that this model is also unable to produce quadratic trends. However, by choosing the formulation (77) the parameters γ_0 and γ_1 can vary freely and consequently even the polynomially cointegrating I(0) relations may contain linear trends and hence will be trend stationary. This appears to be especially useful with respect to hypothesis testing about the cointegration rank when deterministics are considered in the processes.

9. Estimation and hypothesis testing using the Johansen procedure

In empirical applications dealing with I(2) variables in systems, the Johansen I(2) procedure seems to be dominating. We will here give some of the main results for this procedure. Also there is a growing number of empirical contributions. Understanding the complex nature of the models and the hypotheses to be defined in the various spaces of different integration order is difficult. We start by presenting a natural hierarchical ordering of the testable hypotheses which is essential in understanding the subsequent issues related to estimation and hypothesis testing.

9.1. *A hierarchical ordering of testable sub-models*

As we have seen in section 8.2 the I(1) and I(2) models result from particular restrictions of the general VAR model which may be formulated either as in (59) or as in (62). In table 7 the various sub-models that can be formulated in the I(1) model are displayed, and in table 8 the sub-models of the I(2) VAR are reported separately given a fixed value of r, that is, the cointegration rank defined from the I(1) model is fixed. The structure of the two tables are basically the same but the focus in each case is on the I(1) and I(2) reduced rank conditions, respectively. Notice in particular, that the least restricted model is H_p, the model H_0 is a VAR in first differences (no I(0) relations), and finally the model H_{00} is a VAR in second differences (all p relations are I(2)). All the intermediate cases describe situations with cointegration.

Observe also that a superscript '0', for instance in H_r^0, is used to indicate the submodel of H_r where α and β have full rank, r. No superscript indicates that the

Table 7. Hypotheses in the I(1) model

	Restriction	Parameter space	Comments
H_p	None	$(\Pi, \Gamma_1, \Gamma_2, \ldots, \Gamma_{k-1}, \Omega)$	VAR in levels
H_r	$\Pi = \alpha\beta', \alpha, \beta\ p \times r, r = 0, 1, \ldots, p$	$(\alpha, \beta, \Gamma_1, \Gamma_2, \ldots, \Gamma_{k-1}, \Omega)$	Reduced rank
H_0	$\Pi = 0$	$(\Gamma_1, \Gamma_2, \ldots, \Gamma_{k-1}, \Omega)$	VAR in first differences
H_r^0	$\Pi = \alpha\beta'$, $\text{rank}(\alpha\beta') = r$	$(\alpha, \beta, \Gamma_1, \Gamma_2, \ldots, \Gamma_{k-1}, \Omega)$	α, β of full rank r

The relation between the various hypotheses:

$$H_r = \cup_{i=0}^{r} H_i^0$$
$$H_0 \subset H_1 \subset \ldots \subset H_p$$

rank of the matrices is less than or equal to r: $H_r = \cup_{i=0}^{r} H_i^0$. The sub-models $H_{r,s}$ are indexed in a similar way.

Table 9 is taken from Johansen (1995a) and shows how the various I(1) and I(2) sub-models are related. In particular, it should be noticed that by moving from H_{00} to the right, down to H_{10} to the right, and so on, defines models which become less and less restricted as one proceeds.

9.2. *Determining the integration indices*

The ordering of hypotheses defined in section (9.1) is useful in determining the integration indices, that is, the dimension of each of the I(d) spaces, $d = 0, 1, 2$. This is the focus of the present section whilst the subsequent section addresses hypotheses about the parameters and the cointegration spaces after the integration indices have been fixed.

Table 8. Hypotheses in the I(2) model. All hypotheses are conditional on rank$(\alpha\beta') = r$.

	Restriction	Parameter space	Comments
$H_{r,p-r}$	No further	$(\alpha, \beta, \Gamma, \Psi_1, \Psi_2, \ldots, \Psi_{k-2}, \Omega)$	Cointegrated I(1) VAR model. $H_{r,p-r} = H_r^0$
$H_{r,s}$	$\alpha_\perp' \Gamma \beta_\perp = \xi\eta', \xi, \eta$ $(p-r) \times s, s = 0, 1, \ldots, p-r$	$(\alpha, \beta, \Gamma, \Psi_1, \Psi_2, \ldots, \Psi_{k-2}, \Omega)$ subject to restriction	Reduced rank of I(2) model
$H_{r,0}$	$\Gamma = 0$	$(\alpha, \beta, \Psi_1, \Psi_2, \ldots, \Psi_{k-2}, \Omega)$	No I(1) trends
$H_{r,s}^0$	$\alpha_\perp' \Gamma \beta_\perp = \xi\eta'$, rank$(\xi\eta') = s$	$(\alpha, \beta, \Gamma, \Psi_1, \Psi_2, \ldots, \Psi_{k-2}, \Omega)$ subject to restriction	ξ, η of full rank s

The relation between the various hypotheses:

$$H_{r,s} = \cup_{i=0}^{s} H_{r,i}^0$$
$$H_{r,0} \subset H_{r,1} \subset \ldots \subset H_{r,p-r} = H_r^0 \subset H_r$$

Table 9. The relations between the various I(1) and I(2) models.

$p-r$	r													
p	0	H_{00}	$\subset$	H_{01}	$\subset$	$\ldots$	$\subset$	$H_{0,p-1}$	$\subset$	$H_{0,p}$	$= H_0^0$	$\subset$	H_0
													$\cap$
$p-1$	1			H_{10}	$\subset$	$\ldots$	$\subset$	$H_{1,p-2}$	$\subset$	$H_{1,p-1}$	$= H_1^0$	$\subset$	H_1
													$\cap$
											$\vdots$		$\vdots$
													$\cap$
1	$p-1$							$H_{p-1,0}$	$\subset$	$H_{p-1,1}$	$= H_{p-1}^0$	$\subset$	H_p
$p-r-s$		p		$p-1$		$\ldots$		1		0			

Source: Johansen (1995a)

It is well known from the I(1) analysis, see Johansen (1988, 1991), that likelihood analysis of the models H_r can be conducted as a combination of regression and reduced rank regression;[31] regression is conducted to filter the data such that nuisance parameters are eliminated whereas reduced rank regression explicitly aims for determining the cointegration rank. The I(2) analysis is discussed in Johansen (1995a, 1997) and follows a similar train of thought, but now two reduced rank conditions need to be examined, i.e. the restrictions (63) and (64) which define the I(2) model $H_{r,s}$. However, the analysis is further complicated by the fact that the second reduced rank condition associated with the matrix $\alpha'_{\perp}\Gamma\beta_{\perp}=\xi\eta'$ depends upon the first reduced rank condition of $\Pi=\alpha\beta'$. Joint estimation of the indices r and s which define these matrices is therefore rather complicated. Instead, Johansen has suggested a two step procedure; the basic structure of the reduced rank problems is the following:

Step 1 consists of solving the reduced rank problem associated with $\Pi=\alpha\beta'$ and calculating for *each* value of $r=0,\dots,p-1$, the estimates $\hat{\alpha}_r, \hat{\beta}_r, \hat{\alpha}_{r\perp}$ and $\hat{\beta}_{r\perp}$. Subscript r indicates for which value of r the calculated estimates.

Step 2 considers subsequently the reduced rank regression problem associated with $\alpha'_{\perp}\Gamma\beta_{\perp}=\xi\eta'$ which is solved for $s=0,1,\dots,p-r-1$, by replacing the unknown matrices $\alpha_{\perp}$ and $\beta_{\perp}$ by the estimates obtained in step 1. Note that estimates are available for each value of r.

From this triangular array of sub-models corresponding to the hypotheses $H^0_{r,s}$ it remains to be determined which values of r and s to choose. To do so we first need to be specific about the reduced rank regression problems of steps 1 and 2. I will not go into technical details about this, but just note that the reduced rank problem of step 1 amounts to solving an eigenvalue problem after the influence of the nuisance parameters Γ, Ψ_i, $i=1,2,k-2$, has been eliminated by prefiltering.[32] The eigenvalue problem delivers the eigenvalues $1>\hat{\lambda}_1>\hat{\lambda}_2>\dots>\hat{\lambda}_p>0$ with the associated eigenvectors $(v_1, v_2, \dots, v_p)$. The Maximum Likelihood (ML) estimator of β for a given value of r is then given by $(\hat{\beta}_r=(v_1, v_2, \dots, v_r)$, that is, the eigenvectors corresponding to the r largest eigenvalues. The estimates $\hat{\alpha}_r$ can also be found. The maximized value of the likelihood function can be shown to be proportional to

$$L_{\max}^{-2/T} \propto \prod_{i=1}^{r}(1-\hat{\lambda}_i) \tag{78}$$

and hence the likelihood ratio (LR) test, $Q(H_r|H_p)$ of the I(1) model H_r with rank$\Pi \leqslant r$ against the unrestricted VAR, H_p, is given by

$$Q_r = -2\ln Q(H_r\,|\,H_p) = -T\sum_{i=r+1}^{p}\ln(1-\hat{\lambda}_i), \quad r=0,\dots,p-1. \tag{79}$$

By the presence of I(1) (but no I(2)) trends the distribution of this statistic is the Johansen trace statistic well known from the I(1) analysis. Unfortunately the distribution will be different by the presence of I(2) trends and since the number of these is unknown we cannot use the Q_r statistic to determine r in practice. Instead we have to proceed to step 2 of the procedure after Q_r is calculated for each possible value of $r = 0, \ldots, p-1$.

In step 2 the variables are transformed using the estimates $\hat{\alpha}_r, \hat{\beta}_r, \hat{\alpha}_{r\perp}$, and $\hat{\beta}_{r\perp}$ which replace the unknown population parameters in the subsequent calculations. The reduced rank regression problem now consists of regressing $\hat{\alpha}'_{r\perp}\Delta^2 x_t$ on $\hat{\beta}'_{r\perp}\Delta x_{t-1}$ after appropriate prefiltering has been made of the series.[33] Again this problem can be formulated as a particular eigenvalue problem yielding the eigenvalues $1 > \hat{\rho}_1 > \hat{\rho}_2 > \ldots > \hat{\rho}_{p-r} > 0$ and eigenvectors $(w_1, w_2, \ldots, w_{p-r})$. The ML estimate of η is obtained as $\hat{\eta} = (w_1, w_2, \ldots, w_s)$. A solution can be found for ξ as well. For given values of r, α, and β the contribution to the likelihood function is proportional to

$$L_{\max}^{-2/T} \propto \prod_{i=1}^{s} (1 - \hat{\rho}_i). \tag{80}$$

Therefore, the LR test of the models $H_{r,s}$ conditional on the model H_r^0, is given by

$$Q_{r,s} = -2 \ln Q(H_{r,s} \mid H_r^0) = -T \sum_{i=s+1}^{p-r} \ln(1 - \hat{\rho}_i), \quad s = 0, \ldots, p-r-1. \tag{81}$$

This test assumes that r is known and conditional on the value of r the distribution is again given by the I(1) Johansen trace statistic. But since r is unknown in practice it is more relevant to test $H_{r,s}$ (corresponding to the models with $r \leqslant p$, and $s \leqslant p - r$) against H_p (the unrestricted VAR) by focusing on the statistic

$$S_{r,s} = -2 \ln Q(H_{r,s} | H_p) = Q_{r,s} + Q_r. \tag{82}$$

This is valid since the hypotheses are nested. Johansen (1995a) shows that the distribution of $S_{r,s}$ is given by the sum of the trace of functionals of standard Brownian motions and integrated standard Brownian motion processes. In fact, this corresponds to multivariate versions of the Hasza-Fuller distribution discussed in section 5.1 within a univariate context. Generally $S_{r,s}$ will depend upon the integration indices, s and $p - r - s$, i.e. the number of I(1) and I(2) trends in the system. The distributions for the case with no deterministics in the model are given in Johansen (1995a, table 3).

The $S_{r,s}$ statistic can be used to determine the integration indices. The model $H_{r,s}$ is rejected if $H_{i,j}$ is rejected for all $i < r$ and $j \leqslant s$. The idea is therefore to use the hierarchical ordering given in table 9 from left to right and from top to bottom, i.e. following the sequence starting with H_{00} to the right, down to H_{10} to the right *etc*. The integration indices $\hat{r}, \hat{s}$ are determined as the first pair of r, s which is not being rejected.[34]

It can be shown that this order of testing hypotheses which become less and less restricted is a consistent procedure and with a type-1 error which can be controlled by choice of the significance level.[35]

Deterministic components. As previously mentioned, Paruolo (1994, 1996) focuses on the VAR model discussed above augmented with an intercept μ. Basically the presence of an unrestricted intercept is accommodated for by correcting the regressors and the regressand for an intercept prior to the reduced rank regression problems. In Paruolo (1996, table 13), the asymptotic critical values for the corresponding $S_{r,s}$ test with μ being unrestricted are reported. If restrictions are wanted on the intercept such that there is no quadratic trends in the data, $\mu_2 = 0$, or no linear trend, $\mu_1 = \mu_2 = 0$, then the trending behaviour of the different models has to be decided jointly with the determination of the integration indices. Due to the complexity of this analysis it will not be pursued here, but the interested reader is referred to Paruolo (1996) for the details. Note, however, that when the restriction $\mu_2 = 0$ is imposed yet another set of critical values needs to be used to validate the analysis, Paruolo (1996, table 6). If $\mu_1 = \mu_2 = 0$ is imposed in estimation neither linear nor quadratic trends are allowed for and Paruolo's table 5 should be used to determine the integration indices in this case.[36]

In practical situations the factor representation of Rahbek *et al.* (1998) given in (77) seems to be the most appropriate as the benchmark for tests about the cointegration rank. In their VAR model the presence of quadratic trends are excluded but linear trends are allowed, even in the cointegration space. The common stochastic trends representation (77) can be reparametrized such that the model reads

$$\Delta^2 x_t = \alpha\beta^{*\prime} x^*_{t-1} - \Gamma\Delta x_{t-1} + \mu_0 + \sum_{i=1}^{k-2} \Psi_i \Delta^2 x_{t-i} + \varepsilon_t \tag{83}$$

where $\beta^{*\prime} = (\beta', \beta'_0)$ and $x^*_{t-1} = (x'_{t-1}, t)$ and with a particular restriction on the intercept term μ_0. How exactly the parameters μ_0, β_0 of (83) are related with the parameters γ_0, γ_1 of the model (77) can be seen from their paper. The procedure adopted to determine the integration indices for the case with no deterministics can be straightforwardly extended to cover the above situation. Variables just need to be appropriately redefined (as seen in (83)) by taking into account the restrictions on μ_0. LR statistics in each step of the analysis define the LR test of $H^*_{r,s}$ against H^*_p (a '*' signifies that linear trends are allowed in the various directions) and is given by

$$S^*_{r,s} = Q^*_{r,s} + Q^*_{r\cdot} \tag{84}$$

Rahbek *et al.* (1998) report the distribution of this statistic as well as the relevant asymptotic critical values (their tables 1 and 4).

Interestingly, the distributions are similar with respect to the actual deterministic components present (given, of course, that there are no quadratic trends). Hence, after the cointegration indices have been fixed, it is rather simple to test whether the trend-stationarity of the cointegration relations implied by (83) is actually satisfied by the data. Absence of the trends means that $\beta_0 = 0$ and hence the idea is to compare the likelihood values for the model (83) and the restricted model which is obtained by replacing x^*_t by x_t. The likelihood ratio test is given by

$$Q_{\beta_0=0} = T\sum_{i=1}^{r} \ln((1-\hat{\lambda}_i^*)/(1-\hat{\lambda}_i)) \tag{85}$$

where $\hat{\lambda}_i^*$ and $\hat{\lambda}_i$ correspond to the first step eigenvalues for the restricted and unrestricted models, respectively. The test is asymptotic χ^2 with r degrees of freedom.

9.3. *Examples. Estimation of the integration indices and cointegration relations in the various data sets*[37]

German hyperinflation, 1920:1–1923:6.

The Cagan model predicts that for the pair ($p = 2$) of time series, m_t and p_t, $s = 0$, and $r = 1$, that is, one I(0) relation and $p - r - s = 1$ I(2) trend. For the present data set a VAR(3) was estimated with a constant restricted not to produce quadratic trends. This corresponds to the model (73) with $\mu_2 = 0$. The $S_{r,s}$-trace statistics (82) which are associated with the hierarchical hypotheses in table 9 are displayed in table 10.

According to the hierarchical principle the first hypothesis tested is H_{00}. The test value is 45.09 and is clearly significant.[38] The next test yields 14.38 which is insignificant. The conclusion is therefore that $r = 0$ and $s = 1$, that is, m_t and p_t have a common I(2) trend but there is no polynomial cointegration with Δm_t or Δp_t.

US housing data set, 1968:1–1994:12.

A VAR with 12 lags was estimated for the cumulated housing starts and housing completion series. The choice of 12 lags was found to whiten the errors reasonably well. Note that when time series are potentially multicointegrated in the sense of Granger and Lee, the appropriate way of defining the VAR, according to Engsted and Johansen (1997), is to consider the VAR for the integrated time series, see also Engsted and Haldrup (1998). Since the cumulated

Table 10. Joint tests of the cointegration indices. German hyperinflation data set, 1920:1–1923:6.

$p-r$	r	$S_{r,s}$		Q_r
2	0	45.09***	**14.38**	13.03
		36.12	*22.60*	*15.41*
1	1		5.55	2.94
			12.93	*3.84*
$p-r-s$		2	1	0

Note: Numbers in italics are 95 per cent quantiles, (Paruolo (1996), table 6.). r and $p - r - s$ are the number of I(0) and I(2) components.

series will have a trend by construction I decided to allow for a trend also amongst the I(0) relations as in (52), c.f. the Rahbek *et al.* (1998) specification. Table 11 summarizes the results.

As seen the first hypothesis which cannot be rejected at the 90% level suggests the indices $(r, s) = (1, 0)$. Hence the system has one I(2) trend and a single multicointegrating relation. This relation corresponds to Eq. (69) and is given by

$$\sum_{j=1}^{t} y_j - 0.972 \sum_{j=1}^{t} x_j - 3.908 y_t - 4.022 x_t + const + trend \sim \mathrm{I}(0)$$

so the estimate of the percentage of housing construction starts never being completed is 2.8%. The value Lee (1996) imposed a priori was 2%.

Danish money demand data set, 1974:1–1993:4.

The present information set is of course much larger than in the previous two examples which naturally complicates the structural analysis of the equilibrium relations. The analysis presented here is for the purpose of illustration and a more detailed analysis can be found in Juselius (1998) who also consider the possibility of structural shifts in the data. For ease of exposition we abstract from such generalizations. A VAR(4) model was fitted to the data set consisting of the variables $\mathrm{x}_t = (m_t, p_t, y_t, i_{bt}, i_{dt})'$. The analysis allowed for seasonal dummy variables and an intercept restricted such that quadratic trends $(\mu_2 = 0)$ were excluded. Table 12 shows the test results.

In this case it is seen that the hierarchical test procedure suggests one I(2) trend and 4 cointegrating relations,[39] $(r, s) = (4, 0)$. Observe that this implies a total number of two unit roots in the entire VAR model.

It is easy to see that the variables constituting the I(2) trend is some combination of the m_t and p_t variables. The I(2) directions are given by $\beta_2' \mathrm{x}_t$ and in the present case this is estimated as $\hat{\beta}_2' \mathrm{x}_t = (1, 1.07, -0.02, 0.01, 0.01)\mathrm{x}_t$. In fact, the I(2) trend is close to an average of the m_t and p_t series.

Since we assume there is a total of 4 stationary relations it may show useful to separate these into the $r - (p - r - s) = 4 - (5 - 4 - 0) = 3$ relations $\delta_\perp' \beta' \mathrm{x}_t$

Table 11. Joint tests of the cointegration indices. US Housing data set, 1968:1–1994:12.

$p-r$	r		$S_{r,s}$	Q_r
2	0	76.90***	32.72*	22.55*
		47.60	*34.36*	*25.43*
1	1		**13.90**	4.20
			19.87	*12.49*
$p-r-s$		2	1	0

Note: Numbers in italics are 95 per cent quantiles, (Rahbek *et al.* (1998), tables 1 and 4). r and $p - r - s$ are the number of I(0) and I(2) components.

Table 12. Joint tests of the cointegration indices. Danish money data set 1974:1–1993:4.

$p-r$	r			$S_{r,s}$			Q_r
5	0	252.64***	206.70***	163.58***	133.88***	114.65***	100.12
		171.89	*142.57*	*117.63*	*97.97*	*81.93*	*68.52*
4	1		180.20***	137.12***	95.32***	76.70***	61.59***
			116.31	*91.41*	*72.99*	*57.95*	*47.21*
3	2			111.43***	69.02***	41.45**	32.31**
				70.87	*51.35*	*38.82*	*29.68*
2	3				57.29***	29.47***	15.36*
					36.12	*22.60*	*15.41*
1	4					**10.55**	5.63
						12.93	*3.84*
$p-r-s$		5	4	3	2	1	0

Note: Numbers in italics are 95 per cent quantiles, (Paruolo(1996), table 6). r and $p-r-s$ are the number of I(0) and I(2) components.

which are I(0) without the differences, and the remaining single relation $\delta'\beta'x_t - \delta'\delta\beta_2'\Delta x_t$ which is polynomially cointegrating, see (70)–(71) and table 6. By appropriate choice of normalization it can be found that

$$\delta_\perp'\beta'x_t = \begin{pmatrix} 1 & -1.22 & -0.18 & -4.49 & 48.18 \\ -0.95 & 1 & 0.36 & -27.08 & 27.80 \\ -0.51 & 0.51 & 1 & -6.17 & 6.46 \end{pmatrix} (m_t, p_t, y_t, i_{bt}, i_{dt})'$$

$$\delta'\beta'x_t - \delta'\delta\beta_2'\Delta x_t = (1 \quad 1.18 \quad 6.54 \quad -9.94 \quad -270.94)x_t - (215.99 \quad 231.52 \quad -3.99 \quad 2.57 \quad 1.61)\Delta x_t.$$

Of course, one should be careful about making structural interpretations based on the above estimates since the single cointegrating relations are unidentified. However, the estimates suggest several overidentfying restrictions. For instance one may consider addressing a real specification of the money variable, at least this seems to hold for the first three relations. Moreover, the second and third relation suggests a specification where the difference between the bond and deposit rates is considered, and finally the polynomially cointegrating relation, due to the magnitude of the parameters, seems to suggest a cointegrating relationship between real money growth, $\Delta(m_t - p_t)$ and the deposit rate, i_{dt}. These hypotheses are of course testable.

9.4. *Hypothesis testing of the model parameters*

When the cointegration ranks have been determined it is of interest to test restrictions on the cointegration vectors and the adjustment coefficients. Since the cointegration and non-stationary relations are defined such that e.g. β_1 and β_2 are not in the space spanned by β, it is clear that any restriction on β will have implications for the other vectors as well. When using the two step procedure this becomes apparent since the analysis of the vectors β_1 and β_2 is considered after the choice of β has been made.

Recently Johansen (1997) considered a particular parametrization of the Gaussian VAR model (62) which allows all model parameters to vary freely. This makes the likelihood analysis simpler as the model can be formulated as a general non-linear regressions problem upon which ML estimates can be obtained. Interestingly, it can be shown that the computationally simpler two step procedure is fully efficient in estimating the I(2) model, see also Paruolo (1997) for the model with a constant. This means that likelihood ratio tests concerning hypotheses on β from the I(1) analysis are valid although I(2) components are present and hence the distributions are asymptotically χ^2 distributed.

However, in discussing hypotheses on the model parameters it is important to realize, that β and α are unidentified as any non-singular matrix ζ can be chosen whereby $\alpha\zeta$ and $\zeta^{-1}\beta'$ will give the same value of $\Pi = \alpha\beta'$. Therefore, in order to interpret the single cointegration vectors, (exactly) identifying restrictions need to be imposed on β. An easy way of doing this is to normalize the single vectors such that the cointegration relations can be solved, for instance by chosing the identification scheme $\beta_c = (\mathrm{I}_r : \mathrm{B}')'$. Of course any exactly identifying restrictions can be chosen; generally the restrictions can be phrased as $\beta_c = \beta(\mathrm{c}'\beta)^{-1}$.

In doing so Johansen (1995a) shows that[40]

$$T(\hat{\beta}_c - \beta) \longrightarrow \int_{\Xi} N(0, \Xi)\,\mathrm{d}P(\Xi), \tag{86}$$

that is, the distribution is mixed Gaussian with Ξ being the mixing variate matrix. An estimate of the covariance matrix can be obtained by

$$(\mathrm{I} - \hat{\beta}_c\mathrm{c}')\left[\sum_{t=1}^{T} \mathrm{R}_t\mathrm{R}_t'\right]^{-1}(\mathrm{I} - \mathrm{c}\hat{\beta}_c') \otimes (\hat{\alpha}_c'\hat{\Omega}^{-1}\hat{\alpha}_c)^{-1} \tag{87}$$

where R_t is the vector of residuals from the regression of x_{t-1} on lagged first differences (and deterministics). This result means that for the normalization chosen it is easy to do asymptotic inference on the single coefficients associated with β_c by using the standard normal distribution for single t tests.[41]

With respect to the other cointegration parameters similar identification problems arise but of course these problems cannot be solved independently as the parameters are linked together in a particular way. For instance, observe that the parameter δ associated with polynomial cointegration can be defined from $\alpha\delta\beta_2'$ in the representation (72) but only the product of the matrices is identified from the outset. However, whenever α and β_2 are identified also δ is identified. But this means that the whole identification problem for δ is solved when $(\beta, \beta_1, \beta_2)$ are identified since the identification of β also identifies[42] α.

The estimator of δ can be shown to be super-consistent, but unfortunately it appears that inference about δ can be less easily carried out as the distribution of the estimator is not mixed Gaussian. Any test involving this parameter is therefore difficult, see Boswijk (1997) and Paruolo (1997) for details.

Finally, also the estimate of β_1 can be shown to be T-consistent and mixed Gaussian. However, the β directions are probably the most interesting relations from an economic perspective.

With respect to general hypotheses of *overidentifying restrictions* on the cointegration relations (apart from restrictions involving the polynomial cointegration parameter δ), these can for instance be of the form

$$\beta = (\mathrm{H}_1\phi_1, \mathrm{H}_2\phi_2) \tag{88}$$

where different restrictions are imposed on the single vectors. ϕ_i are the freely varying parameters of the restricted model. The restrictions mean that also the other cointegration relations are restricted as β_1 and β_2 are defined orthogonal to β. In practice likelihood inference is based on solving the eigenvalue problems for the constrained model. LR tests can now be conducted by comparing the restricted and unrestricted eigenvalues like in the trend test (85). The LR-test statistic is χ^2 distributed with degrees of freedom corresponding to the number of over-identifying restrictions.

Similarly hypothesis testing can be undertaken with respect to the adjustment coefficients. In the I(1) analysis such tests are frequently associated with testing for weak exogeneity. In this analysis, if rows of the α matrix are found to have zero elements, it means that the corresponding variables can be treated as weakly exogenous with respect to the cointegration parameters, such that a partial system can be analyzed without loss of efficiency. Paruolo and Rahbek (1996) have developed the theory for the I(2) model. Generally they find that the weak exogeneity restrictions can take many different forms depending on the parametrization of the model. For instance, in the parametrization (62) the $(p-m)$ dimensional process $\mathrm{b}'\mathrm{x}_t$ is weakly exogenous for the cointegration parameters (β, β_1, δ) when $\mathrm{b}'\Pi = \mathrm{b}'\Gamma = 0$. A necessary condition for this to be the case is that the weakly exogenous process has dimension such that $m \geqslant r+s$. In general the maximum number of weakly exogenous variables can be shown to equal the number of I(2) trends $p-r-s$. In empirical studies this number is frequently found to be rather small; a negative implication of this is that it becomes difficult to formulate reduced partial models without loosing efficiency. The likelihood analysis and testing strategies are discussed in Paruolo and Rahbek's paper which the interested reader can consult for the details.

9.5. *Examples. Testing hypotheses on the cointegration relations in the Danish money demand data set*

In section 9.3 different restrictions of the cointegrated I(2) VAR for the Danish money demand data set were suggested. Here I briefly demonstrate how the hypothesis that a real specification of money demand will suffice in the specification of the model. If such a restriction can be validly imposed the entire analysis simplifies considerably since in place of m_t and p_t the standard I(1) analysis can be carried out for the variables $[(m_t - p_t), y_t, \Delta p_t, i_{bt}, i_{dt}]$.

The hypotheses tested correspond to considering in (88) the same restrictions

$H_i = H$, for all $i = 1, 2, \ldots, 4$. In the present case H is given by

$$H = \begin{pmatrix} 1 & 0 & 0 & 0 \\ -1 & 0 & 0 & 0 \\ 0 & 1 & 0 & 0 \\ 0 & 0 & 1 & 0 \\ 0 & 0 & 0 & 1 \end{pmatrix}$$

and ϕ_i are 4×1 matrices of parameters. Note that this set of hypotheses does not identify the model structure; this would require different restrictions on each of the cointegration relations.

The LR test of the above hypothesis yields the test value $LR^* = 2.53$ and is distributed as $\chi^2(4)$ and hence is insignificant. The I(1) analysis for the transformed (real) system is carefully analyzed in Juselius (1998).

10. Other results for I(2) variables in systems

This section addresses very briefly some remaining results applying to I(2) systems.

In sections 8 and 9 I have focused attention on the I(2) analysis relating to the Gaussian VAR model. In a recent paper Chang (1997) generalizes Chang and Phillips (1995) and addresses the problem about efficiently estimating (in Phillips' (1991) sense) VAR models when the model has an unknown mixture of I(0), I(1), and I(2) components, i.e. no prior or pretest information is required with respect to the number of unit roots and the integration indices. Chang shows that his estimator (denoted the *residual-based fully modified* -VAR (RBFM-VAR) estimator, see also Chang and Phillips (1997)) is identical to that of the maximum likelihood estimator under Gaussian assumptions with the precise knowledge about the order of unit roots in individual series and the cointegrating relationships in the model. Simulations show that the estimator is behaving well in large samples, and reasonably well in finite samples.

The triangular system representation was introduced in section 7 and has been the benchmark representation for a number theoretical studies of I(2) systems. For instance, Stock and Watson (1993) used the representation (assuming known integration indices) in order to propose a likelihood-based estimation method by augmenting the single equations by leads and lags of the differenced series. Within this framework they showed that their estimator is asymptotically efficient, even when the errors are not necessarily Gaussian. Kitamura (1995) showed, for particular cointegrated I(2) models, how optimal inference applies when other formulations of triangular systems are used.

Although different representations of multivariate systems are typically derived to facilitate statistical analysis, these may also be of separate interest as they provide different insights into the different features of such systems. Many different representations including common stochastic trends, triangular, and error correction representations can be derived from the so-called Smith-McMillan form of a rational polynomial matrix, see Kailath (1980). This tool has been applied to I(1) models, see Yoo (1986) and Hylleberg and Mizon (1989) as well as to models exhibiting seasonal cointegration, see Engle and Yoo (1991) and Hylleberg *et al.* (1993). In the context of I(2) systems this approach has been considered by, *inter alia*, Engle and Yoo (1991) and Haldrup and Salmon (1998).

11. Final comments

In this paper I have provided a survey of recent developments in the econometric analysis of time series models involving I(2) series. The review has deliberately been selective, but I have tried to address the topics I believe are potentially useful for practitioners. Especially with respect to multivariate analysis there exist other contributions to this literature, for instance Gregoir and Laroque (1993, 1994) have derived a rather comprehensive and self-contained procedure for models with polynomial cointegration which includes all of the elements: representation, estimation and hypothesis testing. In relation to the multivariate analysis I decided to focus especially on the Johansen procedure since this has proven to be the most commonly used technique in empirical applications.

It is important to realize the limitations of the I(2) analysis since in general the I(2) property is found to describe only a limited number of time series like e.g. nominal time series and stock variables. However, as I have demonstrated there are in fact many economic theories and models indicating that relations may exist between I(2) and I(1) variables. When I(2) series are potentially present it is important to consider what to do next since inappropriate treatment of the I(2) components may invalidate the I(1) analysis. Sometimes it may be useful to transform the time series *a priori* such that I(2)-ness is excluded, for instance by defining economic models in real rather than in nominal terms or by including the differenced I(2) variables in the analysis. When such transformations are not obvious or it is desirable to test the restrictions on the data, the I(2) analysis becomes especially important.

Acknowledgements

This review paper was written while the author was visiting the European University Institute in Florence in the spring 1997. I would like to thank the Department of Economics for its hospitality during my stay. A longer and more detailed version of the paper can be obtained from the author upon request. The comments and suggestions of three referees and the editor are acknowledged. I also appreciate several stimulating discussions and comments on I(2) issues with Peter Boswijk, Clive Granger, H.C. Kongsted, Søren Johansen, Katarina Juselius, Paolo Paruolo, Anders Rahbek, and Andreu Sansó i Roselló. Some of the data and computer programs used in the applications were kindly made available to me by Tom Engsted, Katarina Juselius, Tae-Hwy Lee, and Byungchul Yu.

Notes

1. At this stage we assume (for simplicity) that each component of x_t is I(d). Later we will permit x_t to have components of different orders of integration and with d refering to the components of maximal integration order.
2. Note that since we have a mixture of I(1) and I(2) variables cointegrating the cointegration possibility (3) actually goes beyond the original definition of cointegration given in Engle and Granger (1987). When case (3) occurs I will just refer to x_{1t}, x_{2t} as being I(2) cointegrated and hence indicating that the maximial order of integration of the relevant variables is I(2).
3. In Engsted and Haldrup (1997) we assume y_t^* is determined from a vector of forcing I(1) and I(2) variables.
4. For instance Engsted (1993) and Engsted and Haldrup (1997) show how Cagan's model and the LQAC model can be formally tested by extending the method initially suggested by Campbell and Shiller (1987) for present value relations.
5. In a recent paper Engsted and Johansen (1997) have extended Granger and Lee's notion of multicointegration to general VAR models and formalized the link existing between I(2)- and multicointegrated systems. See also Engsted *et al.* (1997).
6. Despite the equivalence, I will continue in the following to discriminate between I(2) (and polynomial) cointegration and multicointegration since the latter concept fundamentally is a property which occurs amongst I(1) variables with an obvious economic interpretation. The fact that the system can be formulated as an I(2) system is a different technical issue.
7. It is rather easy to see why the Dickey-Fuller distribution of the t-ratio applies when $|\alpha_2|<1$, because when x_t is I(1) the regression (19) can be equivalently written in terms of Δx_t regressed on x_{t-1} and lags of Δx_t, that is, the usual augmented Dickey-Fuller regression.
8. In Boswijk *et al.* (1997) a similar procedure is used in testing for multiple unit roots in periodic models.
9. Actually Dickey and Pantula's procedure is more general than outlined here as they consider d to be larger than 2. For practical purposes $d \leqslant 2$ so their analysis simplifies considerably in the current presentation.
10. Note, however, that any unit root test for a single unit root can be applied sequentially in this procedure.
11. In the augmentation of the tests lags of the second differenced variables were included to remove autocorrelation. Some of the series seemed to be weakly heteroscedastic but this is not seriously invalidating the tests.
    The Dickey-Pantula test and the Hasza-Fuller test can be easily calculated from standard econometrics software packages. A GAUSS procedure to calculate the Sen-Dickey symmetric F test can be obtained from the author upon request.
12. Shin and Kim (1997) also consider using in place of $\hat{\varepsilon}_t$ the series $\Delta^2 y_t = \varepsilon_t$ which they argue provide improved size of their semiparametric test.
13. GAUSS routines to calculate the semi-parametric tests can be obtained from the author upon request.
14. It is notationally convenient to focus just on I(1) variables x_{1t} and I(2) variables x_{2t}. However, all the subsequent results are not qualitatively affected by assuming that part of x_{1t} could in fact be Δx_{2t}.
15. The multivariate version of this regression equation, i.e. when y_t is a vector, has been intensively studied by Park and Phillips (1989) for the case where $u_t \sim$ I(0).
16. For technical reasons R is assumed to be such that no cross-restrictions are imposed on coefficients corresponding to regressors of different orders of integration.
17. The asymptotic properties of the residual based 'cointegration' augmented Dickey-Fuller test and the Phillips Z-test have been analyzed extensively by Engle and Yoo (1987) and Phillips and Ouliaris (1990).

18. Note that from a cointegration point of view, one of the I(1) regressors y_t or x_{1t} may be excluded from the regression since these series are themselves cointegrated.
19. From an economic perspective Δp_t is perhaps the most reasonable variable to consider since Δp_t is just inflation which may act as the opportunity costs of holding money.
20. Sometimes it may be of interest to consider non-linear least squares estimation of cointegrated models. One such example is the LQAC model with driving I(2) variables, see section 3.1 and in particular Eq. (7). Engsted and Haldrup (1997) discuss different issues concerning the estimation and testing of this particular model.
21. We need to emphasize once more that the analysis relies on the assumption that it is known that only one cointegration relation exists amongst the variables.
22. Some special cases where mirror image distributions of the regressors are obtained can be found in Haldrup (1994b).
23. In Haldrup (1994b) I describe another situation where normality applies asymptotically. That is, when the single series are dominated by deterministic trends and there is full I(0) cointegration and the trends are cotrending. By 'cotrending' of the deterministic components I mean that when weighted by the cointegration vector, some or all of the higher order trends will vanish. In this case, given that the regression model does not include the higher trends, asymptotic Gaussian distributions result. This generalizes a similar result by West (1988) for the I(1) model.
24. A GAUSS procedure to conduct the Choi *et al.* (1997) CCR procedure for I(2) variables is available from the author upon request.
25. If comparisons with the Gaussian VAR model is wanted it may be useful to assume that u_t is i.i.d. $N(0, \Omega)$ as in Boswijk (1997).
26. The specification (58) allows variables to be integrated of different orders. Generally, x_t is said to be $I(d)$, if d is the smallest positive integer for which $\Delta^d x_t$ is a stationary process and $\Delta^{d-1} x_t$ is a nonstationary process.
27. Observe that if some variables in x_t are I(0) these will be elements of $\beta' x_t$, i.e. cointegration vectors of the form $(0, \ldots, 1, \ldots 0)$ can lie in the space spanned by the columns of β.
28. A further condition for the system to be I(2), but not higher order integrated, is that $\Theta = (\Gamma\bar{\beta}\bar{\alpha}'\Gamma + I - \sum_{i=1}^{k-2} \Psi_i)$ is a full rank matrix. This can be seen immediately from the definition of C_2 below.
29. In the stochastic trends representation we have excluded nuisance parameters which follow from the presence of the initial conditions, see Johansen (1995b) for details.
30. Paruolo (1996) discusses the model under the maintained assumption that $\mu_2 = 0$ so no quadratic trends occur in the model. Within this set-up linear trends will only arise in the I(1) and I(2) directions.
31. A detailed discussion of the reduced rank regression technique is beyond the scope of the present survey. The reader is assumed to be familiar with this tool from the I(1) analysis. Since the notation is rather involved for the I(2) model I prefer to describe non-technically this part of the analysis.
32. That is, $\Delta^2 x_t$ and x_{t-1} are regressed on $\Delta x_{t-1}, \Delta^2 x_{t-j}$, (and maybe a constant) for $j = 1, \ldots, k-2$, and regression residuals are used in the subsequent reduced rank regression analysis.
33. The variables $\hat{\alpha}'_{r\perp}\Delta^2 x_t$ and $\hat{\beta}'_{r\perp}\Delta x_{t-1}$ are corrected for the influence of $\hat{\beta}'_r\Delta x_{t-1}$ and lagged second differences of the variables. In fact, the basic regression model can be written as (ignoring '$\hat{}$' and subscript 'r') $\alpha'_{\perp}\Delta^2 x_t = -\alpha'_{\perp}\Gamma\bar{\beta}(\beta'\Delta x_{t-1}) - \xi\eta'(\beta'_{\perp}\Delta x_{t-1}) + \alpha_{\perp}\Theta z_t + \alpha'_{\perp}\varepsilon_t$ where $z_t = (\Delta^2 x'_{t-1}, \ldots, \Delta^2 x'_{t-k+2})$. This shows that the regression explicitly contains the parameters ξ and η.
34. Note that although the above procedure is referred to as a two-step procedure, the integration indices are in fact determined jointly.
35. Remember, by first testing r using the statistic Q_r and then proceeding to fitting s by the statistic $Q_{r,s}$ gives rise to an incorrect size in the first step of the procedure given that I(2) trends are present.

36. When trends and integration indeces are determined jointly the sequence of testing still follows the hierarchical ordering shown in table 9. However, now there exist submodels of the hypotheses given in table 9, corresponding to the restrictions made on the deterministic components. For instance the most restricted model has $\mu_1 = \mu_2 = 0$. Under this restriction, if all hypotheses H_{ij} are rejected by using the usual sequence of testing the hypotheses one proceeds to the model with $\mu_2 = 0$. This model is naturally less restricted. Under this maintained model the same sequence of tests is used for the new model. The first model which cannot reject the hypothesis for given restrictions of the deterministic components determines the integration indeces.
37. All calculations concerning the I(2) VAR analysis has been based on the I(2) platform of the CATS in RATS programme. The programme is written by Clara M. Jørgensen and can be downloaded from http://www.estima.com/procs/i2index.htm.
38. Generally one should be rather careful about using the various asymptotic critical values when the sample size is small. In finite samples there may happen to be serious discrepancies from the limiting distributions.
39. Note that, in fact, the presence of more than a single cointegration relation invalidates the single equation analysis previously conducted.
40. Similar results apply to models with deterministics components, see e.g. Paruolo (1996,1997) and Rahbek *et al.* (1998). Note that in certain directions (orthogonal to (β, β_1)) the rate of normalization in (86) is going to be T^2 by the presence of I(2) components, but this does not change the basic result that the scaled estimators will follow a mixed Gaussian distribution.
41. Note, however, that this facility is not yet available in the CATS in RATS I(2) procedure.
42. Remember that once β and η are estimated the identification of β_1 follows from the relationship $\beta_1 = \overline{\beta}_{\perp}\eta$. Similarly, we have $\beta_2 = \beta_{\perp}\eta_{\perp}$. Note also that when β_c is identified by $\beta_c = \beta(c'\beta)^{-1}$ also α can be identified as $\alpha_c = \alpha\beta' c$ since $\alpha_c\beta_c' = \alpha\beta$.

References

Andrews, D. W. K. (1991) Heteroskedasticity and Autocorrelation Consistent Covariance Matrix Estimation. *Econometrica* 59, 817–858.

Billingsley, P. (1968) *Convergence of probability measures*. New York: Wiley.

Banerjee, A., L. Cockerell, and B. Russell (1998) An I(2) analysis of inflation and the markup. Working paper, University of Oxford.

Boswijk, H. P. (1997) Mixed normality and ancillarity in I(2) systems. Conditionally accepted for *Econometric Theory*.

Boswijk, H. P., P. H. Franses, and N. Haldrup (1997) Multiple unit roots in periodic autoregression. *Journal of Econometrics*, 80, 167–193.

Cagan, P. (1956) The monetary dynamics of hyperinflation. In Milton Friedman (ed.), *Studies in the quantity theory of money*. 25–120. The University of Chicago Press.

Campbell, J. Y. (1987) Does saving anticipate declining labour income? An alternative test of the permanent income hypothesis. *Econometrica*, 55, 1249–1273.

Campbell, J. Y., and R. J. Shiller (1987) Cointegration and tests of present value models. *Journal of Political Economy*, 95, 1052–1088.

Casella, A. (1989) Testing for rational bubbles with exogenous or endogenous fundamentals. The German hyperinflation once more. *Journal of Monetary Economics*, 24, 109–122.

Chang, Y. (1997) Vector autoregressions with unknown mixtures of I(0), I(1), and I(2) components. Working paper, Dept. of Economics, Rice University.

Chang, Y. and P. C. B. Phillips (1995) Time series regression with mixtures of integrated processes. *Econometric Theory*, 11, 1033–1094.

Choi, I. J. Y. Park, and B. Yu (1997) Canonical cointegration regression and testing for cointegration in the presence of I(1) and I(2) variables. *Econometric Theory*, forthcoming.

Dickey, D. A., and W. A. Fuller (1979) Distribution of the estimators for autoregressive time series with a unit root. *Journal of American Statistical Association*, 74, 427–431.

Dickey, D. A. and S. G. Pantula (1987) Determining the order of differencing in autoregressive processes. *Journal of Business and Economic Statistics*, 5, 455–461.

Diebold, F. X., and M. Nerlove (1990) Unit roots in economic time series: A selective survey. *Advances in Econometrics*, 8, 3–69.

Dolado, J. J., T. Jenkinson (1990) Cointegration and unit roots. *Journal of Economic Surveys*, 4, 249–273.

Dolado, J. J., J. W. Galbraith, and A. Banerjee (1991) Estimating intertemporal quadratic adjustment cost models with integrated series. *International Economic Review*, 32, 919–36.

Engle, R. F., and C. W. J. Granger (1987) Co-integration and error correction: Representation, estimation and testing. *Econometrica*, 55, 2, 251–276.

Engle, R. F., and S. Yoo (1987) Forecasting and testing in cointegrated systems. *Journal of Econometrics*, 35, 143–159.

Engle, R. F. and B. S. Yoo (1991) Cointegrated economic time series: A survey with new results. In C. W. J. Granger, and R. F. Engle (eds.). *Long-run economic relations. Readings in cointegration.* Oxford: Oxford University Press.

Engle, R. F., C. W. J. Granger, S. Hylleberg, and H. S. Lee (1993) Seasonal cointegration: The Japanese consumption function. *Journal of Econometrics*, 55, 275–298.

Engsted, T. (1993) Cointegration and Cagan's model of hyperinflation under rational expectations. *Journal of Money, Credit, and Banking*, 25, 350–360.

Engsted, T. (1994) The classic European hyperinflations revisited: Testing the Cagan model using a cointegrated VAR approach. *Economica*, 61, 331–343.

Engsted, T., and N. Haldrup (1994) The linear quadratic adjustment cost model and the demand for labour. *Journal of Applied Econometrics*, 9, (supplement), S145–S159.

Engsted, T. and N. Haldrup (1997) Estimating the LQAC Model with I(2) Variables. Forthcoming in *Journal of Applied Econometrics*.

Engsted, T. and N. Haldrup (1998) Multicointegration in stock-flows models. Forthcoming in *Oxford Bulletin of Economics and Statistics*.

Engsted, T., J. Gonzalo, and N. Haldrup (1997) Testing for multicointegration. *Economics Letters*, 56, 259–266.

Engsted, T., and S. Johansen (1997) Granger's representation theorem and multicointegration. EUI Working papers, ECO No. 97/15, European University Institute, Florence.

Fuller, W. A. (1976) Introduction to statistical time series, New York, John Wiley & Sons.

Goodfriend, M. S. (1982) An alternative method of estimating the Cagan money demand function in hyperinflation under rational expectations. *Journal of Monetary Economics*, 9, 43–57.

Granger, C. W. J. (1997) On modelling the long run in applied economics. *Economic Journal*, 107, 169–177.

Granger, C. W. J., and T. Lee (1989) Investigation of production, sales and inventory relations using multicointegration and non-symmetric error correction models. *Journal of Applied Econometrics*, 4 (supplement), S145–S159.

Granger, C. W. J., and T. Lee (1990) Multicointegration. In *Advances in Econometrics.*, Vol. 8, ed. by G. F. Rhodes and T. B. Fomby, Greenwich, CT: JAI Press, 71–84.

Granger, C. W. J., and P. Newbold (1974) Spurious regressions in econometrics. *Journal of Econometrics*, 26, 1045–1066.

Gregoir, S. and G. Laroque (1993) Multivariate time series: a polynomial error correction theory. *Econometric Theory*, 9, 329–342.

Gregoir, S. and G. Laroque (1994) Polynomial cointegration: Estimation and tests. *Journal of Econometrics*, 63, 183–214.

Gregory, A. W., A. R. Pagan, and G. W. Smith (1993) Estimating linear quadratic models with integrated processes. In P. C. B. Phillips (ed.), *Models, Methods, and Applications in Econometrics*. Oxford: Basil Blackwell. 220–39.

Haldrup, N. (1994a) Semi-parametric tests for double unit roots. *Journal of Business and Economic Statistics*, 12, 109–122.

Haldrup, N. (1994b) The asymptotics of single-equation cointegration regressions with I(1) and I(2) variables. *Journal of Econometrics*, 63, 153–81.

Haldrup, N. and M. Salmon (1998) Representations of I(2) Cointegrated Systems using the Smith-McMillan Form. *Journal of Econometrics*, 84, 303–325.

Hallman, J. J., R. D. Porter, and D. H. Small (1991) Is the price level tied to the M2 monetary aggregate in the long run?, *American Economic Review*, 81, 841–858.

Hamilton, J. (1994) *Time Series Analysis*. Princeton University Press: Princeton, NJ.

Harvey, A. C. (1981) *Time Series Models*. London: Philip Allen.

Hasza, D. P. (1977) Estimation in nonstationary time series. Unpublished Ph.D. thesis. Iowa state University, Dept. of Statistics.

Hasza, D. P. and W. A. Fuller (1979) Estimation of autoregressive processes with unit roots. *The Annals of Statistics*, 7, 1106–1120.

Hendry, D. F. and T. von-Ungern Sternberg (1981) Liquidity and inflation effects of consumer expenditure. In A. S. Deaton (ed.), *Essays in the theory and measurement of consumers' behaviour*. Cambridge University Press.

Holt, C. C., F. Modigliani, J. F. Muth, and H. Simon (1960) *Planning production inventories, and work force*. Prentice Hall, Englewood Cliffs.

Hylleberg, S., and G. E. Mizon (1989) Cointegration and error correction mechanisms. *Economic Journal*, 99, 113–125.

Hylleberg, S., R. F. Engle, C. W. J. Granger, and B. S. Yoo (1990) Seasonal integration and cointegration. *Journal of Econometrics*, 44, 215–238.

Johansen, S. (1988) Statistical analysis of cointegration vectors. *Journal of Economic Dynamics and Control*, 8, 231–254.

Johansen, S. (1991) Estimation and hypothesis testing of cointegration vectors in Gaussian vector autoregressive models. *Econometrica*, 59, 1551–1580.

Johansen, S. (1992a) Testing weak exogeneity and the order of cointegration in UK money demand data. *Journal of Policy Modeling*, 14, 313–334.

Johansen, S. (1992b) A representation of vector autoregressive processes integrated of order 2. *Econometric Theory*, 8, 188–202.

Johansen, S. (1995a) A statistical analysis of cointegration for I(2) variables. Econometric Theory, 11, 25–59.

Johansen, S. (1995b) *Likelihood-based inference in Cointegrated Vector Autoregressive Models*. Oxford: Oxford University Press.

Johansen, S. (1997) A likelihood analysis of the I(2) model. *Scandinavian Journal of Statistics*, forthcoming.

Johansen, S., and K. Juselius (1990) Maximum likelihood estimation and inference on cointegration with applications to money demand. *Oxford Bulletin of Economics and Statistics*, 52, 169–210.

Johansen, S., and K. Juselius (1992) Testing structural hypotheses in a multivariate cointegration analysis of the PPP and the UIP for UK. *Journal of Econometrics*, 53, 211–244.

Juselius, K. (1992) Domestic and foreign effects on prices in an open economy: The case of Denmark. *Journal of Policy Modeling*, 14, 401–428.

Juselius, K. (1994) On the duality between long-run relations and common trends in the I(1) versus I(2) model. An application to aggregate money holdings. *Econometric Reviews*, 13, 151–178.

Juselius, K. (1995a) Do purchasing power parity and uncovered interest rate parity hold in the long run? An example of likelihood inference in a multivariate time-series model. *Journal of Econometrics*, 69, 211–240.

Juselius, K. (1995b) Predictable and unpredictable components of the longrun growth in nominal prices. *Mathematics and Computers in Simulation*, 39, 257–263.

Juselius, K. (1996) An empirical analysis of the changing role of the German Bundesbank after 1983. *Oxford Bulletin of Economics and Statistics*, 58, 791–819.

Juselius, K. (1998) A structured VAR in Denmark under changing monetary regimes. *Journal of Business and Economic Statistics*, 16(4), 400–411.

Juselius, K., and C. Hargreaves (1992) Long-run relations in Australian monetary data. In: C. Hargreaves (ed.), *Macroeconomic modelling of the long run*. Vermont: Edward Elgar.

Kailath, T. (1980) *Linear Systems*. Prentice-Hall, Englewood Cliffs, NJ.

Kennan, J. (1979) The estimation of partial adjustment models with rational expectations. *Econometrica*, 47, 1441–1455.

King, R. G., C. I. Plosser, J. H. Stock, and M. W. Watson (1991) Stochastic trends and economic fluctuations. *American Economic Review*, 81, 819–840.

Kitamura, Y. (1995) Estimation of cointegrated systems with I(2) processes. *Econometric Theory*, 11, 1–24.

Lee, T.-H. (1992) Stock-flow relationships in housing construction. *Oxford Bulletin of Economics and Statistics*, 54, 419–430.

Lee, T.-H. (1996) Stock adjustment for multicointegrated series. *Empirical Economics*, 21, 633–639.

McKinnon, J. G. (1991) Critical values for cointegration tests. In R. F. Engle, and C. W. J. Granger (eds), *Long run Economic Relationships*. Oxford: Oxford University Press, 267–276.

Muscatelli, V. A., and S. Hurn (1992) Cointegration and dynamic time series models. *Journal of Economic Surveys*, 6, 1–43.

Newey, W. and K. D. West (1987) A simple positive semi-definite heteroscedasticity and autocorrelation consistent covariance matrix. *Econometrica* 55, 703–708.

Pantula, S. G. (1989) Testing for unit roots in time series data. *Econometric Theory*, 5, 256–271.

Park, J. Y. (1992) Canonical cointegration regression. *Econometrica*, 60, 119–143.

Park, J. Y., and P. C. B. Phillips (1988) Statistical inference in regressions with integrated processes: Part 1. *Econometric Theory*, 4, 468–498.

Park, J. Y. and P. C. B. Phillips (1989) Statistical inference in regressions with integrated processes: Part 2. *Econometric Theory*, 5, 95–131.

Paruolo, P. (1994) The role of the drift in I(2) systems. *Journal of the Italian Statistical Society*, 3, 65–96.

Paruolo, P. (1996) On the determination of integration indices in I(2) systems. *Journal of Econometrics*, 72, 313–356.

Paruolo, P. (1997) Asymptotic efficiency of the two stage estimator in I(2) systems. *Econometric Theory*, forthcoming.

Paruolo, P., and A. Rahbek (1996) Weak exogeneity in I(2) systems. Working paper.

Peseran, M. H. (1991) Costly adjustment under rational expectations: A generalization. *Review of Economics and Statistics*, 73, 353–358.

Phillips, A. W. (1954) Stabilization policy in the closed economy. *Economic Journal*, 64, 290–323.

Phillips, P. C. B. (1986) Understanding spurious regressions in econometrics. *Journal of Econometrics*, 33, 311–340.

Phillips, P. C. B. (1991) Optimal inference in cointegrated systems. *Econometrica*, 59, 283–306.

Phillips, P. C. B. (1987) Time series regression with unit root. *Econometrica*, 55, 277–302.

Phillips, P. C. B., and S. Ouliaris (1990) Asymptotic properties of residual based tests for cointegration. *Econometrica*, 58, 165–193.

Phillips, P. C. B. and P. Perron (1988) Testing for a unit root in time series regression. *Biometrika*, 75, 335–346.

Price, S. (1992) Forward looking price setting in UK manufacturing. *Economic Journal*, 102, 497–505.

Rahbek, A., C. Jørgensen, and H. C. Kongsted (1998) Trend-stationarity in the I(2) cointegration model. Forthcoming in *Journal of Econometrics*.

Salmon, M. (1988) Error correction models, cointegration and the internal model principle. *Journal of Economic Dynamics and Control*, 12, 523–549.

Sargent, T. J. (1977) The demand for money during hyperinflation under rational expectations I. *International Economic Review*, 14, 59–82.

Sargent, T. J. (1978) Estimation of dynamic labor demand schedules under rational expectations. *Journal of Political Economy*, 86, 1009–1044.

Schwert, G. W. (1989) Tests for unit roots: A Monte Carlo investigation. *Journal of Business and Economic Statistics*, 7, 147–159.

Sen, D. L. (1986) Robustness of single unit root test statistics in the presence of multiple unit roots. Unpublished Ph.D. thesis, North Carolina state University, Dept. of statistics.

Sen, D. L. and D. A. Dickey (1987) Symmetric test for second differencing in univariate time series. *Journal of Business and Economic Statistics*, 5, 463–473.

Shin, Y. (1994) A residual based test of the null of cointegration against the alternative of no cointegration. *Econometric Theory*, 10, 91–115.

Shin, D. W., and H. J. Kim (1997) Semiparametric tests for double unit roots based on symmetric estimators. *Journal of Business and Economic Statistics*, forthcoming.

Stock, J. H. (1994) Unit Roots, Structural Breaks and Trends. In Engle, R. F., and D. L. McFadden (eds.), *Handbook of Econometrics*, 4, ch. 46, 2739–2841.

Stock, J. H. and M. W. Watson (1988) Testing for common trends. *Journal of the American Statistical Association*, 83, 1097–1107.

Stock, J. H. and M. W. Watson (1993) A simple estimator of cointegrating vectors in higher order integrated systems. *Econometrica*, 61, 783–820.

Taylor, M. P. (1991) The hyperinflation model of money demand revisited. *Journal of Money, Credit, and Banking*, 23, 327–56.

Watson, M. W. (1994) Vector Autoregressions and Cointegration. In Engle, R. F., and D. L. McFadden (eds.), *Handbook of Econometrics*, 4, ch. 47, 2843–2915.

West, K. (1988) Asymptotic normality when regressors have a unit root. *Econometrica*, 56, 1397–1417.

White, H. (1984) *Asymptotic Theory for Econometricians*. Orlando: Academic Press.

White, J. S. (1958) The limiting distribution of the serial correlation coefficient in the explosive case. *Annals of Mathematical Statistics*, 29, 1188–1197.

Yoo, S. (1986) Multi-cointegrated time series and a generalized error correction model. UCSD Discussion paper.

COINTEGRATION ANALYSIS OF SEASONAL TIME SERIES

Philip Hans Franses

Erasmus University, Rotterdam

Michael McAleer

University of Western Australia and Osaka University

Abstract. This paper reviews various recent approaches to cointegration analysis of seasonal time series. In addition to the usual decisions concerning data transformations and univariate time series properties, it is necessary to decide how seasonal variation is included in the multivariate model and how standard cointegration methods should accordingly be modified. Seasonal cointegration and periodic cointegration methods are discussed, as are some of their recent refinements. An overview of further research topics is also provided.

Keywords. Seasonal time series; Cointegration; Periodic models; Unit roots.

1. Introduction

Since the beginning of the 1990's, there has been a renewed interest in modelling seasonal time series, where the observations have not been seasonally adjusted. Several statistical agencies produce and distribute both adjusted and unadjusted data, which enables researchers to analyze the raw unadjusted data. It is generally felt that seasonal patterns in economic time series are not only caused by calendar time or the climate, but also that the behaviour of economic agents is somehow reflected through seasonal variation. The collection of papers in Hylleberg (1992) indicates the relevance of modelling seasonality, see also Ghysels (1994). Studies that explicitly advocate the use of unadjusted data are Miron (1996) and Franses (1996a), among others. Miron (1996), for example, had argued that there are economic reasons why seasonal and business cycle variations in macroeconomic variables are linked.

Many macroeconomic time series are trended, and there seems to exist a consensus that these trends can best be described by econometric time series models with stochastic trends (or unit roots). An examination of the graphs of key economic variables indicates that several economic variables tend to move together, that is, they seem to have one or more common trends. The analysis of common trends is called cointegration analysis. In this paper we focus on common trends when the variables are seasonally observed but are not seasonally adjusted. Without loss of generality, the analysis is confined to quarterly data, although we will pay some attention to other frequencies toward the end of this paper. The effects of seasonally adjusting the data prior to cointegration analysis will be discussed in the relevant sections.

This review highlights the main distinguishing properties of various methods of estimation and testing, without elaborating on the technical details. Some of the empirical applications in the available literature are also reviewed. Most methods are developed and applied in the literature, and we refer to the relevant studies, where appropriate. The survey is directed toward practitioners who, when faced with a set of quarterly observed economic time series variables, aim to construct a cointegration model which can be used for tackling important economic questions. It is not our intention to provide a hierarchy of models based on some designated quality measures, especially as we believe that several models can be useful for the same problem. Instead, we review a large number of decisions with which a practitioner is faced, and show how alternative decisions can lead to alternative empirical models.

The focus will primarily be on the VAR model, since this appears to be the most useful for cointegration analysis. Valuable surveys are given in Johansen (1995) and Banerjee *et al.* (1993). Before turning to multivariate analysis in Section 3, we first consider some of the prior decisions that have to be made for univariate time series in Section 2. These decisions concern the choice of appropriate data transformation and the presence of unit roots in univariate series. This last issue is important as the outcome of univariate analysis determines the next step in the analysis of cointegration among a set of time series. In Section 3 we review cointegration when seasonality can be captured mainly by constant seasonal dummy variables, or by seasonal or periodic cointegration. It is assumed here that any seasonal variation can thus be captured by adding or modifying regressors in the conditional mean component of the time series. Hence, we do not explicitly discuss seasonality in the variance, although the methods presented below can be modified in a straightforward manner if required. In Section 4, we provide a survey of further research topics. Finally, in Section 5, we provide some concluding remarks.

It is assumed that the reader has a working knowledge of the basic concepts of time series modelling. These concepts include autoregressive [AR], moving average [MA], and ARMA models, autocorrelation functions, identification, diagnostic measures for residual autocorrelation, testing for unit roots in AR models, and forecasting from ARMA models. Introductory texts on time series analysis are Hamilton (1994), Franses (1998a), and Mills (1990), among others. For multivariate time series analysis, the reader is assumed to be familiar with concepts such as vector autoregression [VAR], unit roots in VARs, and testing for cointegration. The introductory texts above contain material on VARs, but a more comprehensive treatment is given in Lütkepohl (1991).

2. Decisions for univariate time series

In the section we pay particular attention to two important decisions a practitioner needs to make prior to analysing cointegration in a VAR model: (*i*) the transformation of the data; and (*ii*) the unit root properties of all the univariate time series to be considered.

The economically relevant questions for which cointegration analysis can prove most useful typically concern macroeconomic models of money demand, consumption, and unemployment. Standard money demand equations include variables such as M1 or M2, prices, interest rates and income. In this context, attention focuses on log M1 (where log denotes natural logarithms), inflation, which is the growth rate (or log difference) of prices, and GDP as a measure of income. Models of consumption typically include income, prices, and a measure of wealth, while models for unemployment tend to include income, wages and interest rates. Although far from exhaustive, this brief summary indicates that practitioners in macroeconomics typically face an analysis of four to six quarterly observed variables. Given the increased reliability of the data delivered by statistical agencies since the 1960's, it is often seen that empirical studies use approximately three to four decades of quarterly data. This amounts to 120 to 160 observations for each time series.

Cointegration analysis is most reliable in cases where there are not too many variables (see for example Gonzalo and Pitarakis (1994)). As modelling seasonality comes at the substantial cost of increasing the number of parameters, we recommend applying the cointegration methods below to a limited set of variables. Notice that the increase in the number of parameters may be viewed as one drawback in analyzing seasonally unadjusted data, in contrast to using seasonally adjusted data. However, adjusted data have their own shortcomings, for example, different persistence properties (see Jaeger and Kunst (1990)), and spurious nonlinear features (see Ghysels *et al.* (1996)).

2.1. *Data transformations*

Many macroeconomic variables are now collected on a monthly or quarterly basis. Some variables can readily be observed (for example, interest rates), but observations on other variables have to be estimated on the basis of surveys (for example, GDP). Although many financial time series can be obtained at frequencies higher than the monthly frequency, most macroeconomic variables are observable monthly. When such monthly data (or sometimes even quarterly data) were not available for periods in the 1960's or 1970's, the relevant data were constructed using backward extrapolation and interpolation. What this means is that the officially-published quarterly unadjusted figures for macroeconomic variables have proceeded through a process of estimation, averaging, aggregation, correction and, also, new definition. It is difficult to obtain precise insights as to how the data were generated, so it is assumed in this paper that the practitioner uses the data in the format in which they are published in official statistical publications. In what follows, the focus is on officially published, quarterly observed, seasonally unadjusted data, and these are denoted as x_t, $t = 1, 2, \ldots, n$.

The next difficult question that often needs to be answered in practice concerns the transformation of x_t, prior to further analysis. There seems to be a consensus in applied macroeconomics (but not necessarily, for example, in applied marketing research) to use the natural logarithmic (or log) transformation for all time series, except those which are measured as rates (for example, the inflation rate and unemployment rate). Important reasons for the use of the log transformation are that exponential growth in levels becomes linear growth in the transformed series, the variance can be stabilized, aberrant observations can become less influential, and the parameters in linear models for log transformed time series can be interpreted straightforwardly as constant elasticities. Notice that the log transformation is applied primarily for convenience, as one rarely tests for exponential growth (against, for example, quadratic growth, which would require the transformation $x_t^{1/2}$), or for unstable variance. Moreover, it is questionable if constant elasticities are reasonable to assume for a sample spanning several decades. In fact, many nonlinear models such as regime-switching models and neural network models allow for time-varying elasticities across key macroeconomic variables, and these models appear to be quite useful in some cases.

Recently, it has been questioned with more formal methods whether using the log transformation is sensible in practice. One reason for these concerns is that the stochastic trend (or unit root) properties of the data are affected by this transformation (see Granger and Hallman (1991), among others). Franses and McAleer (1998) propose a modified test for a unit root in nonseasonal time series, which allows for an investigation of the adequacy of the log transformation. Their approach can be extended to the seasonal case. An outcome of such an extension is that currently available parametric tests for unit roots in seasonal time series yield outcomes which can differ between x_t and $\log x_t$, so that the outcomes of the tests are sensitive to the transformation used. Franses and Taylor (1998) give an example of differing numbers of seasonal unit roots for log M4 and M4.

To provide intuition, consider a seasonal time series x_t with increasing seasonal variation, which means that the distance between the observations in quarter s ($s = 1, 2, 3, 4$) and in quarter q ($q = 1, 2, 3, 4$, $q \neq s$) increases over time. If this occurs with an exponential pace, one may consider the log transformation to reduce the variance and to obtain linear growth. One possible result is that the observations on $\log x_t$ in quarters s and q ($q \neq s$) are equidistant. A model which can be useful to describe such data is given in equation (1) below. It may well be, however, that the trends in the quarters are not identical, an example being industrial production in countries with severe weather conditions. In winter it may be virtually impossible to produce large quantities, but in other seasons, one may observe increasing production due to improved facilities. In this case, one has so-called diverging seasonal trends. One way of describing these is to assume so-called seasonal unit roots (see below) in models for the untransformed series x_t. An alternative is to consider seasonal deterministic trends.

In this paper we will abstain from a detailed discussion of the effects of taking logs, and focus on $y_t = \log x_t$. The main reason for this is that the available multivariate methods to be discussed below are developed for time series for which $\log x_t$, amounts to the optimal transformation. Allowing for other (or no) data transformations will change these methods substantially, and is viewed as an important separate topic for further research. In the multivariate models in Section 3, we will use the notation $y_{i,t} = \log x_{i,t}$ for $i = 1, \ldots, k$, but in the next subsection, notation is saved by using y_t.

2.2. *Univariate time series properties*

In this subsection, we review briefly the analysis of univariate time series processes, with a specific focus on seasonal variation and unit roots. More elaborate surveys on this topic appear in, for example, Franses (1996a, 1998b).

2.2.1. *Constant seasonality*

The simplest model for a quarterly log transformed time series, y_t, is given by Miron (1996), among others, as

$$\Delta_1 y_t = \delta_1 D_{1,t} + \delta_2 D_{2,t} + \delta_3 D_{3,t} + \delta_4 D_{4,t} + u_t, \tag{1}$$

where u_t is an unknown AR (or ARMA) time series, Δ_1, is the differencing operator defined by $\Delta_h y_t = (1 - L^h) y_t = y_t - y_{t-h}$, for $h = 1, 2, \ldots, L$ denotes the lag operator, and the $D_{s,t}$ are seasonal dummy variables, which take the value 1 when t corresponds with season s, and 0 otherwise, for $s = 1, 2, 3, 4$. Even though the AR model for u_t may include variables at lags 2, 4, or 8, one is tempted to interpret the contribution of the four seasonal dummies as the 'amount of seasonality'. Typically, it is found that the R^2 of the regression in (1) is as high as 0.8 or 0.9 for many macroeconomic time series variables (see Miron (1996) for further details).

It should be emphasized here that (1) can also seem to provide a useful data description in case the data can be described by the models to be given in subsections 2.2.2 and 2.2.3. Hence, the R^2 of a regression such as (1) can be spuriously high (see Franses *et al.* (1995)). Moreover, when the data are generated by $\Delta_4 y_t = \varepsilon_t$, with ε_t a standard white noise process, the δ_s parameters in (1) are not even identified. Abeysinghe (1994) shows that an improper interpretation of seasonal intercept terms may also lead to spurious multivariate relations. On the other hand, if the Δ_1 filter suffices to transform y_t to stationarity, where perhaps (1) should be modified to allow for seasonal mean shifts as in Franses and Vogelsang (1998), the R^2 for (1) can be interpreted as the amount of deterministic seasonality. If so, one tends to find that more than 50 per cent of the seasonal variation appears to be deterministic.

When a univariate time series, y_t, can be adequately described by (1), that is, the residuals from (1) are approximately white noise, it has constant seasonality. The seasonal dummy variables may not contribute at all significantly (which is, for example, the case for many interest rates), in which case the spurious inclusion of seasonal dummies will lead to a loss of efficiency. Additionally, as the y_t series need to be differenced by Δ_1, it is said to have a single zero-frequency unit root (see, for example, Hamilton (1994)). A time series variable that has these properties can be included in the cointegration analysis without further transformation, and does not need to be analysed further using univariate methods.

For many macroeconomic time series, the currently available tests do not suggest that (1) amounts to an accurate description of the data. In fact, it is usually found that the Δ_1 filter does not suffice, or that the u_t process contains highly persistent seasonal terms. Most univariate and multivariate models to be discussed below focus on this so-called stochastic seasonal variation.

2.2.2. *Seasonal unit roots and seasonal integration*

There is now substantial empirical evidence which shows that a large part of the seasonal variation is far from constant over time (see Canova and Hansen (1995) and Hylleberg (1994), among others). One way to transform a time series to accommodate this evolving seasonality is to apply the Δ_4 filter for quarterly data. If this differencing filter is required to transform y_t to yield stationarity, the series are said to be seasonally integrated. This differencing filter amounts to an assumption about the number of seasonal and nonseasonal unit roots. This can be seen by writing $\Delta_S = (1 - L^S)$ for any S (given here as 4) and solving the equation $(1 - z^S) = 0$ or $\exp(Si\phi) = 1$, for z or ϕ. Its general solution is given by $\{\cos(2\pi k/S) + i \sin(2\pi k/S)\}$ for $k = 0, 1, 2, \ldots$, thereby yielding S different solutions, all of which lie on the unit circle. The first solution, 1, is the non-seasonal unit root, and the $S - 1$ other solutions are seasonal unit roots (see Hylleberg *et al.* (1990) [hereafter HEGY]). In the case $S = 4$, Δ_4 assumes the roots 1, -1, i and $-i$.

In some cases the assumption or four unit roots may be excessive, in which case one can use the HEGY test method to examine the empirical adequacy of Δ_4. The HEGY approach is based on an expansion of the polynomial $\phi_p(L)$ of an AR(p) model for y_t, namely:

$$\phi_p(L) = -\pi_1 L\phi_1(L) + \pi_2 L\phi_2(L) + (\pi_3 L + \pi_4)L\phi_3(L) + \phi^*{}_{p-4}(L)\phi_4(L), \quad (2)$$

where the $\phi_i(L)$ polynomials ($i = 1, 2, 3, 4$) are defined by:

$$\phi_1(L) = (1 + L)(1 + L^2) = (1 + L + L^2 + L^3) \quad (3)$$

$$\phi_2(L) = (1 - L)(1 + L^2) = (1 - L + L^2 - L^3) \quad (4)$$

$$\phi_3(L) = (1 - L)(1 + L) = (1 - L^2) \quad (5)$$

$$\phi_4(L) = (1 - L)(1 + L)(1 + L^2) = (1 - L^4). \quad (6)$$

Without loss of generality, suppose that $\phi^*_{p-4}(L) = 1$. Then $\pi_1 = 0$ implies that $\phi_p(L)$ can be decomposed as $\phi_{p-1}(L)(1 - L)$, since all its components contain $(1 - L)$. If it is assumed that y_t is described by a certain AR time series process, that is $\phi_p(L)y_t = \mu_t + \varepsilon_t$, where μ_t is usually given as:

$$\mu_t = \sum_{s=1}^{4} \delta_s D_{s,t} + \beta t, \quad (7)$$

in which t is a deterministic trend variable, then the HEGY auxiliary regression to test for nonseasonal and seasonal unit roots in quarterly series is given by

$$\phi^*_{p-4}(L)z_{4,t} = \mu_t + \pi_1 z_{1,t-1} + \pi_2 z_{2,t-1} + \pi_3 z_{3,t-2} + \pi_4 z_{3,t-1} + \varepsilon_t, \tag{8}$$

where $z_{1,t} = \phi_1(L)y_t$, $z_{2,t} = -\phi_2(L)y_t$, $z_{3,t} = -\phi_3(L)y_t$ and $z_{4,t} = \phi_4(L)y_t$, with the $\phi_i(L)$ polynomials defined as above. Smith and Taylor (1998) extend (8) by allowing (7) to have seasonal trends $\beta_s t$ instead of βt.

Estimation of (8) by OLS yields estimates $\hat{\pi}_i$ $(i = 1, 2, 3, 4)$, where the order of the AR polynomial $\phi^*_{p-4}(L)$ can be determined using a variety of methods. The method that is often recommended in practice is described in Hall (1994), which is to decide on the significance of lag $p-4$, then of lag $p-3$, and so on. Sometimes this order selection issue has a nontrivial impact on the final decision as to the number of unit roots (see Taylor (1997) for an elaborate study).

Testing for the significance of the $\hat{\pi}_i$ implies testing for (seasonal) unit roots. There are no seasonal unit roots if $\hat{\pi}_2$ and $\hat{\pi}_3$ (or $\hat{\pi}_4$) differ significantly from zero. If $\pi_1 = 0$, the presence of the nonseasonal unit root 1 cannot be rejected. The corresponding t– and F-test statistics are not distributed as standard normal under the respective null hypotheses. Asymptotic theory and simulated critical values appear in HEGY and Engle *et al.* (1993). A recent comprehensive treatment is given in Smith and Taylor (1998).

Notice that the HEGY test procedure assumes the validity of an AR model for y_t. Simulation results in Ghysels *et al.* (1994) show that, when y_t is generated by the so-called airline model, that is $\Delta_1\Delta_4 y_t = (1-\theta_1 L)(1-\theta_4 L^4)\varepsilon_t$, with θ_4 taking large positive values, the HEGY tests have improper size. This is a substantial drawback of the HEGY method since the airline model is often found to yield a seemingly adequate description of seasonal data. The methods proposed in Psaradakis (1997) and Breitung and Franses (1998) aim to overcome this drawback, but simulation results in these studies show that the gain in improved size often leads to a loss of power. Of course, this is a problem for unit root testing, in general, and solutions still have to be developed.

The HEGY test has been applied in many studies to a wide variety of macroeconomic time series for many industrialized countries. There is no space to review all the empirical findings, but the main findings typically are as follows: (*i*) the double differencing filter assumed in the airline model is redundant, that is, most quarterly time series contain at most 4 unit roots (see specifically Osborn (1990)); and (*ii*) many time series have only one or two seasonal unit roots, in addition to the nonseasonal unit root. These results also imply that seasonal filters like Δ_4^2 for data in logarithms are unlikely to be useful, while they may be for time series in levels (see Franses and Taylor (1998)).

The seasonal unit root results for the individual series should be taken seriously in the next step of multivariate analysis. When two time series have specific unit roots, while a linear combination of them does not, then these series are cointegrated. Naturally, cointegration may also apply to seasonal unit roots, and the multivariate model is then referred to as the seasonal cointegration model. When two or more time series are examined, it is quite likely that the individual series are found to have differing seasonal unit root properties. To keep matters simple, the most common practical procedure in such a case is to assume that all the time series require the Δ_4 filter. After the unit root properties of the multivariate model have been fixed, one may focus again on the properties of certain individual time series.

2.2.3. *Periodic models and periodic integration*

The AR models in (1) and (8) all have time-invariant parameters. Hence, seasonal variation is absorbed by the lagged variables, and evolving seasonality appears through unit roots at the seasonal frequencies. An alternative class of models (see, for example, Franses (1996b)), which appears to be useful in practice, allows the AR parameters to vary according to the quarter. In other words, a periodic autoregression [PAR] extends the nonperiodic AR model by allowing the AR parameters to vary with the quarters (see Tiao and Grupe (1980) for an early reference). The PAR model assumes that the observations in each of the seasons can be described using a different model. A PAR of order p [PAR(p)] can be written as:

$$y_t = \mu_t + \phi_{1,s} y_{t-1} + \cdots + \phi_{p,s} y_{t-p} + \varepsilon_t, \tag{9}$$

with

$$\mu_t = \sum_{s=1}^{4} \mu_s D_{s,t} + \sum_{s=1}^{4} \tau_s D_{s,t} t. \tag{10}$$

The order p in (9) is the maximum of all p_s, where p_s denotes the order of the AR process for season s. Obviously, the number of autoregressive parameters in a PAR(p) model for a seasonal time series is 4 times greater than that in a nonperiodic AR(p) model.

The parameters in (9) can be estimated by OLS. Model selection criteria are useful to decide on the value of p, in practice. Simulations suggest that the Akaike and Schwarz criteria can be useful for this purpose, while the F-test for additional lags also provides accurate results. Even though a PAR(p) model has four times as many parameters as the AR(p) model, practical experience with PAR(p) models, however, suggests that there is a trade-off between the order p in a nonperiodic AR model and the intra-year variation that is accommodated by the PAR model. In other words, PAR(2) and PAR(3) models often fit the data well, according to diagnostics on residual autocorrelation, while AR models of order 8 to 12 seem to be required for the same time series. Although the nonperiodic AR models contain many parameters, the application of a diagnostic for periodic residual autocorrelation still has power, and often indicates the statistical adequacy of a PAR model (see Franses (1996b) for further details). In sum, this suggests two specification strategies for PAR models. The first is to estimate a PAR model where p is set at a value that is suitable for a nonperiodic AR model, and then to test for appropriate parameter restrictions (like $\phi_{i,s} = \phi_i$ for all s). The second strategy is to consider an AR model, and test for periodic variation in the residuals. If the relevant null hypothesis is rejected, one can proceed with specifying a PAR model and use the selection criteria discussed above. There is also a third possibility, which is to treat the selection between a PAR(k) model and an AR(p) model (with $k>p$) as a non-nested testing problem. Further research is needed to see whether this last approach can yield better results. Some empirical evidence in this regard is given in section 2.2.4 below.

In order to test for a single unit root, Boswijk and Franses (1996) show that it is convenient to rewrite (9) as the following nonlinear regression:

$$y_t = \sum_{s=1}^{4} \alpha_s D_{s,t} y_{t-1} + \sum_{i=1}^{p-1} \sum_{s=1}^{4} \beta_{i,s} D_{s,t} (y_{t-1} - \alpha_{s-i} y_{t-i-1}) + \sum_{s=1}^{4} \mu_s D_{s,t} + \sum_{s=1}^{4} \tau_s D_{s,t} t + \varepsilon_t. \tag{11}$$

Boswijk *et al.* (1997) propose alternative versions of (11) to test for seasonal unit roots in a periodic model. There is a single unit root if the restriction $\alpha_1\alpha_2\alpha_3\alpha_4 = 1$ cannot be rejected. Notice that the α_s parameters also appear in the periodic differencing filter on the right-hand side of (11). A test for this hypothesis can be shown to follow the Johansen distribution, depending on the inclusion of the appropriate intercepts and trends (proofs of this result are given in Boswijk and Franses (1996)). Conditional on the restriction $\alpha_1\alpha_2\alpha_3\alpha_4 = 1$, tests for the hypotheses H_0: $\alpha_s = 1$ and H_0: $\alpha_s = -1$ for $s = 1, 2, 3$, follow the standard $\chi^2(3)$ distribution. When both hypotheses are rejected, y_t is said to be periodically integrated. If $\alpha_s = 1$ is not rejected, y_t has the unit root 1; when $\alpha_s = -1$, y_t has the seasonal unit root -1.

Ghysels *et al.* (1996) develop tests for the hypothesis $\alpha_s = 1$ in (11) without imposing the restriction $\alpha_1\alpha_2\alpha_3\alpha_4 = 1$. The test follows a distribution which is a mixture of Dickey–Fuller and χ^2. Boswijk *et al.* (1997) provide a unifying framework to test for seasonal and nonseasonal unit roots in PAR models, and their tests do not require tables with new critical values. In any case, both studies are in agreement concerning the presence of seasonal unit roots. After allowing for periodicity in the AR parameters, the empirical evidence for seasonal unit roots disappears, which again indicates that one can consider either seasonal unit root models or periodic integration models.

The application of the above procedures to empirical data shows that many macroeconomic variables can be described by a periodic integration model (see Franses (1996b) and Wells (1997), among others). It is not surprising that data that can be described by (variants of) the airline model and the seasonal unit root model can also be described by a periodic integration model. To provide some intuition, consider the following PAR(1) model with a unit root:

$$y_t = \alpha_s y_{t-1} + \varepsilon_t \qquad \text{with } \alpha_1\alpha_2\alpha_3\alpha_4 = 1, \tag{12}$$

which can be written after recursive substitution as

$$y_t - y_{t-4} = \varepsilon_t + \alpha_s \varepsilon_{t-1} + \alpha_s \alpha_{s-1} \varepsilon_{t-2} + \alpha_s \alpha_{s-1} \alpha_{s-2} \varepsilon_{t-3}. \tag{13}$$

When α_s takes values close to 1, taking first differences of (13) results in:

$$\Delta_1\Delta_4 y_t \approx \varepsilon_t - \eta_s \varepsilon_{t-4}, \quad (14)$$

which, in turn, can be approximated by an airline-type model. In terms of forecasting, however, it may be better to retain the PAR model, since such a model can result in improved forecasting (Novales and Flores de Fruto (1997), among others).

2.2.4. *Non-nested models and structural breaks*

Consider the logarithms of quarterly real GNP series for Austria which has been chosen since, as will be shown below, a periodically integrated model can be fitted to this time series. Consider the quarterly real GNP series for Austria over the sample period 1964.1–1988.4 (100 observations). In figure 1 are given the quarterly y_t series, and in figure 2 are given the annual $Y_{s,T}$ series, where $Y_{s,T}$ is the observation in season s in year T, $T=1,\ldots,N$ $(N=n/4)$. It can be observed, especially from figure 2, that the seasonal fluctuations seem to change slowly over time. In fact, the observations in quarter 3 seem to shift from close to those in quarter 4 to those in quarter 2. Furthermore, the y_t series display a trending pattern.

In figures 3 and 4 are displayed similar graphs as in the previous two figures, but for the corresponding $(1-L)y_t$ time series. The annual time series in figure 4 are $Y_{s,T} - Y_{s-1,T}$ for $s=2,3,4$ (denoted as dys) and $Y_{1,T} - Y_{4,T-1}$. Figures 3 and 4

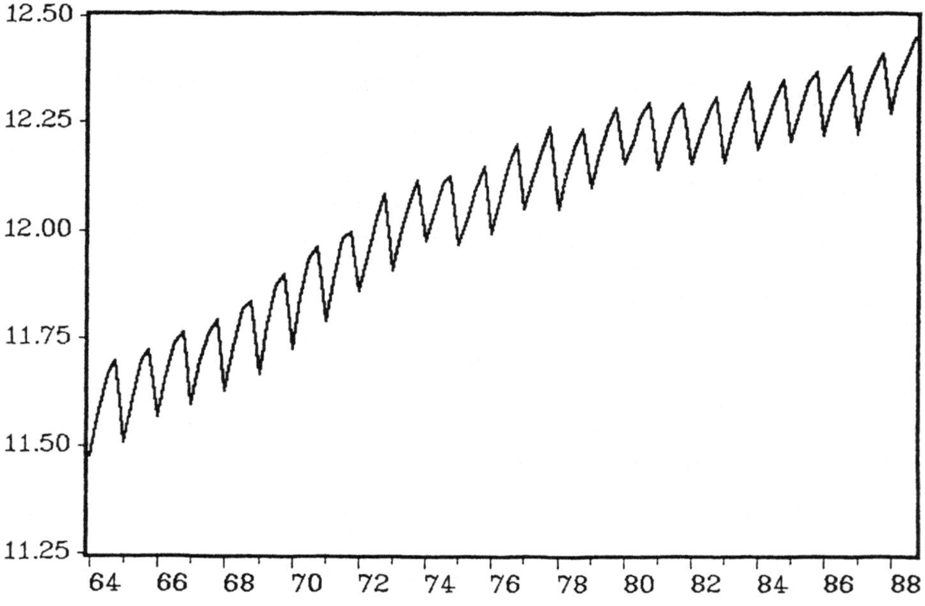

Figure 1. Real GNP in Austria, 1964.1–1988.4

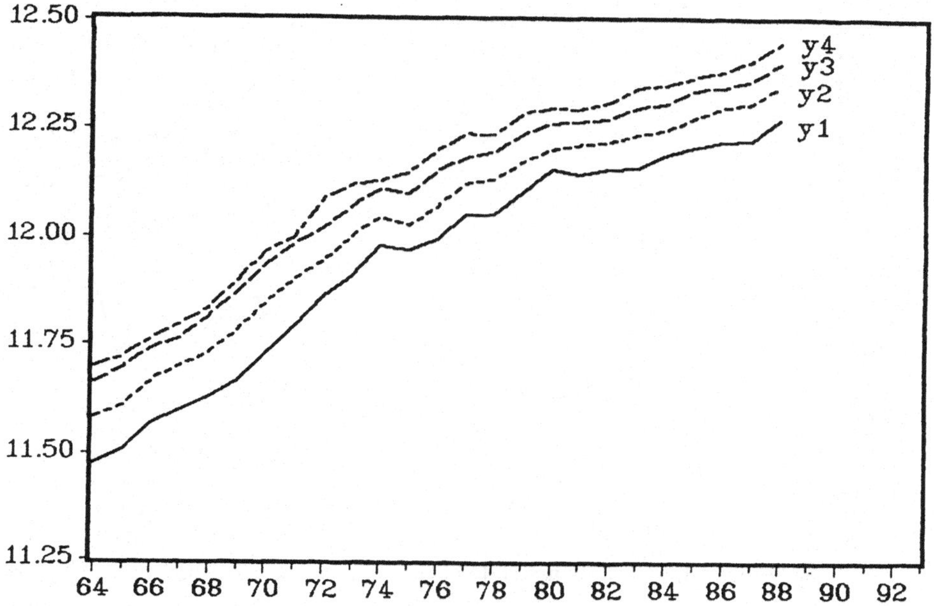

Figure 2. Quarterly real GNP in Austria, 1964–1988

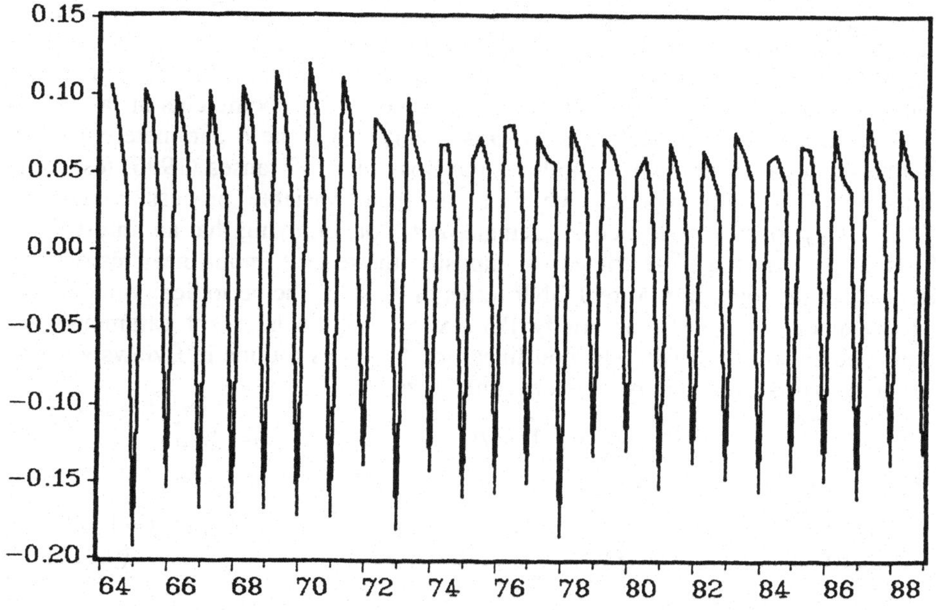

Figure 3. First differences of real GNP in Austria

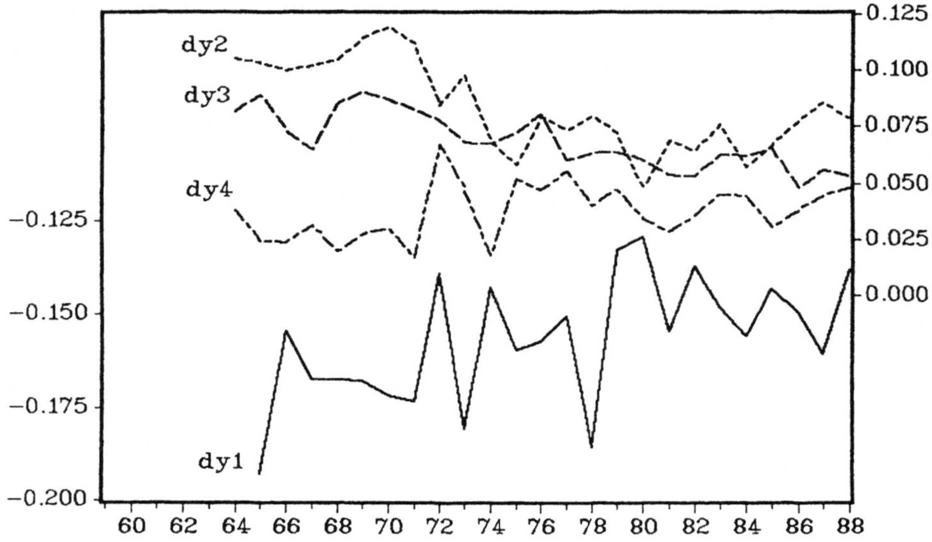

Figure 4. Quarterly first differences of real GNP in Austria

indicate that the $(1-L)y_t$ time series seem to evolve in a reasonably constant manner over time, except for a possible break; somewhere over the period 1972–1974. Note, for example, from figure 4 that the $Y_{4,T}-Y_{3,T}$ and the $Y_{2,T}-Y_{1,T}$ series approach the $Y_{3,T}-Y_{2,T}$ series in 1972, and that the relative patterns seem to be constant before and after that period.

The analysis for Austria is initiated by fitting a PAR(p) model. Model selection criteria, namely F-type tests for the significance of the coefficients at lag $p+1$, indicate that an appropriate value for p is 2, and that some β parameters in (11) can be set equal to zero. Upon applying the Boswijk and Franses (1996) test for a unit root in the Y_T process, which is the four variable process containing $Y_{1,T},\dots,Y_{4,T}$, there is evidence of a single unit root, implying that an unrestricted PAR(2) process can be restricted by imposing the relevant non-linear restriction. Hence, for the logarithm of real GNP series of Austria, the periodically integrated AR(2) model (PIAR(2), or briefly PI), except for the intercept parameters, is estimated as follows (using the non-linear least squares routine in Eviews version 2.0, and setting irrelevant parameters equal to zero):

$$\text{PI model:}\quad (1-\alpha_s L)y_t = \mu_s + \beta_{1s}(1-\alpha_{s-1}L)y_{t-1} + \varepsilon_t,$$

where

$$\hat{\alpha}_2 = \underset{(0.009)}{0.950} \qquad \hat{\alpha}_3 = \underset{(0.008)}{0.972} \qquad \hat{\alpha}_4 = \underset{(0.010)}{1.033} \qquad \hat{\alpha}_1 = 1/(\hat{\alpha}_2\hat{\alpha}_3\hat{\alpha}_4) = \underset{(0.011)}{1.048}$$

$$\hat{\beta}_{11} = \underset{(0.201)}{-0.473} \qquad \hat{\beta}_{12} = \underset{(0.172)}{-0.328}$$

where the asymptotic standard errors are given in parentheses. Although the estimate of the β_{12} parameter may seem insignificant, deletion of the corresponding variable results in an inadequate model through serial correlation of the residuals. An $F(3, 90)$ test for the hypothesis that $\alpha_s = \alpha$ for all s yields a value of 17.701, which implies a rejection of the null hypothesis. This model, as well as all subsequent models for this series, passes LM-type diagnostic checks for residual autocorrelation of orders 1 and 4, for periodic residual autocorrelation of order 1, for normality, and for the absence of ARCH effects of orders 1 and 4.

Based on the visual evidence in figures 1 to 4, one may hypothesize that a structural shift occurred in either 1972.1, 1973.1 or 1974.1. If one wants to abstain from periodic models, and also given that the α_s parameters above are close to unity, one may want to consider the following descriptive model:

$$\text{I-model:} \quad (1 - B)y_t = \delta_s + I_{(t>\tau)}\delta_s^* + \beta_{1s}(1 - B)y_{t-1} + \varepsilon_t.$$

Fitting this model to the Austrian data, we find that it passes the standard diagnostic checks.

The general model that nests the above PI- and I-models has 13 parameters to be estimated. In table 1 are reported the corresponding values of the F_{PI} and F_I test statistics for the nested case. The PI model is rejected because of the significant values of the F_{Pi} statistics against the general model. On the other hand, the F_i test statistics are not significant at conventional significance levels, so that the I hypothesis is not rejected. Furthermore, the hypothesis that the δ_s^* are equal to zero and that the α_s are equal to one is rejected, with F test values of 12.882, 10.653 and 10.9 for τ at 1972.1, 1973.1 and 1974.1, respectively. In sum, these nested testing results suggest that the I-model is preferred to the PI-model. The evidence against periodic integration seems to be most convincing when a structural break is established at 1972.1. The non-nested testing results (see Franses and McAleer (1997) for more details) summarized in table 1 indicate a similar conclusion, with the t_{Pi} statistics all being highly significant and the t_i statistics being insignificant. Again this illustrates that several alternative descriptive models (with or without structural shifts) may seem to describe the same data.

Table 1. Empirical results for real GNP in Austria

	Nested tests		Non-nested tests	
τ	F_{Pi}	F_i	t_{Pi}	t_i
1972.1	6.200**	2.761	5.830**	−0.136
1973.1	3.747**	2.788	3.194**	0.689
1974.1	4.017**	2.946	3.351**	0.871

** Significant at the 1% level.

2.2.5. *Conclusion*

At present there is as yet no consensus as to which of the above models yields the best data description. There is ample evidence in favour of evolving seasonal fluctuations, and hence indications that the constant seasonality model can be dismissed. However, for some purposes, the model in (1) may be preferred, as it amounts to a very simple description. For short-term forecasting of univariate time series, the seasonal unit root model and the periodic integration model tend to perform much better than does the constant seasonality model. There is no decisive evidence yet that one model should be preferred to the other, and the choice appears to be a matter of taste and/or economic theory. In fact, there are several theoretical studies which lead to the use of periodic models (see Osborn (1988) and Todd (1990), among others).

Whatever the choice of univariate models, each of these almost uniquely leads to a multivariate approach to cointegration analysis. To the best of our knowledge, there have been no attempts yet to place the three multivariate approaches into a single framework. Hence, we will follow the available literature and, in the next section, review the three prevalent approaches to cointegration analysis of seasonal time series.

3. Three approaches to cointegration

In this section we review three methods of cointegration analysis of seasonal time series, where each follows from the empirical results for the univariate time series. In Section 3.1, we discuss the cointegration method when seasonality in the individual series seems (approximately) constant. In Section 3.2, cointegration analysis is discussed when there are seasonal unit roots. Finally, in Section 3.3, the focus is on cointegration among series with periodic properties.

Cointegration analysis is considered for Vector AR [VAR] models. There are many other approaches, but a VAR seems the most useful for a unifying structure. A VAR is used to summarize the dynamic behavior of k univariate time series, denoted as $y_{1,t}$, $y_{2,t}$ to $y_{k,t}$, which are stacked in the vector time series Y_t, where $Y_t = (y_{1,t}, y_{2,t}, \ldots, y_{k,t})'$. Additionally, e_t denotes the $k \times 1$ error time series defined by $e_t = (e_{1,t}, e_{2,t}, \ldots, e_{k,t})'$.

3.1. *Constant seasonal variation*

When seasonal variation is (approximately) constant, one can include four seasonal dummy variables in the VAR(p) model for Y_t, that is:

$$Y_t = \Upsilon_1 D_{1,t} + \cdots + \Upsilon_4 D_{4,t} + \Phi_1 Y_{t-1} + \Phi_2 Y_{t-2} + \cdots + \Phi_p Y_{t-p} + e_t, \tag{15}$$

where Φ_i $(i = 1, \ldots, p)$ and Υ_1, Υ_2, Υ_3, and Υ_4 contain parameters. As indicated in Johansen (1995), to facilitate the analysis of the asymptotic distribution of the various test statistics, it is sensible to take the seasonal dummies as deviations from their means, namely, to consider $D^*_{s,t} = D_{s,t} - n^{-1} \sum_{t=1}^{n} D_{s,t}$. For practical purposes, one can use (15).

Cointegration analysis can simply be performed by considering a rewritten version of (15), that is:

$$\Delta_1 Y_t = \Upsilon_1 D_{1,t} + \cdots + \Upsilon_4 D_{4,t} + \Pi Y_{t-p} + \Gamma_1 \Delta_1 Y_{t-1} + \cdots + \Gamma_{p-1} \Delta_1 Y_{t-p+1} + e_t, \quad (16)$$

where Δ_1 denotes the first differencing operator, and:

$$\Gamma_i = (\Phi_1 + \Phi_2 + \cdots + \Phi_i) - I_k, \qquad \text{for } i = 1, 2, \ldots, p-1, \quad (17)$$

$$\Pi = \Phi_1 + \Phi_2 + \cdots + \Phi_p - I_k. \quad (18)$$

The $k \times k$ matrix Π contains the information on possible cointegrating relations between the k elements of Y_t. Notice that when $\sum_{i=1}^{p} \Phi_i$ has eigenvalues close to or equal to unity, Π has eigenvalues close to or equal to 0. The latter implies that the matrix Π is close to rank deficiency, and hence there may be cointegration. An elegant statistical method to investigate whether the rank of Π differs from zero or from k is summarized in Johansen (1995).

In the VAR model in (16), there are three interesting cases: (*i*) the matrix Π can be the zero (or null) matrix, which implies that the rank of Π is 0; (*ii*) the matrix Π can have full rank k; (*iii*) the matrix Π can have deficient rank r, that is $0 < \text{rank}\ \Pi = r < k$. In the third case, Π can be decomposed as $\Pi = \alpha\beta'$, where α and β are $k \times r$ matrices. The matrix β contains the r cointegrating relations, while the matrix α contains the adjustment parameters. Again, the α and β matrices are not unique, and hence it is more appropriate to state that the columns of β span the space with cointegration vectors.

The Johansen maximum likelihood cointegration method examines the rank of Π using the reduced rank regression technique based on canonical correlations. The idea for using this technique is to determine those particular linear combinations $\beta_j' Y_t$ ($j = 1, 2, .., r$) which have the largest partial correlations with any linear combination of the stationary variables $\Delta_1 y_{1,t}, \Delta_1 y_{2,t}, \ldots, \Delta_1 y_{k,t}$. For (16), this amounts to the following computations. First, one regresses $\Delta_1 Y_t$ and Y_{t-p} on four seasonal dummy variables and the lagged $\Delta_1 Y_{t-1}$ through $\Delta_1 Y_{t-p+1}$ variables. This results in $k \times 1$ vectors of residuals, r_{0t} and r_{1t}, and the $k \times k$ residual product matrices:

$$S_{ij} = (1/n) \sum_{t=1}^{n} r_{it} r_{jt}', \qquad \text{for } i, j = 0, 1, \quad (19)$$

respectively, where n now denotes the number of effective observations. The next step is to solve the eigenvalue problem

$$| \lambda S_{11} - S_{10} S_{00}^{-1} S_{01} | = 0, \quad (20)$$

which gives the eigenvalues $\hat{\lambda}_1 \geqslant \cdots \geqslant \hat{\lambda}_k$ and the corresponding eigenvectors $\hat{\beta}_1, \ldots, \hat{\beta}_k$. A test for the rank of Π can now be performed by checking the values $\hat{\lambda}_i$. The first test proposed for the number of cointegrating relations is the *Trace* test statistic:

$$Trace = -n \sum_{i=r+1}^{k} \log(1 - \hat{\lambda}_i). \tag{21}$$

The null hypothesis for this test is that there are at most r cointegrating relations. One starts with testing for no cointegration ($r = 0$) versus at most one such relation ($r < 1$). If this null is rejected, one tests whether there is at most 1 cointegration relation versus 2. When finally the null hypothesis of at most $r = k - 1$ cointegration relations is rejected, one has found that the Y_t vector series is stationary.

Another useful test is given by evaluating the estimated eigenvalues themselves, namely:

$$\lambda_{\max} = -n \log(1 - \hat{\lambda}_r), \tag{22}$$

which tests the null hypothesis of $r - 1$ against r cointegration relations. Asymptotic distributions and critical values of the test statistics are summarized in Johansen (1995).

When there are r cointegrating relations among k time series, there are $k - r$ common stochastic trends (see Engle and Granger (1987)). A simple method to estimate the stochastic trends is proposed in Gonzalo and Granger (1995) which exploits the duality of cointegration and stochastic trends (see also Johansen (1995)). The above canonical correlation method can naturally be reversed to find the combinations which have minimum partial correlation. Gonzalo and Granger (1995) show that the relevant eigenvalue problem then becomes:

$$|\lambda S_{00} - S_{01} S_{10}^{-1} S_{10}| = 0, \tag{23}$$

which is the dual version of (20). The solutions to (23) are the same eigenvalues $\hat{\lambda}_1, \ldots, \hat{\lambda}_k$ as before, but now one obtains eigenvectors $\hat{w}_1, \ldots, \hat{w}_k$, which are different from the cointegration vectors. Gonzalo and Granger (1995) show that, in the case of r cointegrating relations, stochastic trend variables can be constructed as $\hat{w}'_{r+1}Y_t, \ldots, \hat{w}'_k Y_t$.

Without any further restrictions, the estimated stochastic trends for the unrestricted model in (16) will display seasonal variation. This is because it is unlikely that (23) will yield a combination $\hat{w}'_j Y_t$, which does not display seasonal variation. If one wants to obtain stochastic trends which do not show deterministic seasonal variation, the above procedure should be modified slightly. For simplicity, consider a VAR(1) model with cointegration, that is,

$$\Delta_1 Y_t = \Upsilon_1 D_{1,t} + \cdots + \Upsilon_4 D_{4,t} + \alpha\beta' Y_{t-1} + e_t. \tag{24}$$

Denote $\alpha_\perp$ as the orthogonal complement of α. Johansen (1995) allows that $\alpha'_\perp Y_t$ is one possible choice for the stochastic trends. Premultiplying (24) by $\alpha'_\perp$ gives:

$$\alpha'_\perp Y_t = \alpha'_\perp Y_{t-1} + \alpha'_\perp \Upsilon_1 D_{1,t} + \cdots + \alpha'_\perp \Upsilon_4 D_{4,t} + \alpha'_\perp e_t, \tag{25}$$

which shows that $\alpha'_\perp Y_t$ is a random walk with seasonally varying growth rates. If one wants to have stochastic trends without seasonal variation, one may rewrite (24) as:

$$\Delta_1 Y_t = \Upsilon + \alpha\beta'(Y_{t-1} + \Psi_1 D_{1,t} + \Psi_2 D_{2,t} + \Psi_3 D_{3,t}) + e_t, \tag{26}$$

where Υ is a common intercept, and corresponds to the parameter for the $D_{1,t} + D_{2,t} + D_{3,t} + D_{4,t}$ variable. In order to analyze (26), one should also regress the three dummy variables on the $\Delta_1 Y_{t-1}, \ldots, \Delta_1 Y_{t-p+1}$ variables, resulting in S_{ij} matrices of dimension $(k+3) \times (k+3)$. The asymptotic distribution of the test statistics and the corresponding critical values are not yet available.

Extending the approach taken in Ghysels and Perron (1993) for univariate unit root testing, Otero and Smith (1996) use simulations to investigate the effects of seasonal adjustment. The latter authors generate data from models as in (15), albeit without including specific parameters for seasonal dummies, and apply single-equation cointegration methods to investigate the empirical powers of the relevant tests. It is found that seasonally adjusting cointegrated time series leads to weaker evidence for cointegration.

3.2. *Seasonal cointegration*

If the individual univariate time series have one or more seasonal unit roots, there are two possible strategies. The first is to investigate if appropriately transformed time series have a. common unit root. For example, if it is found that $(1 - L^2)y_{1,t}$ and $(1 - L^4)y_{2,t}$ are suitably transformed series, one can examine if $y_{1,t}$ and $(1 + L_2)y_{2,t}$ have the roots 1 and/or -1 in common. This approach may be useful for a limited set of variables, but in many cases there are two disadvantages: (*i*) there may be many possible combinations of variables to check; and (*ii*) it is possible that a different asymptotic theory is required in each case. Hence, it is not surprising that this first strategy is rarely applied in practice.

A more convenient strategy is to allow for the possible presence of all seasonal unit roots in a first step, and to investigate the redundancy of any unit roots after the cointegration rank has been determined. Within the framework of the VAR(p) model, Lee (1992) develops a Johansen-type of analysis for cointegration. Under the assumption that $p \geqslant 4$, (15) can be rewritten as:

$$\begin{aligned}\Delta_4 Y_t = {} & \Upsilon_1 D_{1,t} + \cdots + \Upsilon_4 D_{4,t} + \Gamma_1 \Delta_4 Y_{t-1} + \cdots + \Gamma_{p-4}\Delta_4 Y_{t-(p-4)} \\ & + \Pi_1 Y_{1,t-1} + \Pi_2 Y_{2,t-1} + \Pi_3 Y_{3,t-2} + \Pi_4 Y_{3,t-1} + e_t,\end{aligned} \tag{27}$$

where

$$Y_{1t} = (1 + L + L^2 + L^3)Y_t \qquad \text{(zero frequency)}$$

$$Y_{2,t} = (1 - L + L^2 - L^3)Y_t \qquad \text{(bi-annual frequency, } \pi/2\text{)},$$

$$Y_{3,t} = (1 - L^2)Y_t. \qquad \text{(annual frequency, } \pi\text{)}.$$

The ranks of the $k \times k$ matrices $\Pi_1 = \alpha_1\beta'_1$, $\Pi_2 = \alpha_2\beta'_2, \Pi_3 = \alpha_3\beta'_3$ and $\Pi_4 = \alpha_4\beta'_4$ determine the cointegration relations at a certain frequency. Lee (1992) argues that seasonal cointegration at the $\pi/2$ frequency can also be checked using Π_3

only. As for the Johansen approach, one can now construct residual processes from the regressions of $\Delta_4 Y_t$ and $Y_{1,t-1}$, $Y_{2,t-1}$ $Y_{3,t-2}$ and $Y_{3,t-1}$ on lagged $\Delta_4 Y_t$ and deterministic terms, and construct the relevant moment matrices. Solving eigenvalue problems results in sets of estimated eigenvalues which can be checked for their significance using trace test statistics. Simulated critical values appear in Lee and Siklos (1995). Recently, Johansen and Schaumburg (1997) developed the asymptotic theory for the maximum likelihood method, which is slightly different from the theory presented in Lee (1992) although the asymptotic distribution of the estimators remains the same.

In one of the first rigorous applications of seasonal cointegration analysis within the VAR framework, Kunst (1993a) finds many common seasonal trends across sets of variables for several countries. His findings show that quarterly macroeconomic variables may have more in common that just a long-run trend (see also Kunst (1993b)).

Recently, many more applications of the Johansen-type analysis of (27) have appeared. Herwartz and Reimers (1996) analyze German M3 money demand for the period 1975.1–1995.4 and find cointegration at the zero and annual frequencies among M3, GDP, long term interest rate and GDP inflator. The authors interpret the estimated cointegrating vectors at both frequencies as evidence against price homogeneity. Another application to money demand is given in Bohl (1998), where German M2, GDP and the long-term interest rate are analyzed for the period 1960.1–1996.4. The author also analyzes the corresponding seasonally adjusted data. Using the seasonal cointegration method for the unadjusted data, the author finds a stable long-run relation among the three variables, whereas no such relation can be found for the adjusted data. Furthermore, Lee and Siklos (1997) find the opposite result in their analysis of quarterly money and output data for the US. Seasonally adjusted data are found to have a cointegration relationship at the zero frequency, while the unadjusted data are only cointegrated at the bi-annual seasonal frequency. The latter two studies clearly show how different findings for adjusted and unadjusted data can be obtained. Finally, similar conclusions are drawn in Ermini and Chang (1996), where the joint hypothesis of rationality and money neutrality is investigated for Korea. Using data for the period 1970.1–1991.4, the authors reject the joint hypothesis for unadjusted data analyzed in a seasonal cointegration framework, while the hypothesis cannot be rejected (at the 5% level) for adjusted data. Hence, an economically relevant hypothesis can receive mixed evidence, depending on the type of data that are used.

There are also several applications of VAR-based seasonal cointegration analysis to consumption functions. Reimers (1997a) uses data on real private consumption, real disposable income and real net financial wealth of private households for West Germany for the period 1960.1–1993.4. The author finds cointegration at all frequencies. Instead of trying to interpret the estimated vectors, the author proposes to analyze the impulse response functions of the time series, given the adequacy of the seasonally cointegrated VAR. It is found that wealth innovations are very important, and also that the impulse response functions of consumption and income display substantial seasonality. Lee and Siklos (1993) analyze US consumption and income data for the period 1947.1–1991.2 using a seasonal cointegration model. They find cointegration at the zero frequency between non-durable consumption and disposable income, while the null hypothesis of no cointegration cannot be rejected for the adjusted data. Finally, Ermini (1997) investigates the DHSY model of Davidson *et al.* (1978), using seasonal cointegration techniques. In contrast to the findings in Davidson *et al.* (1978), seasonal cointegration analysis implies the rejection of a number of economically relevant hypotheses.

Seasonal cointegration analysis based on (27) has two drawbacks, which may be viewed as potentially inconvenient in practice. The first is that the estimated cointegrating vectors at the seasonal frequencies may be difficult to interpret, especially when these vectors are not the same as those at the non-seasonal frequency. This drawback becomes even more relevant for seasonal cointegration analysis of monthly data (see Sanso *et al.* (1997)). Additionally, Osborn (1993) shows that the seasonal cointegration model can imply a dynamic structure which can be viewed as practically implausible. In a simulation study, Reimers (1997b) shows that seasonal cointegration vectors may be difficult to estimate with precision which, in turn, leads to the observation that a VAR model with seasonal dummies may yield better short-run forecasts. On the other hand, for longer horizons, the seasonal cointegration model appears preferable.

A second drawback of the analysis of (27) is that the intercepts yield different interpretations under seasonal cointegration restrictions. In fact, when there is cointegration at both seasonal frequencies with different vector coefficients, unrestricted seasonal intercepts in (27) imply expanding cycles, which may be implausible from an economic perspective. Notice, however, that for untransformed data (that is, without logs), these diverging trends may again become plausible. To overcome this drawback, Franses and Kunst (1998a) impose specific restrictions on the parameters in (27), resulting in:

$$\begin{aligned}\Delta_4 Y_t = {} & \mu + \Gamma_1 \Delta_4 Y_{t-1} + \cdots + \Gamma_{p-4}\Delta_4 Y_{t-(p-4)} \\ & + \alpha_1 \beta_1' Y_{1,t-1} + \alpha_2\{\beta_2' Y_{2,t-1} + a\cdot\cos[\pi(t-1)]\} \\ & + \alpha_3\{\beta_3' Y_{3,t-2} + b\cdot\cos[\pi(t-1)/2] + c\cos[\pi(t-2)/2]\} + e_t.\end{aligned} \tag{28}$$

To determine the number of columns of β_1, β_2 and β_3, Franses and Kunst (1998a) propose a partial analysis, that is, first β_1 is estimated conditional on the other variables, then β_2, and finally β_3. Johansen and Schaumburg (1997) include a related discussion of seasonal intercepts, and propose an alternative method of estimation. Kunst and Franses (1998) document that (28) can yield better forecasts than (27).

If not too many variables are analyzed, and if it is known which variables are of greater interest than others, one may use the bivariate cointegration approach proposed in Engle *et al.* (1993) [EGHL] (see also Engle *et al.* (1989)). This method is a natural extension of the Engle and Granger (1987) method for cointegration. EGHL apply their method to consumption and income data for Japan and find seasonal cointegration at the annual frequency.

Finally, it should be mentioned that Joyeux (1992) and Cubbada (1995) develop nonparametric seasonal cointegration tests along the lines of Phillips and Ouliaris (1988). These techniques, however, have not yet been widely applied in practice.

3.3. *Periodic cointegration*

When the individual time series display periodic autoregressive behaviour, one may want to consider a multivariate extension of periodic integration, that is, a periodic cointegration model. This form of cointegration analysis has not yet been fully developed, and, hence, applications are not widespread. A starting point for periodic cointegration analysis can be the periodic VAR, that is:

$$Y_t = \Upsilon_1 D_{1,t} + \cdots + \Upsilon_4 D_{4,t} + \Phi_{1,s} Y_{t-1} + \cdots + \Phi_{p,s} Y_{t-p} + e_t, \tag{29}$$

where the index s for $\Phi_{j,s}$ $(j = 1, 2, \ldots, p)$ indicates that the matrices contain parameters which vary with the seasons. Notice that this means that each matrix implies $4k \times 4k$ parameters. Given the trade-off between periodicity and the number of lags, as discussed in Section 2.2.3, p tends to be set at 1 or 2 in practice (see Franses (1996b)), although one may also opt for including only lags at 4, 8, and so on.

For a set of periodically integrated time series, each individual series requires its own periodic differencing filter, $(1 - \alpha_s L)$, with $\alpha_1\alpha_2\alpha_3\alpha_4 = 1$. The differencing filters have to be estimated from the data. Let ∇ denote the multivariate periodic differencing operator, such that ∇Y_t is a periodically stationary vector time series. Model (29) can be written in error correction format as:

$$\nabla Y_t = \Upsilon_1 D_{1,t} + \cdots + \Upsilon_4 D_{4,t} + \Gamma_{1,s} \nabla Y_{t-1} + \cdots + \Gamma_{p,s} \nabla Y_{t-p+1} + \Pi_s Y_{t-p} + e_t, \tag{30}$$

which entails long-run relations between the elements of Y_t summarized in Π_s. With cointegration, this long-run impact matrix can be decomposed as $\Pi_s = \alpha_s \beta_s'$, where α_s and β_s are $k \times r_s$ matrices. Notice that the rank of Π can vary with the seasons. Proceeding along the same lines discussed in Section 3.1 for equations (19) and (20), that is, conditioning on lagged ∇Y_t variables, an eigenvalue problem must he solved for each season. Franses and Paap (1995) apply this procedure and find that long-run relations between German consumption and income vary across the seasons using quarterly data.

There are at least two drawbacks of a Johansen-type approach applied to (30) for each of the four seasons. The first is that (30) allows the cointegrating vectors to take different values in different seasons. From an economic perspective, this may be unrealistic since it assumes that the individual series display seasonally diverging trends. Again, notice that these trends are plausible for time series which are not transformed by taking logarithms. At present, there exist two methods to ensure that the long-run relations across the k variables do not vary with the seasons, while the adjustment parameters can still take seasonally-varying values. The first method is proposed in Franses and Paap (1995), and applied in Franses (1996b), and amounts to extracting the estimated stochastic trends from the individual series, and then applying cointegration analysis to the new variables. To extract the stochastic trends, it is proposed to apply the Gonzalo–Granger method (see (23)) to the 4×1 vector series Y_T containing $Y_{1,T}$, $Y_{2,T}$, Y_{3T} and $Y_{4,T}$. As the individual time series are periodically integrated (of order 1), that is, there is only a single unit root in each Y_T (see Franses (1996b, Chapter 8) for details), there is also only a single stochastic trend. The estimated weights on the $Y_{s,T}$ series for this trend result in $y^*_{i,T}$ series, for $i = 1, 2, \ldots, k$. Since $y^*_{i,T}$ is observed annually, the next round of cointegration analysis for these k series yields cointegration relations which are the same for all quarters. These relations can be included in (30) and the adjustment parameters can then be estimated.

An alternative method, which tries to overcome the interpretability issue for the cointegration parameters, is given by simply assuming another periodic VAR representation. Hence instead of (29), Franses and Kleibergen (1997) propose a periodic VAR of the form:

$$\begin{aligned} Y_t = \Upsilon_1 D_{1,t} + \cdots + \Upsilon_4 D_{4,t} & \\ + \Phi_{1,s} Y_{t-1} + \Psi_{1,s} Y_{t-5} + \cdots + \Psi_{p,s} Y_{t-4p-1} + u_t. & \end{aligned} \tag{31}$$

Deleting the intra-year lag structure, that is, deleting lags at 2, 3, and 4, 6, 7 and 8, and so on, it is possible to obtain an explicit expression for the long-run matrix Π_s and its decomposed version $\alpha_s \beta$, in case of cointegration. Franses and Kleibergen (1997) use GMM to estimate the parameters in α_s and β. A potential practical problem with their method is that $\hat{u}_t$ may not be a vector white noise process, not even for high values of p in (31).

A second drawback; in analyzing (29) is that it includes a large number of parameters, which may render cointegration estimators inefficient. It may also not be necessary to have so many parameters in each equation. If there are priors as to which variables are of particular interest, one may resort to single-equation cointegration methods, while allowing for periodicity in the parameters. Boswijk and Franses (1995) extend the approach of Boswijk (1994) by considering (for the case of two variables):

$$\Delta_4 y_{1,t} = \sum_{s=1}^{4} \delta_s D_{s,t} + \sum_{s=1}^{4} \alpha_s D_{s,t}(y_{1,t-4} - \beta_s y_{2,t-4}) + \varepsilon_t, \tag{32}$$

where (32) can be expanded with lagged $\Delta_4 y_{1,t}$ and current and lagged $\Delta_4 y_{2,t}$ values. A similar model was also proposed in Birchenhall *et al.* (1989), but without the asymptotic theory. Cointegration testing can be performed by using Wald-type tests for the joint significance of $y_{1,t-4}$ and $y_{2,t-4}$. Boswijk and Franses (1995) provide tables with the relevant critical values. Conditional on cointegration, one can consider testing hypotheses regarding the β_s and α_s, such as $\beta_s = \beta$. Boswijk and Franses (1995) apply this method to consumption and income in Sweden, and find cointegration in the second and fourth quarters, see also Löf (1998). However, when adjusted data are used, no evidence of cointegration is found. Hence, again seasonally adjusted data again yield different results on the long-run relations between important macroeconomic variables. Finally, Herwartz (1997) studies the forecasting performance of periodic cointegration models.

A final remark in this section concerns model (32), as well as the other periodic cointegration models. It is important to incorporate the fact that not all differencing filters can be applied to the individual variables. For example, model (32) cannot include $\Delta_1 y_{1,t}$ (instead of $\Delta_4 y_{1,t}$), $\Delta_1 y_{2,t}$ and the long-run relations, $y_{1,t} - \beta_s y_{2,t}$, because the differencing filters in $\Delta_1 y_{1,t}$ and $\Delta_1 y_{2,t}$ assume $(1, -1)$ cointegrating relations between their individual $Y_{s,T}$ components. Consequently, the only possible long-run relation between $y_{1,t}$ and $y_{2,t}$ should be nonperiodic, so that only $y_{1,t} - \beta y_{2,t}$ can be a cointegrating relationship. Instead, when $\Delta_4 y_{2,t}$ is considered, there may indeed be a periodic cointegration relation (see Franses (1995) for further details).

4. Further research topics

In previous sections we have already indicated further research topics concerning cointegration analysis of seasonal time series. In this section we will add a few more, limiting attention to those important problems which a practitioner may face.

4.1. *Monthly or weekly data*

Asset return time series that are observed at minute or daily intervals are well known to display seasonal variation. This variation often amounts to high average values of returns or volatility at the beginning and end of a day, or on Mondays and Fridays. Seasonal variation in asset returns is approximately deterministic and, in case one wishes to analyze cointegration across stock market indices (that is, not the returns themselves, as these are stationary), one can use the techniques discussed in Section 3.1.

The analysis of weekly or monthly macroeconomic data can be expected to be much more complicated. This difficulty arises because seasonal variation in macroeconomic data tends to evolve over time, and subsequent cointegration analysis should take the univariate properties of the data into account. Suppose there is an interest in seasonal unit root models, then monthly data may have 11 seasonal unit roots and weekly data 51. These huge numbers obviously cause problems in practice for analyzing vector time series.

There would seem to be three plausible strategies for reducing the potentially large number of parameters in multivariate models for, say, weekly data. The first is simply to focus on only relevant intra-year cycles (or, equivalently, on only a few seasonal unit roots). Hence, the irrelevant unit roots are filtered out, and specific covariance matrix estimators can be designed to correct for any overdifferencing. In terms of quarterly data, this would imply, for example, that one analyzes all variables after differencing by $(1 + L^2)$.

A second strategy is to design models with cycles in cycles, so to say. One may assume a 4-weekly cycle within a 13-period cycle within a year. The auxiliary test regression for seasonal unit roots in Section 2.2.2 should then be modified accordingly.

A third approach to reduce parameters is to impose parametric restrictions. For example, weekly data may require 52 seasonal dummy variables and hence 52 free parameters. Imposing a certain smooth function on these parameters may reduce the number to be estimated dramatically. This approach should certainly be useful for periodic models for weekly data, where a PAR(p) model requires $52(p + 1)$ parameters.

4.2. *Data transformations*

As was discussed in Section 2.1, it is common practice to use logarithms of macroeconomic data. There are several arguments, such as convenience, in favour of taking logs, but, in general, there are no strong theoretical reasons for doing so. In fact, if one wishes to forecast the growth rate of x_t, one can also construct a model for x_t, generate forecasts for x_{t+1}, and calculate $(x_{t+1} - x_t)/x_t$, instead of modelling $\Delta_1 \log x_t$. Another potential problem is that not all time series take only positive values, which has led to definitions of the trade balance as log(exports) minus log (imports), instead of the more conventional and natural exports minus imports.

It is well known that the log transformation is not harmless for unit root analysis. Granger and Hallman (1991) show that the Dickey–Fuller (1979) (DF) test is sensitive to alternative functions and that the outcomes may result in different conclusions for different data transformations. They propose a rank-based unit root test, which remains useful given monotonic data transformations. Franses and McAleer (1998) propose a modified Dickey–Fuller test for the augmented DF (ADF) auxiliary regression equation, which is informative as to whether the log transformation is appropriate. If a variable added to the ADF auxiliary regression is significant, the log transformation is questionable. Extensions of this method to the HEGY regression and the test regression for periodic integration would be worthwhile.

If formal or informal methods suggest that the log transformation is not adequate, and untransformed data are preferred, the cointegration methods reviewed above may need modifications. In fact, without logs the data may have diverging seasonal trends. As discussed in Section 3.2, the standard seasonal cointegration model in (27) without restrictions on the seasonal intercepts already allows for diverging trends. However, to ensure that the asymptotic distributions of test statistics are invariant, the seasonal cointegration model should include additional deterministic seasonal trend terms, as in (10). In fact, this amounts to extending the procedures in Smith and Taylor (1998) to the multivariate case. Obviously, the same comments apply for periodic cointegration analysis.

4.3. *Nonlinearity*

Several macroeconomic time series display nonlinear features, for example, industrial production (some nonlinearity) and unemployment (substantial nonlinearity). These variables typically also have substantial seasonality. An important question is how one should design useful models for univariate time series to incorporate both of these features. Franses (1998c) extends the Smooth Transition AR [STAR] model of Teräsvirta (1994) to include a second transition function for the seasonal dummies. A natural subsequent issue is how such a complicated univariate model can be developed for a multivariate framework.

4.4. *Common seasonal patterns*

Using regressions as in (1), Beaulieu *et al.* (1992) and Miron (1996) document that quarterly real GNP in several countries seem to display strikingly common features. The estimates of the seasonal dummy parameters in (1) take similar values in certain quarters. It may now be of interest to see whether there is also statistical evidence in favour of the observed regularity in the quarterly growth rates. Engle and Hylleberg (1996) suggest a method that uses canonical correlation techniques (as for cointegration), where these are applied to constructed variables that are assumed to 'contain seasonality'. One possible drawback of this method is the same as that of cointegration in a VAR model, that is, if the number of variables becomes too large, the tests lose their practical usefulness.

Franses and Kunst (1998b) propose an alternative method for examining common seasonal patterns, which uses panel estimation techniques. The idea is to consider (a slightly more elaborate version of:

$$\Delta_1 y_{jt} = \delta_{1j} D_{1,t} + \delta_{2j} D_{2,t} + \delta_{3j} D_{3,t} + \delta_{4j} D_{4,t} + u_{jt}, \tag{33}$$

for countries $j = 1, 2, \ldots, m$. Panel estimators and pooling methods can reveal if the δ_{sj} parameters have certain common values. The method can also be used when u_{jt} has seasonal unit roots for some j, or when it is generated by a PAR process. Practical experience with this method is limited, and greater investigation is needed to examine its usefulness.

5. Final remarks

In this paper we surveyed three methods for cointegration analysis of seasonal (specifically, quarterly) time series. It was argued that each method is suggested by the properties of the individual univariate time series at hand, and that there is no consensus as to which approach is best. At present, there are also no clear winners in terms of forecasting or policy implications. It is also possible that models with an incorrect number of seasonal unit roots may forecast better (see Clements and Hendry (1997) and Reimers (1997b)). Future studies should shed more light on these issues. There does exist broad consensus however on the notion that seasonally adjusted data tend to yield inferences that are not in general agreement with the results obtained for unadjusted data. Long-run relations between key macroeconomic variables either appear or disappear for adjusted data. It seems, therefore, that further research is needed to study the impact of using seasonally adjusted time series.

Acknowledgements

The second author wishes to acknowledge the financial support of the Australian Research Council and the Japan Society for the Promotion of Science.

References

Abeysinghe, T. (1994) Deterministic seasonal models and spurious regressions. *Journal of Econometrics*, 61, 259–272.

Banerjee, A., Dolado, J., Galbraith, J. W. and Hendry, D. F. (1993) *Cointegration, Error Correction, and the Econometric Analysis of Nonstationary Data*, Oxford: Oxford University Press.

Beaulieu, J. J., MacKie-Mason, J. K. and Miron, J. A. (1992) Why do countries and industries with large seasonal cycles also have large business cycles?. *Quarterly Journal of Economics*, 107, 621–656.

Birchenhall, C. R., Bladen-Hovell, R. C., Chui, A. P. L., Osborn, D. R. and Smith, J. P. (1989) A seasonal model of consumption. *Economic Journal*, 99, 837–843.

Bohl, M. T. (1998) Nonstationary stochastic seasonality and the German M2 money demand function. *European Economic Review*, to appear.

Boswijk, H. P. (1994) Testing for an unstable root in conditional and structural error correction models, *Journal of Econometrics*, 63, 37–60.

Boswijk, H. P. and Franses, P. H. (1995) Periodic cointegration: representation and inference. *Review of Economics and Statistics*, 77, 436–454.

Boswijk, H. P. and Franses, P. H. (1996) Unit roots in periodic autoregressions. *Journal of Time Series Analysis*, 17, 221–245.

Boswijk, H. P., Franses, P. H. and Haldrup, N. (1997) Multiple unit roots in periodic autoregression. *Journal of Econometrics*, 80, 167–193.

Breitung, J. and Franses, P. H. (1998) On Phillips–Perron type tests for seasonal unit roots. *Econometric Theory*, 14, 200–221.

Canova, F. and Hansen, B. E. (1995) Are seasonal patterns constant over time?, A test for seasonal stability. *Journal of Business and Economic Statistics*, 13, 237–252.

Clements, M. P. and Hendry, D. F.(1997) An empirical study of seasonal unit roots in forecasting. *International Journal of Forecasting*, 13, 341–355.

Cubbada, C. (1995) A note on testing for seasonal cointegration using principal components in the frequency domain. *Journal of Time Series Analysis*, 16, 499–508.

Davidson, J. H. E., Hendry, D. F., Srba, F. and Yeo, S. (1978) Econometric modelling of the aggregate time-series relationship between consumers' expenditures and income in the United Kingdom. *Economic Journal*, 88, 661–692.

Dickey, D. A. and Fuller, W. A. (1979) Distribution of the estimators for autoregressive time series with a unit root. *Journal of the American Statistical Association*, 74, 427–431.

Engle, R. F. and Granger, C. W. J. (1987) Cointegration and error correction: representation, estimation and testing. *Econometrica*, 55, 2.51–276.

Engle, R. F., Granger, C. W. J. and Hallman, J. J. (1989) Merging short- and long-run forecasts. An application of seasonal cointegration to monthly electricity sales forecasting. *Journal of Econometrics*, 40, 45–62.

Engle, R. F., Granger, C. W. J., Hylleberg, S. and Lee, H. S. (1993) Seasonal cointegration: the Japanese consumption function. *Journal of Econometrics*, 55, 275–298.

Engle, R. F. and Hylleberg, S. (1996) Common seasonal features: global unemployment. *Oxford Bulletin of Economics and Statistics*, 58, 615–630.

Ermini, L. (1997) Testing DHSY as a restricted conditional model of a trivariate seasonally cointegrated system. Unpublished manuscript.

Ermini, L. and Chang, D. (1996) Testing the joint hypothesis of rationality and neutrality under seasonal cointegration: the case of Korea. *Journal of Econometrics*, 74, 363–386.

Franses, P. H. (1995) A vector of quarters representation of a bivariate time series. *Econometric Reviews*, 14, 55–63.

Franses, P. H. (1996a) Recent advances in modelling seasonality. *Journal of Economic Surveys*, 10, 299–345.

Franses, P. H. (1996b) *Periodicity and Stochastic Trends in Economic Time Series*, Oxford: Oxford University Press.

Franses, P. H. (1998a) *Time Series Models for Business and Economic Forecasting*, Cambridge: Cambridge University Press.

Franses, P. H. (1998b) *Modeling seasonality in economic time series*. In A. Ullah and D. E. A. Giles (eds.), *Handbook of Applied Economic Statistics*. New York: Marcel Dekker, 553–577.

Franses, P. H. (1998c) Does seasonality in unemployment change with its nonlinear business cycle? Econometric Institute Report 9809, Erasmus University Rotterdam.

Franses, P. H., Hylleberg, S. and Lee, H, S. (1995) Spurious deterministic seasonality. *Economics Letters*, 48, 249–256.

Franses, P. H. and Kleibergen, F.(1997), Cointegration in periodic VAR models. Unpublished manuscript, Erasmus University Rotterdam.

Franses, P. H. and Kunst, R. M. (1998a) On the role of seasonal intercepts in seasonal cointegration. *Oxford Bulletin of Economics and Statistics*, to appear.

Franses, P. H. and Kunst, R. M. (1998b) Common seasonality in industrial production. Unpublished manuscript.

Franses, P. H. and McAleer, M. (1997) Testing nested and non-nested periodically integrated autoregressive models. *Communications in Statistics: Theory and Methods*, 26, 1461–1475.

Franses, P. H. and McAleer, M. (1998) Testing for unit roots and nonlinear data transformations. *Journal of Time Series Analysis*, 19, 147–164.

Franses, P. H. and Paap, R. (1995) Seasonality and stochastic trends in German consumption and income, 1960.1–1987.4. *Empirical Economics*, 20, 109–132.

Franses, P. H. and Taylor, A. M. R. (1998) Determining the order of differencing in seasonal time series processes. Unpublished manuscript, Erasmus University Rotterdam.

Franses, P. H. and Vogelsang, T. J. (1998) On seasonal cycles, unit roots and mean shifts. *Review of Economics and Statistics*, 80, 231–240.

Ghysels, E. (1994) *On the economics and econometrics of seasonality*. In C. A. Sims (ed.) *Advances in Econometrics, Sixth World Congress of the Econometric Society*. Cambridge: Cambridge University Press.

Ghysels, E., Granger, C. W. J. and Siklos, P. B. (1996) Is seasonal adjustment a linear or nonlinear data-filtering process? (with discussion). *Journal of Business and Economic Statistics*, 14, 374–397.

Ghysels, E., Hall, A. and Lee, H. S. (1996) On periodic structures and testing for seasonal unit roots, *Journal of the American Statistical Association*, 91, 1551–1559.

Ghysels, E., Lee, H. S. and Noh, J. (1994) Testing for unit roots in seasonal time series. Some theoretical extensions and a Monte Carlo investigation. *Journal of Econometrics*, 62, 415–442.

Ghysels, E. and Perron, P. (1993) The effects of seasonal adjustment filters on tests for a unit root. *Journal of Econometrics*, 55, 57–98.

Gonzalo, J. and Pitarakis, J. Y. (1994) Comovements in large systems. Department of Economics Working Paper 33, Boston University.

Gonzalo, J. and Granger, C. W. J. (1995) Estimation of common long-memory components in cointegrated systems. *Journal of Business and Economic Statistics*, 13, 27–36.

Granger, C. W. J. and Hallman, J. J. (1991) Nonlinear transformations of integrated time series. *Journal of Time Series Analysis*, 12, 207–224.

Hall, A. (1994) Testing for a unit root in time series with pretest data-based model selection. *Journal of Business and Economic Statistics*, 12, 461–470.

Hamilton, J. D. (1994) *Time Series Analysis*. Princeton: Princeton University Press.

Herwartz, H. (1997) Performance of periodic error correction models in forecasting consumption data. *International Journal of Forecasting*, 13, 421–431.

Herwartz, H. and Reimers, H. E. (1996), Seasonal cointegration analysis for German M3 money demand. Discussion paper 78, Humboldt University Berlin.

Hylleberg, S. (1992) (ed.), *Modelling Seasonality*, Oxford: Oxford University Press.

Hylleberg, S. (1994), *Modelling Seasonal Variation*. In Hargreaves, C. P. (ed.), *Nonstationary Time Series Analysis and Cointegration*. Oxford: Oxford University Press, 153–178.

Hylleberg, S., Engle, R. F., Granger, C. W. J. and Yoo, B. S. (1990) Seasonal integration and cointegration. *Journal of Econometrics*, 44, 215–238.

Jaeger, A. and Kunst, R. M. (1990) Seasonal adjustment and measuring persistence in output. *Journal of Applied Econometrics*, 5, 47–58.

Johansen, S. (1995) *Likelihood-Based Inference in Cointegrated Vector Autoregressive Models*. Oxford: Oxford University Press.

Johansen, S. and Schaumburg, E. (1997) Likelihood analysis of seasonal cointegration. EUI Working PAper, ECO 97/16, European University Institute, Florence.

Joyeux, R. (1992) Tests for seasonal cointegration using principal components. *Journal of Time Series Analysis*, 13, 109–118.

Kunst, R. M. (1993a) Seasonal cointegration in macroeconomic systems: case studies for small and large European countries. *Review of Economics and Statistics*, 75, 325–330.

Kunst, R. M. (1993b) Seasonal cointegration, common seasonals, and forecasting seasonal series. *Empirical Economics*, 18, 761–776.

Kunst, R. M. and Franses, P. H. (1998) The impact of seasonal constants on forecasting seasonally cointegrated time series. *Journal of Forecasting*, 17, 109–124.

Lee, H. S. (1992) Maximum likelihood inference on cointegration and seasonal cointegration. *Journal of Econometrics*, 54, 351–365.

Lee, H. S. and Siklos, P. L. (1993) The influence of seasonal adjustment on the Canadian consumption function, 1947–1991. *Canadian Journal of Economics*, 26, 575–589.

Lee, H. S. and Siklos, P. L. (1995) A note on the critical values for the maximum likelihood (seasonal) cointegration tests. *Economics Letters*, 49, 137–145.

Lee, H. S. and Siklos, P. L. (1997) The role of seasonality in economic time series: reinterpreting money–output causality in U.S. data. *International Journal of Forecasting*, 13, 381–391.

Löf, Mårten (1998) A periodic cointegration model for Swedish private consumption. Paper presented at the 18th International Symposium on Forecasting, Edinburgh.

Lütkepohl, H. (1991) *Introduction to Multiple Time Series Analysis*, Berlin: Springer-Verlag.

Mills, T. C. (1990) *Time Series Techniques for Economists*, Cambridge: Cambridge University Press.

Miron, J. A. (1996) *The Economics of Seasonal Cycles*, Cambridge: MIT Press.

Novales, A. and Flores de Fruto, R. (1997) Forecasting with periodic models: a

comparison with time invariant coefficient models. *International Journal of Forecasting*, 13, 393–405.
Osborn, D. R. (1988) Seasonality and habit persistence in a life-cycle model of consumption. *Journal of Applied Econometrics*, 3, 255–266.
Osborn, D. R. (1990) A survey of seasonality in UK macroeconomic variables. *International Journal of Forecasting*, 6, 327–336.
Osborn, D. R. (1993) Discussion of 'seasonal cointegration'. *Journal of Econometrics*, 55, 299–303.
Otero, J. and Smith, J. (1996) The effects of seasonal adjustment linear filters on cointegrating equations: a Monte Carlo investigation. Research Paper 456, Department of Economics, University Warwick.
Phillips, P. C. B. and Ouliaris, S. (1988) Testing for cointegration using principal components methods. *Journal of Economic Dynamics and Control*, 12, 205–230.
Psaradakis, Z. (1997) Testing for unit roots in time series with nearly deterministic seasonal variation. *Econometric Reviews*, 16, 421–440.
Reimers, H. E. (1997a) Seasonal cointegration analysis of German consumption function. *Empirical Economics*, 22, 205–231.
Reimers, H. E. (1997b) Forecasting of seasonal cointegrated processes. *International Journal of Forecasting*, 13, 369–380.
Sanso, A., Surinach, J. and Artis, M. (1997) A two-step procedure for the estimation and testing of seasonal cointegration in monthly data. Unpublished manuscript, University of Barcelona.
Smith, R. J. and Taylor, A. M. R. (1998) Additional critical values and asymptotic representation for seasonal unit roots tests. *Journal of Econometrics*, 85, 269–288.
Taylor, A. M. R. (1997) On the practical problems of computing seasonal unit root tests. *International Journal of Forecasting*, 13, 307–318.
Teräsvirta, T. (1994) Specification, estimation, and evaluation of smooth transition autoregressive models. *Journal of the American Statistical Association*, 89, 208–218.
Tiao, C. C. and Grupe, M. R. (1980), Hidden periodic autoregressive-moving average models in time series data. *Biometrika*, 67, 365–373.
Todd, R. (1990) Periodic linear quadratic methods for modeling seasonality. *Journal of Economic Dynamics and Control*, 14, 763–795.
Wells, J. M. (1997) Modelling seasonal patterns and long-run trends in U.S. time series. *International Journal of Forecasting*, 13, 407–420.

AUTHOR INDEX

Note – Page numbers in *italics* indicate the page on which the full reference will be found.

SUBJECT INDEX

9 780631 211983